A Manual for Writers of Research Papers, Theses, and Dissertations

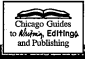

A Manual for Writers of Research Papers, Theses, and Dissertations

Chicago Style for Students and Researchers

7th edition

Kate L. Turabian

Revised by Wayne C. Booth, Gregory G. Colomb,
Joseph M. Williams, and University of Chicago Press
Editorial Staff

The University of Chicago Press • Chicago and London

Portions of this book have been adapted from *The Craft of Research,* 2nd edition, by Wayne C. Booth, Gregory G. Colomb, and Joseph M. Williams, © 1995, 2003 by The University of Chicago; and from *The Chicago Manual of Style,* 15th edition, © 1982, 1993, 2003 by The University of Chicago.

The University of Chicago Press, Chicago 60637
The University of Chicago Press, Ltd., London
© 2007 by The University of Chicago
All rights reserved. Published 2007
Printed in the United States of America

16 15 14 13 12 11 10 09 08 07   1 2 3 4 5

ISBN-13: 978-0-226-82336-2 (cloth)
ISBN-13: 978-0-226-82337-9 (paper)
ISBN-10: 0-226-82336-9 (cloth)
ISBN-10: 0-226-82337-7 (paper)

Library of Congress Cataloging-in-Publication Data

Turabian, Kate L.
    A manual for writers of research papers, theses, and dissertations : Chicago style for students and researchers / Kate L. Turabian; revised by Wayne C. Booth, Gregory G. Colomb, Joseph M. Williams, and University of Chicago Press editorial staff. — 7th ed.
        p.   cm.
    "Portions of this book have been adapted from *The Craft of Research,* 2nd edition, by Wayne C. Booth, Gregory G. Colomb, and Joseph M. Williams, © 1995, 2003 by The University of Chicago; and from *The Chicago Manual of Style,* 15th edition, © 1982, 1993, 2003 by The University of Chicago."
    Includes bibliographical references and index.
    ISBN-13: 978-0-226-82336-2 (cloth : alk. paper)
    ISBN-13: 978-0-226-82337-9 (pbk. : alk. paper)
    ISBN-10: 0-226-82336-9 (cloth : alk. paper)
    ISBN-10: 0-226-82337-7 (pbk. : alk. paper)
    1. Dissertations, Academic—Handbooks, manuals, etc.   2. Academic writing—Handbooks, manuals, etc. I. Title.

LB2369.T8 2007
808.02—dc22

                                                              2006025443

⊛ The paper used in this publication meets the minimum requirements of the American National Standard for Information Sciences—Permanence of Paper for Printed Library Materials, ANSI Z39.48-1992.

Contents

Part I   Research and Writing: From Planning to Production

Wayne C. Booth, Gregory G. Colomb, and Joseph M. Williams

Part II   Source Citation

Part III Style

A Note to Students

Now in its seventh edition, *A Manual for Writers of Research Papers, Theses, and Dissertations* has helped generations of students successfully research, write, and submit their papers. Most commonly known to its dedicated users as "Turabian," the name of the original author, *A Manual for Writers* is the authoritative student resource on "Chicago style."

If you are writing a research paper, you may be told to follow Chicago style for citations and for issues of mechanics, such as capitalization and abbreviations. Chicago style is widely used by students in all disciplines. For citations, you may use one of two styles recommended by Chicago. In the humanities and some social sciences, you will likely use notes-bibliography style, while in the natural and physical sciences (and some social sciences) you may use parenthetical citations–reference list (or "author-date") style. *A Manual for Writers* explains and illustrates both styles.

In addition to detailed information on Chicago style, this seventh edition includes a new part by Wayne C. Booth, Gregory G. Colomb, and Joseph M. Williams that covers every step of the research and writing process. This section provides practical advice to help you formulate the right questions, read critically, build arguments, and revise your draft.

Preface

Students writing research papers, theses, and dissertations in today's colleges and universities inhabit a world filled with electronic technologies that were unimagined in 1937—the year Kate L. Turabian, University of Chicago's dissertation secretary, assembled a booklet of guidelines for student writers. The availability of Internet sources and word-processing software has changed the way students conduct research and write up the results. But these technologies have not altered the basic task of the student writer: doing well-designed research and presenting it clearly and accurately, while following accepted academic standards for citation, style, and format.

Turabian's 1937 booklet reflected guidelines found in *A Manual of Style*, 10th edition—an already classic resource for writers and editors published by the University of Chicago Press. The Press began distributing Turabian's booklet in 1947 and first published the work in book form in 1955, under the title *A Manual for Writers of Term Papers, Theses, and Dissertations*. Turabian revised the work twice more, updating it to meet students' needs and to reflect the latest recommendations of the *Manual of Style*. In time, Turabian's book has become a standard reference for students of all levels at universities and colleges across the country. Turabian died in 1987 at age ninety-four, a few months after publication of the fifth edition. For that edition, as well as the sixth (1996), the Press invited editorial staff to carry out the revisions.

For this seventh edition, Wayne C. Booth, Gregory G. Colomb, and Joseph M. Williams have expanded the focus of the book. The new part 1, "Research and Writing: From Planning to Production," is adapted from their *Craft of Research* (Chicago: University of Chicago Press, 2003). This part offers a step-by-step guide to the process of research and its reporting, a topic not previously covered in this manual but inseparable from source citation, writing style, and the mechanics of paper preparation. Among the topics covered are the nature of research, finding and engaging sources, taking notes, developing an argument, drafting and revising, and presenting evidence in tables and figures. Also included is a discussion of presenting research in alternative forums. In this part, the authors write in a familiar, collegial voice to engage readers in a complex topic. Students undertaking research projects at all levels will benefit from reading this part, though advanced researchers may wish to skim chapters 1–4.

The rest of the book covers the same topics as past editions, but has been extensively revised to follow the recommendations in *The Chicago Manual of Style,* 15th edition (2003), to incorporate current technology as it affects all aspects of student writing, to provide updated examples, and to be easier to read and use.

Reflecting the close connection between the research process and the need for careful and appropriate citation form, "Source Citation" now appears as part 2 of the manual. In this part, chapter 15 offers an overview of scholarly citation, including its relationship not just to good research practices but to the ethics of research. Students using notes-bibliography style for citations (common in the humanities and some social sciences) should then read chapter 16 for a discussion of the basic form for citations and consult chapter 17 as needed for a wide range of source examples. Students using parenthetical citations–reference list style (common in most social sciences and in the natural and physical sciences) will find the same types of information in chapters 18 and 19. Both sets of chapters include updated examples and new coverage of how to cite online and other electronic sources.

Part 3, "Style," addresses issues that occupied the first half of previous editions of the manual. Coverage of spelling and punctuation has been divided into separate chapters, as has treatment of numbers and abbreviations. The chapter on names, special terms, and titles of works has been expanded. The final two chapters in this section treat the mechanics of using quotations and graphics (tables and figures), topics that are discussed from a rhetorical perspective in part 1. Student writers may wish to read these chapters in their entirety or consult them for guidance on particular points.

The recommendations in parts 2 and 3 diverge in a few instances from those in *The Chicago Manual of Style,* but the differences are matters of degree, not substance. In certain cases, this manual recommends just one editorial style where *CMOS* recommends two or more. Sometimes the choice is a matter of simplicity (as in the rules for headline-style capitalization presented in chapter 22); other times it reflects what is appropriate for student papers, as opposed to published works (as in the requirement of access dates with *all* citations from online sources). The chapters on citation include new types of sources, such as Weblogs, that have emerged since 2003 and thus are not treated in the current edition of *CMOS.* These recommendations logically extend principles set forth in *CMOS.*

The appendix gathers in one place the material on paper format and submission that formed the core of Kate Turabian's original booklet. In the years since, this material has become the primary authority for dissertation offices throughout the nation. In revising this material, the Press sought the advice of dissertation officials at a variety of public and private universities, including those named in the acknowledgments section. While continuing to emphasize the importance of consistency, the guidelines now allow more flexibility in matters such as the placement of page numbers and the typography of titles, reflecting the capabilities of current word-processing software. The sample pages presented are new and are adapted from exemplary dissertations submitted to the University of Chicago since 2000. This appendix is intended primarily for students writing PhD dissertations and master's and undergraduate theses, but the sections on format requirements and electronic file preparation also apply to those writing class papers.

The guidelines in this manual offer practical solutions to a wide range of issues encountered by student writers, but they may be supplemented—or even overruled—by the conventions of specific disciplines or the preferences of particular institutions or departments. All of the chapters on style and format remind students to review the requirements of their university, department, or instructor, which take precedence over the guidelines presented here. The expanded bibliography, organized by subject area, lists sources for research and style issues specific to particular disciplines.

Acknowledgments

Revising a book that has been used by millions of students over seventy years is no small task. The challenge of bringing Kate Turabian's creation into the twenty-first century was taken up first by Linda J. Halvorson, then editorial director for reference books at the University of Chicago Press, who recognized how the needs of the student writer had changed since the publication of the sixth edition in 1996 and developed a revision plan to address those changing needs.

The key to this plan was assembling a revision team that understood how the Turabian tradition could be reshaped for students researching and writing papers in an electronic age. Wayne C. Booth, Gregory G. Colomb, and Joseph M. Williams contributed their expertise both as teachers and as authors of numerous books on the subject of research and writing, including *The Craft of Research*. The Press's editorial staff was represented on the revision team first by Margaret Perkins, now director of manuscript editing at the *New England Journal of Medicine*, and later by Mary E. Laur, senior project editor for reference books. Both had played critical roles in the preparation of *The Chicago Manual of Style*, 15th edition, from which parts 2 and 3 of this book are adapted.

Throughout the revision process, the manuscript (partial and complete) benefited from the advice of reviewers with expertise in various aspects of student research and writing, including Susan Allan (*American Journal of Sociology*), Christopher S. Allen (international affairs, University of Georgia), Anna Nibley Baker (HealthInsight), Howard Becker (San Francisco), Paul S. Boyer (history, University of Wisconsin–Madison), Christopher Buck (writing, rhetoric, and American cultures, Michigan State University), David Campbell (political science, University of Notre Dame), Erik Carlson (University of Chicago Press), Michael D. Coogan (religious studies, Stonehill College), Daniel Greene (U.S. Holocaust Memorial Museum), Anne Kelly Knowles (geography, Middlebury College), Lewis Lancaster (East Asian languages and cultures, University of California–Berkeley), Luke Eric Lassiter (humanities, Marshall University Graduate College), James Leloudis (history, University of North Carolina–Chapel Hill), Kurt Mosser (philosophy, University of Dayton), Gerald Mulderig (English, DePaul University), Emily S. Rosenberg (history, University of California–Irvine), Anita Samen (University of Chicago Press), Paul

Stoller (anthropology and sociology, West Chester University), Anne B. Thistle (biological science, Florida State University), and Richard Valelly (political science, Swarthmore College).

The successors of Kate Turabian at a variety of public and private universities offered valuable insights on dissertation preparation and submission. Reviewers of the appendix included Philippa K. Carter from the University of Pittsburgh; Matthew Hill from the University of Maryland, College Park; Elena Hsiao-ching Hsu from the University of Wisconsin–Madison; Johanna E. D. Parker from the University of Illinois at Urbana-Champaign; and Christine Quigley from Georgetown University. The current occupant of Turabian's own position at the University of Chicago, Colleen Mullarkey, reviewed the manuscript in its entirety and also helped identify the exemplary dissertations from which the sample pages in the appendix are drawn. The authors of these dissertations, who granted permission for their text to be used, are identified in the captions of the relevant figures.

Turning the manuscript into a book required the efforts of another team at the Press. Carol Fisher Saller edited the manuscript, Randolph Petilos proofread the pages, and Victoria Baker prepared the index. Michael Brehm provided the design, while Sylvia Mendoza Hecimovich supervised the production. Christopher Rhodes offered editorial assistance throughout the project. Carol Kasper, Ellen Gibson, and Laura Anderson brought the finished product to market.

The loss of Wayne Booth when the manuscript was nearly complete touched everyone involved with the project, which will stand as his last new work.

PART I

Research and Writing

From Planning to Production

Wayne C. Booth, Gregory G. Colomb, and
Joseph M. Williams

Overview of Part I

We know how challenged you can feel when you start a substantial research project, whether it's a PhD dissertation, a BA or master's thesis, or just a long class paper. But you can handle any project if you break it into its parts, then work on them one step at a time. This part shows you how to do that.

We first discuss the aims of research and what readers will expect of any research report. Then we focus on how to find a research question whose answer is worth your time and your readers' attention; how to find and use information from sources to back up your answer; then how to plan, draft, and revise your report so your readers will think your answer is based on sound reasoning and reliable evidence.

Several themes run through this part.

- You can't plunge into a project blindly; you must plan it, then keep the whole process in mind as you take each step. So think big, but break the process down into small goals that you can meet one at a time.
- Your best research will begin with a question that *you* want to answer. But you must then imagine readers asking a question of their own: *So what if you don't answer it? Why should I care?*
- From the outset, you should try to write every day, not just to take notes on your sources but to clarify what you think of them. You should also write down your own developing ideas to get them out of the cozy warmth of your head into the cold light of day, where you can see if they still make sense. You probably won't use much of this writing in your final draft, but it is essential preparation for it.
- No matter how carefully you do your research, readers will judge it by how well you report it, so you must know what they will look for in a clearly written report that earns their respect.

If you're an advanced researcher, skim chapters 1–4. You will see there much that's familiar, but if you're also teaching, it may help you explain what you know to your students more effectively. (Many experienced researchers report that chapters 5–12 have helped them not only explain to others how to do research and report it, but also to draft and revise their own reports more quickly and effectively.)

If you're just starting your career in research, you'll find every chapter of part 1 useful. Skim it all for an overview of the process; then as you work through your project, reread chapters relevant to your immediate task.

You may feel that the steps described here are too many to remember, but you can manage them if you take them one at a time, and as you do more research, they'll become habits of mind. Don't think, however, that you must follow these steps in exactly the order we present them. Researchers regularly think ahead to future steps as they work through earlier ones and revisit earlier steps as they deal with a later one. (That explains why we so often refer you ahead to anticipate a later stage in the process and back to revisit an earlier one.) And even the most systematic researcher has unexpected insights that send her off in a new direction. Work from a plan, but be ready to depart from it, even to discard it for a new one.

If you're a very new researcher, you may also think that some matters we discuss are beyond your immediate needs. We know that a ten-page class paper differs from a PhD dissertation. But both require a kind of thinking that even the newest researcher can start practicing. You begin your journey toward full competence when you not only know what lies ahead but can also start practicing the skills that experienced researchers began to learn when they were where you are now.

No book can prepare you for every aspect of a research project. And this one won't help you with the specific methodologies in fields such as psychology, economics, or philosophy, much less physics, chemistry, or biology. Nor does it tell you how to adapt what you learn about academic research to business or professional settings.

But it does provide an overview of the processes and habits of mind that underlie all research, wherever it's done, and of the plans you must make to assemble a report, draft it, and revise it. With that knowledge and help from your teachers, you'll come to feel in control of your projects, not intimidated by them, and eventually you'll learn to manage even the most complex projects on your own, in both the academic and the professional worlds.

The first step in learning the skills of sound research is to understand how experienced researchers think about its aims.

1 What Research Is and How Researchers Think about It

You do research every time you ask a question and look for facts to answer it, whether the question is as simple as finding a plumber or as profound as discovering the origin of life. When only you care about the answer or when others need just a quick report of it, you probably won't write it out. But you must report your research in writing when others will accept your claims only after they study how you reached them. In fact, reports of research tell us most of what we can reliably believe about our world—that once there were dinosaurs, that germs cause disease, even that the earth is round.

You may think your report will add little to the world's knowledge. Maybe so. But done well, it will add a lot to yours and to your ability to do the next report. You may also think that your future lies not in scholarly research but in business or a profession. But research is as important outside the academy as in, and in most ways it is the same. So as you practice the craft of academic research now, you prepare yourself to do research that one day will be important at least to those you work with, perhaps to us all.

As you learn to do your own research, you also learn to use—and judge—that of others. In every profession, researchers must read and evaluate reports before they make a decision, a job you'll do better only after you've learned how others will judge yours. This book focuses on research in the academic world, but every day, we read or hear about research that can affect our lives. Before we believe those reports, though, we must think about them critically to determine whether they are based on evidence and reasoning that we can trust.

To be sure, we can *reach* good conclusions in ways other than through reasons and evidence: we can rely on tradition and authority or on intuition, spiritual insight, even on our most visceral emotions. But when we try to *explain* to others not just why we believe our claims but why they should too, we must do more than just state an opinion and describe our feelings.

That is how a *research* report differs from other kinds of persuasive writing: it must rest on shared facts that readers accept as truths independent of your feelings and beliefs. They must be able to follow your reasoning from evidence that they accept to the claim you draw from it. Your success as a researcher thus depends not just on how well you gather and analyze data, but on how clearly you report your reasoning so that your readers can test and judge it before making your claims part of their knowledge and understanding.

1.1   How Researchers Think about Their Aims

All researchers gather facts and information, what we're calling *data*. But depending on their aims and experience, they use those data in different ways. Some researchers gather data on a topic—*stories about the Battle of the Alamo,* for example—just to satisfy a personal interest (or a teacher's assignment).

Most researchers, however, want us to know more than just facts. So they don't look for just any data on a topic; they look for specific data that they can use as evidence to test and support an answer to a question that their topic inspired them to ask, such as *Why has the Alamo story become a national legend?*

Experienced researchers, however, know that they must do more than convince us that their answer is sound. They must also show us why their question was worth asking, how its answer helps us understand some bigger issue in a new way. *If we can figure out why the Alamo story has become a national legend, we might then answer a larger question: How have regional myths shaped our national character?*

You can judge how closely your thinking tracks that of an experienced researcher by describing your project in a sentence like this:

1. I am working on the topic of X (*stories about the Battle of the Alamo*),
    2. because I want to find out Y (*why its story became a national legend*),
        3. so that I can help others understand Z (*how such regional myths have shaped our national character*).

That sentence is worth a close look because it describes not just the progress of your research but your personal growth as a researcher.

1. "I am working on the topic of . . . " Researchers often begin with a simple topic like *the Battle of the Alamo,* either because it was assigned, because something about it puzzles them, or because it merely sparks an interest. But inexperienced researchers too often stop there, leaving themselves with nothing but a topic to guide their work. They mound up hundreds of notes, but have no way to decide what data to keep and what to discard. When it comes time to write, they dump everything into a report that reads like a grab bag of random facts. If those facts are new to readers who happen to be interested in the topic, they might read the report. But even those readers will want to know *what those facts add up to.*

2. " . . . because I want to find out how or why . . . " More experienced researchers usually begin not with just a topic but with a research question, such as *Why has the story of the Alamo become a national legend?* And they know that readers will think their facts add up to something only when those facts serve as evidence to support its answer. Indeed, only with a question can a researcher know which facts to look for and which to keep—not just those that support an answer, but also those that test or even discredit it. When he thinks he has enough evidence to support his answer and can respond to data that seem to contradict it, he writes a report first to test his own thinking, then to share his answer with others so that they can test it too.

3. " . . . so that I can help others understand . . . " The most successful researchers, however, realize that readers want to know not only that an answer is sound but why the question was worth asking. So they anticipate that readers will ask a question of their own: *So what? Why should I care why the Alamo story has become a legend?* That *So what?* can vex even the most experienced researcher, but every researcher must try to answer it before it's asked: *If we can find that out, we might better understand the bigger question of how such stories shape our national character.*

But a shrewd researcher doesn't stop there. She anticipates her readers' asking *So what?* again by looking for another, still larger answer: *And if we can understand what has shaped our national character, we might understand better who we Americans think we are. And before you ask, when we know that, we might better understand why others in the world judge us as they do.* The most successful researchers know that readers care about a question only when they think that its answer might encourage them to say not *So what?* but *That's worth knowing!*

In short, not all questions are equally good. We might ask how many cats slept in the Alamo the night before the battle, but so what if we find out? It is hard to see how an answer would help us think about any larger issue worth understanding, so it's a question that's probably not worth asking (though as we'll see, we could be wrong about that).

Three Kinds of Questions That Researchers Ask
Experienced researchers also know that different readers expect them to ask and answer different kinds of questions. The most common questions in academic work are *conceptual.* The ones most common in the professions are *practical.*

1.2.1 Conceptual Questions: *What Should We Think?*
A question is conceptual when your answer to *So what?* doesn't tell readers what to *do,* but helps them *understand* some issue:

1. I am working on the topic of X,
    2. because I want to find out how/why/whether Y, (*So what if you do?*)
        3. so that I can help others *understand* how/why/whether Z.

If you were explaining your research, the conversation might go like this:

I'm working on the topic of risk evaluation.

Why?

Because I want to find out how ordinary people evaluate the risk that they will be hurt by terrorism.

So what if you do?

Once I do, we might better understand the bigger question of how emotional and rational factors interact to influence the way ordinary thinkers think about risk.

Researchers in the humanities and the social and natural sciences work mostly on conceptual questions, such as *How did Shakespeare's political environment influence his plays? What caused the extinction of most large North American mammals? What are comets made of?* The answers to those questions don't tell us how to change the world, but they do help us understand it better.

To be sure, the answer to a conceptual question often turns out to be unexpectedly relevant to solving a practical problem. And before we can solve any important practical problem, we usually must do conceptual research to understand it better. But in most of the academic world, the primary aim of most researchers is only to improve our understanding.

1.2.2   Practical Questions: *What Should We Do?*

You pose a different kind of question—call it a *practical* one—when your answer to *So what?* tells readers what to *do* to change or fix some trouble-some or at least improvable situation:

1. I am working on the topic of X,
    2. because I want to find out Y, (*So what if you do?*)
        3. so that I can tell readers *what to do* to fix/improve Z.

You would explain your work on a practical question like this:

I'm working on the topic of communicating risk effectively.

Why?

Because I want to find out what psychological factors cause ordinary Americans to exaggerate their personal risk from a terrorist attack.

So what if you do?

Then I can tell the government how to counteract those factors when they communicate with the public about the real risk of terrorism.

Practical questions are most common outside the academic world, especially in business. In academic fields such as health care and engineering, researchers sometimes ask practical questions, but more often they ask a third kind of question that's neither purely practical nor purely conceptual: call it an *applied research* question.

1.2.3   Applied Questions: *What Must We Understand before We Know What to Do?*

Often, we know we must do *something* to solve a practical problem, but before we can know what that is, we must do research to understand the problem better. We can call that kind of research *applied.* With this middle kind of question, the third step raises a question whose answer is not the solution to a practical problem, but only a step toward it.

I want to find out how Americans have changed their daily lives in response to the terrorist attacks on 9/11.

So what if you do?

Then we can understand the psychological factors that cause ordinary Americans to exaggerate their personal risk from a terrorist attack.

So what if you do?

Then we can understand how to reduce the effects of those psychological factors.

So what if you do?

Then perhaps the government can use that information to communicate more effectively the real risk from terrorism.

Applied questions are common in academic fields such as business, engineering, and medicine and in companies and government agencies that do research to understand what must be known before they can solve a problem.

1.2.4 Choosing the Right Kind of Question

Some new researchers dislike purely conceptual research questions because they think they're too "theoretical" or irrelevant to the "real" world. So they try to cobble an implausible practical use onto a conceptual answer: *When we know how race shaped the political impact of the Alamo stories, we can understand how racism has been used to foster patriotism and thereby eliminate racist appeals to patriotism in relation to conflicts in the Middle East.*

That impulse is understandable. But unless you've been assigned an applied or practical problem, resist it. You are unlikely to solve any significant practical problem in a class paper, and in any case, most of the academic world sees its mission not as fixing the problems of the world directly, but as understanding them better (which may or may not help fix them).

1.2.5 The Special Challenge of Conceptual Questions: Answering *So What?*

With most practical questions, we don't have to answer *So what?* because the benefit is usually obvious. Even most applied questions imply the practical benefits of their answers: few readers would question why a researcher is trying to understand what causes Alzheimer's. With conceptual questions, however, the answer to *So what?* is often not obvious at all, even to an experienced researcher: *So what if Shakespeare had Lady Macbeth die offstage rather than on? So what if some cultures use masks in their religious rituals and others don't? Why is it important to know that?*

For a research paper in an introductory course, your instructor may be satisfied with any plausible answer to *So what?* So if early in your research career you find yourself struggling with that question, don't take it as a sign of failure, much less as evidence that you're not ready to do the work. In fact, you might not discover the answer to *So what?* until you've drafted your report, maybe not even until you've finished it. And even then, maybe the answer will matter only to you.

But if your project is a thesis or dissertation, it's not just an advisor that you have to satisfy. Your answer must also satisfy those in your field (represented by your advisor) who will judge your work not just by the quality of your answer, but by the significance of your question. Experienced researchers know that some readers, perhaps many, will read their report and think *I don't agree.* They accept that as an inevitable part of sharing research on significant issues. What they can't accept is *I don't care.*

So as hard as it will be, the more often you imagine others asking *So what?* and the more often you try to answer it, if only to your own satisfaction, the more confident you can be that eventually you'll learn to succeed at every experienced researcher's toughest task—to convince your readers that your report is worth their time. (In chapter 10, we discuss how to write an introduction that motivates your readers at least to start reading your report.)

2   Moving from a Topic to a Question to a Working Hypothesis

A research project is more than collecting data. You start it before you log on to the Internet or head for the library, and you continue it long after you have all the data you think you need. In that process, you face countless specific tasks, but they all aim at just five general goals. You must do the following:

- Ask a question worth answering.
- Find an answer that you can support with good reasons.
- Find reliable evidence to support your reasons.
- Draft a report that makes a good case for your answer.
- Revise that draft until readers will think you met the first four goals.

You might even post those five goals in your workspace.

    Research projects would be easy if you could march straight through those steps. But as you've discovered (or soon will), research and its reporting are never straightforward. As you do one task, you'll have to look ahead to others or revisit an earlier one. You'll change topics as you read, search for more data as you draft, perhaps even discover a new question as you revise. Research is looping, messy, and unpredictable. But it's manageable if you have a plan, even when you know you'll depart from it.

2.1 Find a Question in Your Topic

Researchers begin projects in different ways. Many experienced ones begin with a question that others in their field want to answer: *What caused the extinction of most large North American mammals?* Others begin with just a vague intellectual itch that they have to scratch. They might not know what puzzles them about giant sloths and mastodons, but they're willing to spend time finding out whether they can translate their itch into a question worth answering.

They know, moreover, that the best research question is not one whose answer others want to know just for its own sake; it is one that helps them understand some larger issue (*So what?* again). For example, if we knew why North American sloths disappeared, we might be able to answer a larger question that puzzles many historical anthropologists: *Did early Native Americans live in harmony with nature, as some believe, or did they hunt its largest creatures to extinction? (And if we knew that, then we might also understand. . . .)*

Then there are those questions that just pop into a researcher's mind with no hint of where they'll lead, sometimes about matters so seemingly trivial that only the researcher thinks they're worth answering: *Why does a coffee spill dry up in the form of a ring?* Such a question might lead nowhere, but you can't know that until you see its answer. In fact, the scientist puzzled by coffee rings made discoveries about the behavior of fluids that others in his field thought important—and that paint manufacturers found valuable. So who knows where you might go with a question like *How many cats slept in the Alamo the night before the battle?* You can't know until you get there.

In fact, a researcher's most valuable ability is the knack of being puzzled by ordinary things: like the shape of coffee rings; or why Shakespeare has Lady Macbeth die offstage rather than on; or why your eyebrows don't grow as long as the hair on your head. Cultivate the ability to see what's odd in the commonplace and you'll never lack for research projects, as either a student or a professional.

If you have a topic, skip to 2.1.3 to find questions in it. If you already have a question or two, skip to 2.1.4 to test them by the criteria listed there. If you're still looking for a topic, here's a plan to help you search for one.

2.1.1   Search Your Interests

If you can pick any topic appropriate to your field, ask these questions:

- What topics do you already know something about? You can learn more.
- What would you like to know more about? A place? A person? A time? An object? An idea? A process?
- Can you find a discussion list on the Web about issues that interest you?
- What issues in your field have you debated with others, then found that you couldn't back up your views with good reasons and evidence?
- What issues do people outside your field misunderstand?
- What topic is your instructor working on? Would she like you to explore a part of it? Don't be too shy to ask.
- Does your library have rich resources in some field? Ask your instructor or a librarian.
- What other courses will you take in your field or out of it? Find a text-book, and skim it for study questions.
- If you have a job in mind, what kind of research report might help you get it? Employers often ask for samples of an applicant's work.

You can also consult print sources for ideas:

- Skim the topics in specialized indexes in your field such as *Philosopher's Index, Geographical Abstracts, Women's Studies Abstracts,* and so on (in the bibliography, see items in category 2 in your field).
- Skim a journal that reviews the year's work in your field (in the bibliography, see items in category 2 in your field).

Academic research is meant to be shared, but the understanding it brings is also valuable to you alone. So think ahead: look for a project that might help you a year from now. Keep in mind, though, that you may be in for a long relationship with your topic. If so, be sure it interests you enough to get you through the inevitable rocky stretches.

2.1.2   Make Your Topic Manageable

If you pick a topic whose name sounds like an encyclopedia entry—*bridges, birds, masks*—you'll find so many sources that you could spend a lifetime reading them. You must carve out of your topic a manageable piece. You can start before you head to the library by limiting your topic to reflect a special interest in it: What is it about, say, masks that made you choose them? What particular aspect of them interests or puzzles you? Think about your topic in a context that you know something about, then add words and phrases to reflect that knowledge:

masks in religious ceremonies

masks as symbols in Hopi religious ceremonies

mudhead masks as symbols of sky spirits in Hopi fertility ceremonies

You might not be able to focus your topic until after you start reading about it. That takes time, so start early (you can do much of this preliminary work online):

- Begin with an overview of your topic in a general encyclopedia (in the bibliography, see items in category 2 in the general references); then read about it in a specialized one (see items in category 2 in your field).
- Skim a survey of your topic (encyclopedia entries usually cite a few).
- Skim subheads under your topic in an annual bibliography in your field (in the bibliography, see items in category 4 in your field). That will also give you a start on a reading list.
- Search the Internet for the topic (but be cautious about what you find; see 3.4.3).

Especially useful are topics that spark debate: *Fisher claims that Halloween masks reveal children's archetypal fears, but do they?* Even if you can't resolve the debate, you can learn how such debates are conducted (for more on this, see 3.1.2).

2.1.3 Question Your Topic

Do this not just once, early on, but throughout your project. Ask questions as you read, especially *how* and *why* (see also 4.1.1–4.1.2). Try the following kinds of questions (the categories are loose and overlap, so don't worry about keeping them distinct).

1. Ask how the topic fits into a larger context (historical, social, cultural, geographic, functional, economic, and so on):
   - How does your topic fit into a larger story? *What came before masks? How did masks come into being? Why? What changes have they caused in other parts of their social or geographic setting? How and why did that happen? Why have masks become a part of Halloween? How and why have masks helped make Halloween the biggest American holiday after Christmas?*
   - How is your topic a functioning part of a larger system? *How do masks reflect the values of specific societies and cultures? What roles do masks play in Hopi dances? In scary movies? In masquerade parties? For what purposes are masks used other than disguise? How has the booming market for kachina masks influenced traditional designs?*

    ◻ How does your topic compare to and contrast with other topics like it? *How do masks in Native American ceremonies differ from those in Africa? What do Halloween masks have to do with Mardi Gras masks? How are masks and cosmetic surgery alike?*

2. Ask questions about the nature of the thing itself, as an independent entity:

    ▣ How has your topic changed through time? Why? What is its future? *How have Halloween masks changed? Why? How have Native American masks changed? Why?*

    ▣ How do the parts of your topic fit together as a system? *What parts of a mask are most significant in Hopi ceremonies? Why? Why do some masks cover only the eyes? Why do so few masks cover just the bottom half of the face?*

    ▣ How many different categories of your topic are there? *What are the different kinds of Halloween masks? What are the different qualities of masks? What are the different functions of Halloween masks?*

3. Turn positive questions into a negative ones: *Why have masks* not *become a part of Christmas? How do Native American masks* not *differ from those in Africa? What parts of masks are typically* not *significant in religious ceremonies?*

4. Ask speculative questions: *Why are masks common in African religions but not in Western ones? Why are children more comfortable wearing Halloween masks than are most adults? Why don't hunters in camouflage wear masks?*

5. Ask *What if?* questions: How would things be different if your topic never existed, disappeared, or were put into a new context? *What if no one ever wore masks except for safety reasons? What if everyone wore masks in public? What if movies and TV were like Greek plays and all the actors wore masks? What if it were customary to wear masks on blind dates? In marriage ceremonies? At funerals?*

6. Ask questions that reflect disagreements with a source: If a source makes a claim you think is weakly supported or even wrong, make that disagreement a question (see also 4.1.2). *Martinez claims that carnival masks uniquely allow wearers to escape social norms. But I think religious masks also allow wearers to escape from the material realm to the spiritual. Is there a larger pattern of all masks creating a sense of alternative forms of social or spiritual life?*

7. Ask questions that build on agreement: If a source offers a claim you think is persuasive, ask questions that extend its reach (see also 4.1.1). *Elias shows that masked balls became popular in eighteenth-century Lon-*

don in response to anxiety about social mobility. Is the same anxiety responsible for similar developments in other European capitals? You can also ask a question that supports the same claim with additional evidence. *Elias supports his claim about masked balls entirely with published sources. Is it also supported by evidence from unpublished sources such as letters and diaries?*

8. Ask questions analogous to those that others have asked about similar topics. *Smith analyzed the Battle of Gettysburg from an economic point of view. What would an economic analysis of the Battle of the Alamo turn up?*

9. Look for questions that other researchers pose but don't answer. Many journal articles end with a paragraph or two about open questions, ideas for more research, and so on. You might not be able to do all the research they suggest, but you might carve out a piece of it.

10. Find a Web discussion list on your topic, then "lurk," just reading the exchanges to understand the kinds of questions those on the list discuss. If you can't find a list using a search engine, ask a teacher or visit the Web site of professional organizations in your field. Look for questions that spark your interest. You can even ask a question of the list so long as it is very specific and narrowly focused, but wait until you see whether questions from students are welcomed.

2.1.4 Evaluate Your Questions

Not all answers are equally useful, so evaluate your questions and scrap those that are unlikely to yield interesting answers. Reconsider when the following is true.

1. You can answer the question too easily.
   - You can look it up: *What masks are used in Navajo dances?*
   - You can summarize a source: *What does Fisher say about masks and fears?*

2. You can't find good evidence to support the answer.
   - No relevant facts exist: *Are Mayan masks modeled on space aliens?*
   - The question is based on preference or taste: *Are Balinese or Mayan masks more beautiful?*
   - You must read too many sources: *How are masks made?* You don't want to plow through countless reports to find the best evidence (this usually results from a question that's too broad).
   - You can't get the sources that your readers think are crucial. In even moderately advanced projects, you'll be expected to work with the best sources available; for a thesis and dissertation, they're essential. If you can't obtain those sources, find another question.

3. You can't plausibly disprove the answer.

    □ The answer seems self-evident because the evidence overwhelmingly favors one answer. *How important are masks in Inuit culture?* The answer is obvious: *Very.* If you can't imagine disproving a claim, then proving it is pointless. (On the other hand, world-class reputations have been won by those who questioned a claim that seemed self-evidently true—for instance, that the sun went around the earth—and dared to disprove it.)

Don't reject a question because you think someone must already have asked it. Until you know, pursue its answer as if you asked first. Even if someone has answered it, you might come up with a better answer or at least one with a new slant. In fact, in the humanities and social sciences the best questions usually have more than one good answer. You can also organize your project around comparing and contrasting competing answers and supporting the best one (see 6.2.5).

The point is to find a question that you want to answer. Too many students, both graduate and undergraduate, think that the aim of education is to memorize settled answers to someone else's questions. It is not. It is to learn to find your own answers to your own questions. To do that, you must learn to wonder about things, to let them puzzle you, particularly about things that seem most commonplace.

2.2 Propose Some Working Answers

Before you get deep into your project, try one more step. It is one that some beginners resist but that experienced researchers usually attempt. Once you have a question, imagine some plausible answers, no matter how sketchy or speculative. At this stage, don't worry whether they're right. That comes later.

For example, suppose you ask, *Why do some religions use masks in ceremonies while others don't?* You might speculate,

Maybe cultures with many spirits need masks to distinguish them.

Maybe masks are common in cultures that mix religion and medicine.

Maybe religions originating in the Middle East were influenced by the Jewish prohibition against idolatry.

Even a general answer can suggest something worth studying:

Maybe it has to do with the role of masks in nonreligious areas of a culture.

Try to imagine at least one plausible answer, no matter how tentative or speculative. If after lots of research you can't confirm it, you can organize your report around why that answer seemed reasonable at the time but turned out to be wrong, and so isn't worth the time of other researchers. That in itself can be a valuable contribution to the conversation on your topic. (See 10.1.1–10.1.2 for how to use an apparently good idea that turns out to be wrong.)

In fact, look for two or three plausible answers. Even if you prefer one, you can improve it by testing it against the others, and in any event, you can't show that an answer is right if you can't also show why others are wrong. Even early in the project, write out your answers as clearly and as fully as you can. It is too easy to think that you have a clear idea when you don't. Putting a foggy idea into words is the best way to clarify it, or to discover that you can't.

2.2.1   Decide on a Working Hypothesis

If one answer seems promising, call it your *working hypothesis* and use it to guide your research. You can, of course, look for evidence with no more than a question to guide you, because any question limits the number of plausible answers. But even the most tentative working hypothesis helps you to think ahead, especially about the *kind* of evidence that you'll need to support it. Will you need numbers? quotations? observations? images? historical facts? More important, what kind of evidence would *disprove* your hypothesis? Answer those questions, and you know the kind of data to watch for and to keep. In fact, until you have a hypothesis, you can't know whether any data you collect are relevant to any question worth asking.

If you can't imagine any working hypothesis, reconsider your question. Review your list of exploratory questions to find one that you can answer; if you skipped that step, go back to 2.1.3. You may even decide to start over with a new topic. That costs time in the short run, but it may save you from a failed project. If you're working on a thesis or dissertation, you can wait longer to firm up a hypothesis while you read and ponder, but don't get deeply into your project without at least the glimmer of a possible answer.

Under no circumstances put off thinking about a hypothesis until you begin drafting your report or, worse, until you've almost finished it. You might not settle on the best answer to your question until you've written your last page: writing, even revising, is itself an act of discovery. Just don't wait until that last page to start thinking about *some* answer.

2.2.2   Beware the Risks in a Working Hypothesis

It is a bad idea to settle on a final answer too soon. But many new researchers and some experienced ones are afraid to consider *any* working hypothesis early in their project, even one they hold lightly, because they fear it might bias their thinking. There is some risk of that, but a working hypothesis need not close your mind to a better one. Even the most objective scientist devises an experiment to test for just a few predicted outcomes, often just one. In fact, researchers who don't state a hypothesis usually have one in mind, but don't want to seem publicly committed to it, lest it turn out wrong.

A working hypothesis is a risk only if it blinds you to a better one or if you can't give it up when the evidence says you should. So as in all relationships, don't fall too hard for your first hypothesis: the more you like it, the less easily you'll see its flaws. Despite that risk, it's better to start with a flawed hypothesis than with none at all.

2.2.3   If You Can't Find an Answer, Argue for Your Question

We have focused on questions so much that you might think that your project fails if you can't answer yours. In fact, much important research explains why a question no one has asked should be, even though the researcher can't answer it: *Do turtles dream? Why is yawning contagious but being sleepy isn't? Or is it?* Such reports focus on why the question is important and what a good answer might look like. Or you may find that someone has answered your question, but incompletely or even, if you're lucky, incorrectly. If you can't find the right answer, you help readers by showing that a widely accepted one is wrong. (See 10.1.2 for how to use this plan in your introduction.)

Only when you ask question after question will you develop the critical imagination you'll need in any profession you follow. In fact, as experienced researchers know, most issues have few, if any, final answers, because there are no final questions. They know that it's as important to ask a new question as it is to answer an old one, and that one day their new question will become old and yield to a newer researcher's still newer one.

Your job is to become that newer researcher.

2.3   Build a Storyboard to Plan and Guide Your Work

For a short paper, you might not need a detailed plan—a sketch of an outline might do. But for a long project, you'll usually need more, especially for one as long as a thesis or dissertation. The first plan that comes to mind is usually an outline, with its *I*'s and *II*'s and *A*'s and *B*'s and so on (see 23.4.2). If you prefer an outline, use one, especially if your project is relatively short. The problem is that an outline can force you to specify too much too soon and so lock up a final form before you've done your best thinking.

To avoid that risk, many researchers, including those outside the academic world, plan long reports on a *storyboard*. A storyboard is like an outline spread over several pages, with lots of space for adding data and ideas as you go. It is more flexible than an outline: it can help you plan your search for evidence, organize your argument, write a first draft, and test a final one. As opposed to lines in an outline, you can physically move storyboard pages around without having to print a new plan every time you try out a new organization. You can spread its pages across a wall, group related pages, and put minor sections below major ones to create a "picture" of your project that shows you at a glance the design of the whole and your progress through it.

2.3.1 State Your Question and Working Hypotheses

To start a storyboard, state at the top of its first page your question and working hypothesis as exactly as you can. Then add plausible alternatives to help you see more clearly its limits and strengths. Add new hypotheses as you think of them, and cross off those you prove wrong. But save them, because you might be able to use one of them in your introduction (see 10.1.1).

2.3.2 State Your Reasons

Put at the top of separate pages each reason that might support your best hypothesis, even if you have only one or two (for more on reasons, see 5.4.2). Imagine explaining your project to a friend. You say, *I want to show that Alamo stories helped develop a unique Texan identity,* and your friend asks, *Why do you think so?* Your reasons are the general statements that you offer to support your answer: *Well, first, the stories distorted facts to emphasize what became central to Texan identity; second, the stories were first used to show that Texas (and the Wild West) was a new kind of frontier; third, . . .* and so on.

If you can think of only one or two reasons (you'll usually need more), put placeholders at the tops of pages: *Reason 3: Something about Alamo stories making Texans feel special.* If you know only *how* you want a reason to support your answer, state that: *Reason 4: Something to show that Alamo stories were more than just myth.* Each reason, of course, needs support, so for each reason, ask *Why do I think that? What evidence will I need to prove it?* That will help you focus your search for evidence (see 2.3.3 and 5.4.2).

If you're new to your topic or early in your project, your reasons may be only educated guesses that you'll change; if you don't, you might not be self-critical enough. But a list of reasons, no matter how speculative, is the best framework to guide your research and focus your thinking, and certainly better than no reasons at all.

2.3.3   Sketch in the *Kind* of Evidence You Should Look For

Every field prefers its own kinds of evidence—numbers, quotations, observations, historical facts, images, and so on. So for each reason, sketch the kind of evidence that you think you'll need to support it. Even imagine what the most convincing evidence would look like. If you can't imagine the kind of evidence you'll need, leave that part of the page blank, then read secondary sources to find out the kind of evidence that researchers in your field favor (see 3.1.2).

2.3.4   Look at the Whole

Lay the pages on a table or tape them on a wall. Then step back and look at their order. When you plan a first draft, you must put its parts in some order, so you might as well think about one now. Can you see a logic in your order? cause and effect? narrative time? relative importance? complexity? length? (See 6.2.5 for more principles of order.) Try out different orders. This storyboard isn't your final plan; it's only a tool to guide your thinking and organize what you find.

When you fill a page, try drafting that section, because writing out your ideas can improve your thinking at every stage of your project.

Someday, you may have the leisure to amble through sources, reading just what interests you. Such random browsing has opened up important lines of research. But if your report is due in a month or so, you can't wait for lightning to strike; you need a plan. A storyboard is a simple and reliable device to help you create one.

2.4   Organize a Writing Support Group

A down side of scholarly research is its isolation. Except for group projects, you'll read, think, and write mostly alone. But it doesn't have to be that way, at least not entirely. Look for someone other than your instructor or advisor who will talk with you about your progress, review your drafts, even pester you about how much you have written. That might be a generous friend, but look first for another writer so that you can comment on each other's ideas and drafts.

Better yet is a writing group of four or five people working on their own projects who meet regularly to discuss one another's work. Early on, start each meeting with a summary of each person's project in that three-part sentence: *I'm working on the topic of X, because I want to find out Y, so that I (and you) can better understand Z.* As your projects develop, start with an "elevator story," a short summary of your research that you might give someone in the elevator on the way to the meeting. It should include that three-part sentence, a working hypothesis, and the major reasons supporting it (see 13.4).

In later stages, the group shares outlines and drafts so that they can serve as surrogate readers to anticipate how your final readers will respond. If your group has a problem with your draft, so will your final readers. They can even help you brainstorm when you bog down. But for most writers, a writing group is most valuable for the discipline it imposes. It is easier to meet a schedule when you know you must report your progress to others.

Writing groups are standard practice for theses or dissertations. But the rules may differ for a class paper. Some teachers think that a group or writing partner might provide more help than is appropriate, so be clear with your instructor what your group will do. If you don't, she may decide the assistance you have received is inappropriate (see 7.10).

3 Finding Useful Sources

Once you have at least a question and perhaps a working hypothesis along with a few tentative reasons for supporting it, you can start looking for the data you'll need to support your reasons and test your hypothesis. In this chapter we explain how to find those data and in the next how to work with them. But don't think of finding sources and reading them as separate steps. Once you have a promising source, read it to find other sources. And as you fill your storyboard with notes, you'll discover gaps and new questions that only more sources can fill. So while we discuss finding and using sources as two steps, you'll more often do them repeatedly and simultaneously.

3.1 Understand the Kinds of Sources Readers Expect You to Use

Depending on your experience, readers will expect you to use different levels of sources, called *primary, secondary,* and *tertiary* (think first-, second-, and thirdhand). These aren't sharply defined categories, but they roughly characterize how researchers think about most sources.

3.1.1 Consult Primary Sources for Evidence

In fields such as literary studies, the arts, and history, primary sources are original works—diaries, letters, manuscripts, images, films, film scripts, recordings, and musical scores created by writers, artists, composers, and so on. Those sources provide data—the words, images, and sounds that you use as evidence to support your reasons. Data can also be objects: coins, clothing, tools, and other artifacts from the period or belonging to a person you're studying.

In fields such as economics, psychology, chemistry, and so on, researchers typically collect data through observation and experiment. In others, researchers gather evidence through interviews. (To conduct effective interviews, you must use reliable methods for eliciting and recording the information you collect.) In such fields, evidence consists of the data that researchers collect. The primary sources for those collected data are the publications that first publish them, ranging from government and commercial databases to scholarly journals.

Experienced researchers look for data in primary sources first. If, for example, you were writing on Alamo stories, you'd try to find sources written at the time—letters, diaries, eyewitness reports, and so on.

3.1.2 Read Secondary Sources to Learn from Other Researchers

Secondary sources are books and articles that analyze primary sources, usually written by and for other researchers. A report in a scholarly journal analyzing Alamo stories would be a secondary source for researchers working on those stories. Secondary sources also include specialized encyclopedias and dictionaries that offer essays written by scholars in a field. You use secondary sources for three purposes:

1. To Keep Up with Current Research. Researchers read secondary sources to keep up with the work of other researchers, to inform and refine their thinking, and to motivate their own work by adding to a published line of research.

2. To Find Other Points of View. A research report is not complete until the researcher acknowledges and responds to the views of others and to his readers' predictable questions and disagreements (see 5.4.3). You can find most of those other points of view in secondary sources. What alternatives to your ideas do they offer? What evidence do they cite that you must acknowledge? Some new researchers think they weaken their case if they mention any view opposing their own. The truth is the opposite. When you acknowledge competing views, you show readers that you not only know those views but can confidently respond to them (for more on this, see 5.4.3).

   More important, you must use those competing views to improve your own. You can't understand what you think until you understand why a rational person might think differently. So as you look for sources, don't look just for those that support your views. Be alert as well for those that contradict them.

3. To Find Models for Your Own Research and Analysis. You can use secondary sources to find out not just *what* others have written about your topic, but *how* they have written about it, as models for the form and style of your own report. Imagine a secondary source as a colleague talking to you about your topic. As you respond, you'd want to sound like someone who knows the field, and so you'd try to learn how she reasons, the language she uses, the kinds of evidence she offers, and the kinds she rarely or never uses. The "conversation" would be in writing, so you'd even imitate stylistic details such as whether she writes in long paragraphs or breaks up her pages with subheads and bullet points (common in the social sciences, less common in the humanities).

You can also use a secondary source as a model for your conceptual analysis. If, for example, you were analyzing Alamo stories, you might study how a source treats Custer's Last Stand. Is its approach psychological, social, historical, political? Its particular reasons or evidence will probably be irrelevant to your project, but you might support your answer with the same kinds of data and reasoning, perhaps even following the same organization.

So if you come across a source that's not exactly on your topic but treats one like it, skim it to see how that researcher thinks about his material and presents it. (You don't have to cite that source if you use only its general logic, but you may cite it to give your own approach more authority.)

Researchers use data reported in secondary sources only when they can't find them in primary sources. Then they're cautious about using those secondary sources, because secondhand reports of data have a high error rate. If you're doing very advanced work, check the accuracy of important quotations, facts, or numbers from secondary sources. Those who publish in respected places rarely misreport deliberately, but they make careless mistakes more often than nonexperts think or experts admit.

Of course, if you were studying how the Alamo story has been analyzed, then secondary sources offering those analyses would be your primary sources.

If you're new to a field, you may find secondary sources hard to read: they assume a lot of background knowledge, and many aren't clearly written (see 11.2). If you're working on a topic new to you, you might begin with an overview in a specialized encyclopedia or reliable tertiary source.

3.1.3 Read Tertiary Sources for Introductory Overviews

Tertiary sources are based on secondary sources, usually written for nonspecialists. They include general encyclopedias and dictionaries, as well as newspapers and magazines like *Time* and the *Atlantic Monthly* and commercial books written for a general audience. Well-edited general encyclopedias offer a quick overview of many topics. Beware, however, of online encyclopedias, such as *Wikipedia*, that rely on anonymous contributions rather than on carefully edited entries written by established researchers. *Wikipedia* has proved to be relatively accurate in the sciences, but overall it is uneven and sometimes wrong. Never cite it as an authoritative source.

Be similarly cautious about using magazine and newspaper articles. Some describe research reported in secondary sources reliably, but most oversimplify, or worse, misreport it. You would, of course, treat such a source as primary if you were studying how it deals with a topic, such as gender bias in the *Encyclopedia Britannica* or hoaxes in *Wikipedia*.

Once you understand kinds of sources, you can begin looking for them.

3.2 Record Your Sources Fully, Accurately, and Appropriately

Before you look for sources, you should know how to cite the ones you find. Your readers will trust your report only if they trust your evidence, and they won't trust your evidence if they can't find your sources. Your first obligation as a researcher is to cite your sources accurately and fully so that your readers can find them.

3.2.1 Determine Your Citation Style

Most fields require a specific citation style. The two most common ones are described in detail in part 2:

- *notes-bibliography style* (or simply *bibliography style*), used widely in the humanities and in some social sciences (see chapters 16 and 17)
- *parenthetical citations–reference list style* (or simply *reference list style*), used in most social sciences and in the natural sciences (see chapters 18 and 19)

If you are uncertain which style to use, consult your instructor. Before you start compiling your list of sources, read the general introduction to citations in chapter 15, then depending on the citation style you are required to use, read the introduction to bibliography style (chapter 16) or reference list style (chapter 18).

3.2.2 Record Bibliographic Data

To save time and avoid errors, record all the citation information you will need when you first find a source. Most of this information appears on the title page of a book or at the head of a journal article. The specific information you need depends on the type of source, but for each source, record at least the following:

- Who wrote or assembled the source?
  - author(s)
  - editor(s)
  - translator(s)
- What data identify the source?
  - title and subtitle
  - title and subtitle of any larger work that contains the source (such as a collection, journal, or newspaper)
  - page numbers if the source appears in a larger work
  - volume number
  - issue number
  - edition number
  - URL and date you accessed the material, for online sources
- Who published the source and when?
  - publisher's name
  - place of publication
  - date of publication

For your own use, you might record Library of Congress call numbers. You don't include them in bibliographic citations, but you may find them helpful if you must consult the source again.

At some point, you'll need to format this bibliographic information into your required citation style, so you should record your sources in that style now. You can find templates and examples for bibliography style in figure 16.1 and chapter 17; for reference list style, refer to figure 18.1 and chapter 19.

As you record these data, you'll be tempted to take shortcuts, because it's boring work, and rules about periods, commas, and parentheses can feel like nit-picking. But nothing labels you a beginner faster than citations that are inappropriate, or worse, incomplete or inaccurate. So get in the habit of recording bibliographic data for a source fully, accurately, and appropriately the moment you handle it. There are computer programs that automatically format citations for you. They are useful aids, but they cannot substitute for your own knowledge of proper citation forms and methods, and not all of the software works perfectly.

3.3 Search for Sources Systematically

As you search for sources, you must be knowledgeably systematic, because if you miss an important one, you'll lose credibility.

3.3.1 Look for Someone Who Knows Something about Your Topic

You might start by asking around to find someone who knows something about your topic and standard reference works on it: advanced students, faculty, even people outside the academic community. You might look up your topic in the yellow pages of the phonebook. You won't always find someone, but you might get lucky.

3.3.2 Skim the Internet

Before college, many students do research only on the Web, because their high school libraries are small and they need to find only a few sources. In college, you can still do some preliminary work with a scholarly search engine such as Google Scholar. It will give you a rough idea of the kinds of sources available. If your library catalog is online, you can also start there (see 3.3.6 below). But if you search just the Internet, you'll miss important sources that you'll find only by poking around in your library. Once again, you'll work most efficiently if you have a plan.

3.3.3 Talk to Reference Librarians

If you don't know how to find what you need, ask a librarian. Most college libraries offer tours of reference rooms and special collections, and short seminars on how to search the catalog, databases, and other sources of information. If you're a new researcher, seize every opportunity to learn online search techniques in your field.

You can also talk to librarians who specialize in your area. They won't find sources for you, but they will help you look for them. If you have a research question, share it: *I'm looking for data on X because I want to find out.* . . . If you have a working hypothesis and reasons, share them too: *I'm looking for data to show Y [your reason] because I want to claim Z [your hypothesis].* Rehearse your questions to avoid wasting your time and theirs.

3.3.4 Browse in Your Reference Area

Researchers in all fields share common values and habits of thought, but every field has its own ways of doing things. To learn about the ways of your field, browse the shelves in your library's reference room that hold guides to your field's particular research methods, databases, and special resources (in the bibliography, see items in category 3 in your field). At least familiarize yourself with the following resources (in the bibliography, see category 4 for lists of sources in your field; many are also online):

- a bibliography of works published each year in your field, such as *Philosopher's Index* or *Education Index*
- summary bibliographies of works on a specific topic collected over several years (*Bibliographic Index* is a bibliography of bibliographies)
- collections of abstracts that summarize articles in newspapers and in professional journals
- reviews of the year's work; look for a title in your field beginning with *Reviews in* . . .
- for new fields, Web sites maintained by individuals or scholarly associations

If you know even a little of the secondary literature on your topic, you can begin looking for more substantive sources (skip to 3.3.7–3.3.8). If you don't, you might start with some specialized reference works.

3.3.5 Skim a Few Specialized Reference Works

Start by looking up your topic in a relevant specialized encyclopedia or dictionary such as the *Encyclopedia of Philosophy* or the *Concise Oxford Dictionary of Literary Terms,* where you may find an overview of your topic and often a list of standard primary and secondary sources (in the bibliography, see items in categories 1 and 2 in your field).

3.3.6 Search Your Library Catalog

SUBJECT HEADINGS IN BOOKS. As soon as you find one recent book relevant to your topic, look it up in your library's online catalog to find its Library of Congress subject headings; they will be at the bottom of the entry. For example, the online entry for this book includes these two topics:

1. Dissertations, Academic. 2. Academic writing.

You can click on the subject headings to find other books on the same topics. Many of those sources will have still more subject headings that can lead you to still more sources; it can turn into an endless trail.

KEYWORDS. Also search your online catalog using keywords from your question or working hypothesis—*Alamo, Texas independence, James Bowie.* If you find too many titles, start with those published in the last ten years by well-known university presses. For a wider selection, search WorldCat if your library subscribes. Otherwise, search the Library of Congress catalog at http://www.loc.gov. It has links to large university catalogs. Start early if you expect to get books on interlibrary loan.

ARTICLES. If most sources on your topic are articles, locate a recent one in your library's online databases. Its database entry will include a list of keywords. Search for them to find more articles on your topic. In most cases, you can just click on them. Some databases also provide abstracts of journal articles. Use these keywords to search the library catalog, as well.

3.3.7 Search Guides to Periodical Literature

If you've done research before, you're probably familiar with annual guides such as *Readers' Guide to Periodical Literature,* which cites sources such as magazines and newspapers. Most specialized fields also have yearly guides to secondary sources, such as *Art Abstracts, Historical Abstracts, and Abstracts in Anthropology* (in the bibliography, see items in category 4 in your field). Most are available online or on CDs.

All those resources will direct you to more sources, but none of them can substitute for the kind of in-library search that turns up an unexpectedly useful source.

3.3.8 Browse the Shelves

You might think that online research is faster than walking around your library. But it can be slower, and if you work only online, you may miss crucial sources that you'll find only in the library. More important, you'll miss the benefits of serendipity—a chance encounter with a source that you find only in person.

If you're allowed in the stacks (where all the books that you can check out are kept), find the shelf with books on your topic. Then scan the titles on that shelf and the ones above, below, and on either side. Then turn around and skim titles behind you; you never know. When you spot a promising title, especially on a university press book with a new binding, skim its table of contents, then its index for keywords related to your question or its answer. Then skim its bibliography for titles that look relevant to your project. You can do all that faster with books on a shelf than you can online.

If the book looks promising, skim its preface or introduction. If it still looks promising, set it aside for a closer look. Even if it doesn't seem relevant, record its Library of Congress call number and bibliographic data (author, title, publisher, date of publication and so on; see part 2 of this manual for the details), and in a few words summarize what the book seems to be about. A month later, you might realize that it's more useful than you thought.

You can check tables of contents for many journals online, but browsing in the journals area of a library can be more productive. Find the journals that have promising articles. Skim tables of contents for the prior ten years. Most volumes include a yearly summary table of contents. Then take a quick look at the journals shelved nearby. Skim their most recent tables of contents. You will be surprised at how often you find a relevant article that you would have missed had you done your work entirely online.

If you are new to a field, you can get a rough impression of the academic quality of a journal by its look. If it's on glossy paper with lots of illustrations, even advertisements, it might be more journalistic than scholarly. Those are not infallible signs of unreliable scholarship, but they are worth considering.

3.3.9   For Advanced Projects, Follow Bibliographic Trails

If you're into advanced work, use the bibliographies in your sources to find new sources and use their bibliographies in turn to find more. Do this:

- Skim bibliographies of recent books on your topic; look at any work mentioned in all or most of them, along with other publications by its author.
- If you find a source useful, skim its index for authors mentioned on four or more pages.
- Look for reviews of research in the first few paragraphs of journal articles.
- Look for recent PhD dissertations even marginally on your topic. Almost every dissertation reviews research in its first or second chapter.

New sources are best, but you may discover an old one with data long neglected.

3.4   Evaluate Sources for Relevance and Reliability

You will probably find more sources than you can use, so you must evaluate their usefulness by skimming quickly for two criteria: relevance and reliability.

3.4.1   Evaluate the Relevance of Sources

Once you decide a book might be relevant, skim it systematically:

- If its index lists keywords related to your question or its answers, skim the pages on which those words occur.
- Skim its introduction, especially its last page, where writers often outline their text.
- Skim its last chapter, especially the first and last six or seven pages.
- If you have time, do the same for chapters that look relevant, especially those for which the index lists many of your keywords.
- If the source is a collection of articles, skim the editor's introduction.

(Be sure that you're looking at a book's most recent edition. Over time, researchers change their views, refining them, even rejecting earlier ones.) If you're doing advanced work, read book reviews of promising sources (see section 4 of the bibliography of resources in your field).

If your source is a journal article, do this:

- Read its abstract, if any.
- Skim the last two or three paragraphs of the introduction (or other opening section) and all of any section called "Conclusion."
- If the article has no separate introduction or conclusion, skim its first and last few paragraphs.
- Skim the first paragraph or two after each subhead, if any.

If your source is online, do this:

- If it looks like a printed article, follow the steps for a journal article.
- Skim any section labeled "Introduction," "Overview," "Summary," or the like. If there is none, look for a link labeled "About the Site" or something similar.
- If the site has a link labeled "Site Map" or "Index," follow it and check the list, looking for keywords related to your question or its answers. Click to skim those pages.
- If the site has a "search" resource, type in keywords from your topic.

3.4.2   Evaluate the Reliability of Print Sources

You can't judge a source until you read it, but there are signs of its reliability:

1. Is the author a reputable scholar? Most publications cite an author's academic credentials; you can find more with a search engine. Most established scholars are reliable, but be cautious if the topic is a contested social issue such as gun control or abortion. Even reputable scholars

can have axes to grind, especially if their research is supported by a special interest group.

2. Is the source current? Many reputable scholars write books and articles popularizing the research of others. But by the time you read them, these tertiary sources may be out of date. How fast a source dates varies by subject, so check with someone who knows your field. For journal articles in the social sciences, more than ten years is pushing the limit. For books, figure fifteen or so. Publications in the humanities have a longer life span.

3. Is the source published by a reputable press? You can trust most university presses, especially those at well-known schools. Before they publish a manuscript, they ask experts to review it (a process called *peer review*). You can also trust some commercial presses in some fields, such as Norton in literature, Ablex in sciences, or West in the law. Be skeptical of a commercial book that makes sensational claims, even if its author has a PhD after his name.

4. Was the article peer-reviewed? Most scholarly journals, both print and online, publish only peer-reviewed articles. Few commercial magazines use peer review, and fewer still check an author's facts. If a report hasn't been peer-reviewed, use it cautiously.

5. Has the source received good reviews? If the source is a book published more than a year ago, it may have been reviewed in a journal in the field. Many fields have indexes to published reviews that tell you how others evaluate a source. (See the bibliography.)

6. Has the source been frequently cited by others? You can roughly estimate how influential a source is by how often others cite it. To determine that, consult a citation index (in the bibliography, see section 4 in your field).

Those signs don't guarantee that a source is reliable, but they should give you reasonable confidence in it. If you can't find reliable sources, acknowledge the limits of the ones you have. Of course, you may find an exciting research problem when you discover that a source thought to be reliable is not.

3.4.3 Evaluate the Reliability of Online Sources

Evaluate online sources as you do those in print, but more cautiously. The number of reliable Web sources grows every day, but they are still islands in a swamp of misinformation. If you find data available only on the Web, look for sites or online publications with these signs of reliability:

1. The site is sponsored by a reputable organization. Some sites supported by individuals are reliable; most are not.

2. It is related to a reliable professional journal.
3. It supplements reliable print sources. Some journals use the Web to host discussions among authors and readers, to offer data too new to be in libraries, to archive data not in articles, or to present illustrations too expensive to print. Many government and academic databases are only online.
4. It avoids heated advocacy for or against a contested social issue.
5. It does not make wild claims, attack other researchers, use abusive language, or make errors of spelling, punctuation, and grammar.
6. It indicates when the site was last updated. If it has no date, be cautious.

Trust a site only if careful readers would trust those who maintain it. If you don't know who maintains it, be skeptical.

Online services now provide reliable editions of many older texts. You'll also find well-edited texts at many university sites. It's "one-stop shopping"; you never have to move from your chair. Online services are, however, far less complete than most university libraries, and using them will teach you nothing about doing research in a real library. Some day, everything ever printed will be available online (a future that gives some researchers mixed feelings). But until then, surfing the Web doesn't replace prowling the stacks.

3.5 Look beyond the Usual Kinds of References

If you are writing a class paper, you'll usually have to focus narrowly on the kinds of sources typically used in your field. But if you are doing an advanced project such as an MA thesis or PhD dissertation, find an opportunity to search beyond them. If, for example, you were doing a project on the economic effects of agricultural changes on London grain markets in 1600, you might read some Elizabethan plays, look at pictures of working-class life, or look for commentary by religious figures on social behavior. Conversely, if you were working on visual representations of daily life in London, you might work up the economic history of the period and place. You can't do this in the limited time you have for short papers, but when you have months to work on a major project, try to look beyond the standard kinds of references relevant to your question. When you do, you enrich not only your specific analysis but your range of intellectual reference and your ability to synthesize diverse kinds of data, a crucial competence of an inquiring mind.

4 Engaging Sources

Once you find a source worth a close look, don't read it mechanically, just mining it for data to record. Note-taking is not clerical work. When you take notes on a source thoughtfully, you engage not just its words and ideas, but its implications, consequences, shortcomings, and new possibilities. Engage your source as if its writer were sitting with you, eager for a conversation (it's how you should imagine your readers engaging you).

4.1 Read Generously to Understand, Then Critically to Engage and Evaluate

For an advanced project, take the time to read your most promising sources twice, first quickly and generously to understand them on their own terms. If you disagree too soon, you can misunderstand or exaggerate a weakness.

Then reread them slowly and critically, as if you were amiably but pointedly questioning a friend; imagine his or her answers, then question them. If you disagree, don't just reject a source: read it in ways that will encourage your own original thinking.

You probably won't be able to engage your sources fully until after you've done some reading and developed a few ideas of your own. But from the outset, be alert for ways to read your sources not passively, as a consumer, but actively and creatively, as an engaged partner. At some point, better earlier than later, you must look for ways to go *beyond* your sources, even when you agree with them.

4.1.1 Look for Creative Agreement

It is a happy moment when a source confirms your views. But if you just passively agree, you won't develop any of your own ideas. So try to extend what your source claims: What new cases might it cover? What new insights can it provide? Is there confirming evidence your source hasn't considered? Here are some ways to agree creatively.

OFFER ADDITIONAL SUPPORT. You have new evidence to support a source's claim.

Smith uses anecdotal evidence to show that the Alamo story had mythic status beyond Texas, but a study of big-city newspapers offers better evidence.

1. Source supports a claim with old evidence, but maybe you can offer new evidence.
2. Source supports a claim with weak evidence, but maybe you can offer stronger evidence.

CONFIRM UNSUPPORTED CLAIMS. You can prove something that a source has only assumed or speculated.

Smith recommends visualization to improve sports performance, but a study of the mental activities of athletes shows why that is good advice.

1. Source only speculates that X might be true, but maybe you can offer evidence to show that it definitely is.
2. Source assumes that X is true, but maybe you can prove it.

APPLY A CLAIM MORE WIDELY. You can extend a position to new areas.

Smith has shown that medical students learn physiological processes better when they are explained with many metaphors rather than by just one. The same appears to be true for engineers learning physical processes.

1. Source correctly applies his claim to one situation, but maybe it can apply to new ones.
2. Source claims that X is true in a specific situation, but maybe it's true in general.

4.1.2   Look for Creative Disagreement

It is even more important to note when you disagree with a source, because that might suggest a working hypothesis for your whole report. So instead of just noting that you disagree with its views, use that disagreement to encourage your own productive thinking. Here are some kinds of disagreement (these aren't sharply defined categories; many overlap).

CONTRADICTIONS OF KIND. A source says something is one kind of thing, but maybe it's another kind.

Smith says that certain religious groups are considered "cults" because of their strange beliefs, but those beliefs are no different in kind from standard religions.

1. Source claims that X is a kind of Y (or like it), but maybe it's not.
2. Source claims that X always has Y as one its features or qualities, but maybe it doesn't.
3. Source claims that X is normal/good/significant/useful/moral/interesting/. . . , but maybe it's not.

(You can reverse those claims and the ones that follow to state the opposite: though a source says X is *not* a kind of Y, you can show that it is.)

PART-WHOLE CONTRADICTIONS. You can show that a source mistakes how the parts of something are related.

Smith has argued that sports are crucial to an educated person, but in fact athletics has no place in college.

1. Source claims that X is a part of Y, but maybe it's not.
2. Source claims that part of X relates to another of its parts in a certain way, but maybe it doesn't.
3. Source claims that every X has Y as one of its parts, but maybe it doesn't.

DEVELOPMENTAL OR HISTORICAL CONTRADICTIONS. You can show that a source mistakes the origin and development of a topic.

Smith argues that the world population will continue to rise, but it will not.

1. Source claims that *X* is changing, but maybe it's not.
2. Source claims that *X* originated in *Y*, but maybe it didn't.
3. Source claims that *X* develops in a certain way, but maybe it doesn't.

EXTERNAL CAUSE-EFFECT CONTRADICTIONS. You can show that a source mistakes a causal relationship:

Smith claims that juveniles can be stopped from becoming criminals by "boot camps." But evidence shows that it makes them more likely to become criminals.

1. Source claims that *X* causes *Y*, but maybe it doesn't.
2. Source claims that *X* causes *Y*, but maybe they are both caused by *Z*.
3. Source claims that *X* is sufficient to cause *Y*, but maybe it's not.
4. Source claims that *X* causes only *Y*, but maybe it also causes *Z*.

CONTRADICTIONS OF PERSPECTIVE. Most contradictions don't change a conceptual framework, but when you can contradict a standard view of things, you urge others to think in a new way.

Smith assumes that advertising is a purely economic function, but it also serves as a laboratory for new art forms.

1. Source discusses *X* in the context of or from the point of view of *Y*, but maybe a new context or point of view reveals a new truth (the new or old context can be social, political, philosophical, historical, economic, ethical, gender specific, etc.).
2. Source analyzes *X* using theory/value system *Y*, but maybe you can analyze *X* from a new point of view and see it in a new way.

As we said, you probably won't be able to engage sources in these ways until after you've read enough to form some views of your own. But if you keep these ways of thinking in mind as you begin to read, you'll engage your sources sooner and more productively.

Of course, once you discover that you can productively agree or disagree with a source, you should then ask *So what?* So what if you can show that while Smith claims that Easterners did not embrace the story of the Alamo enthusiastically, in fact many did?

4.2 | Take Notes Systematically

Like the other steps in a research project, note-taking goes better with a plan.

Figure 4.1. Example of a note card

4.2.1 Create Templates for Notes

You will take notes more reliably if you set up a system that encourages you to think beyond the mere content of your sources by analyzing and organizing that content into useful categories. A few instructors still recommend taking notes in longhand on 3 × 5 cards, as in figure 4.1. A card like that may seem old-fashioned, but it provides a template for efficient note-taking, even if you take notes on a laptop. (Start a new page for each general idea or claim that you record from a source.) Here is a plan for such a template:

■ At the top of each new page, create a space for bibliographic data (author, short title, page number).
■ Create another space at the top for keywords (see upper right above). Those words will later will let you sort and re-sort your notes by subject matter (for more on keywords, see 4.3.4).
■ Create different places on each new page for different kinds of notes. You might even label the places (see fig. 4.1, with places for a *Claim, Data,* and *My Qs*).
■ In particular, create a section specifically dedicated to *your own* responses, agreements, disagreements, speculations, and so on. That will encourage you to do more than simply record the content of what you read.
■ When you quote the words of a source, record them in a distinctive color

or font size and style so that you can recognize quotations at a glance, *and* enclose them in large quotation marks in case the file loses its formatting.
- When you paraphrase a passage (see 4.2.2), record the paraphrase in a distinctive color or font so that you can't possibly mistake it for your own ideas, and enclose it in curly brackets (in case the file loses its formatting).

If you can't take notes directly on a computer, make paper copies of the template.

4.2.2 Know When to Summarize, Paraphrase, or Quote

It would take you forever to transcribe the exact words of every source you might want to use, so you must know when not to quote, but to summarize or paraphrase.

Summarize when you need only the general point of a passage, section, or even whole article or book. Summary is useful for general context or related but not specifically relevant data or views. A summary of a source never serves as good evidence (see 5.4.2 for more on evidence).

Paraphrase when you can represent what a source says more clearly or pointedly than it does. Paraphrase doesn't mean just changing a word or two. You must use *your own* words and *your own* phrasing to replace most of the words and phrasing of the passage (see 7.9.2). A paraphrase is never as good evidence as a direct quotation.

Record exact quotations when they serve these purposes:

- The quoted words constitute evidence that backs up your reasons. If, for example, you wanted to claim that different regions responded to the Battle of the Alamo differently, you would quote exact words from different newspapers. You would paraphrase them if you needed only their general sentiments.
- The words are from an authority who backs up your view.
- They are strikingly original.
- They express your ideas so compellingly that the quotation can frame the rest of your discussion.
- They state a view that you disagree with, and to be fair you want to state that view exactly.

If you don't record important words now, you can't quote them later. So copy or photocopy passages more often than you think you'll need (for more on photocopying, see 4.3.1). *Never* abbreviate a quotation thinking you can accurately reconstruct it later. You can't. If you misquote, you fatally undermine your credibility, so double check your quote against the original. Then check it again.

4.2.3   Guard against Inadvertent Plagiarism

Sloppy note-taking has caused grief for students and professionals alike, ranging from ridicule for trivial errors to professional exile for inadvertent plagiarism. To avoid that risk, commit to heart these two iron rules for recording information in notes:

- *Always* unambiguously identify words and ideas from a source so that weeks or months later you cannot possibly mistake them for your own. As recommended above, record quotations and paraphrases with quotation marks, as well as in a font that unambiguously distinguishes them from your own ideas.
- *Never* paraphrase a source so closely that a reader can match the phrasing and sense of your words with those in your source (see 7.9.2).

In fact, rather than retyping quotations of more than a few lines, download or photocopy them. Add to the top of the downloaded or photocopied page the name of the source and keywords for sorting.

This is important: *never* assume that you can use what you find online without citing its source, even if it's free and publicly available. *Nothing* releases you from the duty to acknowledge your use of *anything* you did not personally create yourself. (For more on plagiarism, see 7.9.)

4.3   Take Useful Notes

Readers will judge your report not just by the quality of your sources and how accurately you report them, but also by how deeply you engage them. To do that, you must take notes in a way that not only reflects but encourages a growing understanding of your project.

4.3.1   Use Note-Taking to Advance Your Thinking

Many inexperienced researchers think that note-taking is a matter of merely recording data. Once they find a source, they download or photocopy pages or write down exactly what's on them. Recording and photocopying can help you quote or paraphrase accurately, but if that's all you do, if you don't *engage* your sources actively, you will simply accumulate a lot of inert data that are likely to be equally inert in your report.

If you photocopy lots of text, annotate it in a way that engages your critical thinking. Start by picking out those sentences that express crucial elements in a chapter or article (its claim, major reasons, and so on). Highlight or label them in the margin. Then mark ideas or data that you expect to include in your report. (If you use a highlighter, use different colors to indicate these different elements.)

Then on the back of the photocopied pages, summarize what you've highlighted or sketch a response to it, or make notes in the margin that help you interpret the highlighting. The more you write *about* a source now, the better you will understand and remember it later.

4.3.2 Take Notes Relevant to Your Question and Working Hypothesis

To make your notes most useful, record not just the facts that you think you can use as evidence, but data that help you explain those facts and their relationship to your claim. You can create a notes template to help you remember to look for several different kinds of information (see 4.2.1).

The first three items are directly relevant to your working hypothesis:

- reasons that support your hypothesis or suggest a new one
- evidence that supports your reasons
- views that undermine or even contradict your hypothesis

Do not limit your notes to supporting data. You will need to respond to data that qualify or even contradict your hypothesis when you make your case in support of it (see 5.4.3).

These next items might not support or challenge your hypothesis, but they may help you explain its context or simply make your report more readable:

- historical background of your question, what authorities have said about it, particularly earlier research (see 6.2.2 and 10.1.1)
- historical or contemporary context that explains the importance of your question
- important definitions and principles of analysis
- analogies, comparisons, and anecdotes that might not directly support your hypothesis but do explain or illustrate complicated issues or simply make your analysis more interesting
- strikingly original language relevant to your topic

4.3.3 Record Relevant Context

Those who misreport sources deliberately are dishonest, but an honest researcher can mislead inadvertently if she merely records words and ignores their role or qualifications. To guard against misleading your reader, follow these guidelines:

1. Do not assume that a source agrees with a writer when the source summarizes that writer's line of reasoning. Quote only what a source believes, not its account of someone else's beliefs, unless that account is relevant.
2. Record why sources agree, because why they agree can be as important as why they don't. Two psychologists might agree that teenage

drinking is caused by social influences, but one might cite family background, the other peer pressure.

3. Record the context of a quotation. When you note an important conclusion, record the author's line of reasoning:

Not: Bartolli (p. 123): The war was caused . . . by Z.

But: Bartolli: The war was caused by Y and Z (p. 123), but the most important was Z
(p. 123), for two reasons: First, . . . (pp. 124–26); Second, . . . (p. 126)

Even if you care only about a conclusion, you'll use it more accurately if
you record how a writer reached it.

4. Record the scope and confidence of each statement. Do not make a
source seem more certain or expansive than it is. The second sentence
below doesn't report the first fairly or accurately.

One study on the perception of risk (Wilson 1988) suggests a correlation between
high-stakes gambling and single-parent families.

Wilson (1988) says single-parent families cause high-stakes gambling.

5. Record how a source uses a statement. Note whether it's an important
claim, a minor point, a qualification or concession, and so on. Such
distinctions help you avoid mistakes like this:

Original by Jones: We cannot conclude that one event causes another because the
second follows the first. Nor can statistical correlation prove causation. But no one
who has studied the data doubts that smoking is a causal factor in lung cancer.

Misleading report: Jones claims "we cannot conclude that one event causes another
because the second follows the first. Nor can statistical correlation prove causation."
Therefore, statistical evidence is not a reliable indicator that smoking causes lung
cancer.

4.3.4 Categorize Your Notes for Sorting

Finally, a conceptually demanding task: as you take notes, categorize the
content of each one under two or more different keywords (see the upper
right corner of the note card in fig. 4.1). Avoid mechanically using words
only from the note: categorize the note by what it implies, by a general
idea larger than the specific content of the note. Keep a list of the keywords you use, and use the same ones for related notes. Do not create a
new keyword for every new note.

This step is crucial because it forces you to distill the content of a
note down to a word or two, and if you take notes on a computer, those
keywords will let you instantly group related notes with a single *Find-*

command. If you use more than one keyword, you can recombine your notes in different ways to discover new relationships (especially important when you feel you are spinning your wheels; see 4.5.3).

4.4 Write as You Read

We've said this before (and will again): writing forces you to think hard, so don't wait to nail down an idea in your mind before you write it out on the page. Experienced researchers know that the more they write, the sooner and better they understand their project. There is good evidence that the most successful researchers set a fixed time to write every day—from fifteen minutes to more than an hour. They might only draft a paragraph that responds to a source, summarizes a line of reasoning, or speculates about a new claim. But they write *something*, not to start a first draft of their report, but to sort out their ideas and maybe discover new ones. If you miss your goals, post a schedule by your computer.

If you write something that seems promising, add it to your storyboard. You will almost certainly revise it for your final draft, maybe even omit it entirely. But even if you reuse little of it, the more you write now, no matter how sketchily, the more easily you'll draft later. Preparatory writing and drafting aren't wholly different, but it's a good idea to think of them as distinct steps.

If you're new to a topic, much of this early writing may be just summary and paraphrase. When you reread it, you might see few of your own ideas and feel discouraged at your lack of original thinking. Don't be. Summarizing and paraphrasing are how we all gain control over new data, new and complicated ideas, even new ways of thinking. Writing out what we are trying to understand is a typical, probably even necessary, stage in just about everyone's learning curve.

4.5 Review Your Progress

Regularly review your notes and storyboard to see where you are and where you have to go. Full pages indicate reasons with support; empty pages indicate work to do. Check whether you think your working hypothesis is still plausible. Do you have good reasons supporting it? Good evidence to support those reasons? Can you add new reasons or evidence?

4.5.1 Search Your Notes for an Answer

We have urged you to find a working hypothesis or at least a question to guide your research. But some writers start with a question so vague that it evaporates as they pursue it. If that happens to you, search your notes for a generalization that might be a candidate for a working hypothesis, then work backward to find the question it answers.

Look first for questions, disagreements, or puzzles in your sources and in your reaction to them (see 2.1.3 and 4.1). What surprises you might surprise others. Try to state that surprise:

I expected the first mythic stories of the Alamo to originate in Texas, but they didn't. They originated in . . .

That tentative hypothesis suggests that the Alamo myth began as a national, not a regional, phenomenon—a modest, but promising start.

If you can't find a hypothesis in your notes, look for a pattern of ideas that might lead you to one. If you gathered data with a vague question, you probably sorted them under predictable keywords. For masks, the categories might be their origins (*African, Indian, Japanese* . . .), uses (*drama, religion, carnival* . . .), materials (*gold, feather, wood,* . . .), and so on. For example:

Egyptians—mummy masks of gold for nobility, wood for others.

Aztecs—masks from gold and jade buried only in the graves of the nobility.

New Guinea tribes—masks for the dead from feathers from rare birds.

Those facts could support a general statement such as, *Mask-making cultures create religious masks from the most valuable material available, especially for the dead.*

Once you can generate two or three such statements, try to formulate a still larger generalization that might include them all:

Many cultures invest great material and human resources in creating masks that represent their deepest values.generalization Egyptians, Aztecs, and Oceanic cultures all created religious masks out of the rarest and most valuable materials. Although in Oceanic cultures most males participate in mask-making, both the Egyptians and Aztecs set aside some of their most talented artists and craftsmen for mask-making.

If you think that some readers might plausibly disagree with that generalization, you might be able to offer it as a claim that corrects their misunderstanding.

4.5.2   Invent the Question

Now comes a tricky part. It's like reverse engineering: you've found the answer to a question that you haven't yet asked, so you have to reason backward to invent the question that your new generalization answers.

In this case, it might be *What signs indicate the significance of masks in the societies of those who make and use them?* As paradoxical as it may seem, experienced researchers often discover their question after they answer it, the problem they should have posed after they solve it.

4.5.3 Re-sort Your Notes

If none of that helps, try re-sorting your notes. When you first selected keywords for your notes, you identified general concepts that could organize not just your evidence but your thinking. If you chose keywords representing those concepts carefully, you can re-sort your notes in different ways to get a new slant on your material. If your keywords no longer seem relevant, review your notes to create new ones and reshuffle again.

4.6 Manage Moments of Normal Panic

This may be the time to address a problem that afflicts even experienced researchers and at some point will probably afflict you. As you shuffle through hundreds of notes and a dozen lines of thought, you start feeling that you're not just spinning your wheels but spiraling down into a black hole of confusion, paralyzed by what seems to be an increasingly complex and ultimately unmanageable task.

The bad news is that there's no sure way to avoid such moments. The good news is that most of us have them and they usually pass. Yours will too if you keep moving along, following your plan, taking on small and manageable tasks instead of trying to confront the complexity of the whole project. It's another reason to start early, to break a big project into its smallest steps, and to set achievable deadlines, such as a daily page quota when you draft.

Many writers try to learn from their research experience by keeping a journal, a diary of what they did and found, the lines of thought they pursued, why they followed some and gave up on others. Writing is a good way to think more clearly about your reading, but it's also a good way to think more clearly about your thinking.

5 ▪ Planning Your Argument

Most of us would rather read than write. There is always another article to read, one more source to track down, just a bit more data to gather. But well before you've done all the research you'd like to do, there comes a point when you must start thinking about the first draft of your report. You might be ready when your storyboard starts to fill up and you're satisfied with how it looks. You will know you're ready when you think you can sketch a reasonable case to support your working hypothesis (see 2.3). If your storyboard is full and you still can't pull together a case strong enough to plan a draft, you may have to rethink your hypothesis, perhaps even your question. But you can't be certain where you stand in that process until you try to plan that first draft.

If you're not an experienced writer, we suggest planning your first draft in two steps:

- Sort your notes into the elements of a research argument.
- Organize those elements into a coherent form.

In this chapter, we explain how to assemble your argument; in the next, how to organize it. As you gain experience, you'll learn to combine those two steps into one.

5.1   What a Research Argument Is and Is Not

The word *argument* has bad associations these days, partly because radio and TV stage so many abrasive ones. But the argument in a research report doesn't try to intimidate an opponent into silence or submission. In fact, there's rarely an "opponent" at all. Like any good argument, a research argument resembles an amiable conversation in which you and your imagined readers reason together to solve a problem whose solution they don't yet accept. That doesn't mean they oppose your claims (though they might). It means only that they won't accept them until they see good reasons based on reliable evidence and until you respond to their reasonable questions and reservations.

In face-to-face conversation, making (not *having*) a cooperative argument is easy: you state your reasons and evidence not as a lecturer would to a silent audience, but as you would engage talkative friends sitting around a table with you: you offer a claim and some reasons to believe it; they probe for details, raise objections, or offer their points of view; you respond, perhaps with questions of your own; and they ask more questions. At its best, it's an amiable but thoughtful back-and-forth that develops and tests the best case that you and they can make *together*.

In writing, that kind of cooperation is harder, because you usually write alone (unless you're in a writing group; see 2.4), and so you must not only answer your imagined readers' questions, but *ask them on their behalf*—as often and as sharply as real readers will. But your aim isn't just to think up clever rhetorical strategies that will persuade readers to accept your claim regardless of how good it is. It is to test your claim and especially its support, so that when you submit your report to your readers, you offer them the best case you can make. In a good research report, readers hear traces of that imagined conversation.

Now as we've said, reasoning based on evidence isn't the only way to reach a sound conclusion, sometimes not even the best way. We often make good decisions by relying on intuition, feelings, or spiritual insight. But when we try to *explain* why we believe our claims are sound and why others should too, we have no way to *demonstrate* how we reached them, because we can't offer intuitions or feelings as evidence for readers to evaluate. We can only say we had them and ask readers to take our claim on faith, a request that thoughtful readers rarely grant.

When you make a research argument, however, you must lay out your reasons and evidence so that your readers can consider them; then you must imagine both their questions and your answers. That sounds harder than it is.

5.2   Build Your Argument around Answers to Readers' Questions

It is easy to imagine the kind of conversation you must have with your readers, because you have them every day:

A: I hear you had a hard time last semester. How do you think this one will go? *[A poses a problem in the form of a question.]*

B: Better, I hope. *[B answers the question.]*

A: Why so? *[A asks for a reason to believe B's answer.]*

B: I'm taking courses in my major. *[B offers a reason.]*

A: Like what? *[A asks for evidence to back up B's reason.]*

B: History of Art, Intro to Design. *[B offers evidence to back up his reason.]*

A: Why will taking courses in your major make a difference? *[A doesn't see the relevance of B's reason to his claim that he will do better.]*

B: When I take courses I'm interested in, I work harder. *[B offers a general principle that relates his reason to his claim that he will do better.]*

A: What about that math course you have to take? *[A objects to B's reason.]*

B: I know I had to drop it last time I took it, but I found a good tutor. *[B acknowledges A's objection and responds to it.]*

If you can see yourself as *A* or *B*, you'll find nothing new in the argument of a research report, because you build one out of the answers to those same five questions.

- What is your claim?
- What reasons support it?
- What evidence supports those reasons?
- How do you respond to objections and alternative views?
- How are your reasons relevant to your claim?

If you ask and answer those five questions, you can't be sure that your readers will accept your claim, but you make it more likely that they'll take it—and you—seriously.

5.3   Turn Your Working Hypothesis into a *Claim*

We described the early stages of research as finding a question and imagining a tentative answer. We called that answer your *working hypothesis.* Now as we discuss building an argument to support that hypothesis, we change our terminology a last time. When you think you can write a report that backs up your hypothesis with good reasons and evidence, you'll present that hypothesis as your argument's *claim*. Your claim is the center of your argument, the point of your report (some teachers call it a *thesis*).

5.4 Assemble the Elements of Your Argument

At the core of your argument are three elements: your claim, your reasons for accepting it, and the evidence that supports those reasons. To that core, you'll add one and perhaps two more elements: one responds to questions, objections, and alternative points of view; the other answers those who do not understand how your reasons are *relevant* to your claim.

5.4.1 State and Evaluate Your Claim

Start a new first page of your storyboard (or outline). At the bottom, state your claim in a sentence or two. Be as specific as you can, because the words in this claim will help you plan and execute your draft. Avoid vague value words like *important, interesting, significant,* and the like. Compare

Masks play a significant role in many religious ceremonies.

In cultures from pre-Columbian America to Africa and Asia, masks allow religious celebrants to bring deities to life so that worshipers experience them directly.

Now judge the *significance* of your claim (*So what?* again). A significant claim doesn't make a reader think *I know that,* but rather *Really? How interesting. What makes you think so?* (Review 2.1.4.) These next two claims are too trivial to justify reading, much less writing, a report to back them up:

This report discusses teaching popular legends such as the Battle of the Alamo to elementary school students. (*So what if it does?*)

Teaching our national history through popular legends such as the Battle of the Alamo is common in elementary education. (*So what if it is?*)

Of course, what your readers will count as interesting depends on what they know, and if you're early in your research career, that's something you can't predict. If you're writing one of your first reports, assume that your most important reader is you. It is enough if *you alone* think your answer is significant, if it makes you think, *Well, I didn't know that when I started.* If, however, you think your own claim is vague or trivial, you're not ready to assemble an argument to support it, because you have no reason to make one.

5.4.2 Support Your Claim with Reasons and Evidence

It may seem obvious that you must back up a claim with reasons and evidence, but it's easy to confuse those two words because we often use them as if they meant the same thing:

What reasons do you base your claim on?

What evidence do you base your claim on?

But they mean different things:

- We think up logical reasons, but we collect hard evidence; we don't collect hard reasons and think up logical evidence. And we base reasons on evidence; we don't base evidence on reasons.
- A reason is abstract, and you don't have to cite its source (if you thought of it). Evidence usually comes from outside your mind, so you must always cite its source, even if you found it through your own observation or experiment; then you must show what you did to find it.
- Reasons need the support of evidence; evidence should need no support beyond a reference to a reliable source.

The problem is that what you think is a true fact and therefore hard evidence, your readers might not. For example, suppose a researcher offers this claim and reason:

Early Alamo stories reflected values already in the American character.claim The story almost instantly became a legend of American heroic sacrifice.reason

To support that reason, she offers this "hard" evidence:

Soon after the battle, many newspapers used the story to celebrate our heroic national character.evidence

If readers accept that statement as a fact, they may accept it as evidence. But skeptical readers, the kind you should expect (even hope for), are likely to ask *How soon is "soon?" How many is "many?" Which papers? In news stories or editorials? What exactly did they say? How many papers didn't mention it?*

To be sure, readers may accept a claim based only on a reason, if that reason seems self-evidently true or is from a trusted authority:

We are all created equal,reason so no one has a natural right to govern us.claim

In fact, instructors in introductory courses often accept reasons supported only by what authoritative sources say: *Wilson says* X *about religious masks, Yang says* Y, *Schmidt says* Z. But in advanced work, readers expect more.

They want evidence drawn not from a secondary source but from primary sources or your own observation.

Review your storyboard: Can you support each reason with what your readers will think is evidence of the right kind, quantity, and quality and is appropriate to their field? Might your readers think that what you offer as evidence needs more support? Or a better source? If so, you must find more data or acknowledge the limits of what you have.

Your claim, reasons, and evidence make up the core of your argument, but it needs at least one more element, maybe two.

5.4.3 Acknowledge and Respond to Readers' Points of View

You may wish it weren't so, but your best readers will be the most critical; they'll read fairly, but not accept everything you write at face value. They will think of questions, raise objections, and imagine alternatives. In conversation, you can respond to questions as others ask them. But in writing, you must not only answer those questions, but ask them. If you don't, you'll seem not to know or, worse, not to care, about your readers' views.

Readers raise two kinds of questions; try to imagine and respond to both.

1. The first kind of question points to problems *inside* your argument, usually its evidence. Imagine a reader making any of these criticisms, then construct a miniargument in response:

   ▫ Your evidence is from an unreliable or out-of-date source.
   ▫ It is inaccurate.
   ▫ It is insufficient.
   ▫ It doesn't fairly represent all the evidence available.
   ▫ It is the wrong kind of evidence for our field.
   ▫ It is irrelevant, because it does not *count* as evidence.

Then imagine these kinds of objections to your reasons and how you would answer them:

■ Your reasons are inconsistent or contradictory.
■ They are too weak or too few to support your claim.
■ They are irrelevant to your claim (we discuss this matter in 5.4.4).

2. The second kind of question raises problems from *outside* your argument. Those who see the world differently are likely to define terms differently, reason differently, even offer evidence that you think is irrelevant. If you and your readers see the world differently, you must acknowledge and respond to these issues, as well. Do not treat these dif-

fering points of view simply as objections. You will lose readers if you argue that your view is right and theirs is wrong. Instead, acknowledge the differences, then compare them so that readers can understand your argument on its own terms. They still might not agree, but you'll show them that you understand and respect their views; they are then more likely to try to understand and respect yours.

If you're a new researcher, you'll find these questions hard to imagine because you might not know how your readers' views differ from your own. Even so, try to think of some plausible questions and objections; it's important to get into the habit of asking yourself *What could cast doubt on my claim?* But if you're writing a thesis or dissertation, you must know the issues that others in your field are likely to raise. So however experienced you are, practice imagining and responding to disagreements. Even if you just go through the motions, you'll cultivate a habit of mind that your readers will respect and that may keep you from jumping to questionable conclusions.

Add those acknowledgments and responses to your storyboard where you think readers will raise them.

5.4.4   Establish the Relevance of Your Reasons

Even experienced researchers find this last element of argument hard to grasp, harder to use, and even harder to explain. It is called a *warrant*. You add a warrant to your argument when you think a reader might reject your claim not because a reason supporting it is factually wrong or is based on insufficient evidence, but because it's *irrelevant* and so doesn't count as a reason at all.

For example, imagine a researcher writes this:

The Alamo stories spread quickly~claim~ because in 1836 this country wasn't yet a confident player on the world stage.~reason~

Imagine that she suspects that her readers will likely object, *It's true that the Alamo stories spread quickly and that in 1836 this country wasn't a confident player on the world stage. But I don't see how not being confident is relevant to the story spreading quickly.* The writer can't respond simply by offering more evidence that this country was not a confident player on the world stage or that the stories in fact spread quickly: her reader already accepts both as true. Instead, she has to explain the *relevance* of that reason—*why* its truth supports the truth of her claim.

To do that, she needs a warrant. Warrants are very difficult to grasp, but anyone writing a research argument must understand how they work, because readers so often object that while they might agree that a researcher's reason may be true or his evidence accurate, nevertheless, they disagree with his claim *because the reason is irrelevant to that claim or the evidence is irrelevant to its reason.*

HOW A WARRANT WORKS IN A CASUAL CONVERSATION. Suppose you make this little argument to a new friend from a faraway land:

It's 5° below zero_{reason} so you should wear a hat._{claim}

To most of us, the reason seems obviously to support the claim and so needs no explanation of its relevance. But suppose your friend asks this odd question:

So what if it is 5° below? Why does that mean I should wear a hat?

That question challenges not the *truth* of the reason (it is 5° below), but its *relevance* to the claim (you should wear a hat). You might think it odd that anyone would ask that question, but you could answer with a general principle:

Well, when it's cold, people should dress warmly.

That sentence is a warrant. It states a general principle based on our experience in the world: when a certain general condition exists (*it's cold*), we're justified in saying that a certain general consequence regularly follows (*people should dress warmly*). We think that the general warrant justifies our specific claim that our friend should wear a hat on the basis of our specific reason that it's 5° below, because we're reasoning according to this principle of logic: if a general condition and its consequence are true, then specific instances of it must also be true.

In more detail, it works like this (warning: what follows may sound like a lesson in logic 101):

- In the warrant, the general condition is *it's cold*. It regularly leads us to draw a general consequence: *people should dress warmly.* We state that as a true and general principle, *When it's cold, people should dress warmly.*
- The specific reason, *it's 5° below,* is a valid instance of the general condition *it's cold.*
- The specific claim, *you should wear a hat,* is a valid instance of the general consequence, *people should dress warmly.*
- Since the general principle stated in the warrant is true and the reason and claim are valid instances of it, we're "warranted" to assert as true and valid the claim, *wear a hat.*

But now suppose six months later you visit your friend and he says this:

It's above 80° tonight,reason so wear a long-sleeved shirt.claim

That might baffle you: How could the reason (*it's above 80°*) be relevant to the claim (*wear a long-sleeved shirt*)? You might imagine this general principle as a warrant:

When it's a warm night, people should dress warmly.

But that isn't true. And if you think the warrant isn't true, you'll deny that the reason supports the claim, because it's irrelevant to it.

But suppose your friend adds this:

Around here, when it's a warm night, you should protect your arms from insect bites.

Now the argument would make sense, but only if you believe all this:

- The warrant is true (*when it's a warm night, you should protect your arms from insect bites*).
- The reason is true (*it's above 80° tonight*).
- The reason is a valid instance of the general condition (*80° is a valid instance of being warm*).
- The claim is a valid instance of the general consequence (*wearing a long-sleeved shirt is a valid instance of protecting your arms from insect bites*).
- No unstated limitations or exceptions apply (*a cold snap didn't kill all insects the night before, the person can't use insect repellant instead, and so on*).

If you believe all that, then you should accept the argument that when it's 80° at night, it's a good idea to wear a long-sleeved shirt, at least at that time and place.

We all know countless such principles, and we learn more every day. If we didn't, we couldn't make our way through our daily lives. In fact, we express our folk wisdom in the form of warrants, but we call them proverbs: *When the cat's away, the mice will play. Out of sight, out of mind. Cold hands, warm heart.*

HOW A WARRANT WORKS IN AN ACADEMIC ARGUMENT. Here is a more scholarly example, but it works in the same way:

Encyclopedias must not have been widely owned in early nineteenth century America,claim because wills rarely mentioned them.reason

Assume the reason is true: there is lots of evidence that encyclopedias were in fact rarely mentioned in early nineteenth-century wills. Even so, a reader might wonder why that statement is *relevant* to the claim: *You may be right that most such wills didn't mention encyclopedias, but so what? I don't see how that is relevant to your claim that few people owned one.* If a writer expects that question, he must anticipate it by offering a warrant, a general principle that shows how his reason is relevant to his claim.

That warrant might be stated like this:

When a valued object wasn't mentioned in early nineteenth-century wills, it usually wasn't part of the estate._{warrant} Wills at that time rarely mentioned encyclopedias,_{reason} so few people must have owned one._{claim}

We would accept the claim as sound *if and only if* we believe the following:

- The warrant is true.
- The reason is both true and a valid instance of the general condition of the warrant (encyclopedias were instances of valued objects).
- The claim is a valid instance of the general consequence of the warrant (not owning an encyclopedia is a valid instance of something valuable not being part of an estate).

And if the researcher feared that a reader might doubt any of those conditions, she would have to make an argument supporting it.

But that's not the end of the problem: is the warrant true *always and without exception?* Readers might wonder whether in some parts of the country wills mentioned only land and buildings, or whether few people made wills in the first place. If the writer thought that readers might wonder about such qualifications, she would have to make yet another argument showing that those exceptions don't apply.

Now you can see why we so rarely settle arguments about complex issues: even when we agree on the evidence, we can still disagree over how to reason about it.

TESTING THE RELEVANCE OF A REASON TO A CLAIM. To test the relevance of a reason to a claim, construct a warrant that bridges them. First, state the reason and claim, in that order. Here's the original reason and claim from the beginning of this section:

In 1836, this country wasn't a confident player on the world stage,_{reason} so the Alamo stories spread quickly._{claim}

Now construct a general principle that includes that reason and claim. Warrants come in all sorts of forms, but the most convenient is the *When– then* pattern. This warrant "covers" the reason and claim.

When a country lacks confidence, it quickly embraces stories of heroic military events.

When this **General Condition** exists,		this **General Consequence** follows._{warrant}
*When a country lacks confidence,*_{general condition}		*it quickly embraces stories of heroic military events.*_{general consequence}
*In 1836, this country wasn't a confident player on the world stage*_{specific reason}	so	*the story of the Alamo spread quickly.*_{specific claim}
This **Specific Condition** exists,_{reason}	so	this **Specific Consequence** follows._{claim}

Figure 5.1. Argument structure

We can formally represent those relationships as in figure 5.1.

To accept that claim, readers must accept the following:

- The warrant is true.
- The specific reason is true.
- The specific reason is a valid instance of the general condition side of the warrant.
- The specific claim is a valid instance of the general consequence side of the warrant.
- No limiting conditions keep the warrant from applying.

If the writer thought that readers might deny the truth of that warrant or reason, she would have to make an argument supporting it. If she thought they might think the reason or claim wasn't a valid instance of the warrant, she'd have to make yet another argument that it was.

As you gain experience, you'll learn to check arguments in your head, but until then you might try to sketch out warrants for your most debatable reasons. After you test a warrant, add it to your storyboard where you think readers will need it. If you need to support a warrant with an argument, outline it there.

WHY WARRANTS ARE ESPECIALLY DIFFICULT FOR RESEARCHERS NEW TO A FIELD. If you're new in a field, you may find warrants difficult for these reasons:

- Advanced researchers rarely spell out their principles of reasoning because they know their colleagues take them for granted. New researchers must figure them out on their own. (It's like hearing someone say, "Wear a long-sleeved shirt because it's above 80° tonight.")
- Warrants typically have exceptions that experts also take for granted and therefore rarely state, forcing new researchers to figure them out, as well.
- Experts also know when *not* to state an obvious warrant or its limitations, one more thing new researchers must learn on their own. For example, if an expert wrote *It's early June, so we can expect that we'll soon pay more for gasoline,* he wouldn't state the obvious warrant: *When summer approaches, gas prices rise.*

If you offer a well-known but rarely stated warrant, you'll seem condescending or naïve. But if you fail to state one that readers need, you'll seem illogical. The trick is learning when readers need one and when they don't. That takes time.

So don't be dismayed if warrants seem confusing; they're difficult even for experienced writers. But knowing about them should encourage you to ask this crucial question: in addition to the *truth* of your reasons and evidence, will your readers see their *relevance* to your claim? If they might not, you must make an argument demonstrating it.

5.5 Distinguish Arguments Based on Evidence from Arguments Based on Warrants

Finally, it's important to note that there are two kinds of arguments that readers judge in different ways:

- One infers a claim from a reason and warrant. The claim in that kind of argument is believed to be *certainly* true.
- The other bases a claim on reasons based on evidence. The claim in that kind of argument is considered to be *probably* true.

As paradoxical as it may seem, researchers put more faith in the second kind of argument, the kind based on evidence, than in the first.

This argument presents a claim based on a reason based on evidence:

Needle-exchange programs contribute to increased drug usage.claim When their participants realize that they can avoid the risk of disease from infected needles, they feel encouraged to use more drugs.reason A study of those who participated in one such program reported that 34% of the participants increased their use of drugs from 1.7 to 2.1 times a week because they said they felt protected from needle-transmitted diseases.evidence

If we consider the evidence to be both sound and sufficient (we might not), then the claim seems reasonable, though by no means certain, because someone might find new and better evidence that contradicts the evidence offered here.

This next argument makes the same claim based on the same reason, but the claim is supported not by evidence but by logic. The claim must be true if the warrant and reason are true and if the reason and claim are valid instances of the warrant:

Needle-exchange programs contribute to increased drug usage.claim When participants realize that they can avoid the risk of disease from infected needles, they feel encouraged to use more drugs.reason **Whenever the consequences of risky behavior are reduced, people engage in it more often.**warrant

But we have to believe that the warrant is always true in all cases everywhere, a claim that most of us would—or should—deny. Few of us drive recklessly because cars have seat belts and collapsible steering columns.

All arguments rely on warrants, but readers of a *research* argument are more likely to trust a claim when it's not inferred from a principle but rather is based on evidence, because no matter how plausible general principles seem, they have too many exceptions, qualifications, and limitations. Those who make claims based on what they think are unassailable principles too often miss those complications, because they are convinced that their principles must be right, regardless of evidence to the contrary, and if their principles are right, so are their inferences. Such arguments are more ideological than factual. So support your claims with as much evidence as you can, even when you think you have the power of logic on your side. Add a warrant to nail down an inference, but base the inference on evidence, as well.

5.6   Assemble an Argument

Here is a small argument that fits together all five parts:

TV aimed at children can aid their intellectual development, but that contribution has been offset by a factor that could damage their emotional development—too much violence.claim Parents agree that example is an important influence on a child's development. That's why parents tell their children stories about heroes. It seems plausible, then, that when children see degrading behavior, they will be affected by it as well.warrant In a single day, children see countless examples of violence.reason Every day, the average child watches almost four hours of TV and sees about twelve acts of violence (Smith 1992).evidence Tarnov has shown that children don't confuse cartoon violence with real life (2003).acknowledgment of alternative point of view But that may make children more vulnerable to violence in other shows. If they only distinguish between cartoons and people, they may think real actors engaged in graphic violence represent real life._{response} We cannot ignore the possibility that TV violence encourages the development of violent adults._{claim restated}

Most of those elements could be expanded to fill many paragraphs.

Arguments in different fields look different, but they all consist of answers to just these five questions:

- What are you claiming?
- What are your reasons?
- What evidence supports your reasons?
- But what about other points of view?
- How are your reasons relevant to your claim?

Your storyboard should answer those questions many times. If it doesn't, your report will seem incomplete and unconvincing.

6 │ Planning a First Draft

Once you assemble your argument, you might be ready to draft it. But experienced writers know that the time they invest in planning a draft more than pays off when they write it. To draft effectively, though, you need more than just the elements of a sound argument; you need a plan to assemble them into a coherent one. Some plans, however, are better than others.

6.1   Avoid Unhelpful Plans

Avoid certain approaches.

1. Do not organize your report as a narrative of your project, especially not as a mystery story, with your claim revealed at the end. Few readers care what you found first, then problems you overcame, then leads you pursued, on and on to the end. You see signs of that in language like *The first issue was . . . , Then I compared. . . . Finally I conclude.*

2. Do not patch together a series of quotations, summaries of sources, or downloads from the Web. Teachers want to see *your* thinking, not that of others. They especially dislike reports that read like a collage of Web

screens. Do that, and you'll seem not only an amateur but worse, possibly a plagiarist (see 7.9).

3. Do not mechanically organize your report around the terms of your assignment or topic. If your assignment lists issues to cover, don't think you must address them in the order given. If you were asked or you decide to compare and contrast Freud's and Jung's analyses of the imagination, you would not have to organize your report in two parts, the first on Freud, the second on Jung. It would be more productive to break those two big topics into their parts, then organize your report around them (for more on this, see 6.2.5–6.2.6).

6.2 Create a Plan That Meets Your Readers' Needs

Some fields stipulate the plan of a report. Readers in the experimental sciences, for example, expect reports to follow some version of this:

Introduction—Methods and Materials—Results—Discussion—Conclusion

If you must follow a preset plan, ask your instructor or find a secondary source for a model. But if you must create your own, it must make sense not just to you, but *visibly* to your readers. To create that visible form, go back to your storyboard or outline.

6.2.1 Converting a Storyboard into an Outline

If you prefer to work from an outline, you can turn your storyboard into one:

- Start with a sentence numbered *I* that states your claim.
- Add complete sentences under it numbered *II, III, . . .* , each of which states a reason supporting your claim.
- Under each reason, use capital letters to list sentences summarizing your evidence; then list by numbers the evidence itself. For example (the data are invented for the illustration):

I. Introduction: Value of classroom computers is uncertain.
II. Different uses have different effects.
    A. All uses increase number of words produced.
        1. Study 1: 950 vs. 780
        2. Study 2: 1,103 vs. 922
    B. Labs allow students to interact.
III. Studies show limited benefit on revision.
    A. Study A: writers on computers are more wordy.
        1. Average of 2.3 more words per sentence
        2. Average of 20% more words per essay

B. Study B: writers need hard copy to revise effectively.
  1. 22% fewer typos when done on hard copy vs. computer screen
  2. 2.26% fewer spelling errors
IV. Conclusion: Too soon to tell how much computers improve learning.
  A. Few reliable empirical studies.
  B. Little history because many programs are in transition.

The sketchiest outline is just phrases, with no formal layers of I, A, 1, and so on.

Introduction: benefits uncertain
Different uses/different effects
  More words
  More interaction
Revision studies
  Study A longer sentences
  Study B longer essays
Conclusion: Too soon to judge effects

When you start a project, a sketch may be the best you can do, and for a short project it may be all you need, so long as you know the point of each item. But an outline of complete sentences is usually more useful. More useful yet is a storyboard, especially for a long project.

6.2.2   Sketch a Working Introduction

Be ready to write your introduction twice, first a sketchy one for yourself; then a final one for your readers after you've revised your draft and know what you have written. That final introduction will usually have four parts, so you might as well build your working introduction to anticipate them (see chapter 9).

1. *Briefly* sketch the research you've read that is *specifically* relevant to your topic. In 5.4.1, we suggested that you write your claim at the bottom of a new first page of your storyboard. Now, at the top, *sketch* the prior research that you intend to extend, modify, or correct. Do not list all the research remotely relevant to your topic. Many semi-experienced researchers list scores of reports, thinking they'll impress readers with their diligence. But an endless list of irrelevant references is less impressive than it is annoying. If you were working on Alamo stories, for example, you wouldn't cite every historical analysis of the battle, but only the specific research that you intend to extend, modify, or correct.

List your sources in an order useful to your readers. If their historical sequence is important, list them chronologically. If not, group them by some other principle: their quality, significance, point of view. Then order those groups in whatever way best helps your readers understand them (see 6.2.5 for principles of order). Under no circumstances list your sources in the order you happened to read them or now remember them.

2. Rephrase your question as a lack of knowledge or gap in understanding. After you sketch that research, tell readers what part of it you will extend, modify, or correct. Do that by restating your question as something that the research has gotten wrong, explained poorly, or failed to consider.

Why is the Alamo story so important in our national mythology?
→ Few historians have tried to explain why the Alamo story has become so important in our national mythology.

Writers do this almost always and in many ways, so as you read, note how your sources do it.

3. If you can, sketch an answer to *So what if we don't find out?* What larger issue will your readers not understand if you don't answer your research question?

If we understood how such stories became national legends, we would better understand our national values, perhaps even what makes us distinct.

At this point, you may find any larger significance hard to imagine. Add it if you can, but don't spend a lot of time on it; we'll return to it (see 10.1.3).

4. Revise and position your claim. You wrote your claim on the first page of your storyboard. Now decide if that's where you want to leave it. You have two choices for where to state it in your report:
   ▫ at the end of your introduction and again close to the beginning of your conclusion
   ▫ only in your conclusion, as a kind of climax to your reasoning

If you've done few advanced projects, we urge you to state your claim at the end of your introduction and again near the beginning of your conclusion. When readers see a claim early, at the end of your introduction, they know where you're taking them and so can read what follows faster, understand it better, and remember it longer. When you put your claim first, it also helps keep you on track.

Some new researchers fear that if they reveal their claim in their introduction, readers will be bored and stop reading. Others worry about repeating themselves. Both fears are baseless. If you ask an interesting question, readers will want to see how well you can support its answer.

If you leave your claim at the bottom of your introduction page, restate a version of it at the top of a new conclusion page at the end of your storyboard. If you can, make this concluding claim more specific than the one in the introduction.

In some fields, writers conventionally state their claim only in a final section headed *Discussion* or *Conclusion*. In those cases, many readers just skim the introduction, then jump to the conclusion. So for that kind of reader, write your introduction in a way that introduces not only the body of your paper, but your conclusion, as well.

If you decide to announce your claim only in your conclusion, move it to the top of a new conclusion page. But if you do, you'll need another sentence to replace it at the end of your introduction, one that launches your reader into the body of your report. That sentence should include the key terms that you use throughout your report (see 6.2.3).

We suggest that you write that launching sentence when you draft your final introduction (see 10.1.4). So for now, make a place for it at the bottom of the introduction page of your storyboard, either by sketching a rough version of it or making a note to add it later.

Some writers add a "road map" at the end their introduction, laying out the organization of their report:

In part 1, I discuss. . . . Part 2 addresses the issue of. . . . Part 3 examines . . .

Readers differ on this. Road maps are common in the social sciences, but many in the humanities find them clumsy. Even if your readers might object, you can add a road map to your storyboard to guide your drafting, then cut it from your final draft. If you keep it, make it short.

6.2.3 Identify Key Terms Expressing Concepts That Unite the Report and Distinguish Its Parts

To feel that your report is coherent, readers must see a few central concepts running through all of its parts. But readers won't recognize those repeated concepts if you refer to them in many different words. Readers need to see specific terms that repeatedly refer to those concepts, not every time you mention one, but often enough that readers can't miss them. Those terms running through the whole might include the words you used to categorize your notes, but they must include important words from your question and claim. Readers must also see more specific concepts in each part that distinguish that part from all other parts.

Before you start drafting, therefore, identify the key concepts that you intend to run through your whole report and select the term that you will use most often to refer to each one. Then do the same for the concepts that distinguish each section from other sections. As you draft, you may find new ones and drop some old ones, but you'll write more coherently if you keep your most important terms and concepts in the front of your mind.

Here is a specific method to identify the global concepts that unite the whole report:

1. On the introduction and conclusion pages of your storyboard, circle four or five words that express your most important concepts. You should find those words in the most explicit statement of your claim.
   - ▣ Ignore words obviously connected to your topic: *Alamo, battle, defeat.*
   - ▢ Focus on concepts that *you* bring to the argument and intend to develop: *aftermath of defeat, triumph in loss, heroic ideals, sacrifice, national spirit,* and so on.

2. For each concept, select a key term that you can repeat through the body of your paper. It can be one of your circled words or a new one. List those key terms on a separate page. If you find few words that can serve as key terms, your claim may be too general (review 5.4.1).

You can follow the same procedure to find the key terms that unify each section. Look at the reason you stated at the top of each reason page, and circle its important words. Some of those words should be related to the words circled in the introduction and conclusion. The rest should identify concepts that distinguish that section from others. Select a key term for each key concept.

Now, as you draft, keep in front of you both the general terms that should run through your whole report and the specific terms that distinguish each section from other sections. They will help you keep yourself—and thus your readers—on track. If later you find yourself writing something that lacks those terms, don't just wrench yourself back to them. In the act of drafting, you might be discovering something new.

6.2.4 Use Key Terms to Create Subheads That Uniquely Identify Each Section
Even if reports in your field don't use subheads (see A.2.2 in the appendix), we recommend that you use them in your drafts. Create them out of the key terms you identified in 6.2.3. If you cannot find key terms to distinguish a section, look closely at how you think it contributes to the whole. Readers may think it repetitive or irrelevant.

If your field avoids subheads, use them to keep yourself on track, then delete them from your last draft.

6.2.5 Order Your Reasons
Finding a good order for the sections of a report can be the hardest part of planning. When you assembled your argument, you may not have put

your reasons in any particular order (one benefit of a storyboard). But when you plan a draft, you must impose on them some order that best meets your readers' needs. That is not easy, especially when you're writing on a new topic in a new field.

When you're not sure how best to order your reasons, consider these options:

- Comparison and contrast. This is the form you'd choose if you were comparing two or more entities, concepts, or objects.

  But there are two ways to compare and contrast, and one is usually better than the other. If, for example, you were comparing whether Hopi masks have more religious symbolism than Inuit masks, you might decide to devote the first half of your paper to Inuit masks and the second to Hopi masks. This organization, however, too often results in a pair of unrelated summaries. Try breaking the topics into their conceptual parts. In the case of masks, it would be their symbolic representation, design features, stages of evolution, and so on.

  There are several other standard ways to order your ideas. Two focus on the subject matter:

- Chronological. This is the simplest: earlier-to-later or cause-to-effect.
- Part-by-part. If you can break your topic into its constituent parts, you can deal with each part in turn, but you must still order those parts in some way that helps readers understand them.

  You can also organize the parts from the point of view of your readers' ability to understand them:

- Short to long, simple to complex. Most readers prefer to deal with less complex issues before they work through more complex ones.
- More familiar to less familiar. Most readers prefer to read what they know about before they read what they don't.
- Less contestable to more contestable. Most readers move more easily from what they agree with to what they don't.
- Less important to more important (or vice versa). Readers prefer to read more important reasons first, but those reasons may have more impact when they come last.
- Earlier understanding as a basis for later understanding. Readers may have to understand some events, principles, definitions, and so on before they understand another thing.

  Often, these principles cooperate: what readers agree with and most easily understand might also be shortest and most familiar. But they may also conflict: reasons that readers understand most easily might be the ones they reject most quickly; what you think is your most decisive reason might to readers seem least familiar. No rules here, only principles of choice.

Whatever order you choose, it should reflect your readers' needs, not the order that the material seems to impose on itself (as in an obvious compare-contrast organization), and least of all the order in which ideas occurred to you.

6.2.6 Make Your Order Clear with Transitional Words

Be certain that your readers can recognize the order you chose. Start each page of reasons in your storyboard with words that make the *principle* of order clear: *First, Second, Later, Finally, More important, A more complex issue is, As a result.* Don't worry if these words feel awkwardly obvious. At this point, they're more for your benefit than for your readers'. You can revise or even delete the clumsy ones from your final draft.

6.2.7 Sketch a Brief Introduction to Each Section and Subsection

Just as your whole report needs an introduction that frames what follows, so does each of its sections. If a section is only a page or two, you need just a short paragraph; for a section several pages long, you might need to sketch in two or more paragraphs. This opening segment should introduce the key terms that are special to its section, ideally in a sentence at its end expressing its point. That point might be a reason, a response to a different point of view, or a warrant you must explain. In a section that you think will be longer than five pages or so, you might state its point both at the end of its introduction and again in a conclusion.

6.2.8 For Each Section, Sketch in Evidence, Acknowledgments, Warrants, and Summaries

In their relevant sections, sketch out the parts of your argument. Remember that many of those parts will themselves make a point that must be supported by smaller arguments.

EVIDENCE. Most sections consist primarily of evidence supporting reasons. Sketch the evidence after the reason it supports. If you have different kinds of evidence supporting the same reason, group and order them in a way that makes sense to your readers.

EXPLANATIONS OF EVIDENCE. You may have to explain your evidence—where it came from, why it's reliable, exactly how it supports a reason. Usually, these explanations follow the evidence, but you can sketch them before if that seems more logical.

ACKNOWLEDGMENTS AND RESPONSES. Imagine what readers might object to and where, then sketch a response. Responses are typically subarguments with at least a claim and reasons, often including evidence and even another response to an imagined objection to your response.

WARRANTS. If you think you need a warrant to justify the relevance of a reason, develop it before you state the reason. (If you're using a warrant only for emphasis, put it after the reason.) If you think readers will question the truth of the warrant, sketch a mini-argument to support it. If readers might think that your reason or claim isn't a valid instance of the warrant, sketch an argument that it is.

SUMMARIES. If your paper is more than twenty or so pages, you might briefly summarize the progress of your argument at the end of each major section, especially if your report is fact-heavy in dates, names, events, or numbers. One fact after another can blur the line of an argument. What have you established in this section? How does your argument shape up thus far? If in your final draft those summaries seem too obvious, cut them.

Writers in different fields may arrange these elements in slightly different ways, but the elements themselves and their principles of organization are the same in every field and profession. And what is key in every report, regardless of field, is that you must order the parts of your argument not merely to reflect your own thinking, but to help your readers understand it.

6.2.9   Sketch a Working Conclusion

You should have stated your concluding claim at the top of the conclusion page of your storyboard. If you can add to the significance of that claim (another answer to *So what?*), sketch it after the claim (see 10.3 for more on conclusions).

6.3   File Away Leftovers

Once you have a first plan, you may discover that you have a lot of material left that doesn't fit into it. Resist the impulse to shoehorn leftovers into your report in the belief that if you found it, your readers should read it. In fact, if you don't have more leftovers than what you used, you may not have done enough research. File away leftovers for future use. They may contain the seeds of another project.

7 Drafting Your Report

Some writers think that once they have an outline or storyboard, they can draft by just grinding out sentences. If you've written a lot to explore your ideas, you may even think that you can plug that preliminary writing into a draft. Experienced writers know better. They know two things: exploratory writing is crucial but often not right for a draft, and thoughtful drafting can be an act of discovery that planning and storyboarding can prepare them for, but never replace. In fact, most writers don't know what they *can* think until they see it appear in words before them. Indeed, you experience one of the most exciting moments in research when you discover yourself expressing ideas that you did not know you had until that moment.

So don't look upon drafting as merely translating a storyboard or outline into words. If you draft with an open mind, you can discover lines of thought that you couldn't have imagined before you started. But like other steps in the process, even surprises work better with a plan.

7.1 Draft in the Way That Feels Most Comfortable

Writers draft in different ways. Some are slow and careful: they have to get every paragraph right before they start the next one. To do that, they need a meticulous plan. So if you draft slowly, plan carefully. Other writers let the words flow, skipping ahead when they get stuck, omitting quotations, statistics, and so on that they can plug in later. If they are stopped by a stylistic issue such as whether to represent numbers in words or numerals, they insert a [?] and keep on writing until they run out of gas, then go back and fix it. But quick drafters need lots of time to revise. So if you draft quickly, start early. Draft in whatever way works for you, but experienced writers usually draft quickly, then revise extensively.

7.2 Develop Productive Drafting Habits

Most of us learn to write in the least efficient way—under pressure, rushing to meet a deadline, with a quick draft the night before and maybe a few minutes in the morning for proofreading. That rarely works for a short paper, almost never for a longer one. You need time and a plan that sets small, achievable goals but keeps your eye on the whole.

Most important, draft regularly and often, not in marathon sessions that dull your thinking and kill your interest. Set a small goal and a reasonable quota of words for each session, and stick to it. When you resume drafting, you need not start where you left off: review your storyboard to decide what you're ready to draft today. Review how it will fit into its section and the whole: *What reason does this section support? Where does it fit in the overall logic? Which key terms state the concepts that distinguish this section?* If you're blocked, skip to another section. Whatever you do, don't substitute more reading for writing. Chronic procrastinators are usually so intimidated by the size of their project that it paralyzes them, and they just keep putting off getting started. You can overcome that destructive habit by breaking your project into small, achievable goals (see 7.11).

7.3 Use Your Key Terms to Keep Yourself on Track

As you draft, keep in front of you a separate list of the key terms for your general concepts that should run through your whole report. From time to time, check how often you've used those words, both those that run through the whole report and those that distinguish one section from another. But don't let those words stifle fresh thinking. If you find yourself wandering, let yourself go for a while. You may be developing an interesting idea. Follow it until you see where it takes you.

7.4 ◆ Quote, Paraphrase, and Summarize Appropriately

We covered this issue when we discussed note-taking (4.2.2). You should build most of your report out of your own words that reflect your own thinking. Much of the support for that thinking will be in quotations, paraphrases, and summaries. Different fields, however, use them in different proportions. In general, researchers in the humanities quote most often; social and natural scientists typically paraphrase and summarize. But you must decide each case for itself, depending on how you use the information in your argument. Here are some principles:

- Summarize when details are irrelevant or a source isn't important enough to warrant more space.
- Paraphrase when you can state what a source says more clearly or concisely than the source, or when your argument depends on the details of a source but not on its specific words. (Before you paraphrase, however, read 7.9.)
- Quote for these purposes:
  - The words constitute evidence that backs up your reasons.
  - A passage states a view that you disagree with, and to be fair you want to state it exactly.
  - The quoted words are from an authority who backs up your view.
  - They are strikingly original.
  - They express your key concepts so compellingly that the quotation can frame the rest of your discussion.

You must balance quotations, paraphrases, and summaries with your own fresh ideas. Do not merely repeat, or worse, download, words and ideas of others that you stitch together with a few sentences of your own. All teachers have ground their teeth over such reports, dismayed by their lack of original thinking. In an advanced project such as a thesis or dissertation, readers reject a patchwork of borrowings out of hand.

Readers value research only to the degree that they trust its sources. So for every summary, paraphrase, or quotation you use, cite its bibliographic data in the appropriate citation style (see part 2).

7.5 Integrate Quotations into Your Text

You can insert quotations into your text in two ways:

- Run four or fewer quoted lines into your running text.
- Set off five or more lines as an indented block.

You can integrate both run-in and block quotations into your text in two ways:

1. Drop in the quotation as an independent sentence or passage, introduced with a few explanatory words. But avoid introducing all of your questions with just a *says, states, claims,* and so on:

   Diamond says, "The histories of the Fertile Crescent and China . . . hold a salutary lesson for the modern world: circumstances change, and past primacy is no guarantee of future primacy" (417).

Instead, provide some interpretation:

   Diamond suggests that one lesson we can learn from the past is not to expect history to repeat itself. "The histories of the Fertile Crescent and China . . . hold a salutary lesson for the modern world. . . ."

2. Weave the grammar of the quotation into the grammar of your sentence:

   Political leaders should learn from history, but Diamond points out that the "lesson for the modern world" in the history of the Fertile Crescent and China is that "circumstances change, and past primacy is no guarantee of future primacy" (417). So one lesson from history is that you can't count on it to repeat itself.

To make a quoted sentence mesh with yours, you can modify the quotation, so long as you don't change its meaning and you clearly indicate added or changed words with square brackets and deletions with three dots (called *ellipses*). This sentence quotes the original intact:

   Posner focuses on religion not for its spirituality, but for its social functions: "A notable feature of American society is religious pluralism, and we should consider how this relates to the efficacy of governance by social norms in view of the historical importance of religion as both a source and enforcer of such norms" (299).

This version modifies the quotation to fit the grammar of the writer's sentence:

   In his discussion of religious pluralism, Posner says of American society that "a notable feature . . . is [its] religious pluralism." We should consider how its social norms affect "the efficacy of governance . . . in view of the historical importance of religion as both a source and enforcer of such norms" (299).

(See chapter 25 for more on integrating quotations with your text.)

When you refer to a source the first time, use his or her full name. Do not precede it with *Mr., Mrs., Ms.,* or *Professor* (see 24.2.2 for the use of *Dr., Reverend, Senator,* and so on). When you mention a source thereafter, use just the last name:

According to Steven Pinker, "claims about a language instinct . . . have virtually nothing to do with possible genetic differences between people."[1] Pinker goes on to claim that . . .

Except when referring to kings, queens, and popes, never refer to a source by his or her first name. Never this:

According to Steven Pinker, "claims about a language instinct . . . " Steven goes on to claim that . . .

7.6 Use Footnotes and Endnotes Judiciously

If you are using bibliography-style citations (see 3.2.1), you will have to decide as you draft how to use footnotes and endnotes (for their formal requirements, see chapter 16). You must cite every source in a note, of course, but you might also decide to use footnotes and endnotes for substantive material that you don't want to include in the body of your text, but also don't want to omit. (You might also use such substantive notes in combination with parenthetical citations in reference list style; see 18.3.3.)

■ If you cite sources in endnotes, put substantive material in footnotes. Otherwise you force readers to keep flipping to the back of your report to check every endnote to see whether it is substantive or bibliographical.
■ Use substantive footnotes sparingly. If you create too many, you risk making your pages look choppy and broken up.

In any event, keep in mind that many readers ignore substantive footnotes on the principle that information not important enough for you to include in the text is not important enough for them to read in a footnote.

7.7 Interpret Complex or Detailed Evidence before You Offer It

By this point, you may be so sure that your evidence supports your reasons that you'll think readers can't miss its relevance. But evidence never speaks for itself, especially not a long quotation, an image, a table or chart, and so on. You must speak for it by introducing it with a sentence stating what you want your readers to get out of it.

For example, it's hard to see how the quoted lines in this next passage support the introductory sentence:

When Hamlet comes up behind his stepfather Claudius at prayer, he coolly and logically thinks about whether to kill him on the spot.claim

>Now might I do it [kill him] pat, now he is praying:
>And now I'll do't; and so he goes to heaven;
>And so am I reveng'd . . .
>[But this] villain kills my father; and for that,
>I, his sole son, do this same villain send to heaven.
>Why, this is hire and salary, not revenge.evidence

Nothing in those lines obviously refers to cool rationality. Compare this:

When Hamlet comes up behind his stepfather Claudius at prayer, he coolly and logically thinks about whether to kill him on the spot.claim First he wants to kill Claudius immediately, but then he pauses to think: If he kills Claudius while he is praying, he sends his soul to heaven. But he wants Claudius damned to hell, so he coolly decides to kill him later:reason

>Now might I do it [kill him] pat, now he is praying:
>And now I'll do't; and so he goes to heaven;
>And so am I reveng'd . . .
>[But this] villain kills my father; and for that,
>I, his sole son, do this same villain send to heaven.
>Why, this is hire and salary, not revenge.evidence

That kind of explanatory introduction is even more important when you present quantitative evidence in a table or figure (see 8.3.1).

7.8 Be Open to Surprises

If you write as you go and plan your best case before you draft, you're unlikely to be utterly surprised by how your draft develops. Even so, be open to new directions from beginning to end:

- When your drafting starts to head off on a tangent, go with it for a bit to see whether you're on to something better than you planned.
- When reporting your evidence leads you to doubt a reason, don't ignore that feeling. Follow it up.
- When the order of your reasons starts to feel awkward, experiment with new ones, even if you thought you were almost done.
- Even when you reach your final conclusion, you may see how to restate your claim more clearly and pointedly.

If you get better ideas early enough before your deadline, invest the time to make the changes. It is a cheap price for a big improvement.

7.9 Guard against Inadvertent Plagiarism

It will be as you draft that you risk making one of the worst mistakes a researcher can make: you lead readers to think that you're trying to pass off the work of another writer as your own. Do that and you risk being accused of plagiarism, a charge that, if sustained, could mean a failing grade or even expulsion.

Many instructors warn against plagiarism but don't explain it, because they think it is always an act of deliberate dishonesty that needs no explanation. And to be sure, students know they cheat when they put their name on a paper bought on the Internet or copied from a fraternity or sorority file. Most also know they cheat when they pass off as their own page after page copied from a source or downloaded from the Web. For those cases, there's nothing to say beyond *Don't*.

But many students fail to realize that they risk being charged with plagiarism even if they were not intentionally dishonest, but only ignorant or careless. You run that risk when you give readers reason to think that you've done one or more of the following:

- You cited a source but used its exact words without putting them in quotation marks or in a block quotation.
- You paraphrased a source and cited it, but in words so similar to those of your source that they are almost a quotation: anyone could see that you were following the source word-by-word as you paraphrased it.
- You used ideas or methods from a source but failed to cite it.

7.9.1 Signal Every Quotation, Even When You Cite Its Source

Even if you cite your source, readers must know which words are yours and which you quote. You risk a charge of plagiarism if you fail to use quotation marks or a block quotation to signal that you have copied *as little as a single line of words*.

It gets complicated, however, when you copy just a few words. Read this:

> Because technology begets more technology, the importance of an invention's diffusion potentially exceeds the importance of the original invention. Technology's history exemplifies what is termed an autocatalytic process: that is, one that speeds up at a rate that increases with time, because the process catalyzes itself (Diamond 1998, 301).

If you were writing about Jared Diamond's ideas, you would probably have to use some of his words, such as *the importance of an invention*. But you wouldn't put that phrase in quotation marks, because it shows no originality of thought or expression. Two of his phrases, however, are so striking that they do require quotation marks: *technology begets more technology* and *autocatalytic process*. For example,

> The power of technology goes beyond individual inventions because technology "begets more technology." It is, as Diamond puts it, an "autocatalytic process" (301).

Once you cite those words, you can use them again without quotation marks or citation:

> As one invention begets another one and that one still another, the process becomes a self-sustaining catalysis that spreads exponentially across all national boundaries.

This is a gray area: words that seem striking to some readers are commonplace to others. If you use quotation marks for too many common phrases, readers might think you're naïve or insecure, but if you fail to use them when readers think you should, they may suspect you're trying to take credit for language and ideas not your own. Since it's better to seem naïve than dishonest, especially early in your research career, use quotation marks freely. (You must, however, follow the standard practices of your field. For example, lawyers often use the exact language of a statute or judicial opinion with no quotation marks.)

7.9.2   Don't Paraphrase Too Closely

You paraphrase appropriately when you represent an idea in your own words more clearly or pointedly than the source does. But readers will think that you cross the line from fair paraphrase to plagiarism if they can match your words and phrasing with those of your source. For example, these next sentences plagiarize the two sentences you just read:

> Booth, Colomb, and Williams claim that appropriate paraphrase is the use of one's own words to represent an idea to make a passage from a source clearer or more pointed. Readers can accuse a student of plagiarism, however, if his paraphrase is so similar to its source that someone can match words and phrases in the sentence and those in that source.

This next paraphrase borders on plagiarism:

> Appropriate paraphrase rewrites a passage from a source into one's own words to make it clearer or more pointed. Readers think plagiarism occurs when a source is paraphrased so closely that they see parallels between words and phrases. (Booth, Colomb, and Williams, 2007).

This paraphrase does not plagiarize:

> According to Booth, Colomb, and Williams (2007), paraphrase is the use of your own words to represent the ideas of another more clearly. It becomes plagiarism when readers see a word-for-word similarity between a paraphrase and a source.

To avoid seeming to plagiarize by paraphrase, don't read your source as you paraphrase it. Read the passage, look away, think about it for a moment; *then still looking away,* paraphrase it in your own words. Then check whether you can run your finger along your sentence and find the same ideas in the same order in your source. If you can, so can your readers. Try again.

7.9.3 Usually Cite a Source for Ideas Not Your Own

This rule is more complicated than it seems, because most of our own ideas are based on or derived from identifiable sources somewhere in history. Readers don't expect you to find every distant source for every familiar idea, but they do expect you to cite the source for an idea when (1) the idea is associated with a specific person *and* (2) it's new enough not to be part of a field's common knowledge.

For example, psychologists claim that we think and feel in different parts of our brains. But no reader would expect you to cite that idea, because it's no longer associated with a specific source and it's so familiar that no one would think you implied that it was yours. On the other hand, some psychologists argue that emotions are crucial to rational decision making. That idea is so new and so closely tied to particular researchers that you'd have to cite them.

The principle is this: cite a source for an idea not your own whenever an informed reader might think that you're implying that it is your own. Though that seems black and white, it has a big gray area in the middle. When in doubt, check with your instructor.

7.9.4 Don't Plead Ignorance, Misunderstanding, or Innocent Intentions

To be sure, what looks like plagiarism is often just honest ignorance of how to use and cite sources. Some students sincerely believe that they don't have to cite material they have downloaded from the Web if that material is free and publicly available. But they're wrong. The fact that it's public or free is irrelevant. You must cite *anything* you use that was created by someone else.

Many students defend themselves by claiming they didn't *intend* to mislead. The problem is, we read words, not minds. So think of plagiarism not as an *intended* act but as a *perceived* one. Avoid any sign that might give your readers any reason to suspect you of it. Whenever you submit a paper with your name on it, you implicitly promise that you wrote every word that you don't clearly and specifically attribute to someone else.

Here is the best way to think about this: If the person whose work you used read your report, would she recognize any of it as hers, including paraphrases and summaries, or even general ideas or methods? If so, you must cite that source and enclose any sequence of her exact words in quotation marks or set them off in a block quotation.

7.10 Guard against Inappropriate Assistance

Experienced writers regularly show their drafts to others for criticism and suggestions, and you should too. But instructors differ on how much help is appropriate and what help students should acknowledge. When you get help, ask two questions:

1. How much help is appropriate?
   - □ For a class paper, most instructors encourage students to get general criticism and minor editing, but not detailed rewriting or substantive suggestions.
   - □ For a thesis, dissertation, or work submitted for publication, writers get all the help they can from teachers, reviewers, and others so long as they don't become virtual ghost writers.

Between those extremes is a gray area. Ask your instructor where she draws the line, then get all the help you can on the right side of it.

2. What help must you acknowledge in your report?
   - □ For a class paper, you usually aren't required to acknowledge general criticism, minor editing, or help from a school writing tutor, but you must acknowledge help that's special or extensive. Your instructor sets the rules, so ask.
   - □ For a thesis, dissertation, or published work, you're not required to acknowledge routine help, though it's courteous and often politic to do so in a preface (see A.2.1). But you must acknowledge special or extensive editing and cite in a note major ideas or phrases provided by others.

7.11 Work through Chronic Procrastination and Writer's Block

If you can't seem to get started on a first draft or if you struggle to draft more than a few words, you may have writer's block. Some cases arise from serious anxieties about school and its pressures; if that might be you, see a counselor. But most cases have causes you can address:

- You may be stuck because you have no goals or goals that are too high. If so, create a routine and set small, achievable goals. Do not be reluctant to use devices to keep yourself moving, such as a progress chart or regular meetings with a writing partner.
- You may feel so intimidated by the size of the task that you don't know where to begin. If so, follow our suggestions about dividing the process into small, achievable tasks; then focus on doing one small step at a time. Don't dwell on the whole task until you've completed several small parts.
- You may feel that you have to make every sentence or paragraph perfect before you move on to the next one. If so, tell yourself you're not writing a draft but only sketching out some ideas, grit your teeth, then do some quick and dirty writing to get yourself started. You can avoid some of this obsession with perfection if you write along the way, knowing that you aren't writing a first draft. And in any event, we all have to compromise on perfection to get the job done.

If you have problems like these with most of your writing projects, go to the student learning center. There are people there who have worked with every kind of procrastinator and blocked writer and can give you advice tailored to your problem.

On the other hand, some cases of writer's block may really be opportunities to let your ideas simmer in your subconscious while they combine and recombine into something new and surprising. If you're stuck but have time (another reason to start early), do something else for a day or two. Then return to the task to see if you can get back on track.

8 Presenting Evidence in Tables and Figures

If your data are in the form of numbers, most readers grasp them more easily if you present them graphically. But you face many choices of graphic forms, and some forms will suit your data and message better than others. In this chapter, we show you how to choose the right graphic form and design it so that readers can see both what your data are and how they support your argument. (See pp. 414–15 in the bibliography for guides to creating and using graphics; see chapter 26 for details on formatting graphics.)[1]

8.1   Choose Verbal or Visual Representations

Ordinarily, present quantitative data verbally when they include only a few numbers. (See chapter 23 for presenting numbers in text.) Present them graphically when most of your evidence is quantitative or you must communicate a large set of data. But when the data are few and simple, readers can grasp them as easily in a sentence as in a table like table 8.1:

In 1996, on average, men earned $32,144 a year, women $23,710, a difference of $8,434.

---

1. A note on terminology: The terms for graphics vary, so we will stipulate ours. In this chapter, we use the term *graphics* to refer to all visual representations of evidence. Another term sometimes used for such representations is *illustrations*. Traditionally, graphics are divided into *tables* and *figures*. A table is a grid with columns and rows that present data in numbers or words organized by categories. Figures are all other graphic forms, including graphs, charts, photographs, drawings, and diagrams. Figures that present quantitative data are divided into *charts*, typically consisting of bars, circles, points, or other shapes, and *graphs*, typically consisting of continuous lines. For a selection of common figures, see table 8.7.

Table 8.1. Male-female salaries ($),1996

Men	32,144
Women	23,710
Difference	8,434

Table 8.2. Changes in family structure, 1970–2000

Family type	Percentage of total families			
	1970	1980	1990	2000
2 Parents	85	77	73	68
Mother	11	18	22	23
Father	1	2	3	4
No adult	3	4	3	4

But if you present more than four or five numbers in a passage, readers will struggle to keep them straight, particularly if they must compare them, like this:

Between 1970 and 2000, the structure of families changed in two ways. In 1970, 85 percent of families had two parents, but in 1980 that number declined to 77 percent, then to 73 percent in 1990, and to 68 percent in 2000. The number of one-parent families rose, particularly families headed by a mother. In 1970, 11 percent of families were headed by a single mother. In 1980 that number rose to 18 percent, in 1990 to 22 percent, and to 23 percent in 2000. Single fathers headed 1 percent of the families in 1970, 2 percent in 1980, 3 percent in 1990, and 4 percent in 2000. Families with no adult in the home have remained stable at 3–4 percent.

Those data can be presented more effectively in graphic form, as in table 8.2.

8.2 Choose the Most Effective Graphic

When you graphically present data as complex as in that paragraph, you have many choices. The simplest and most common are tables, bar charts, and line graphs, each of which has a distinctive rhetorical effect.

- To emphasize specific values, use a table like table 8.2.
- To emphasize comparisons that can be seen at a glance, use a bar chart like figure 8.1 (p. 84).
- To emphasize trends, use a line graph like figure 8.2 (p. 84).

While each of these forms communicates the same data, readers respond to them in different ways:

- A table seems precise and objective. It emphasizes individual numbers and forces readers to infer relationships or trends (unless you state them in an introductory sentence).

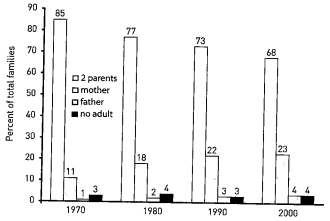

Figure 8.1. Changes in family structure, 1970–2000

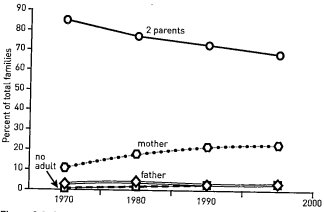

Figure 8.2. Changes in family structure, 1970–2000

■ Both charts and line graphs emphasize a visual image that communicates values less precisely but more quickly than do the exact numbers of a table. But they also differ:

    ▨ A bar chart emphasizes comparisons among discrete items.

    ▨ A line graph emphasizes trends, usually over time.

Choose the graphic form that best achieves the effect you intend, not the first one that comes to mind.

How many choices you should consider depends on your experience. If you're new to quantitative research, limit your choices to basic tables, bar charts, and line graphs. Your computer software may offer more choices, but ignore those that you aren't familiar with.

If you are doing advanced research, readers will expect you to use the graphic form best suited to your point and your kind of data, and to draw from a larger range of choices. In that case, consult table 8.7, which describes the rhetorical uses of other common forms. But you may have to consider more creative ways of representing data if you are writing a dissertation or article in a field that routinely displays complex relationships in large data sets.

8.3 Design Tables and Figures

Computer programs now let you create graphics so dazzling that you might be tempted to let your software make your design decisions. But readers don't care how elaborate your graphics look if they are confusing, misleading, or irrelevant to your point. You have to decide how to make them clear, focused, and relevant, then set your software to reflect that judgment. (See A.3.1 on creating and inserting tables and figures in your paper.)

8.3.1 Frame Each Graphic to Help Your Readers Understand It

A graphic representing complex numbers rarely speaks for itself. You must frame it so that readers know what to see in it and how to understand its relevance to your argument.

1. Introduce tables and figures with a sentence in your text that states how the data support your point. Include in that sentence any specific number that you want readers to focus on. (That number must also appear in the table or figure.)
2. Label every table and figure in a way that describes its data and, if possible, their important relationships. For a table, the label is called a *title* and is set flush left above; for a figure, the label is called a *caption* (or *legend*) and is set flush left below. (For the forms of titles and captions, see chapter 26.) Keep titles and captions short but descriptive enough to indicate the specific nature of the data and to differentiate every graphic from every other one.

   ◻ Avoid making the title or caption a general topic:

   Not: Heads of households
   But: Changes in one- and two-parent heads of households, 1970–2000

   ◻ Use noun phrases; avoid relative clauses in favor of participles:

   Not: Number of families that subscribe to weekly news magazines
   But: Number of families subscribing to weekly news magazines

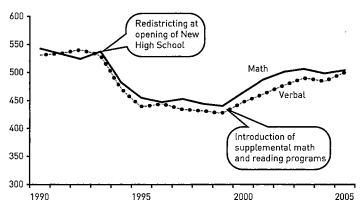

Figure 8.3. SAT scores for Mid-City High, 1990–2005

□ Do not give background information or characterize the implications of the data:

Not: Weaker effects of counseling on depressed children before professional-ization of staff, 1995–2004
But: Effect of counseling on depressed children, 1995–2004

□ Be sure labels distinguish graphics presenting similar data:

Risk factors for high blood pressure among men in Maywood, Illinois

Risk factors for high blood pressure among men in Kingston, Jamaica

3. Put into the table or figure information that helps readers see how the data support your point. For example, if numbers in a table show a trend, and if the size of the change matters, add the change to the final column. Or if a line on a graph changes in response to an influence not mentioned on the graph, as in figure 8.3, add text to the image to explain it:

Although reading and math scores initially declined by almost 100 points following redistricting, that trend was substantially reversed by the introduction of supplemental math and reading programs.

4. Highlight the part of the table or figure that you want readers to focus on, particularly any number or relationship mentioned in the sentence introducing the table or figure. For example, we have to study table 8.3 closely to see how it supports the introductory sentence:

Most predictions about gasoline consumption have proved wrong.

Table 8.3. Gasoline consumption

	1970	1980	1990	2000
Annual miles (000)	9.5	10.3	10.5	11.7
Annual consumption (gal.)	760	760	520	533

Table 8.4. Per capita mileage and gasoline consumption 1970–2000

	1970	1980	1990	2000
Annual miles (000)	9.5	10.3	10.5	11.7
(% change vs. 1970)		8.4%	10.5%	[23.1%]
Annual consumption (gal.)	760	760	520	533
(% change vs. 1970)			(31.5%)	[(31.6%)]

We need another sentence explaining how the numbers relate to the claim, a more informative title, and visual help that focuses us on what to see (table 8.4):

Gasoline consumption did not grow as many had predicted. *Even though Americans drove 23 percent more miles in 2000 than in 1970, they used 32 percent less fuel.*

The added sentence tells us how to interpret the key data in table 8.4, and the highlight tells us where to find it.

8.3.2 **Keep the Image as Simple as Its Content Allows**
Some guides encourage you to put as much data as you can in every graphic, but readers want to see only the data relevant to your point, presented in an image free of distractions:

1. Include only relevant data. If you want to include data just for the record, label it accordingly and put it in an appendix (see A.2.3).
2. Make the grid simple.
   - Graphics
     - Box a graphic only if you group two or more figures.
     - Do not color or shade the background.
     - Never create a three-dimensional background for a two-dimensional graphic. The added depth contributes nothing and can distort how readers judge values.
     - Plot data on three dimensions only when you cannot display the data in any other way and your readers are familiar with such graphs.
   - Tables
     - Never use both horizontal and vertical lines to divide columns and rows. Use light gray lines if you want to direct your reader's eyes in one direction to compare data or if the table is unusually complex. Avoid using

gray lines or shading in anything that will be microfilmed, because the photographed image may be blurred.

  ○ For tables with many rows, lightly shade every fifth row.
  ○ Do not use a font size smaller than nine points for a document that will be microfilmed. Smaller fonts will be illegible.

□ Charts and Graphs

  ○ Use grid lines only if the graphic is complex or readers need to see precise numbers. Make all grid lines light gray, unless the text will be microfilmed.
  ○ Color or shade lines or bars only to show a contrast. Use color only if the text will be printed in color and not photocopied later. (Black-and-white photocopies make many colors look alike.)
  ○ Never create a three-dimensional chart or graph if you can represent the same data in two dimensions. The added depth contributes nothing and can distort how readers judge values.
  ○ Never use iconic bars (for example, images of cars to represent automobile production). They add nothing, can distort how readers judge values, and look amateurish.

3. Use clear labels.

  □ Label rows and columns in tables and both axes in charts and graphs. (See chapter 26 for the punctuation and spelling of labels.)
  □ Use tick marks and labels to indicate intervals on the vertical axis of a graph (see fig. 8.4).
  □ If possible, label lines, bar segments, and the like on the image rather than in a caption set to the side. Use a caption only if labels make the image too complex to read.
  □ When specific numbers matter, add them to bars, segments, or dots on lines.

8.3.3 Follow Guidelines for Tables, Bar Charts, and Line Graphs

TABLES. Tables with lots of data can seem especially dense, so keep their image and content as simple as possible.

■ Order the rows and columns by a principle that lets readers quickly find what you want them to see. Do not automatically choose alphabetic order.
■ Round numbers to relevant values. If differences of less than 1,000 don't matter, then 2,123,499 and 2,124,886 are irrelevantly precise.
■ Sum totals at the bottom of a column or at the end of a row, not at the top or left. Compare tables 8.5 and 8.6. Table 8.5 looks cluttered and its items aren't helpfully organized. In contrast, table 8.6 is clearer because its title is more informative, the table has less distracting visual clutter, and its items are organized to let us see patterns more easily.

Table 8.5. Unemployment in major industrial nations, 1990–2000

	1990	2001	Change
Australia	6.7	6.5	(0.2)
Canada	7.7	5.9	(1.8)
France	9.1	8.8	(0.3)
Germany	5.0	8.1	3.1
Italy	7.0	9.9	2.9
Japan	2.1	4.8	2.7
Sweden	1.8	5.1	3.3
UK	6.9	5.1	(1.8)
USA	5.6	4.2	(1.6)

Table 8.6. Changes in unemployment rates of industrial nations, 1990–2000

English-speaking vs. non-English-speaking nations

	1990	2001	Change
Australia	6.7	6.5	(0.2)
USA	5.6	4.2	(1.6)
Canada	7.7	5.9	(1.8)
UK	6.9	5.1	(1.8)
France	9.1	8.8	(0.3)
Japan	2.1	4.8	2.7
Italy	7.0	9.9	2.9
Germany	5.0	8.1	3.1
Sweden	1.8	5.1	3.3

BAR CHARTS. Bar charts communicate as much by image as by specific numbers. Bars that seem to be arranged in no pattern imply no point, so if possible, group-and arrange bars to give readers an image of an order that matches your point.

For example, look at figure 8.4 (p. 90) in the context of the explanatory sentence before it. The items are listed alphabetically, an order that doesn't help readers see the point. In contrast, figure 8.5 (p. 90) supports the claim with a coherent image.

In standard bar charts, each bar represents 100% of a whole. But sometimes it helps readers if they can see specific values for parts of the whole. You can do that in two ways:

- A "stacked bar" chart subdivides the bars into proportional parts, as in the chart on the left in figure 8.6 (p. 91).
- A "grouped bar" chart uses a separate bar for each part of the whole but groups the bars, as in the chart on the right in figure 8.6.

Use stacked bars only when it's more important to compare whole values than it is to compare their segments. Readers, however, can't easily gauge proportions by eye alone, so if you do use stacked bars, do this:

Most of the desert area in the world is concentrated in North Africa and the Middle East.

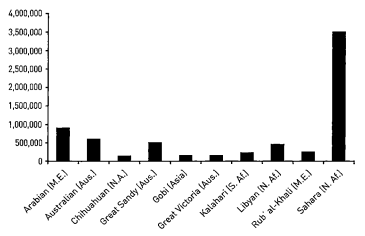

Figure 8.4. World's ten largest deserts

Most of the desert area in the world is concentrated in North Africa and the Middle East.

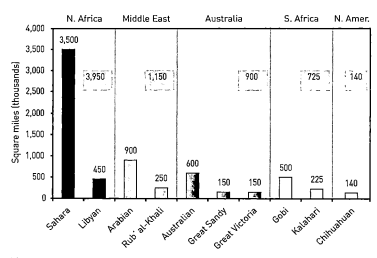

Figure 8.5. World distribution of large deserts

- Arrange segments in a logical order. If possible, put the largest segment at the bottom in the darkest shade.
- Label segments with specific numbers and connect corresponding segments with grey lines to help clarify proportions.

Figure 8.6. Stacked bar chart compared to grouped bar chart

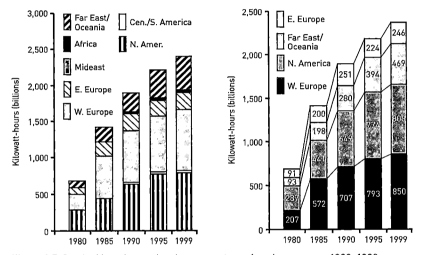

Figure 8.7. Stacked bar charts showing generators of nuclear energy, 1980–1999

Figure 8.7 shows how a stacked bar chart is more readable when irrelevant segments are eliminated and those kept are logically ordered and fully labeled.

A grouped bar chart makes it easy for readers to compare parts of a whole, but difficult to compare different wholes because they must do mental arithmetic. If you group bars because the segments are more important than the wholes, do this:

■ Arrange groups of bars in a logical order; if possible put bars of similar size next to one another (order bars within groups in the same way).

■ Label groups with the number for the whole, either above each group or below the labels on the bottom.

Most data that fit a bar chart can also be represented in a pie chart. It is a popular choice in magazines, tabloids, and annual reports, but it's harder to read than a bar chart, and it invites misinterpretation because readers must mentally compare proportions of segments whose size is hard to judge in the first place. Most researchers consider them amateurish. Use bar charts instead.

LINE GRAPHS. Because a line graph emphasizes trends, readers must see a clear image to interpret it correctly. To create a clear image, do the following:

■ Choose the variable that makes the line go in the direction, up or down, that supports your point. If the good news is a reduction (down) in high school dropouts, you can more effectively represent the same data as an increase in retention (up).

■ Plot more than six lines on one graph only if you cannot make your point in any other way.

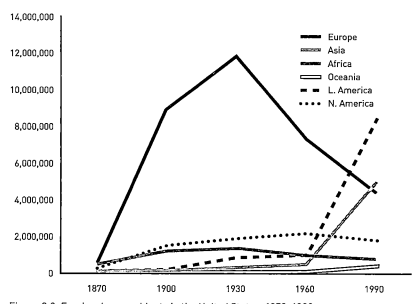

Figure 8.8. Foreign-born residents in the United States, 1870–1990

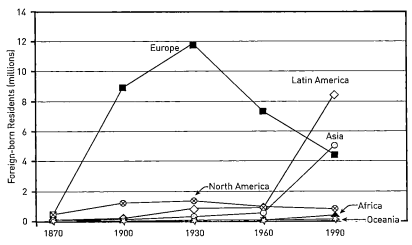

Figure 8.9. Foreign-born residents in the United States, 1870–1990

- Do not depend on different shades of gray to distinguish lines, as in figure 8.8.
- When you create a line graph from only a few values, the lines will be less precise. So if you plot fewer than ten values (called *data points*), indicate that by adding a dot at each data point, as in figure 8.9. If those values are relevant, you can add numbers above the dots. Do not add dots to lines plotted from ten or more data points.

Compare figure 8.8 and figure 8.9. Beyond its general story, figure 8.8 is harder to read because the shades of gray do not distinguish the lines well and because our eyes have to flick back and forth to connect lines with variables and their numbers. Figure 8.9 makes those connections clearer.

These different ways of showing the same data can be confusing. You can cut through that confusion if you first represent the same data in different ways (your computer program will usually let you do that quickly), and then ask someone unfamiliar with the data to judge the representations for impact and clarity. Be sure to introduce the representations with a sentence that states the claim you want the table or figure to support.

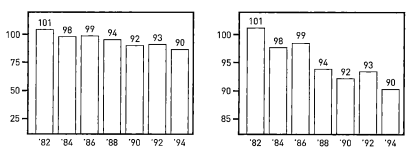

Figure 8.10. Capitol City pollution Index, 1982–1994

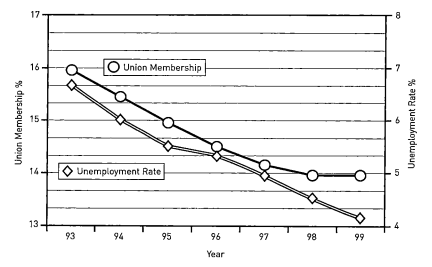

Figure 8.11. Union membership and unemployment rate, 1993–1999

8.4 Communicate Data Ethically

Your graphic must be not only clear, accurate, and relevant, but honest. It should not distort its data or their relationships to make a point. For example, the two bar charts in figure 8.10 display identical data, yet seem to send different messages. The full scale in the figure on the left creates a fairly flat slope, which makes the drop in pollution seem small. The vertical scale in the figure on the right, however, begins not at 0 but at 80. When a scale is that truncated, its drawn-out slope exaggerates small contrasts.

Graphs can also mislead by implying false correlations. Someone

Figure 8.12. Representation of collar counties in State U. undergraduates (percentage of total)

might claim that unemployment goes down when union membership goes down, and offer figure 8.11 as evidence. And indeed, union membership and the unemployment rate seem to move together so closely that a reader might infer they are causally related. But the scale for the left axis (union membership) differs from the scale for the right axis (the unemployment rate). The two scales have been deliberately skewed to make the two declines seem parallel. They may be related, but that distorted image doesn't prove it.

Graphs can also mislead when the image encourages readers to misjudge values. The two charts in figure 8.12 seem to communicate different messages, even though they represent exactly the same data. The charts in figure 8.12 are "stacked area" charts. Despite their visual differences, they represent the same data. These stacked area charts represent differences in values not by the *angles* of the lines, but by the areas *between* them. In both charts, the bands for south, east, and west are roughly the same width throughout, indicating little change in the values they represent. The band for the north, however, widens sharply, representing a large increase in the value it represents. In the chart on the left, readers are likely to misjudge the top three bands, because they are on top of the rising north band, making those bands seem to rise as well. In the chart on the right, on the other hand, those three bands do not rise because they are on the bottom. Now only the band for the north rises.

Here are four guidelines for avoiding visual misrepresentations:

- Do not manipulate a scale to magnify or reduce a contrast.
- Do not use a figure whose image distorts values.
- Do not make a table or figure unnecessarily complex or misleadingly simple.
- If the table or figure supports a point, state it.

Table 8.7. Common graphic forms and their uses

	Data	Rhetorical Uses
Bar Chart 	Compares the value of one variable across a series of items called *cases* (e.g., average salaries for service workers_variable in six companies_cases).	Creates strong visual contrasts among individual cases, emphasizing comparisons. For specific values, add numbers to bars. Can show ranks or trends. Vertical bars (called *columns*) are most common, but bars can be horizontal if cases are numerous or have complex labels. See section 8.3.3.
Bar Chart, Grouped or Split 	Compares the value of one variable, divided into subsets, across a series of cases (e.g., average salaries_variable for men and women service workers_subsets in six companies_cases).	Contrasts subsets within and across individual cases; not useful for comparing total values for cases. For specific values, add numbers to bars. Grouped bars show ranking or trends poorly; useful for time series only if trends are unimportant. See section 8.3.3.
Bar Chart, Stacked 	Compares the value of one variable, divided into two or more subsets, across a series of cases (e.g., harassment complaints_variable segmented by region_subsets in six industries_cases).	Best for comparing totals across cases and subsets *within* cases; difficult to compare subsets *across* cases (use grouped bars). For specific values, add numbers to bars and segments. Useful for time series. Can show ranks or trends for total values only. See section 8.3.3.
Histogram 	Compares two variables, with one segmented into ranges that function like the cases in a bar graph (e.g., service workers_continuous variable whose salary is $0–5,000, $5–10,000, $10–15,000, etc. segmented variable).	Best for comparing segments within continuous data sets. Shows trends, but emphasizes segments (e.g., a sudden spike at $5–10,000 representing part-time workers). For specific values, add numbers to bars.
Image Chart 	Shows value of one or more variables for cases displayed on a map, diagram, or other image (e.g., states_cases colored red or blue to show voting patterns_variable).	Shows the distribution of the data in relation to preexisting categories; deemphasizes specific values. Best when the image is familiar, as in a map or diagram of a process.
Pie Chart 	Shows the proportion of a single variable for a series of cases (e.g., the budget share_variable of U.S. cabinet departments_cases).	Best for comparing one segment to the whole. Useful only with few segments or segments that are very different in size; otherwise comparisons among segments are difficult. For specific values, add numbers to segments. Common in popular venues, frowned on by professionals. See 8.3.3.

Table 8.7. (Continued)

	Data	Rhetorical Uses
Line Graph	Compares continuous variables for one or more cases (e.g., temperature$_{variable}$ and viscosity$_{variable}$ in two fluids$_{cases}$).	Best for showing trends; deemphasizes specific values. Useful for time series. To show specific values, add numbers to data points. To show the significance of a trend, segment the grid (e.g., below or above average performance). See 8.3.3.
Area Chart	Compares two continuous variables for one or more cases (e.g., reading test scores$_{variable}$ over time$_{variable}$ in a school district$_{case}$).	Shows trends; deemphasizes specific values. Can be used for time series. To show specific values, add numbers to data points. Areas below the lines add no information, but will lead some readers to misjudge values. Confusing with multiple lines/areas.
Area Chart; Stacked	Compares two continuous variables for two or more cases (e.g., profit$_{variable}$ over time$_{variable}$ for several products$_{cases}$).	Shows the trend for the total of all cases, plus how much each case contributes to that total. Likely to mislead readers on the value or the trend for any individual case, as explained in section 8.4.
Scatterplot	Compares two variables at multiple data points for a single case (e.g., housing sales$_{variable}$ and distance from downtown$_{variable}$ in one city$_{case}$) or at one data point for multiple cases (e.g., brand loyalty$_{variable}$ and repair frequency$_{variable}$ for ten manufacturers$_{cases}$).	Best for showing the distribution of data, especially when there is no clear trend or when the focus is on outlying data points. If only a few data points are plotted, it allows a focus on individual values.
Bubble Chart	Compares three variables at multiple data points for a single case (e.g., housing sales$_{,variable}$ distance from downtown$_{,variable}$ and prices$_{variable}$ in one city$_{case}$) or at one data point for multiple cases (e.g. image advertising$_{,variable}$ repair frequency$_{,variable}$ and brand loyalty$_{variable}$ for ten manufacturers$_{cases}$).	Emphasizes the relationship between the third variable (bubbles) and the first two; most useful when the question is whether the third variable is a product of the others. Readers easily misjudge relative values shown by bubbles; adding numbers mitigates that problem.

9 Revising Your Draft

Some new researchers think that once they have a draft, they're done. Thoughtful writers know better. They write a first draft not for their readers, but for themselves, to see whether they can make the case they hoped to (or a better one). Then they revise their draft until they think it meets the needs and expectations of their readers. That's hard, because we all know our own work too well to read it as others will. To revise effectively, you must know what readers look for and whether your draft helps them find it. To that end, our advice may seem mechanical. But only when you can analyze your draft objectively can you avoid reading into it what you want your readers to get out of it.

We suggest revising from the top down: first the "outer frame" (introduction and conclusion), then overall organization, then sections, paragraphs, sentences, finally stylistic issues such as spelling and punctuation (for guidance on these issues, see part 3). Of course, no one revises so neatly. All of us fiddle with words as we move paragraphs around and reorganize as we revise a sentence. But you're likely to make the best revisions if you revise from whole to part, even if at the moment you're revising, a part is the only whole you have.

Many experienced researchers find that they can edit hard copy more reliably than they can edit text on their computer screen. You might edit early drafts on the screen, but you may catch more errors and get a better sense of the overall structure of your report if you read at least one later version of it on paper, as your readers will.

9.1 Check Your Introduction, Conclusion, and Claim
Your readers must recognize three things quickly and unambiguously:

- where your introduction ends
- where your conclusion begins
- what sentences in one or both state your claim

To make the first two clearly visible, you might insert a subhead or extra space between your introduction and body and another between the body and conclusion. (Chapter 10 discusses revising your last draft introduction and conclusion in detail, particularly how and where you signal your claim.)

9.2 Make Sure the Body of Your Report Is Coherent

Once you frame your report clearly, check its body. Readers will think your report is coherent when they see the following:

- what key terms run through all sections of the report
- where each section and subsection ends and the next begins
- how each section relates to the one before it
- what role each section plays in the whole
- what sentence in each section and subsection states its point
- what distinctive key terms run through each section

To ensure that your readers will see those features, check for the following:

1. Do key terms run through your whole report?
   - Circle key terms in the claim in your introduction and in your conclusion (review 7.3).
   - Circle those same terms in the body of your report.
   - Underline other words related to concepts named by those circled terms.

If readers don't see your key terms in most paragraphs, they may think your report wanders. Revise by working those terms into parts that lack them. If you underlined many more words than you circled, be sure that readers will recognize how the underlined words relate to the concepts named in your circled key terms. If readers might miss the connections, change some of those related words to the key terms. If you really did stray from your line of reasoning, you have some serious revising to do.

2. Is the beginning of each section and subsection clearly signaled?

You can use subheads to signal transitions from one major section to the next (review 6.2.4). In a long paper, you might add an extra space at the major joints. If you have a problem deciding what words to use in sub-heads or where to put them, your readers will have a bigger one, because they probably won't see your organization. (For styles of different levels of heads, see A.2.2 on p. 397.)

3. Does each major section begin with words that signal how that section relates to the one before it?

Readers must not only recognize where sections begin and end, but understand why they are ordered as they are (see 6.2.5–6.2.6). Signal the logic of your order with words such as *First, Second, More important, The next issue, Some have objected that,* and so on.

4. Is it clear how each section is relevant to the whole?

Of each section, ask *What question does this section answer?* If it doesn't help answer one of the five questions whose answers constitute an argument (see 5.2), think about its relevance: does it create a context, explain a background concept or issue, or help readers in some other way? If you can't explain how a section relates to your claim, consider cutting it.

5. Is the point of each section stated in a sentence at the end of a brief introduction to that section (or at its end)?

If you have a choice, state the point of a section at the end of its introduction. Under no circumstances bury the point of a section in its middle. If a section is longer than four or five pages, you might restate the point at its end.

6. Do the specific terms that distinguish a section run through it?

Just as the key terms that unify your whole report distinguish it from other reports, so should the key terms that distinguish each section and subsection run through and unify that section. Repeat step (1) for each section: find the sentence that expresses its point and identify the key terms that distinguish that section from the others. Then check whether those terms run through that section. If you find no key terms, then your readers might not see what distinct ideas that section contributes to the whole.

9.3 Check Your Paragraphs

Each paragraph should be relevant to the point of its section. And like sections, each paragraph should have a sentence or two introducing it, usually stating its point and including the key concepts that the rest of the paragraph develops. If the opening sentences of a paragraph don't state its point, then its last one must. Order your sentences by some principle and make them relevant to the point of the paragraph (for principles of order, see 6.2.5).

Avoid strings of short paragraphs (fewer than five lines) or very long ones (for most fields, more than half a page). Reserve the use of two- or three-sentence paragraphs for lists, transitions, introductions and conclusions to sections, and statements that you want to emphasize. (We use short paragraphs here so that readers can more easily skim, rarely a consideration in report writing.)

9.4 Let Your Draft Cool, Then Paraphrase It

If you start your project early, you'll have time to let your revised draft cool. What seems good one day often looks different the next. When you return to your draft, don't read it straight through; skim its top-level parts: its introduction, the first paragraph of each major section, and conclusion. Then based on what you have read, paraphrase it for someone who hasn't read it. Does the paraphrase hang together? Does it fairly sum up your argument? Even better, ask someone else to skim your report by reading just its introduction and the introduction to major sections: how well that person summarizes your report will predict how well your readers will understand it.

Finally, always revise in light of a teacher's or advisor's advice. Not only will you annoy anyone who takes time to read a draft and make suggestions, only to see you ignore them, but you'll pass up an opportunity to improve your report. That doesn't mean you must follow every suggestion, but you should consider each one carefully.

10 Writing Your Final Introduction and Conclusion

Once you have a final draft and can see what you have actually written, you can write your final introduction and conclusion. These two framing parts of your report crucially influence how readers will read and remember the rest of it, so it's worth your time to make them as clear and compelling as you can.

Your introduction has three aims. It should do the following:

- put your research in the context of other research
- make readers understand why they should read your report
- give them a framework for understanding it

Most introductions run about 10 percent of the whole (in the sciences they are often shorter).

Your conclusion also has three aims. It should do the following:

- leave readers with a clear idea of your claim
- make readers understand its importance
- suggest further research

Your conclusion should usually be shorter than your introduction. (In theses and dissertations, the introduction and conclusion are usually separate chapters.)

10.1 Draft Your Final Introduction

Different fields seem to introduce reports in different ways, but behind most of them is a pattern with the four parts described in 6.2.2:

1. Opening context or background. When this summarizes relevant research, it's called a *literature review* that puts your project in the context of other research and sets up the next step. Keep it short.
2. A statement of your research question. This is typically a statement of what isn't known or understood or of what is flawed about the research you cited in step 1. It often begins with a *but, however,* or other word signaling a qualification.
3. The significance of your question. This answers *So what?* It is key to motivating your readers.
4. Your claim. This answers your research question expressed in step 2. Here is an abbreviated example (each sentence could be expanded to a paragraph or more):

> For centuries, risk analysts have studied risk as a problem in statistics and the rational uses of probability theory.context But risk communicators have discovered that ordinary people think about risk in ways that seem unrelated to statistically based probabilities.question Until we understand how nonexperts think about risk, an important aspect of human cognition will remain a puzzle.significance It appears that nonexperts judge risk by visualizing worst-case scenarios, then assessing how frightening the image is.claim

10.1.1 Establish a Brief Context of Prior Research

Not every report opens with a survey of research. Some begin directly with a research question stated as something not known or understood, followed by a review of the relevant literature. This is a common strategy when the gap in knowledge or understanding is well known:

> The relationship between secondhand smoke and heart disease is still contested.

But if that gap isn't well known, such an opening can feel abrupt, like this one:

> Researchers do not understand how ordinary people think about risk.

As a rule, writers prepare readers by describing the prior research that their research will extend, modify, or correct. If the report is intended for general readers, the context can be brief:

> We all take risks every day—when we cross the street, eat high-fat food, even when we take a bath. The study of risk began with games of chance, so it has long been treated mathematically. By the twentieth century, researchers used mathematical

tools to study risk in many areas: investments, commercial products, even war. As a result, most researchers think that risk is a statistically quantifiable problem and that decisions about it should be rationally based.

In a report intended for other researchers, this opening context typically describes the specific research that the report will extend or modify. It is important to represent this prior research fairly, so describe it as those researchers would.

Ever since Girolamo Cardano thought about games of chance in quantitative terms in the sixteenth century (Cardano 1545), risk has been treated as a purely mathematical problem. Analyses of risk significantly improved in the seventeenth century when Pascal, Leibniz, and others developed the calculus (Bernstein 1996). In the twentieth century, researchers widened their focus to study risk in all areas of life: investments, consumer products, the environment, even war (Stimson 1990, 1998). These problems, too, have been addressed almost exclusively from a mathematical perspective. [Detailed discussion of contemporary research follows.]

Some reports, especially theses and dissertations, go on like that for pages, citing scores of books and articles only marginally relevant to the topic, usually to show how widely the researcher has read. That kind of survey can provide helpful bibliography to other researchers, especially new ones, but busy readers want to know about only the *specific* research that the researcher intends to extend, modify, or correct.

It is important to represent this prior research fairly and fully: describe it as the researcher you're citing would, even quoting, not selectively or out of context, but as she would represent her own work.

Early in your career, you might not be able to write this review of prior research with much confidence, because you're unlikely to know much of it. If so, imagine your reader as someone like yourself *before* you started your research. What did you then not know? What did you then get wrong that your research has corrected? How has it improved your own flawed understanding? This is where you can use a working hypothesis that you rejected: *It might seem that X is so, but.* . . . (see also 4.1.2).

10.1.2 Restate Your Question as Something Not Known or Fully Understood

After the opening context, state what that prior research hasn't done or how it's incomplete, even wrong. Introduce that qualification or contradiction with *but, however,* or some other term indicating that you're about to modify the received knowledge and understanding that you just surveyed:

Ever since Girolamo Cardano . . . mathematical perspective.context *But risk communicators have discovered that ordinary people think about risk in ways that are irrational and unrelated to statistically realistic probabilities. What is not understood is whether such nonexpert risk assessment is based on random guesses or whether it has systematic properties.*_{question restated}

10.1.3 State the Significance of Your Question

Now you must show your readers the *significance* of answering your research question. Imagine a reader asking that most vexing question, *So what?*, then answer it. Frame your response as a larger cost of not knowing the answer to your research question:

Ever since Girolamo Cardano . . . mathematical perspective._{context} But risk communicators have discovered that. . . . What is not understood is whether such nonexpert risk assessment is based on random guesses or whether it has systematic properties._{question restated} [*So what?*] *Until we understand how risk is understood by nonexperts, an important aspect of human reasoning will remain a puzzle: the kind of cognitive processing that seems systematic but lies outside the range of what is called "rational thinking."*_{significance}

Alternatively, you can phrase the cost as a benefit:

Ever since Girolamo Cardano . . . mathematical perspective._{context} But risk communicators have discovered that. . . . What is not understood is whether such nonexpert risk assessment is based on random guesses or whether it has systematic properties._{question restated} [*So what?*] *If we could understand how ordinary people make decisions about risks in their daily lives, we could better understand a kind of cognitive processing that seems systematic but lies outside the range of what is called "rational thinking."*_{significance}

You may struggle to answer that *So what?* It is a problem that only experience can solve, but the fact is, even experienced researchers can be vexed by it.

10.1.4 State Your Claim

Once you state that something isn't known or understood and why it should be, readers want to see your claim, the answer to your research question (we abbreviate a good deal in what follows):

Ever since Girolamo Cardano . . . mathematical perspective._{context} But risk communicators have discovered that ordinary people think about risk in ways that are systematic but irrational and unrelated to statistically realistic probabilities._{question} [*So what?*] Until we understand how risk is understood by nonexperts, an important kind of human reasoning will remain a puzzle: the kind of cognitive processing that seems systematic but lies outside the range of what is called "rational thinking."_{significance} *It appears that nonexperts assess risk not by assigning quantitative probabilities to events that might occur, but by visualizing worst-case scenarios, then assigning degrees of risk according to how vivid and frightening the image is.*_{claim}

If you have reason to withhold your claim until the end of your paper, write a sentence to conclude your introduction that uses the key terms from that claim and that frames what follows:

It appears that nonexperts assess risk not by assigning quantitative probabilities but by systematically using properties of their visual imagination.promise of claim

Those four steps may seem mechanical, but they constitute the introductions to most research reports in every field, both inside the academic world and out. As you read your sources, especially journal articles, watch for that four-part framework. You will not only learn a range of strategies for writing your own introductions but better understand the ones you read.

10.1.5 Draft a New First Sentence

Some writers find it so difficult to write the first sentence of a report that they fall into clichés. Avoid these:

- Do not repeat the language of your assignment.
- Do not quote a dictionary definition: *Webster defines risk as. . . .*
- Do not pontificate: *For centuries, philosophers have debated the burning question of. . . .* (Good questions speak their own importance.)

If you want to begin with something livelier than prior research, try one or more of these openers (but note the warning that follows):

1. A striking quotation:

As someone once said, calculating risk is like judging beauty: it's all in the eye of the irrational beholder.

2. A striking fact:

Many people drive rather than fly because the vivid image of an airplane crash terrifies them, even though they are many times more likely to die by driving on a highway than by hitting it from the air.

3. A relevant anecdote:

George Miller always drove long distances to meet clients because he believed that the risk of an airplane crash was too great. Even when he broke his back in an automobile accident, he still thought he had made the right calculation. "At least I survived. The odds of surviving an airplane crash are zero!"

You can combine all three:

As someone once said, calculating risk is like judging beauty: it's all in the eye of the irrational beholder. For example, many people drive rather than fly because the vivid image of an airplane crash terrifies them, even though they are more likely to

die by driving on a highway than by hitting it from the air, as witness George Miller.
He always drove long distances to meet clients because he believed that the risk
of an airplane crash was too great. Even when he broke his back in an automobile
accident, he still thought he had made the right calculation. "At least I survived. The
odds of surviving an airplane crash are zero!"

Be sure to include in these openers terms that refer to the key concepts
you'll use when you write the rest of the introduction (and the rest of the
report). In this case, they include *calculating, risk, vivid image, irrational,
more likely.*

Now the warning: Before you write a snappy opening, be sure that
others in your field use them. In some fields, they're considered too journalistic for serious scholarship.

10.2   Draft Your Final Conclusion

If you have no better plan, build your conclusion around the elements of
your introduction, in reverse order.

10.2.1   Restate Your Claim

Restate your claim early in your conclusion, more fully than in your
introduction:

Ordinary people make decisions about risk not on a rational or quantifiable basis,
but on the basis of at least six psychological factors that not only involve emotion but
systematically draw on the power of visual imagination.

At this point, you're probably sure what your claim is, but even so, take
this last chance to rephrase it to make it as specific and complete as you
can.

10.2.2   Point Out a New Significance, a Practical Application, or New Research (or All Three)

After stating your claim, remind readers of its significance, or better, state
a new significance or a practical application of your claim:

These findings suggest a hitherto unsuspected aspect of human cognition, a quantitative logic independent of statistical probabilities involving degrees of precision or
realism in visualization. Once we understand this imaginative but systematic assessment of risk, it should be possible for risk communicators to better explain risk in
everyday life.

Finally, suggest further research. This gesture suggests how the community of researchers can continue the conversation. It mirrors the opening
context:

Although these factors improve our understanding of risk, they do not exhaust the "human" factors in judgments of it. We must also investigate the relevance of age, gender, education, and intelligence. For example, . . .

10.3   Write Your Title Last

Your title is the first thing your readers read; it should be the last thing you write. It should both announce the topic of your report and communicate its conceptual framework, so build it out of the key terms that you earlier circled and underlined (review 9.2). Compare these three titles:

Risk

Thinking about Risk

Irrational but Systematic Risk Assessment: The Role of Visual Imagination in Calculating Relative Risk

The first title is accurate but too general to give us much guidance about what is to come. The second is more specific, but the third uses both a title and subtitle to give us advance notice about the keywords that will appear in what follows. When readers see the keywords in a title turn up again in your introduction and then again throughout your report, they're more likely to feel that its parts hang together. Two-part titles are most useful: they give you plenty of opportunity to use your keywords to announce your key concepts.

At this point, you may be so sick of your report that you want nothing more than to kick it out the door. Resist that impulse; you have one more important task.

11 Revising Sentences

Your last big task is to make your sentences as clear as your ideas allow. On some occasions, you may know your writing is awkward, especially if you're writing about an unfamiliar and complex topic for intimidating readers. In fact, you may even feel you've forgotten how to write clearly at all. You need a plan to revise sentences that you can see need help, but even more, you need a way first to identify those that you think are fine, but that readers might think are not.

We can't tell you how to fix every problem in every sentence, but we can tell you how to deal with those that most often afflict a writer struggling to sound like a "serious scholar," a style that most experienced readers think is just pretentious. Here is a short example:

1a. An understanding of terrorist thinking could achieve improvements in the protection of the public.

However impressive that sounds, the student who wrote it meant only this:

1b. If we understood how terrorists think, we could protect the public better.

To diagnose (1a) and revise it into (1b), however, you must know a few grammatical terms: *noun, verb, active verb, passive verb, whole subject, simple subject, main clause, subordinate clause.* If they're a dim memory, skim a grammar guide before you go on.

11.1 Focus on the First Seven or Eight Words of a Sentence

Just as the key to a clearly written report, section, or paragraph is in its first few sentences, so is the key to a clearly written sentence in its first few words. When readers grasp those first seven or eight words easily, they read what follows faster, understand it better, and remember it longer. It is the difference between these two sentences:

2a. The Federalists' argument in regard to the destabilization of government by popular democracy arose from their belief in the tendency of factions to further their self-interest at the expense of the common good.

2b. The Federalists argued that popular democracy destabilized government, because they believed that factions tended to further their self-interest at the expense of the common good.

To write a sentence like (2b), or to revise one like (2a) into (2b), follow these seven principles:

- Avoid introducing more than a few sentences with long phrases and clauses; get to the subject of your sentence quickly.
- Make subjects short and concrete, ideally naming the character that performs the action expressed by the verb that follows.
- Avoid interrupting the subject and verb with more than a word or two.
- Put key actions in verbs, not in nouns.
- Put information familiar to readers at the beginning of a sentence, new information at the end.
- Choose active or passive verbs to reflect the previous principles.
- Use first person pronouns appropriately.

Those principles add up to this: readers want to get past a short, concrete, familiar subject quickly and easily to a verb expressing a specific action. When you do that, the rest of your sentence will usually take care of itself. To diagnose your own writing, look for those characteristics in it. Skim the first seven or eight words of every sentence. Look closely at sentences that don't meet those criteria, then revise them as follows.

11.1.1 Avoid Long Introductory Phrases and Clauses

Compare these two sentences (introductory phrases are boldfaced; whole subjects italicized):

3a. **In view of claims by researchers on higher education indicating at least one change by most undergraduate students of their major field of study,** *first-year students* seem not well informed about choosing a major field of study.

3b. *Researchers on higher education* claim that *most students* change their major field of study at least once during their undergraduate careers. **If that is so,** then *first-year students* seem not well informed when they choose a major.

Most readers find (3a) harder to read than (3b), because it makes them work through a twenty-four-word phrase before they reach its subject (*first-year students*). In the two sentences in (3b), readers immediately start with a subject, *Researchers,* or reach it after a very short clause, *If that is so.*

The principle is this: start most of your sentences directly with their subjects. Begin only a few sentences with introductory phrases or clauses longer than ten or so words. You can usually revise long introductory phrases and subordinate clauses into their own independent sentences as in (3b).

11.1.2 Make Subjects Short and Concrete

Readers must grasp the subject of a sentence easily, but can't when the subject is long, complex, and abstract. Compare these two sentences (the whole subjects in each are italicized; the one-word simple subject is boldfaced):

4a. *A school system's successful **adoption** of a new reading curriculum for its elementary schools* depends on the demonstration in each school of the commitment of its principal and the cooperation of teachers in setting reasonable goals.

4b. *A school **system*** will successfully adopt a new reading curriculum for elementary schools only when *each **principal*** demonstrates that *she* is committed to it and *teachers* cooperate to set reasonable goals.

In (4a), the whole subject is fourteen words long, and its simple subject is an abstraction—*adoption.* In (4b), the clearer version, the whole subject of every verb is short, and each simple subject is relatively concrete: *school system, each principal, she, teachers.* Moreover, each of those subjects performs the action in its verb: ***system** will adopt, **principal** demonstrates, **she** is committed, **teachers** cooperate.*

The principle is this: readers tend to judge a sentence to be readable when the subject of its verb names the main character in a few concrete words, ideally a character that is also the "doer" of the action expressed by the verb that follows.

But there's a complication: you can often tell clear stories about abstract characters:

> 5. *No skill* is more valued in the professional world than problem solving. *The ability to solve problems quickly* requires us to frame situations in different ways and to find more than one solution. In fact, *effective problem solving* may define general intelligence.

Few readers have trouble with those abstract subjects, because they're short and familiar: *no skill, the ability to solve problems quickly,* and *effective problem solving.* What gives readers trouble is an abstract subject that is long and unfamiliar.

To fix sentences with long, abstract subjects, revise in three steps:

- Identify the main character in the sentence.
- Find its key action, and if it is buried in an abstract noun, make it a verb.
- Make the main character the subject of that new verb.

For example, compare (6a) and (6b) (actions are boldfaced; verbs are capitalized):

> 6a. Without a means for **analyzing interactions** between social class and education in regard to the **creation** of more job opportunities, success in **understanding** economic mobility WILL REMAIN limited.

> 6b. Economists do not entirely UNDERSTAND economic mobility, because they cannot ANALYZE how social class and education INTERACT to CREATE more job opportunities.

In both sentences, the main character is *economists,* but in (6a), that character isn't the subject of any verb; in fact, it's not in the sentence at all: we must infer it from actions buried in nouns: *analyzing* and *understanding* (what economists do). We revise (6a) into (6b) by making the main characters, *economists, social class,* and *education,* subjects of the explicit verbs *understand, analyze, interact,* and *create.*

Readers want subjects to name the main characters in your story, ideally flesh-and-blood characters, and specific verbs to name their key actions.

11.1.3 Avoid Interrupting Subjects and Verbs with More than a Word or Two

Once past a short subject, readers want to get to a verb quickly, so avoid splitting a verb from its subject with long phrases and clauses:

> 7a. Some economists, because they write in a style that is impersonal and objective, do not communicate with lay people easily.

In (7a), the *because* clause separates the subject *some economists* from the verb *do not . . . communicate,* forcing us to suspend our mental breath. To revise, move the interrupting clause to the beginning or end of its sentence, depending on whether it connects more closely to the sentence before or after. When in doubt, put it at the end (for more on this see 11.1.5);

7b. Because some economists write in a style that is impersonal and objective, they do not communicate with lay people easily. This inability to communicate . . .

7c. Some economists do not communicate with lay people easily because they write in a style that is impersonal and objective. They use passive verbs and . . .

Readers manage short interruptions more easily:

8. Few economists *deliberately* write in a style that is impersonal and objective.

11.1.4 Put Key Actions in Verbs, Not in Nouns

Readers want to get to a verb quickly, but they also want that verb to express a key action. So avoid using an empty verb such as *have, do, make,* or *be* to introduce an action buried in an abstract noun. Make the noun a verb.

Compare these two sentences (nouns naming actions are boldfaced; verbs naming actions are capitalized; verbs expressing little action are italicized):

9a. During the early years of the Civil War, the South's **attempt** at **enlisting** Great Britain on its side *was met* with **failure**.

9b. During the early years of the Civil War, the South ATTEMPTED to ENLIST Great Britain on its side, but FAILED.

In (9a), three important actions aren't verbs, but nouns: *attempt, enlisting, failure.* Sentence (9b) seems more direct because it expresses those actions in verbs: *attempted, enlist, failed.*

11.1.5 Put Information Familiar to Readers at the Beginning of a Sentence, New Information at the End

Readers understand a sentence most readily when they grasp its subject easily, and the easiest subject to grasp is not just short and concrete, but *familiar.* Compare how the second sentence in each of the following passages does or doesn't contribute to a sense of "flow":

10a. New questions about the nature of the universe have been raised by scientists studying black holes in space. The collapse of a dead star into a point perhaps no larger than a marble creates a black hole. So much matter squeezed into so little volume changes the fabric of space around it in odd ways.

10b. New questions about the nature of the universe have been raised by scientists studying black holes in space. A black hole is created by the collapse of a dead star into a point no larger than a marble. So much matter squeezed into so little volume changes the fabric of space around it in odd ways.

Most readers think (10b) flows better than (10a), partly because the subject of the second sentence, *A black hole,* is shorter and more concrete than the longer subject of (10a): *The collapse of a dead star into a point perhaps no larger than a marble.* But (10b) also flows better because the order of its ideas is different.

In (10a), the first words of the second sentence express new information:

10a . . . black holes in space. The collapse of a dead star into a point perhaps no larger than a marble creates . . .

Those words about collapsing stars seem to come out of nowhere. But in (10b), the first words echo the end of the previous sentence:

10b . . . black holes in space. A black hole is created when . . .

Moreover, once we make that change, the end of that second sentence introduces the third more cohesively:

10b . . . the collapse of a dead star into a point no larger than a marble. So much matter compressed into so little volume changes . . .

Contrast (10a); the end of its second sentence doesn't flow into the beginning of the third as smoothly:

10a. The collapse of a dead star into a point perhaps no larger than a marble creates a black hole. So much matter squeezed into so little volume changes the fabric of space around it in odd ways.

That is why readers think that passage (10a) feels choppier than (10b): the end of one sentence does not flow smoothly into the beginning of the next.

The corollary of the old-information-first principle is to put new information last, especially new technical terms. So when you introduce one, put it at the end of its sentence. Compare these:

11a. Calcium blockers can control muscle spasms. Sarcomeres are the small units of muscle fibers in which these drugs work. Two filaments, one thick and one thin, are in each sarcomere. The proteins actin and myosin are contained in the thin filament. When actin and myosin interact, your heart contracts.

11b. Muscle spasms can be controlled with drugs known as *calcium blockers.* They work in small units of muscle fibers called *sarcomeres.* Each sarcomere has *two filaments, one thick and one thin.* The thin filament contains *two proteins, actin and myosin.* When actin and myosin interact, your heart contracts.

In (11a), the new technical terms are *calcium blockers, sarcomeres, filaments, the proteins actin and myosin,* but they first appear early in their sentences. In contrast, in (11b), those new terms first appear toward the ends of their sentences. After that, they're old information and so can appear at the beginning of the next sentences.

No principle of writing is more important than this: old before new, familiar information introduces unfamiliar information.

11.1.6 Choose Active or Passive Verbs to Reflect the Previous Principles

You may recall advice to avoid passive verbs—good advice, when a passive verb forces you to write a sentence that contradicts the principles we have discussed, as in the second sentence of this passage:

12a. Global warming may have many catastrophic effects. Tropical diseases and destructive insect life even north of the Canadian border could be increased_{passive} verb by this climatic change.

That second sentence opens with an eleven-word subject conveying new information: *Tropical diseases . . . Canadian border.* It is the subject of a passive verb, *be increased,* and that verb is followed by a short, familiar bit of information from the sentence before: *by this climatic change.* That sentence would be clearer if its verb were active:

12b. Global warming may have many catastrophic effects. This climatic change could increase_{active verb} tropical diseases and destructive insect life even north of the Canadian border.

Now the subject is familiar, and the new information in the longer phrase is at the end. In this case, the active verb is the right choice.

But if you never make a verb passive, you'll write sentences that contradict the old-new principle. We saw an example in (10a):

10a. New questions about the nature of the universe have been raised by scientists studying black holes in space. The collapse of a dead star into a point perhaps no larger than a marble creates_{active verb} a black hole. So much matter squeezed into so little volume changes the fabric of space around it in odd ways.

The verb in the second sentence is active, but the passage flows better when it's passive:

10b. New questions about the nature of the universe have been raised by scientists studying black holes in space. A black hole is created_{passive verb} by the collapse of a dead star into a point no larger than a marble. So much matter squeezed into so little volume changes the fabric of space around it in odd ways.

Readers prefer a subject that is short, concrete, and familiar, regardless of its following verb. So choose active or passive, depending on which gives you the right kind of subject: short, concrete, and familiar. You can best judge how your readers will respond to your writing if you have someone read it back to you. If that person stumbles or seems to drone, you can bet that your readers will like your prose less than you do.

11.1.7   Use First Person Pronouns Appropriately

Almost everyone has heard the advice to avoid using *I* or *we* in academic writing. In fact, opinions differ on this. Some teachers tell students never to use *I*, because it makes their writing "subjective." Others encourage using *I* as a way to make writing more lively and personal.

Most instructors and editors do agree that two uses of *I* should be avoided:

■ Insecure writers begin too many sentences with *I think* or *I believe* (or their equivalent, *In my opinion*). Readers assume that you think and believe what you write, so you don't have to say you do.

■ Inexperienced writers too often narrate their research: *First, I consulted ... , then I examined ... ,* and so on. Readers care less about the story of your research than about its results.

But we believe, and most scholarly journals agree, that the first person is appropriate on two occasions. That last sentence illustrates one of them: *we . . . believe that the first person . . .*

■ An occasional introductory *I (or we) believe* can soften the dogmatic edge of a statement. Compare this blunter, less qualified version:

13. But ~~we believe, and most scholarly journals agree, that~~ the first person is appropriate on two occasions.

The trick is not to hedge so often that you sound uncertain or so rarely that you sound smug.

■ A first person *I* or *we* is also appropriate when it's the subject of a verb naming an action unique to you as the writer of your argument: Verbs referring to such actions typically appear in introductions: *I will show/argue/prove/claim that X,* and in conclusions: *I have demonstrated/concluded that Y.* Since only you can show, prove, or claim what's in your argument, only you can say so with *I:*

14. In this report, I will show that social distinctions at this university are . . .

On the other hand, researchers rarely use the first person for an action that others must repeat to replicate the reported research. Those words include *divide, measure, weigh, examine,* and so on. Researchers rarely write sentences with active verbs like this:

15a. I *calculated* the coefficient of X.

Instead, they're likely to write in the passive, because anyone can do that:

15b. The coefficient of X *was calculated.*

Those same principles apply to *we,* if you're one of two or more authors. But many instructors and editors object to two other uses of *we:*

- the royal *we* used to refer reflexively to the writer
- the all-purpose *we* that refers to people in general

Not this:

16. We must be careful to cite sources when we use data from them. When we read writers who fail to do that, we tend to distrust them.

Finally, though, your instructor decides. If he flatly forbids *I* or *we,* then so be it.

11.2 Diagnose What You Read

Once you understand how readers judge what they read, you know how to write clear prose, but also why so much of what you must read seems so dense. You might struggle with some writing because its content is difficult. But you may also struggle because the writer didn't write clearly. This next passage, for example, is by no means the thickest ever written:

15a. Recognition of the fact that grammars differ from one language to another can serve as the basis for serious consideration of the problems confronting translators of the great works of world literature originally written in a language other than English.

But in half as many words, it means only this:

15b. Once we know that languages have different grammars, we can consider the problems of those who translate great works of literature into English.

So when you struggle to understand some academic writing (and you will), don't blame yourself, at least not first. Diagnose its sentences. If they have long subjects stuffed with abstract nouns expressing new information, the problem is probably not your inability to read easily, but the writer's inability to write clearly. In this case, unfortunately, the more experience you get with academic prose, the greater your risk of imitating it. In fact, it's a common problem in professional writing everywhere, academic or not.

11.3 Choose the Right Word

Another bit of standard advice is *Choose the right word:*

1. Choose the word with the right meaning. *Affect* doesn't mean *effect; elicit* doesn't mean *illicit.* Many handbooks list commonly confused words. If you're an inexperienced writer, invest in one.
2. Choose the word with the right level of usage. If you draft quickly, you risk choosing words that might mean roughly what you think they do, but are too casual for a research report. Someone can *criticize* another writer or *knock* him; a risk can seem *frightening* or *scary.* Those pairs have similar meanings, but most readers judge the second to be a bit loose.

On the other hand, if you try too hard to sound like a real "academic," you risk using words that are too formal. You can *think* or *cogitate, drink* or *imbibe.* Those pairs are close in meaning, but the second in each is too fancy for a report written in ordinary English. Whenever you're tempted to use a word that you think is especially fine, look for a more familiar one.

The obvious advice is to look up words you're not sure of. But they're not the problem; the problem is the ones you are sure of. Worse, no dictionary tells you that a word like *visage* or *perambulate* is too fancy for just about any context. The short-term solution is to ask someone to read your report before you turn it in (but be cautious before accepting too many suggestions; see 7.10). The long-term solution is to read a lot, write a lot, endure a lot of criticism, and learn from it.

11.4 Polish It Off

Before you print out your report, read it one last time to fix errors in grammar, spelling, and punctuation. Many experienced writers read from the last sentence back to the first to keep from getting caught up in the flow of their ideas and missing the words. Do not rely solely on your spell checker. It won't catch correctly spelled but incorrectly used words such as *their/there/they're, it's/its, too/to, accept/except, affect/effect, already/all ready, complement/compliment, principal/principle, discrete/discreet,* and so on. If you've had that kind of problem, do a global search to check on both words. See chapter 20 for more on spelling.

If you used a lot of foreign words, numbers, abbreviations, and so on, check the relevant chapters in part 3 of this manual.

Finally, if your report has a table of contents that lists titles and numbers for chapter and sections, be certain that they *exactly* match the corresponding wording and numbering in the body of your report. If in your text you refer back or forward to other sections or chapters, be sure the references are accurate.

Some students think they should worry about the quality of their writing only in an English course. It is true that instructors in courses other than English are likely to focus more on the content of your report than on its style. But don't think they'll ignore its clarity and coherence. If a history or art instructor criticizes your report because it's badly written, don't plead *But this isn't an English course.* Every course in which you write is an opportunity to practice writing clearly, coherently, and persuasively, a skill that will serve you well for the rest of your life.

11.5 Give It Up and Print It Out

If one thing is harder than starting to write, it's stopping. We all want another day to get the organization right, another hour to tweak the opening paragraph, another minute to . . . you get the idea. If experienced researchers know one more crucial thing about research and its reporting, it's this: nothing you write will ever be perfect, that the benefit of getting the last 1 percent or even 5 percent right is rarely worth the cost. Dissertation students in particular agonize over reaching a standard of perfection that exists largely in their own minds. *No thesis or dissertation has to be utterly perfect; what it has to be is done.* At some point, enough is enough. Give it up and print it out. (But before you turn it in, leaf through it one last time to be sure that it looks the way you want it to: look at page breaks, spacing in margins, positions of tables and figures, and so on.)

You might now think your job is done. In fact, you have one last task: to profit from the comments on your returned paper.

12 Learning from Your Returned Paper

12.1 Find General Principles in Specific Comments

12.2 Talk to Your Instructor

Teachers are baffled and annoyed when a student looks only at the grade on his paper and ignores substantive comments, or, worse, doesn't bother to pick up the paper at all. Since you'll write many reports in your academic and professional life, it's smart to understand how your readers judge them and what you can do next time to earn a better response. For that, you need one more plan.

12.1 Find General Principles in Specific Comments

When you read your teacher's comments, focus on those that you can apply to your next project:

- Look for a pattern of errors in spelling, punctuation, and grammar. If you see one, you know what to work on.
- If your teacher says you made factual errors, check your notes: Did you take bad notes or misreport them? Were you misled by an unreliable source? Whatever you find, you know what to do in your next project.
- If your teacher reports only his judgments of your writing, look for what causes them. If he says your writing is choppy, dense, or awkward, check your sentences using the steps in chapter 11. If he says it's disorganized or wandering, check it against chapter 9. You won't always find what caused the complaints, but when you do you'll know what to work on next time.

12.2 Talk to Your Instructor

If your teacher's comments include words like *disorganized, illogical,* or *unsupported* and you cannot find what triggered them, make an appointment to ask. As with every other step in your project, that visit will go better if you plan and even rehearse it:

- If your teacher marked up spelling, punctuation, and grammar, correct those errors in bold letters *before* you talk to your teacher to show him that you took his comments seriously. In fact, you might jot responses after his comments to show that you've read them closely.

- Don't complain about your grade. Be clear that you want only to understand the comments so that you can do better next time.
- Focus on just a few comments. Rehearse your questions so that they'll seem amiable: not "You say this is disorganized but you don't say why," but rather "Can you help me see where I went wrong with my organization so I can do better next time?"
- Ask your instructor to point to passages that illustrate his judgments and what those passages should have looked like. Do not ask "What didn't you like?" but rather "Where exactly did I go wrong and what could I have done to fix it?"

If your teacher can't clearly explain his judgment, he may have graded your paper impressionistically rather than point by point. If so, bad news: you may learn little from your visit.

You might visit your teacher even if you got an A. It is important to know how you earned it, because your next project is likely to be more challenging and may even make you feel like a beginner again. In fact, don't be surprised if that happens with every new project. It happens to most of us. But with a plan, we usually overcome it, and so can you.

13 Presenting Research in Alternative Forums

You may be too early in your career to think about publishing your work, but you'll probably share some of it as an *oral presentation* to your class. Working up a talk is easier than preparing a written report, but doing it well still requires a plan and some practice. In fact, the ability to stand up and talk about your work clearly and cogently is a skill that you'll find crucial in any career you pursue. If you're working on a PhD dissertation, you probably expect to submit your work for publication eventually, but you should look for opportunities to present it as a talk before you send it off to a professional journal.

In this chapter, we show you how to use your plan for your written text to prepare a talk. We also discuss a hybrid form of presentation called a *poster,* which combines elements of writing and speech. Finally, we discuss how to prepare a conference proposal so that you'll get an invitation to give a talk.

13.1 Plan Your Oral Presentation

Talks have some advantages over writing. You get immediate feedback during the question-and-answer period afterward, responses that may be less severely critical than they would be to your written work, especially if you frame your presentation as only auditioning new ideas or testing new data. But to profit from those responses, you must plan a talk just as carefully as you would a written report.

13.1.1 Narrow Your Focus

You will probably have only about twenty minutes for your talk. (If you are reading, which is rarely a good idea, that means no more than seven to ten double-spaced pages.) So you must boil down your work to its essence or focus on just part of it. Here are three common options:

- Problem statement with a sketch of your argument. If your problem is new, focus on its originality. Start with a short introduction: *Brief literature review* + *Question* + *Consequences of not knowing an answer* + *Claim* (review 9.1); then explain your reasons, summarizing your evidence for each.
- Summary of a subargument. If your argument is too big, focus on a key subargument. Mention your larger problem in your introduction and conclusion, but be clear that you're addressing only part of it.
- Methodology or data report. If you offer a new methodology or source of data, explain why they matter. Start with a brief problem statement, then focus on how your new methods or data solve it.

13.1.2 Understand the Difference between Listeners and Readers

Speakers have endless ways to torment their listeners. Some robotically recite memorized sentences or hunch over pages reading every word, rarely making eye contact with their audience. Others ramble through slides of data, with no more structure than, *And now this slide shows. . . .* Such presenters think passive listeners are like active readers or engaged conversationalists. They are not:

- When we read, we can pause to reflect and puzzle over difficult passages. To keep track of organization, we can look at subheads, even paragraph indentations. If our minds wander, we reread.
- When we converse, we can pose questions as we think of them and ask the other person to clarify a line of reasoning or just to repeat it.

But as listeners in an audience, we can do none of those things. We must be motivated to pay attention, and we need help to follow a complicated line of thought. And if we lose its thread, we may drift off into our own thoughts. So when speaking, you have to be explicit about your purpose and your organization, and if you're reading a paper, you have to make your sentence structure far simpler than in a written report. So favor shorter sentences with consistent subjects (see 11.1.2). Use "I," "we," and "you" a lot. What seems clumsily repetitive to readers is usually welcomed by listeners.

13.2 Design Your Presentation to Be Listened To

To hold your listeners' attention, you must seem to be not lecturing *at* them, but rather amiably conversing *with* them, a skill that does not come easily, because few of us can write as we speak and because most of us need notes to keep us on track. If you must read, read no faster than about two minutes a page (at about three hundred words a page). Time yourself reading more slowly than you ordinarily speak. The top of your head is probably not your most attractive feature, so build in moments when you deliberately look straight out at your audience, especially when you're saying something important. Do that at least once or twice a page.

Far better is to talk from notes, but to do that well you need to prepare them well.

13.2.1 Sketch Your Introduction

For a twenty-minute talk, you get one shot at motivating your audience before they tune out, so prepare your introduction more carefully than any other part of your talk. Base it on the four-part problem statement described in section 10.1, plus a road map. (The times in parentheses are rough estimates.)

Use your notes only to remind yourself of the four parts, not as a word-for-word script. If you can't remember the content, you're not ready to give a talk. Sketch enough in your notes to *remind* yourself of the following:

1. the research that you extend, modify, or correct (no more than a minute)
2. a statement of your research question—the gap in knowledge or understanding that you address (thirty seconds or less)
3. an answer to *So what?* (thirty seconds)

Those three steps are crucial in motivating your listeners. If your question is new or controversial, give it more time. If your listeners know its significance, mention it quickly and go on.

4. Your claim, the answer to your research question (thirty seconds or less)

Listeners need to know your answer up front even more than readers do, so state at least its gist, unless you have a compelling reason to wait for the end. If you do wait, at least forecast your answer.

5. A forecast of the structure of your presentation (ten to twenty seconds). The most useful forecast is a verbal table of contents: "First I will discuss. . . ." That can seem clumsy in print, but listeners need more help than readers do. Repeat that structure as you work through the body of your talk.

Rehearse your introduction, not only to get it right, but to be able to look your audience in the eye as you give it. You can look down at notes later.

All told, spend no more than three minutes or so on your introduction.

13.2.2 Design Notes for the Body of Your Talk So That You Can Understand Them at a Glance

Do not write your notes as complete sentences (much less paragraphs) that you read aloud; notes should help you see at a glance only the structure of your talk and cue what to say at crucial points. So do not cut and paste sentences from a written text; create your notes from scratch.

Use separate pages for each main point. On each page, write out your main points not as topics but as claims, either in a shortened form or (only if you must) in complete sentences. Above it, you might add an explicit transition as the verbal equivalent of a subhead: "The first issue is. . . ."

Visually highlight those main points so that you recognize them instantly. Under them, list as *topics* the evidence that supports them. If your evidence consists of numbers or quotations, you'll probably have to write them out. Otherwise, know your evidence well enough to be able to talk about it directly to your audience.

Organize your points so that you cover the most important ones first. If you run long (most of us do), you can then skip to the next section or even jump to your conclusion without losing anything crucial to your argument. Never build up to a climax that you might not reach. If you must skip something, use the question-and-answer period to return to it.

13.2.3 Model Your Conclusion on Your Introduction

Make your conclusion memorable, because listeners will repeat it when asked, *What did Jones say?* Learn it well enough to present it looking at your audience, without reading from notes. It should have these three parts:

- your claim, in more detail than in your introduction

If listeners are more interested in your reasons or data, summarize them as well.

■ your answer to *So what?*

You can restate an answer from your introduction, but try to add a new one, even if it's speculative.

■ suggestions for more research, what's still to be done

Rehearse your conclusion so that you know exactly how long it takes (no more than a minute or two). Then when you have that time remaining, conclude, even if you haven't finished your last (relatively unimportant) points. If you had to skip one or two points, work them into an answer during the question-and-answer period. If your talk runs short, don't ad lib. If another speaker follows you, make her a gift of your unused time.

13.2.4 Prepare for Questions

If you're lucky, you'll get questions after your talk, so prepare answers for predictable ones. Expect questions about data or sources, especially if you didn't cover them in your talk. If you address matters associated with well-known researchers or schools of research, be ready to expand on how your work relates to them, especially if you contradict or complicate their results or approach. Also be ready to answer questions about a source you never heard of. The best policy is to acknowledge that you haven't seen it, but that you'll check it out. If the question seems friendly, ask why the source is relevant. Don't prepare only defensive answers. Use questions to reemphasize your main points or cover matters that you may have left out.

Listen to every question carefully, then to be sure you understand the question, *pause before you respond and think about it for a moment.* If you don't understand the question, ask the questioner to rephrase it. Don't snap back an answer reflexively and defensively. Good questions are invaluable, even when they seem hostile. Use them to refine your thinking.

13.2.5 Create Handouts

You can read short quotations or important data, but if you have lots of them, create a handout. If you use slides, pass out printed copies. You might hand out an outline of your main points, with white space for notes.

13.3 Plan Your Poster Presentation

A poster is a large board on which you lay out a summary of your research along with your most relevant evidence. Poster sessions are usually held in hallways or in a large room filled with other presenters. People move from poster to poster, asking questions of the presenters. Posters combine the advantages of writing and speaking. Those who read your poster have more control than a listener, and they can rely on prominent visual signals that you use to organize your material—boxes, lines, colors, and larger and smaller titles.

You can design your poster using available software and Web sites that produce a competent final product. For the text itself, however, follow the guidelines for a paper to be read aloud, with two more considerations:

1. Layer your argument. Present your argument visually in three levels of detail:

   ▫ Highlight an abstract or a problem statement and summary at the top of the poster (box it, use larger type, etc.).

   ▫ Under it, list your reasons as subheads in a section that summarizes your argument.

   ▫ Under that, restate your reasons and group evidence under them.

2. Explain all graphs and tables. In addition to a caption on each graphic, add a sentence or two explaining what is important in the data and how they support your reason and claim (review 7.7 and 8.3.1).

13.4 Plan Your Conference Proposal

Conferences are good opportunities to share your work, but to be invited to speak, you usually have to submit a proposal. Write it not as a paragraph-by-paragraph summary of your work, but as a thirty-second "elevator story"—what you would tell someone who asked, as you both stepped into an elevator on the way to your talk, *What are you saying today?* (In fact, a carefully prepared and rehearsed elevator story is especially useful for any conversation about your work, particularly interviews).

An elevator-story has three parts:

- a problem statement that highlights an answer to *So what?*
- a sketch of your claim and major reasons
- a summary of your most important evidence

Conference reviewers are less interested in your exact words than in why anyone should want to listen to them. Your aims are to pose your research question and to answer the reviewer's *So what?* So focus on how your claim contributes to your field of research, especially on what's novel or controversial about it. If you address a question established by previous research, mention it, then focus on your new data or on your new claim, depending on which is more original.

Be aware that reviewers will often know less about your topic than you do and may need help to see the significance of your question. So even after you answer that first *So what?*, ask and answer it again, and if you can, one more time. Whether your role at a conference is to talk or only to listen depends not just on the quality of your research, but on the significance of your question.

14 On the Spirit of Research

As we've said, we can reach good conclusions in many ways other than research: we can rely on intuition, emotion, even spiritual insight. But the truths we reach in those ways are personal. When we ask others to accept and act on them, we can't present our feelings as evidence for them to agree; we can ask only that they take our report of our inner experience—and our claims—on faith.

The truths of research, however, and how we reached them must be available for public study. We base research claims on evidence available to everyone and on principles of reasoning that, we hope, our readers accept as sound. And then those readers test all of that in all the ways that they and others can imagine. That may be a high standard, but it must be if we expect others to base their understanding and actions, even their lives, on what we ask them to believe.

When you accept the principles that shape public, evidence-based belief, you accept two more that can be hard to live by. One concerns our relationship to authority. No more than five centuries ago, the search for better understanding based on *evidence* was often regarded as a threat. Among the powerful, many believed that the important truths were known and that the scholar's job was to preserve and transmit them, certainly not to challenge them. If new facts cast doubt on an old belief, the belief usually trumped the facts. Many who dared to follow evidence to conclusions that challenged authority were banished, imprisoned, and on occasion killed.

Even today, those who reason from evidence can anger those who hold a cherished belief. For example, some historians claim that, based on the sum of the evidence, Thomas Jefferson probably fathered at least one child by his slave, Sally Hemings. Others disagree, not because they have better counterevidence, but because of a fiercely held belief: *a person of Jefferson's stature couldn't do such a thing* (see 5.5). But in the world of research, both academic and professional, good evidence and sound reasoning trump belief every time, or at least they should.

In some parts of the world, it's still considered more important to guard settled beliefs than to test them. But in those places informed by the values of research, we think differently: we believe not only that we *may* question settled beliefs, but that we *must,* no matter how much authority cherishes them—so long as we base our answers on sound reasons based on reliable evidence.

But that principle requires another. When we make a claim, we must expect, even encourage, others to question not just our claim but how we reached it, to ask *Why do you believe that?* It's often hard to welcome such questions, but we're obliged to listen with good will to objections, reservations, and qualifications that collectively imply *I don't agree, at least not yet.* And the more we challenge old ideas, the more we must be ready to acknowledge and answer those questions, because we may be asking others to give up deeply held beliefs.

When some students encounter these values, they find it difficult, even painful, to live by them. Some feel that a challenge to what they believe isn't a lively search for truth, but a personal attack on their deepest values. Others retreat to a cynical skepticism that doubts everything and believes nothing. Others fall into mindless relativism: "We're all entitled to our own beliefs, and so all beliefs are right for those who hold them!" Many turn away from an active life of the mind, rejecting not only answers that might disturb their settled beliefs but even the questions that inspired them.

But in our worlds of work, scholarship, civic action, and even politics, we can't replace tested knowledge and hard-won understanding with personal opinion, a relativistic view of truth, or the comfortable, settled knowledge of "authority."

That does not mean we reject long-held and time-tested beliefs lightly. We replace them only after we're persuaded by sound arguments backed by good reasons based on the best evidence available, and after an amiable but searching give-and-take that tests those arguments as severely as we can. In short, we become *responsible* believers when we can make our own sound arguments that test and evaluate those of others.

You may find it difficult to see all of this at work in a paper written for a class, but despite its cold type, a research report written for any audience is a conversation, imagined to be sure, but still a cooperative but rigorous inquiry into what we should and should not believe.

PART II

Source Citation

15 General Introduction to Citation Practices

The first duty of a researcher is to get the facts right, but a second duty is to tell readers where the facts came from. To that end, researchers must cite the sources of the facts, ideas, or words that they use in their papers.

15.1 Reasons for Citing Your Sources

You cite sources for at least four reasons:

1. *To give credit.* Research is hard work. Some who do it well receive concrete rewards—money, promotions, good grades, degrees, and so on. But no less important is recognition, the pride and prestige of seeing one's name associated with knowledge that others value and use. In fact, for some researchers, that is the only reward. So when you cite the work of another, you give that writer the recognition he or she has earned. (You also guard against a charge of plagiarism; see 7.9.)

2. *To assure readers about the accuracy of your facts.* Researchers cite sources to be fair to other researchers, but also to earn their readers' trust. It is

not enough to get the facts right. You must also tell readers the source of the facts so that they can judge their reliability, even check them if they wish. Readers do not trust a source they do not know and cannot find. If they do not trust your sources, they will not trust your facts; and if they do not trust your facts, they will not trust your argument. You establish the first link in that chain of trust by citing your sources fully, accurately, and appropriately.

3. *To show readers the research tradition that informs your work.* Researchers cite sources whose data they use, but they also cite work that they extend, support, contradict, or correct. These citations help readers not only understand your specific project but connect it to other research in your field.

4. *To help readers follow or extend your research.* Many readers use sources cited in a research paper not to check its reliability but to pursue their own work. So your citations help others not only to follow your footsteps, but to strike out in new directions.

15.2 The Requirements of Citation

To fulfill the requirements of citation, you need to know when to include a source citation in your paper and what information about the source to include.

15.2.1 Situations Requiring Citations

Chapter 7, particularly 7.9, discusses in depth when you should cite materials from other sources. Briefly, you should always provide a citation in the following situations:

- when you *quote exact words* from a source (see also chapter 25 on quotations)
- when you *paraphrase ideas* that are associated with a specific source, even if you don't quote exact words from it
- when you use any idea, data, or method attributable to any source you consulted

As noted in 15.1, you may also use citations to *point readers to sources* that are relevant to a particular portion of your argument but not quoted or paraphrased. Such citations demonstrate that you are familiar with these sources, even if they present claims at odds with your own.

15.2.2 Information Required in Citations

Over the long tradition of citing sources, as researchers in different fields began to write in different ways, they also developed distinctive ways of citing and documenting their sources. When citation methods became standardized, researchers had to choose from not just one or two standards but many.

Citation styles differ in the elements included and in the format of these elements, but they have the same aim: to give readers the information they need to identify and find a source. For most sources, including books, articles, unpublished documents, online sources, and other written material, that information must answer these questions:

- Who wrote, edited, or translated the text (sometimes all three)?
- What data identify the text? This includes the title and subtitle of the work; title of the journal, collection, or series it appears in, as well as volume number, edition number, or other identifying information; and page numbers, URL, or other locating information if the reference is to a specific part of a larger text.
- Who published the text, and when? This includes the name of the publisher and the place and date of publication—or an indication that the document has not been published.

Details vary for other sources, such as sound and video recordings, but they answer the same three questions: Who wrote, edited, translated, or assembled the source? What data identify it? Who published it and when?

Your readers will expect you to use the citation style appropriate to their particular field, not just because they are familiar with this style but because when you use it, you show them that you understand their values and practices. The details, however, are complex: when to use capitals, periods, commas, even where to put a space. But if you do not get these small matters right, many of your readers will question whether they can trust you on the bigger ones. Few researchers try to memorize all these details. Instead, they learn the form of the citations they use most so that they do not need to look them up repeatedly. Then, for citing sources that are less common or have unusual elements, they consult a book like this one.

15.3 Two Citation Styles

This book covers the two most common forms of citation, called *notes-bibliography style,* or simply *bibliography style* (used widely in the humanities and in some social sciences), and *parenthetical citations–reference list style,* or *reference list style* (used in most social sciences and in the natural and physical sciences). If you are not certain which style to use in a paper, consult your instructor.

You may be asked to use different styles in different settings (for example, an art history course and a political science course). Within a specific paper, however, always follow a single style consistently.

If you are new to research, read this section for a brief description of how the two citation styles work. Then, if you are using bibliography style, read chapter 16 for an overview of this style, and refer to chapter 17 for detailed guidelines and examples for citing most types of sources you're likely to consult. If you are using reference list style, the overview and detailed chapters are 18 and 19, respectively.

15.3.1 Bibliography Style

In bibliography-style citations, you signal that you have used a source by placing a superscript number at the end of the sentence in which you refer to it:

He argues that "in an uncertain world, printed materials can be put to use in ways that make them powerful."[1]

You then cite the source of that quotation in a correspondingly numbered note that provides information about the source (author, title, and facts of publication) plus relevant page numbers. Notes are printed at the bottom of the page (called *footnotes*) or in a list collected at the end of your paper (called *endnotes*). All notes have the same general form:

N: 1. Adrian Johns, *The Nature of the Book: Print and Knowledge in the Making* (Chicago: University of Chicago Press, 1998), 623.

If you cite the same text again, you can shorten subsequent notes:

N: 5. Johns, *Nature of the Book*, 384–85.

In most cases, you also list sources at the end of the paper in a *bibliography*. That list normally includes every source you cited in a note and sometimes others you consulted but did not cite. Each bibliography entry includes the same information contained in a full note, but in a slightly different form:

B: Johns, Adrian. *The Nature of the Book: Print and Knowledge in the Making.* Chicago: University of Chicago Press, 1998.

15.3.2 Reference List Style

In reference list–style citations, you signal that you have used a source by placing a *parenthetical citation* (including author, date, and relevant page numbers) next to your reference to it:

He argues that "in an uncertain world, printed materials can be put to use in ways that make them powerful" [Johns 1998, 623].

At the end of the paper, you list all sources in a *reference list*. That list normally includes every source you cited in a parenthetical citation and sometimes others you consulted but did not cite. Each reference list entry includes complete bibliographical information for a source, since parenthetical citations do not. All reference list entries have the same general form:

R: Johns, Adrian. 1998. *The nature of the book: Print and knowledge in the making.* Chicago: Univ. of Chicago Press.

15.4 Citation of Electronic Sources

The standard citation forms evolved in the age of print, but researchers now increasingly rely on sources that are found online or in another electronic medium. These new sources have been used long enough for researchers to have created standard citation forms adapted to their special characteristics, especially their transitory and changeable nature.

15.4.1 Online Sources

Sources available online are inherently less stable than printed sources.

■ Online content can be revised easily, often without any indication that changes have been made. Some sites include revision dates, but many do not. There are no standards for deciding how much change counts as a revision, so a revision date on one Web site may indicate correction of a spelling error while on another it may mark changes in factual data or claims.

■ Many Web sites have no identifiable author, publisher, or sponsor. This makes them the equivalent of any other anonymous source, unlikely to be reliable enough to use without serious qualification (see 3.4.3).

■ Online content may be simultaneously available from more than one site, some more reliable than others.

■ Most online sources are located through a URL (uniform resource locator), but URLs come and go. You cannot be certain that a URL will be available months, weeks, or even days later, making it difficult or impossible for you or your readers to find the content you originally consulted.

In your research, choose online sources carefully. When information is available on multiple Web sites or in multiple media (print and online), consult the most stable and reliable version available, and always cite the version you consulted.

TWO CATEGORIES OF SOURCES. For citations in both styles covered in this book, online sources fall into two categories.

1. Many online sources are like print sources in everything except medium—for example, an article published in an online journal instead of in a printed journal. Other sources of this type include online books, newspaper and magazine articles, and public documents. Cite an online source of this type similarly to a print source, beginning with standard facts of publication (author's name, title, date, and so forth). At the end of the citation, add the URL and the date you accessed the material (see below). You can find examples of how to cite such items under the relevant type of source in chapter 17 (for bibliography style) and chapter 19 (for reference list style).
2. Other types of online sources, such as institutional or personal Web sites and electronic mailing lists, are unique to the medium. Since these sources lack many of the standard facts of publication, they are considered "informally published." To cite such a source, you will need to give as much information as possible about it in addition to the URL and access date (see below). Examples of how to cite these items appear in 17.7 (for bibliography style) and 19.7 (for reference list style).

URLS, PERMANENT SOURCE IDENTIFIERS, AND ACCESS DATES. Although URLs are unstable, they are still the primary locator for online content. Every citation of an online source identified with a URL should include the URL after the facts of publication. If a source uses digital object identifiers (DOIs) or another system of permanent identifiers instead of URLs, use the relevant locator in your citation. For details on listing URLs or other identifiers in your citations, see especially 17.1.7 (for bibliography style) or 19.1.8 (for reference style).

In addition, every citation of an online source should include the date you last accessed it. If the source has changed or been removed from the Web, this date represents the version you consulted more accurately than the URL or other identifier alone. You may also copy an online source you intend to cite onto your hard drive or a CD, so you will have a stable copy that you or your readers can later consult. Chapters 17 and 19 provide many examples of access dates in citations.

SUBSCRIPTION-BASED AND RESTRICTED SITES. Many online databases, jour-
. nals, and other periodicals are accessible by subscription only. Similarly,
some Web sites and Weblogs are restricted to users who have registered or
otherwise applied for access. When citing such sources, you do not need
to identify them as "subscription-based" or "restricted"; simply include
the URL and access date, as for any other online source.

15.4.2 Other Electronic Media

Sources available in other electronic media, such as CD-ROMs, are more
stable than those posted online. Those that are reproduced and distributed in quantity should be cited similarly to published books, with the
addition of information about the medium; see 17.5.8 (for bibliography
style) or 19.5.8 (for reference list style).

If a source is available in more than one electronic medium (for example, online and on CD-ROM), or both electronically and in print form,
consult the most stable version, and always cite the version you consulted.

15.5 ██ Preparation of Citations

You can ease the process of preparing and checking citations if you anticipate what you will need.

- Use the most reliable sources, in their most reliable version. If you find
  second- or thirdhand information, track down the original source.
- If a source is available in multiple versions, always cite the one you actually consulted. There may be small but important differences between the
  versions that could affect the accuracy of your quotations or other references to the source.
- Record all bibliographical information before you take notes. See figure
  16.1 (for bibliography style) or figure 18.1 (for reference list style) for templates showing what information is needed for several common types of
  sources.
- Record page numbers for every quotation and paraphrase.
- As you draft, clearly indicate every place where you may need to cite a
  source. It is much easier to remove an unnecessary citation when you
  revise than to remember where you may have relied on someone else's
  ideas.
- When your draft is in its final form, consult chapter 17 or 19 to ensure
  that each citation is in the correct form, including punctuation and
  spacing. .

- You can assemble your bibliography or reference list either as you consult your sources or as you draft and revise. Be sure to check each detail carefully.

Getting each citation right may be tedious, but as with every other phase of research, if you anticipate what you need and manage the process from the beginning, you can complete even this least exciting part of research faster, more easily, and more reliably.

15.6 A Word on Citation Software

Software companies offer a variety of programs that format bibliographical information according to a specific citation style, including the styles covered in the following chapters. Such a program may save time, but it is not a substitute for knowing the underlying principles of the style. Morever, citation and bibliographic management software varies widely in quality and might not reflect the small changes in citation styles that occur over time (for example, the addition of different electronic sources). If you use such software, you should always review the resulting citations for accuracy and completeness.

16 Notes-Bibliography Style: The Basic Form

A citation style used widely in the humanities and in some social sciences is the *notes-bibliography style,* or *bibliography style* for short. This chapter presents an overview of the basic pattern for citations in bibliography style, including bibliography entries, full notes, shortened notes, and parenthetical notes. Examples of notes are identified with an N; examples of bibliography entries are identified with a B.

In bibliography style, you signal that you have used a source by placing a superscript number at the end of the sentence in which you refer to that source:

According to one scholar, "The railroads had made Chicago the most important meeting place between East and West."[4]

You then cite the source of that quotation in a correspondingly numbered note that provides information about the source (author, title, and facts of publication) plus relevant page numbers. Notes are printed at the bottom of the page (called *footnotes*) or in a list collected at the end of your paper, called (*endnotes*). All notes have the same general form:

N: 4. William Cronon, *Nature's Metropolis: Chicago and the Great West* (New York: W. W. Norton & Company, 1991), 92–93.

If you cite the same text again, you can shorten subsequent notes:

N: 8. Cronon, *Nature's Metropolis*, 383.

In most cases, you also list sources at the end of the paper in a *bibliography*. That list normally includes every source you cited in a note and sometimes others you consulted but did not cite. Each bibliography entry includes the same information contained in a full note, but in a slightly different form:

B: Cronon, William. *Nature's Metropolis: Chicago and the Great West*. New York: W. W. Norton & Company, 1991.

Readers expect you to follow the rules for correct citations exactly. These rules cover not only what data you must include and their order, but also punctuation, capitalization, italicizing, and so on. To get your citations right, you must pay close attention to many minute details that few researchers can easily remember. The next chapter provides a ready reference guide to those details.

16.1 Basic Patterns

Although sources and their citations come in almost endless variety, you are likely to use only a few kinds. While you may need to look up details to cite some unusual sources, you can easily learn the basic patterns for the few kinds you will use most often. You can then create templates that will help you record bibliographical data quickly and reliably as you read.

The rest of this section describes the basic patterns, and figure 16.1 provides templates for and examples of several common types of sources. Chapter 17 includes examples of a wide range of sources, including exceptions to the patterns discussed here.

Figure 16.1. Templates for notes and bibliography entries

The following templates show which elements should be included and their order when citing several common types of sources in notes (N) and bibliographies (B). They also show punctuation, capitalization of titles, and typography of the elements. Gray shading shows abbreviations (or their spelled-out versions) and other terms as they would actually appear in a citation. *XX* stands in for page numbers actually cited, *YY* for a full span of page numbers for an article or a chapter.

For further examples, explanations, and variations, see chapter 17. For templates of shortened note forms, see figure 16.2.

Books

1. Single Author or Editor

N: Note Number. Author's First and Last Names, *Title of Book: Subtitle of Book* (Place of Publication: Publisher's Name, Date of Publication), XX–XX.

1. Jared Diamond, *Guns, Germs, and Steel: The Fates of Human Societies* (New York: W. W. Norton and Company, 1997), 47–48.

B: Author's Last Name, Author's First Name. *Title of Book: Subtitle of Book.* Place of Publication: Publisher's Name, Date of Publication.

Diamond, Jared. *Guns, Germs, and Steel: The Fates of Human Societies.* New York: W. W. Norton and Company, 1997.

For a book with an editor instead of an author, adapt the pattern as follows:

N: Note Number. Editor's First and Last Names, ed. *Title of Book* . . .

7. Mark A. Noll, ed., *Religion and American Politics* . . .

B: Editor's Last Name, Editor's First Name, ed. *Title of Book* . . .

Noll, Mark A., ed. *Religion and American Politics* . . .

2. Multiple Authors

For a book with two authors, use the following pattern:

N: Note Number. Author #1's First and Last Names and Author #2's First and Last Names, *Title of Book: Subtitle of Book* (Place of Publication: Publisher's Name, Date of Publication), XX–XX.

2. Kai Bird and Martin J. Sherwin, *American Prometheus: The Triumph and Tragedy of J. Robert Oppenheimer* (New York: Alfred A. Knopf, 2005), 52.

B: Author #1's Last Name, Author #1's First Name, and Author #2's First and Last Names. *Title of Book: Subtitle of Book.* Place of Publication: Publisher's Name, Date of Publication.

Bird, Kai, and Martin J. Sherwin. *American Prometheus: The Triumph and Tragedy of J. Robert Oppenheimer.* New York: Alfred A. Knopf, 2005.

For a book with three authors, adapt the pattern as follows:

N: Note Number. Author #1's First and Last Names, Author #2's First and Last Names, and Author #3's First and Last Names, *Title of Book* . . .

5. Joyce Appleby, Lynn Hunt, and Margaret Jacob, *Telling the Truth about History* . . .

Figure 16.1. Templates for notes and bibliography entries *(continued)*

B: Author #1's Last Name, Author #1's First Name, Author #2's First and Last Names, [and] Author #3's First and Last Names. *Title of Book* . . .

Appleby, Joyce, Lynn Hunt, and Margaret Jacob. *Telling the Truth about History* . . .

For a book with four or more authors, adapt the note pattern only as follows:

N: Note Number. Author #1's First and Last Names [et al.], *Title of Book* . . .

15. Jacquelyn Dowd Hall et al., *Like a Family* . . .

3. Author(s) Plus Editor or Translator

For a book with an author plus an editor, use the following pattern:

N: Note Number. Author's First and Last Names, *Title of Book: Subtitle of Book,* [ed.] Editor's First and Last Names (Place of Publication: Publisher's Name, Date of Publication), XX–XX.

9. J. B. Harley, *The New Nature of Maps: Essays in the History of Cartography,* ed. Paul Laxton (Baltimore: Johns Hopkins University Press, 2002), 132–33.

B: Author's Last Name, Author's First Name. *Title of Book: Subtitle of Book.* [Edited by] Editor's First and Last Names. Place of Publication: Publisher's Name, Date of Publication.

Harley, J. B. *The New Nature of Maps: Essays in the History of Cartography.* Edited by Paul Laxton. Baltimore: Johns Hopkins University Press, 2002.

If a book has a translator instead of an editor, substitute the words *trans.* and *Translated by* and the translator's name for the editor data.

4. Edition Number

N: Note Number. Author's First and Last Names, *Title of Book: Subtitle of Book,* Edition Number [ed.] (Place of Publication: Publisher's Name, Date of Publication), XX–XX.

11. Roger Daniels, *Coming to America: A History of Immigration and Ethnicity in American Life,* 2nd ed. (New York: Harper Perennial, 2002), 84.

B: Author's Last Name, Author's First Name. *Title of Book: Subtitle of Book.* Edition Number [ed.] Place of Publication: Publisher's Name, Date of Publication.

Daniels, Roger. *Coming to America: A History of Immigration and Ethnicity in American Life.* 2nd ed. New York: Harper Perennial, 2002.

5. Single Chapter in an Edited Book

N: Note Number. Chapter Author's First and Last Names, "Title of Chapter: Subtitle of Chapter," [in] *Title of Book: Subtitle of Book,* [ed.] Editor's First and Last Names (Place of Publication: Publisher's Name, Date of Publication), XX–XX.

15. Anne Whiston Spirn, "Constructing Nature: The Legacy of Frederick Law Olmsted," in *Uncommon Ground: Rethinking the Human Place in Nature,* ed. William Cronon (New York: W. W. Norton and Company, 1996), 101.

Figure 16.1. Templates for notes and bibliography entries *(continued)*

B: Chapter Author's Last Name, Chapter Author's First Name. "Title of Chapter: Subtitle of Chapter." In *Title of Book: Subtitle of Book,* edited by Editor's First and Last Names, YY–YY. Place of Publication: Publisher's Name, Date of Publication.

> Spirn, Anne Whiston. "Constructing Nature: The Legacy of Frederick Law Olmsted." In *Uncommon Ground: Rethinking the Human Place in Nature,* edited by William Cronon, 91–113. New York: W. W. Norton and Company, 1996.

Journal Articles

6. Journal Article in Print

N: Note Number. Author's First and Last Names, "Title of Article: Subtitle of Article," *Title of Journal* Volume Number (Date of Publication): XX–XX.

> 4. Pramod K. Nayar, "Marvelous Excesses: English Travel Writing and India, 1680–1727," *Journal of British Studies* 44, no. 2 (April 2005): 213.

B: Author's Last Name, Author's First Name. "Title of Article: Subtitle of Article." *Title of Journal* Volume Number (Date of Publication): YY–YY.

> Nayar, Pramod K. "Marvelous Excesses: English Travel Writing and India, 1680–1727." *Journal of British Studies* 44, no. 2 (April 2005): 213–38.

For an article with multiple authors, follow the relevant pattern for authors' names in template 2.

7. Journal Article Online

N: Note Number. Author's First and Last Names, "Title of Article: Subtitle of Article," *Title of Journal* Volume Number (Date of Publication), under "Descriptive Locator," URL (accessed Date of Access).

> 4. Daniel A. McFarland, "Resistance as a Social Drama: A Study of Change-oriented Encounters," *American Journal of Sociology* 109, no. 6 (May 2004), under "Settings," http://www.journals.uchicago.edu/AJS/journal/issues/v109n6/050199/050199.html (accessed May 3, 2006).

B: Author's Last Name, Author's First Name. "Title of Article: Subtitle of Article." *Title of Journal* Volume Number (Date of Publication). URL (accessed Date of Access).

> McFarland, Daniel A. "Resistance as a Social Drama: A Study of Change-oriented Encounters." *American Journal of Sociology* 109, no. 6 (May 2004). http://www.journals.uchicago.edu/AJS/journal/issues/v109n6/050199/050199.html (accessed May 3, 2006).

16.1.1 Order of Elements

The order of elements in notes and bibliography entries follows the same general pattern for all types of sources: author, title, facts of publication. However, notes present authors' names in standard order (first name first), while bibliography entries present them in inverted order (last name first) for alphabetical listing. Notes citing specific passages usually include page numbers or other locating information; bibliography entries do not, though they do include a full span of page numbers for a source that is part of a larger whole, such as an article or a chapter.

16.1.2 Punctuation

In notes, separate most elements with commas; in bibliography entries, separate them with periods. In notes, enclose facts of publication in parentheses; in bibliography entries, do not. The styles are different because a note is intended to be read like text, where any period would signal the end of a citation. Bibliographies are designed as lists in which each source has its own entry, so periods can be used without confusion to separate the elements of author, title, and publication data.

16.1.3 Capitalization

Capitalize most titles headline style, but capitalize titles in foreign languages sentence style. (See 22.3.1 for both styles.) Capitalize proper nouns in the usual way (see chapter 22).

16.1.4 Typography of Titles

Titles of larger entities (books, journals) are printed in italics; titles of smaller entities (chapters, articles) are printed in roman type and enclosed in quotation marks. Titles of unpublished works (such as dissertations) are printed in roman type and enclosed in quotation marks, even if they are book length.

16.1.5 Numbers

In titles, numbers are spelled out or given in numerals exactly as they are in the original. Page numbers that are in roman numerals in the original are presented in lowercase roman numerals. All other numbers (such as chapter numbers or figure numbers) are given in arabic numerals, even if they are in roman numerals or spelled out in the original.

16.1.6 Abbreviations

In notes, abbreviate terms such as *editor, translator,* and *volume* (*ed., trans.,* and *vol.*). In bibliography entries, these terms are often spelled out when they introduce an element (*Edited by*) but abbreviated when they conclude it (*ed.*). The plural is usually formed by adding *s* (*eds.*) unless the abbreviation ends in an *s* (use *trans.* for both singular and plural).

16.1.7 Indentation

Notes are indented like other paragraphs in the text; all following lines are flush left. Bibliography entries have a hanging indentation: the first line is flush left and all following lines are indented the same space as paragraphs.

16.2 Bibliographies

Papers that use the notes-bibliography citation style typically include both notes and a bibliography listing all sources cited in the notes. Although the same information appears in both notes and bibliographies, readers need it in both places, because they use notes and bibliographies differently. Notes let readers quickly check the source for a particular reference without disrupting the flow of their reading. Bibliographies show readers the extent of your research and its relationship to prior work. Bibliographies also help readers use your sources in their own research. So unless you have only a handful of sources or your instructor tells you otherwise, always include both notes and a bibliography in your papers. If you do not include a bibliography, make sure that your notes present complete information for each source, at least the first time you cite it.

16.2.1 Types of Bibliographies

In most cases, your bibliography should include every work you cite in your text (other than a few special types of sources; see 16.2.3). You may also include works that were important to your thinking but that you did not specifically mention in the text. Label this kind *Bibliography* or *Sources Consulted.* See figure A.15 in the appendix for a sample page of a bibliography.

There are other options:

- *Selected bibliography.* Some bibliographies do not include all works cited in notes, either to save space or omit minor references unlikely to interest readers. You may use a selected bibliography if you have good reasons and your instructor or advisor approves. Label it *Selected Bibliography* and add a headnote that explains your principle of selection.
- *Single-author bibliography.* Some writers list works by one person, usually as a separate list in addition to a standard bibliography, but sometimes as the only bibliography in a single-author study with few other sources. Label such a list *Works of [Author's Name]* or some appropriate descriptive

title (*Published Works of, Writings of,* and so on). You can arrange it chronologically or alphabetically by title. If chronologically, list titles published in the same year alphabetically.

- *Annotated bibliography.* Some writers annotate each bibliography entry with a brief description of the work's contents or relevance to their research. In most cases, if you annotate one entry you should annotate them all. But researchers sometimes annotate only the most important works or those whose relevance to their research may not be evident. If your annotations are brief phrases, add them in brackets after the publication data (note that there is no period within or after the bracketed entry):

B: Toulmin, Stephen. *The Uses of Argument.* Cambridge: Cambridge University Press, 1958. [a seminal text describing argument in nonsymbolic language]

You may also add full-sentence annotations on a new line with paragraph indentation:

B: Toulmin, Stephen. *The Uses of Argument.* Cambridge: Cambridge University Press, 1958.

This is the seminal text in describing the structure of an argument in nonsymbolic language.

16.2.2 Arrangement of Entries

ALPHABETICAL BY AUTHOR. A bibliography is normally a single list of all sources arranged alphabetically by the last name of the author, editor, or whoever is first in each entry. (For alphabetizing foreign names, compound names, and other special cases, see 17.1.1.) Most word processors provide an alphabetical sorting function; if you use it, be sure each entry is followed by a hard return. If you are writing a thesis or dissertation, your department or university may specify that you should alphabetize the entries letters by letter or word by word; see 18.56–59 of the *Chicago Manual of Style,* 15th edition (2003), for an explanation of these two systems.

If your bibliography includes two or more works written, edited, or translated by the same individual, arrange the entries alphabetically by title (ignoring articles such as *a* or *the*). For all entries after the first, replace the individual's name with a long dash called a 3-em dash (see 21.7.3). For edited or translated works, put a comma and the appropriate designation (*ed., trans.,* and so on) after the dash. List all such works before any that the individual coauthored or coedited.

B: Gates, Henry Louis Jr. *America behind the Color Line: Dialogues with African Americans.* New York: Warner Books, 2004.

——, ed. *The Classic Slave Narratives.* New York: Penguin Putnam, 2002.

——. *The Signifying Monkey: A Theory of African-American Literary Criticism.* New York: Oxford University Press, 1989.

Gates, Henry Louis Jr., and Cornel West. *The African American Century: How Black Americans Have Shaped Our Country.* New York: Free Press, 2000.

The same principles apply to works by a single group of authors named in the same order.

B: Marty, Martin E., and R. Scott Appleby, eds. *Accounting for Fundamentalisms.* Chicago: University of Chicago Press, 2004.

——. *The Glory and the Power: The Fundamentalist Challenge to the Modern World.* Boston: Beacon Press, 1992.

Marty, Martin E., and Micah Marty. *When True Simplicity Is Gained: Finding Spiritual Clarity in a Complex World.* Grand Rapids, MI: William B. Eerdmans Publishing Company, 1998.

If a source does not have a named author or editor, alphabetize it based on the first element of the citation, generally a title. Ignore articles such as *a* or *the*.

B: *Account of the Operations of the Great Trigonometrical Survey of India.* 22 vols. Dehra Dun: Survey of India, 1870–1910.

"The Great Trigonometrical Survey of India." *The Calcutta Review* 38 (1863): 26–62.

"State and Prospects of Asia." *The Quarterly Review* 63, no. 126 (March 1839): 369–402.

OTHER THAN ALPHABETICAL. Occasionally, readers will find an order other than alphabetical more useful. Single-author bibliographies are often more usefully arranged chronologically, as are specialized listings such as newspaper articles, archival records, and so on. You may also find it useful to invent an order for a specific purpose—for example, a list of topographical maps arranged by state or region. If you do use an order other than alphabetical or chronological, explain your choice in a headnote.

CATEGORIZED LISTINGS. You may organize a longer bibliography into categories to help readers see related sources as a group. Some common ways of categorizing longer bibliographies into sections include these:

- *By the physical form of sources.* You can create separate lists for manuscripts, archival collections, recordings, and so on.
- *By the primacy of sources.* You can separate primary sources from secondary and tertiary ones, as in a single-author bibliography.
- *By the field of sources.* You can group sources by field, either because your readers will have different interests (as in the bibliography to this book) or

because you mix work from fields not usually combined. For example, a work on the theory and psychology of comic literature might categorize sources: *Theory of Comedy, Psychological Studies, Literary Criticism, Comic Works.*

If you categorize sources, present them either in separate bibliographies or a single one divided into sections. Introduce each separate bibliography or section with a subheading and, if necessary, a headnote. In a single bibliography, use the same principle of order within each section (usually alphabetical), and do not list a source in more than one section unless it clearly could be categorized in two or more ways. If you use different principles of order, create separate bibliographies, each with its own explanatory heading.

16.2.3 Sources That May Be Omitted

By convention, you may omit the following types of sources from a bibliography:

- newspaper articles (see 17.4)
- classical, medieval, and early English literary works (17.5.1) and (in some cases) well-known English-language plays (17.8.7)
- the Bible and other sacred works (17.5.2)
- well-known reference works, such as major dictionaries and encyclopedias (17.5.3)
- brief published items, such as reviews of published works or performances (17.5.4), abstracts (17.5.5), and pamphlets and reports (17.5.6)
- unpublished interviews and personal communications (17.6.3), Weblog entries and comments (17.7.2), and postings to electronic mailing lists (17.7.3)
- individual documents in unpublished manuscript collections (17.6.4)
- many sources in the visual and performing arts, including artworks and other visual sources (17.8.1), live performances (17.8.2), and television and other broadcast programs (17.8.3)
- the U.S. Constitution (17.9.5), legal cases (17.9.7), and some other public documents (17.9)

You may choose to include in your bibliography a specific work from one of these categories that is critical to your argument or frequently cited.

If you use many such sources from a single larger entity—for example, several documents from a single manuscript collection—you may cite the larger entity, as discussed in the relevant sections of chapter 17.

16.3 Notes

Writers use several different kinds of notes, depending on their field, their readers, and the nature of their project. This section explains your options and how to choose among them.

16.3.1 Footnotes versus Endnotes

Your department may specify whether you should use footnotes or end-notes, especially for a thesis or dissertation. If not, you should generally choose footnotes, which are easier to read. Endnotes force readers to flip to the back to check every citation. If you include substantive comments in endnotes (see 16.3.5), readers might ignore them because they cannot tell without turning back which notes are substantive and which only cite sources.

On the other hand, choose endnotes when your footnotes are so long or numerous that they take up too much space on the page, making your report unattractive and difficult to read. Also, endnotes better accommodate tables, quoted poetry, and other matter that requires special typography.

If you use endnotes, you can reduce the risk that readers will miss substantive comments by separating substantive notes from source notes. Number source notes and print them as endnotes. Signal substantive notes with asterisks and other symbols (see 16.3.3) and print them as footnotes. Do not do this if you have more than a few substantive notes.

16.3.2 Referencing Notes in Text

Whenever you refer to or otherwise use material from a source, you must insert into your text a superscript number that directs your reader to a note that gives bibliographical information about that source. For most quotations, put the number immediately following, whether the quotation is run into the text or set off as a block quotation (see 25.2). For some quotations and for general citations, put reference numbers at the end of a sentence or clause, after the terminal punctuation mark, quotation mark, or closing parenthesis.

Magic was a staple of the Kinahan charm.[1]

"This," wrote George Templeton Strong, "is what our tailors can do."[2]

(In an earlier book he had said quite the opposite.)[3]

If, however, the note refers to material before a dash, put the reference number before the dash:

The bias surfaced in the Shotwell series[4]—though not obviously.

Do not include more than one reference number at the same location (such as [5, 6]). Instead, use one number and include all citations or comments in a single note (see 16.3.5).

For aesthetic reasons, do not put note numbers inside or at the end of a title, subtitle, or subhead. If your note applies to the entire chapter, omit the number and put an unnumbered footnote on the first page, before any numbered notes. If a note applies to a section following a subhead, put the reference number after the first sentence in the section.

16.3.3 Numbering Notes

Number notes consecutively, beginning with 1. If your paper has separate chapters, restart each chapter with note 1. Do not skip a number or use numbers such as 5a.

If you use endnotes for source citations but footnotes for substantive comments (see 16.3.1), do not number the footnotes. Instead, label the first footnote on a page with an asterisk (*). If you have more than one footnote on a page, use superscript symbols in the sequence * † ‡ §.

For notes to tables, see 26.2.7.

16.3.4 Formatting Notes

Indent both footnotes and endnotes as you would a paragraph. Begin each note with its reference number, preferably printed not as a superscript but as regular text. Put a period and a space between the number and the text of the note.

If your local guidelines allow it, you may instead use superscripts for reference numbers in notes. You should then begin the text of each note without an intervening period and space. Use this method for notes labeled with symbols (see 16.3.3).

FOOTNOTES. Begin every footnote on the page on which you reference it. Put a short rule between the last line of text and the first footnote on each page, including any notes that run over from previous pages, even if your word processor doesn't do so automatically. If a footnote runs over to the next page, break it in midsentence, so that readers do not think the note is finished and overlook the part on the next page. If you have more than one footnote on a page, begin each subsequent note on its own line, with a blank line before it. See figure A.10 for a sample page of text with footnotes.

ENDNOTES. Endnotes should be listed together after the end of the text and any appendixes but before the bibliography. Start each note on a new line, with a blank line between notes. Label the list *Notes*. If you restart numbering for each chapter, add subheadings to distinguish the notes for each chapter: "Chapter 1" and so forth. See figure A.14 for a sample page of endnotes.

16.3.5 Complex Notes

CITATIONS. If you cite several sources to make a single point, avoid cluttering your text with reference numbers by grouping them into a single note. List the citations in the same order that the references appear in the text; separate citations with semicolons.

Only when we gather the work of several scholars—Walter Sutton's explications of some of Whitman's shorter poems; Paul Fussell's careful study of structure in "Cradle"; S. K. Coffman's close readings of "Crossing Brooklyn Ferry" and "Passage to India"—do we begin to get a sense of both the extent and the specificity of Whitman's forms.[1]

N: 1. Sutton, "The Analysis of Free Verse Form, Illustrated by a Reading of Whitman," *Journal of Aesthetics and Art Criticism* 18 (December 1959): 241–54; Fussell, "Whitman's Curious Warble: Reminiscence and Reconciliation," in *The Presence of Whitman*, ed. R. W. B. Lewis, 28–51; Coffman, "'Crossing Brooklyn Ferry': Note on the Catalog Technique in Whitman's Poetry," *Modern Philology* 51 (May 1954): 225–32; Coffman, "Form and Meaning in Whitman's 'Passage to India,'" *PMLA* 70 (June 1955): 337–49.

It is also useful to group citations when you refer readers to a number of additional sources (called a "string cite"):

N: 2. For accounts of the coherence-making processes of consciousness from, respectively, psychological, neuropsychological, and philosophical points of view, see Bernard J. Baars, *A Cognitive Theory of Consciousness* (New York: Cambridge University Press, 1988); Gerald Edelman, *Bright Air, Brilliant Fire: On the Matter of the Mind* (New York: Basic Books, 1992); and Daniel Dennett, *Consciousness Explained* (Boston: Little Brown, 1991).

CITATIONS AND COMMENTS. If a note includes both a citation and a substantive comment, put the citation first with a period after it, followed by the comment in a separate sentence.

To come to Paris was to experience the simultaneous pleasures of the best contemporary art and the most vibrant art center.[9]

N: 2. Natt, "Paris Art Schools," 269. Gilded Age American artists traveled to other European art centers, most notably Munich, but Paris surpassed all others in size and importance.

When you include a quotation in a note, put the citation after the terminal punctuation of the quotation.

Property qualifications dropped out of U.S. practice for petit juries gradually during the nineteenth century, but remained in force for grand juries in some jurisdictions until the mid-twentieth century.[33]

N: 33. "The grand jury inquires into complaints and accusations brought before it and, based on evidence presented by the state, issues bills of indictment." Kermit Hall, *The Magic Mirror: Law in American History* (New York: Oxford University Press, 1989), 172.

Be judicious in your use of substantive comments in notes. If a point is critical to your argument, include it in the text. If it is peripheral, think carefully about whether it is important enough to mention in a note.

16.4 Short Forms for Notes

In some fields, your instructor may expect you to give full bibliographical data in each note, but in most you can give a complete citation the first time you cite a work and a shortened one in subsequent notes. In a few fields, writers have even begun to use a shortened form for all citations, with complete data listed only in the bibliography.

If you don't know the practice common in your field, consult your local guidelines.

16.4.1 Shortened Notes

A shortened note should include enough information for readers to find the full citation in your bibliography or in an earlier note. The two main choices are *author-only* notes and *author-title* notes. In many fields, writers use the author-title form for all shortened notes; in others, writers use the author-only form for most shortened notes, but the author-title form when they cite more than one work by the same author. If a source does not have an author (or editor), you can use a *title-only* note. Figure 16.2 provides templates for each type of shortened note.

An author-only note includes the author's last name and page numbers (or other locator), separated by a comma and followed by a period. If the work has an editor rather than an author, use the editor's last name but do not add *ed.* An author-title note adds a shortened title composed of up to four distinctive words from the full title. Use a comma to separate the author and the shortened title, and print the title with italics or quotation marks as you would in a full note.

N: 1. Philip Ball, *Bright Earth: Art and the Invention of Color* (New York: Farrar, Straus and Giroux, 2001), 140.
        4. Ball, 204.

or

        4. Ball, *Bright Earth,* 204.

        12. Nancy L. Green, "The Politics of Exit: Reversing the Immigration Paradigm," *Journal of Modern History* 77 (June 2005): 275.
        17. Green, 276.

or

        17. Green, "Politics of Exit," 276.

        20. John Demos, "Real Lives and Other Fictions: Reconsidering Wallace Stegner's *Angle of Repose,*" in *Novel History: Historians and Novelists Confront America's Past (and Each Other),* ed. Mark C. Carnes (New York: Simon and Schuster, 2001), 135.
        22. Demos, 138.

or

        22. Demos, "Real Lives," 138.

For multiple authors or editors, list the last names in the same order in which they appear in a full note.

N: 5. Jan H. Kalicki and David L. Goldwyn, eds., *Energy and Security: Toward a New Foreign Policy Strategy* (Baltimore: Johns Hopkins University Press, 2005), 195–96.
        8. Kalicki and Goldwyn, 204.

or

        8. Kalicki and Goldwyn, *Energy and Security,* 204.

16.4.2 Ibid.

At one time, writers shortened citations in notes by using Latin terms and abbreviations: *idem,* "the same"; *op. cit.,* for *opere citato,* "in the work cited"; and *loc. cit.,* for *loco citato,* "in the place cited." This practice has fallen out of favor, so avoid all Latin citation terms except one—*ibid.,* from *ibidem* or "in the same place." Some writers still use *ibid.* to shorten a citation to a work whose bibliographical data appear in the immediately previous note.

N: 30. Buchan, *Advice to Mothers,* 71.
        31. Ibid., 95.
        32. Ibid.

Figure 16.2. Templates for shortened notes

The following templates show what elements should be included in what order in the three types of shortened notes (see 16.4.1 for when to use each type). They also show punctuation, capitalization of titles, and typography of the elements. Gray shading shows terms as they would actually appear in a citation. *XX* stands in for page numbers cited.

Author-only Notes

1. Single Author

N: Note Number. Author's Last Name, XX–XX.

   2. Diamond, 85–90.

For a work cited by editor or translator instead of author (see 17.1.1), use the editor or translator in place of the author. Do not add *ed.* or *trans.*, as in a full note.

N: Note Number. Editor's or Translator's Last Name, XX–XX.

   9. Noll, 15.

If more than one author has the same last name, distinguish them by adding first names.

N: Note Number. Author's First Name and Last Names, XX–XX.

   12. Philip Smith, 212–13.

2. Two or Three Authors

N: Note Number. Author #1's Last Name and Author #2's Last Name, XX–XX.

   7. Bird and Sherwin, 88–89.

N: Note Number. Author #1's Last Name, Author #2's Last Name, and Author #3's Last Name, XX–XX.

   15. Appleby, Hunt, and Jacob, 140.

3. Four or More Authors

N: Note Number. Author #1's Last Name et al. XX–XX.

   10. Hall et al., 91–93.

Author-Title Notes

4. Books

N: Note Number. Author's Last Name, *Shortened Title*, XX–XX.

   2. Diamond, *Guns, Germs, and Steel*, 85–90.

For books by more than one author, follow the pattern for authors' names in templates 2 and 3.

Figure 16.2. Templates for shortened notes *(continued)*

---

5. Articles

N: Note Number. Author's Last Name, "Shortened Title," XX–XX.

   8. Nayar, "Marvelous Excesses," 225.

For articles by more than one author, follow the pattern for authors' names in templates 2 and 3.

Title-only Notes

6. Books without an Author

N: Note Number. *Shortened Title*, XX–XX.

   11. *Account of Operations*, 252.

7. Articles without an Author

N: Note Number. "Shortened Title," XX–XX.

   17. "Great Trigonometrical Survey," 26–27.

In notes, *ibid.* should be capitalized but not italicized. Since *ibid.* is an abbreviation, it must end with a period; if the citation includes a page number, put a comma after *ibid.* If the page number of a reference is the same as in the previous note, do not include a page number after *ibid.* Do not use *ibid.* after a note that contains more than one citation, and avoid using *ibid.* to refer to footnotes that do not appear on the same page.

16.4.3 Parenthetical Notes

PARENTHETICAL NOTES VERSUS FOOTNOTES OR ENDNOTES. In some situations, you may cite a source within parentheses in the text instead of in a footnote or an endnote. Parenthetical notes give readers a cleaner, more readable text, especially if you have many references to just a few sources.

According to one scholar, "The railroads had made Chicago the most important meeting place between East and West" (Cronon, *Nature's Metropolis*, 92–93).

You may routinely use parenthetical notes for certain types of sources that readers can identify with only a few elements, such as a newspaper article (see 17.4), a legal case (17.9.7), an older literary work (17.5.1), a biblical or other sacred work (17.5.2), or a source in the visual and performing arts (17.8). For most such sources, you should provide a full citation in the bibliography.

In many fields, you may use parenthetical notes if you are discussing a particular work at length and need to cite it frequently. The first time you cite the work, provide full bibliographical data in a footnote or endnote; for subsequent references, use parenthetical notes instead of shortened notes (see 16.4.1). Since this is a new practice in some fields, check with your instructor or advisor before citing sources in this way.

In fields that study language and literature, parenthetical notes have generally replaced footnotes or endnotes for most source citations, including the first reference to each work.

FORMATTING PARENTHETICAL NOTES. Insert a parenthetical note where you would place a reference number for a note: at the end of a quotation, sentence, or clause. The note comes before rather than after any comma, period, or other punctuation mark when the quotation is run into the text. With a block quotation, however, the note follows the terminal punctuation mark (see 25.2.2 for an example).

The fullest parenthetical note includes the same information as the author-title form of a shortened note, with the elements separated by commas. (Note that both the elements and the punctuation are slightly different from those used in parenthetical citations with reference list style, described in chapters 18 and 19; do not confuse or combine the two styles.)

"What on introspection seems to happen immediately and without effort is often a complex symphony of processes that take time to complete" (LeDoux, *Synaptic Self*, 116).

According to an expert, the norms of friendship are different in the workplace (Little, "Norms of Collegiality," 330).

In some fields, writers are expected to use this full form for all parenthetical notes; in others, they are allowed to shorten them, since such notes interrupt the flow of a text. If your field allows shortening, you have three options for most types of sources:

■ *Page numbers only.* You may include in the parentheses only the page number(s) or other locator if readers can readily identify the specific source from your text, either because it is a main object of your study (as in the first example below referring to Harriet Beecher Stowe's *Uncle Tom's Cabin*) or because you mention the author or title in your text.

Poor John!" interposes Stowe's narrative voice. "It was rather natural; and the tears that fell, as he spoke, came as naturally as if he had been a white man" (169).

Ernst Cassirer notes this in *Language and Myth* (59–60).

- *Author and page number.* You should include the author and page number(s) or other locator if readers cannot readily identify the source from your text and you cite only one work by that author.

  While one school claims that "material culture may be the most objective source of information we have concerning America's past" (Deetz, 259), others disagree.

- *Title and page number.* You should include a shortened title and page number(s) or other locator if readers can readily identify the author from your text and you cite more than one work by that author.

  According to Furet, "the Second World War completed what the First had begun—the domination of the great political religions over European public opinion" (*Passing,* 360).

  If you cite a work often, you can abbreviate the title. If the abbreviation is not obvious, you may specify it in the note for its first citation. (If you use more than five such abbreviations in your citations, list them in a separate section of your paper; see A.2.1.)

N: 2. François Furet, *The Passing of an Illusion: The Idea of Communism in the Twentieth Century,* trans. Deborah Furet (Chicago: University of Chicago Press, 1999), 368 (cited in text as *PI*).

According to Furet, "the Second World War completed what the First had begun—the domination of the great political religions over European public opinion" (*PI,* 360).

For newspaper articles and other types of sources in which author, title, and page number are not the key identifying elements (see the relevant sections of chapter 17), modify the parenthetical note style as needed.

In a *New York Times* article on the transitions within the Supreme Court (September 30, 2005), Linda Greenhouse discusses these trends.

17 Notes-Bibliography Style: Citing Specific Types of Sources

Chapter 16 presents an overview of the basic pattern for citations in the notes-bibliography style, including bibliography entries, full notes, shortened notes, and parenthetical notes. If you are not familiar with this citation style, read that chapter before consulting this one.

This chapter provides detailed information on the form of notes and bibliography entries for a wide range of sources. It is organized by type of source. It begins with the most common—books and journal articles—and then addresses other published, unpublished, and recorded sources. The sections on books (17.1) and journal articles (17.2) discuss variations in such elements as authors' names, titles, and URLs in greater depth than sections on less common sources.

Online and other electronic sources that are analogous to print sources (online journal articles, for example) are included under the relevant type of source. Other online sources, considered "informally published" (see 15.4.1), are discussed in 17.7.

Most sections include guidelines and examples for both full notes (identified with an N) and bibliography entries (B). In some cases, the examples show the same work cited in both forms to illustrate the similarities and differences between them; in other cases, they show different works to illustrate variations in elements even within a specific type of source.

To cite a type of source that is not covered in this chapter, consult chapter 17 of the *Chicago Manual of Style,* 15th edition (2003). You may also create your own style, adapted from the principles and examples given here. Most instructors, departments, and universities accept such adaptations, as long as you use them consistently.

17.1   Books

Books reflect a wider range of elements than most other types of published sources. Many of the variations in elements discussed in this section are also relevant to other types of sources.

17.1.1   Author's Name

Give each author's name exactly as it appears on the title page. If the name includes more than one initial, use spaces between them (see 24.2.1).

In notes, list authors' names in standard order (first name first):

N: 1. Philip Ball, *Bright Earth: Art and the Invention of Color* (New York: Farrar, Straus and Giroux, 2001), 140.

6. T. H. Breen, *The Marketplace of Revolution: How Consumer Politics Shaped American Independence* (New York: Oxford University Press, 2004), 48.

8. Elizabeth I, *Collected Works,* ed. Leah S. Marcus, Janel Mueller, and Mary Beth Rose (Chicago: University of Chicago Press, 2000), 102–4.

In bibliography entries, list authors' names in inverted order (last name first), except for some non-English names and other cases explained in "Special Types of Names" below (p. 166).

B: Ball, Philip. *Bright Earth: Art and the Invention of Color.* New York: Farrar, Straus and Giroux, 2001.

Breen, T. H. *The Marketplace of Revolution: How Consumer Politics Shaped American Independence.* New York: Oxford University Press, 2004.

Elizabeth I. *Collected Works.* Edited by Leah S. Marcus, Janel Mueller, and Mary Beth Rose. Chicago: University of Chicago Press, 2000.

MULTIPLE AUTHORS. In a note, for a book with more than one author, list all names in standard order. Use a comma before the *and* in a series of three or more. If there are four or more authors, list only the first author's name followed by *et al.* (with no intervening comma). Put a period after *al.* (an abbreviation for *alii,* "others") but not after *et* (not an abbreviation; the Latin word for "and").

N: 2. Kai Bird and Martin J. Sherwin, *American Prometheus: The Triumph and Tragedy of J. Robert Oppenheimer* (New York: Alfred A. Knopf, 2005), 52.

3. Joyce Appleby, Lynn Hunt, and Margaret Jacob, *Telling the Truth about History* (New York: W. W. Norton & Company, 1994), 135–36.

8. Jacquelyn Dowd Hall et al., *Like a Family: The Making of a Southern Cotton Mill World* (Chapel Hill: University of North Carolina Press, 1987), 114–15.

In a bibliography entry, list the first author's name in inverted order, followed by a comma, and list the rest of the authors in standard order. Include all authors, no matter how many; do not use *et al.*

B: Bird, Kai, and Martin J. Sherwin. *American Prometheus: The Triumph and Tragedy of J. Robert Oppenheimer.* New York: Alfred A. Knopf, 2005.

Appleby, Joyce, Lynn Hunt, and Margaret Jacob. *Telling the Truth about History.* New York: W. W. Norton & Company, 1994.

Hall, Jacquelyn Dowd, James Leloudis, Robert Korstad, Mary Murphy, Lu Ann Jones, and Christopher B. Daly. *Like a Family: The Making of a Southern Cotton Mill World.* Chapel Hill: University of North Carolina Press, 1987.

EDITOR OR TRANSLATOR IN ADDITION TO AN AUTHOR. If a title page lists an editor or a translator in addition to an author, treat the author's name as described above. Add the editor or translator's name after the book's title. If there is a translator as well as an editor, list the names in the same order as on the title page of the original.

In notes, insert the abbreviation *ed.* (never *eds.,* since in this context it means "edited by" rather than "editor") or *trans.* before the editor's or translator's name.

N: 6. Yves Bonnefoy, *New and Selected Poems,* ed. John Naughton and Anthony Rudolf (Chicago: University of Chicago Press, 1995), 35.

7. Rigoberta Menchú, *Crossing Borders,* trans. and ed. Ann Wright (New York:
Verso, 1999), 50–51.

10. Theodor W. Adorno and Walter Benjamin, *The Complete Correspondence, 1928–
1940,* ed. Henri Lonitz, trans. Nicholas Walker (Cambridge, MA: Harvard University
Press, 1999), 212.

In bibliography entries, insert the phrase *Edited by* or *Translated by* before the editor's or translator's name.

B: Bonnefoy, Yves. *New and Selected Poems.* Edited by John Naughton and Anthony Rudolf. Chicago: University of Chicago Press, 1995.

Menchú, Rigoberta. *Crossing Borders.* Translated and edited by Ann Wright. New York:
Verso, 1999.

Adorno, Theodor W., and Walter Benjamin. *The Complete Correspondence, 1928–1940.*
Edited by Henri Lonitz. Translated by Nicholas Walker. Cambridge, MA: Harvard
University Press, 1999.

When a title page identifies an editor or translator with a complicated description, such as "Edited with an Introduction and Notes by" or
"Translated with a Foreword by," you can simplify this phrase to *edited by*
or *translated by* and follow the above examples. In general, if a foreword
or an introduction is written by someone other than the author, you need
not mention that person unless you cite that part specifically (see 17.1.8).
For cases in which the author's name appears in the book's title and the
editor's name appears on the title page instead, see "Additional Authorial
Situations" below (p. 165).

EDITOR OR TRANSLATOR IN PLACE OF AN AUTHOR. When an editor or a translator is listed on a book's title page instead of an author, use that person's
name in the author's slot. Treat it as you would an author's name (see
above), but add the abbreviation *ed.* (plural, *eds.*) or *trans.* (singular or
plural) following the name. If there are multiple editors or translators, follow the principles in "Multiple Authors" (see above, p. 163).

N: 3. Theodore Silverstein, trans., *Sir Gawain and the Green Knight* (Chicago: University of Chicago Press, 1974), 34.

4. Timothy E. Fulop and Albert J. Raboteau, eds., *African-American Religion: Interpretive Essays in History and Culture* (New York: Routledge, 1997), 412–14.

B: Silverstein, Theodore, trans. *Sir Gawain and the Green Knight.* Chicago: University of
Chicago Press, 1974.

Fulop, Timothy E., and Albert J. Raboteau, eds. *African-American Religion: Interpretive
Essays in History and Culture.* New York: Routledge, 1997.

ADDITIONAL AUTHORIAL SITUATIONS. Following are some additional ways authors might be identified in your sources. If you encounter situations not covered here, adapt the pattern that seems most closely related.

■ *Author's name in title.* An author's name may appear in the title or subtitle of a book such as an autobiography. In a note, omit the author's name and begin with the title. In a bibliography entry, however, include the author's name, despite the repetition. Although many such works also have editors, do not list the works under the editor's name except in special cases (for example, in a study of works edited by that individual).

N: 12. *Memoirs of General W. T. Sherman,* ed. Charles Royster (New York: Library of America, 1990), 836.

       15. *Illumination and Night Glare: The Unfinished Autobiography of Carson McCullers,* ed. Carlos L. Dews (Madison: University of Wisconsin Press, 1999), 54.

B: Sherman, W. T. *Memoirs of General W. T. Sherman.* Edited by Charles Royster. New York: Library of America, 1990.

    McCullers, Carson. *Illumination and Night Glare: The Unfinished Autobiography of Carson McCullers.* Edited by Carlos L. Dews. Madison: University of Wisconsin Press, 1999.

■ *Organization as author.* If a publication issued by an organization, association, commission, or corporation has no personal author's name on the title page, list the organization itself as author, even if it is also given as publisher.

N: 9. World Health Organization, *Organization of Services for Mental Health* (Geneva: World Health Organization, 2003), 50.

B: National Commission on Terrorist Attacks upon the United States. *The 9/11 Commission Report.* New York: W. W. Norton & Company, 2004.

■ *Pseudonym.* Treat a widely used pseudonym as if it were the author's real name. If the real name is unknown, add *pseud.* in brackets after the pseudonym.

N: 16. Mark Twain, *The Prince and the Pauper: A Tale for Young People of All Ages* (New York: Harper & Brothers, 1899), 34.

B: Centinel [pseud.]. "Letters." In *The Complete Anti-Federalist,* edited by Herbert J. Storing. Chicago: University of Chicago Press, 1981.

■ *Anonymous author.* If the authorship is known or guessed at but omitted from the book's title page, include the name in brackets (with a question mark to indicate uncertainty). If the author or editor is unknown, avoid the use of *Anonymous* in place of a name, and begin the note or bibliography entry with the title.

N: 22. [Ebenezer Cook?], *Sotweed Redivivus, or The Planter's Looking-Glass* (Annapolis, 1730), 5–6.
       31. *A True and Sincere Declaration of the Purpose and Ends of the Plantation Begun in Virginia, of the Degrees Which It Hath Received, and Means by Which It Hath Been Advanced* (1610), 17.

B: [Cook, Ebenezer?]. *Sotweed Redivivus, or The Planter's Looking-Glass.* Annapolis, 1730.
       A True and Sincere Declaration of the Purpose and Ends of the Plantation Begun in Virginia, of the Degrees Which It Hath Received, and Means by Which It Hath Been Advanced. 1610.

SPECIAL TYPES OF NAMES. Some authors' names consist of more than a readily identifiable "first name" and "last name." For names of well-known historical authors, consult *Merriam-Webster's Biographical Dictionary;* for contemporary authors, consult your library's online catalog. Following are some general principles for alphabetizing such names. In shortened or parenthetical notes, use the last name exactly as inverted (shown below in boldface).

■ *Compound names.* Alphabetize compound last names, including hyphenated names, by the first part of the compound. If a woman uses both her own family name and her husband's but does not hyphenate them, generally alphabetize by the second name. While many foreign languages have predictable patterns for compound names (see below), others—such as French and German—do not.

Kessler-Harris, Alice	**Mies van der Rohe,** Ludwig
Hine, Darlene Clark	**Teilhard de Chardin,** Pierre

■ *Names with particles.* Depending on the language, particles such as *de, di, D',* and *van* may or may not be considered the first part of a last name for alphabetizing. Consult one of the resources noted above if you are unsure about a particular name. Note that particles may be either lowercased or capitalized, and some are followed by an apostrophe.

de Gaulle, Charles	**Beauvoir,** Simone de
di Leonardo, Micaela	**Kooning,** Willem de
Van Rensselaer, Stephen	**Medici,** Lorenzo de'

■ *Names beginning with "Mac," "Saint," or "O'."* Names that begin with *Mac, Saint,* or *O'* can have many variations in abbreviations (*Mc, St.*), spelling (*Sainte, San*), capitalization (*Macmillan, McAllister*), and hyphenation or

apostrophes (*O'Neill* or *Odell; Saint-Gaudens* or *St. Denis*). Alphabetize
all such names based on the letters actually present; do not group them
because they are similar.

- *Names in languages other than English.* Naming conventions in many languages are different from those in English. If your paper involves many names from a particular language, study the conventions for the relevant language.

    Many Spanish last names are compound names, consisting of an individual's paternal and maternal family names and usually joined by the conjunction *y.* Alphabetize such names under the first part.

    Ortega y Gasset, José   Sánchez Mendoza, Juana

    Alphabetize Arabic last names that begin with the particle *al-* or *el-* ("the") under the element following the particle. Names that begin with *Abu, Abd,* and *Ibn* are similar to English names beginning with *Mac* or *Saint* and should be alphabetized under these terms.

    Hakim, Tawfiq al-   Abu Zafar Nadvi, Syed
    Jamal, Muhammad Hamid al-   Ibn Saud, Aziz

    If an author with a Chinese or Japanese name follows traditional usage (family name followed by given name), do not invert the name or insert a comma between the "first" and "last" names. If the author follows westernized usage (given name followed by family name), treat the name as you would an English name.

Traditional usage	Westernized usage
Chao Wu-chi	Tsou, Tang
Yoshida Shigeru	Kurosawa, Noriaki

17.1.2 Title

List complete book titles and subtitles. Italicize both, and separate the
title from the subtitle with a colon. If there are two subtitles, use a colon
before the first and a semicolon before the second.

N: 5. Jan H. Kalicki and David L. Goldwyn, eds., *Energy and Security: Toward a New Foreign Policy Strategy* (Baltimore: Johns Hopkins University Press, 2005), 195–96.

B: Ahmed, Leila. *A Border Passage: From Cairo to America; A Woman's Journey.* New York: Farrar, Straus & Giroux, 1999.

Capitalize most titles and subtitles headline style; that is, capitalize the
first letter of the first and last words of the title and subtitle and all major

words. For foreign-language titles, use sentence-style capitalization; that is, capitalize only the first letter of the first word of the title and subtitle and any proper nouns and proper adjectives thereafter. (See 22.3.1 for a more detailed discussion of the two styles.).

(headline style) *How to Do It: Guides to Good Living for Renaissance Italians*

(sentence style) *De sermone amatorio apud elegiarum scriptores*

Preserve the spelling, hyphenation, and punctuation of the original title, with two exceptions: change words in full capitals (except for initial-isms or acronyms; see chapter 24) to upper- and lowercase, and change an ampersand (&) to *and*. Spell out numbers or give them as numerals according to the original (*Twelfth Century* or *12th Century*) unless there is a good reason to make them consistent with other titles in the list.

For titles of chapters and other parts of a book, see 17.1.8.

SPECIAL ELEMENTS IN TITLES. Several elements in titles require special typography.

■ *Dates.* Use a comma to set off dates in a title or subtitle, even if there is no punctuation in the original source. If the source introduces the dates with a preposition ("from 1920 to 1945") or a colon, follow the usage in the source.

N: 5. Walter A. McDougall, *Freedom Just around the Corner: A New American History, 1525–1828* (New York: HarperCollins, 2004), 333–34.

B: Jellicoe, Geoffrey, and Susan Jellicoe. *The Landscape of Man: Shaping the Environment from Prehistory to the Present Day.* 3rd ed. New York: Thames & Hudson, 1995.

■ *Titles and quotations within titles.* When the title of a work that would normally be italicized appears *within* the italicized title of another, en-close the quoted title in quotation marks. If the title-within-a-title would normally be enclosed in quotation marks, keep the quotation marks.

N: 22. Celia Applegate, *Bach in Berlin: Nation and Culture in Mendelssohn's Revival of the "St. Matthew Passion"* (Ithaca: Cornell University Press, 2005), 25.

B: McHugh, Roland. *Annotations to "Finnegans Wake."* 2nd ed. Baltimore: Johns Hopkins University Press, 1991.

However, when a quotation is used as the entire main title of a book, do not enclose it in quotation marks.

N: 8. Sam Swope, *I Am a Pencil: A Teacher, His Kids, and Their World of Stories* (New York: Henry Holt and Company, 2004), 108–9.

B: Chernoff, John M. *Hustling Is Not Stealing: Stories of an African Bar Girl.* Chicago: University of Chicago Press, 2003.

■ *Italicized terms.* When an italicized title includes terms normally italicized in text, such as species names or names of ships, set the terms in roman type.

N: 7. T. Hugh Pennington, *When Food Kills: BSE,* E. Coli, *and Disaster Science* (New York: Oxford University Press, 2003), 15.

B: Lech, Raymond B. *The Tragic Fate of the* U.S.S. Indianapolis: *The U.S. Navy's Worst Disaster at Sea.* New York: Cooper Square Press, 2001.

■ *Question marks and exclamation points.* When a title or a subtitle ends with a question mark or an exclamation point, no other punctuation follows.

N: 26. Thomas Frank, *What's the Matter with Kansas? How Conservatives Won the Heart of America* (New York: Metropolitan Books, 2004), 250–51.

B: Aaron, Henry. *Why Is Welfare So Hard to Reform?* Washington, DC: Brookings Institution Press, 1973.

OLDER TITLES. For titles of works published in the eighteenth century or earlier, retain the original punctuation and spelling. Also retain the original capitalization, even if it does not follow headline style. Words in all capital letters, however, should be given an initial capital only. If the title is very long, you may shorten it, giving enough information for readers to find the full title in a library or publisher's catalog. Indicate omissions in such titles by three ellipsis dots within a title. If the omission comes at the end of a title in a bibliography entry, use four dots (three ellipsis dots and a period; see 25.3.2).

N: 19. John Ray, *Observations Topographical, Moral, and Physiological: Made in a Journey Through part of the Low-Countries, Germany, Italy, and France: with A Catalogue of Plants not Native of England . . . Whereunto is added A Brief Account of Francis Willughby, Esq., his Voyage through a great part of Spain* ([London], 1673), 15.

B: Escalante, Bernardino. *A Discourse of the Navigation which the Portugales doe make to the Realmes and Provinces of the East Partes of the Worlde. . . .* Translated by John Frampton. London, 1579.

NON-ENGLISH TITLES. Use sentence-style capitalization for non-English titles, following the capitalization principles for proper nouns and adjectives within the relevant language. If you are unfamiliar with these principles, consult a reliable source.

N: 3. Danielle Maisonneuve, Jean-François Lamarche, and Yves St-Amand, *Les relations publiques: Dans une société en mouvance* (Sainte-Foy, QC: Presses de l'Université de Québec, 1998), 15.

6. Ljiljana Piletic Stojanovic, ed. *Gutfreund i ceski kubizam* (Belgrade: Muzej savremene umetnosti, 1971), 54–55.

B: Krone-Schmalz, Gabriele. *In Wahrheit sind wir stärker: Frauenalltag in der Sowjetunion.* Frankfurt am Main: Fischer Taschenbuch Verlag, 1992.

If you add the English translation of a title, place it after the original. Enclose it in brackets, without italics or quotation marks, and capitalize it sentence style.

N: 7. Henryk Wereszycki, *Koniec sojuszu trzech cesarzy* [The end of the Three Emperors' League] (Warsaw: PWN, 1977), 5.

B: *Zhongguo renkou tongji nianjian 1996* [China population statistics yearbook 1996]. Beijing: Zhongguo tongji chubanshe, 1996.

If you need to cite both the original and a translation, use one of the following forms, depending on whether you want to focus readers on the original or the translation.

B: Furet, François. *Le passé d'une illusion.* Paris: Éditions Robert Laffont, 1995. Translated by Deborah Furet as *The Passing of an Illusion* (Chicago: University of Chicago Press, 1999).

or

Furet, François. *The Passing of an Illusion.* Translated by Deborah Furet. Chicago: University of Chicago Press, 1999. Originally published as *Le passé d'une illusion* (Paris: Éditions Robert Laffont, 1995).

17.1.3 Edition

The term *edition* has several meanings, all based on the fact that some works are published more than once with changes in content and/or format. If you cite a book published in more than one edition, always indicate which edition you consulted because editions may differ. (If none of the markers described below apply to a book, you can assume it is a first edition, a fact that is not cited.)

REVISED EDITIONS. When a book is reissued with significant content changes, it may be called a "revised" edition or a "second" (or subsequent) edition. This information usually appears on the book's title page and is repeated, along with the date of the edition, on the copyright page.

When you cite an edition other than the first, include the number or description of the edition after the title. Abbreviate such wording as "Second Edition, Revised and Enlarged" as *2nd ed.;* abbreviate "Revised Edition" as *rev. ed.* Include the publication date only of the edition you are citing, not of any previous editions (see 17.1.6).

N: 1. Paul J. Bolt, Damon V. Coletta, and Collins G. Shackelford Jr., *American Defense Policy,* 8th ed. (Baltimore: Johns Hopkins University Press, 2005), 157–58.

B: Daniels, Roger. *Coming to America: A History of Immigration and Ethnicity in American Life.* 2nd ed. New York: Harper Perennial, 2002.

Babb, Florence. *Between Field and Cooking Pot: The Political Economy of Marketwomen in Peru.* Rev. ed. Austin: University of Texas Press, 1989.

REPRINT EDITIONS. A book may also be reissued in a new format—for example, in a paperback edition (by the original publisher or a different publisher), or in electronic form (see 17.1.10). Even though the contents of the book might be minimally changed from the original, cite the reprint edition if you consulted it. You may wish to indicate that it is a reprint, especially if it was published more than a year or two after the original edition or is a modern printing of a classic work. In this case, include the publication dates of both the original and the edition you are citing (see 17.1.6).

N: 23. Peter Ward Fay, *The Opium War, 1840–1842* (1975; repr., Chapel Hill: University of North Carolina Press, 1997), 67–68.

B: Emerson, Ralph Waldo. *Nature.* 1836. Reprint, Boston: Beacon, 1985.

17.1.4 Volume

If a book is part of a multivolume work, include this information in your citations.

SPECIFIC VOLUME. How you cite a specific volume in a multivolume work depends on whether the volume has a title different from the work as a whole. If so, list the title of the specific volume, followed by both the volume number and the general title. Abbreviate *vol.* and use arabic numbers for volume numbers.

N: 10. Jaroslav Pelikan, *Christian Doctrine and Modern Culture (Since 1700),* vol. 5 of *The Christian Tradition: A History of the Development of Doctrine* (Chicago: University of Chicago Press, 1989), 16.

B: Pelikan, Jaroslav. *Christian Doctrine and Modern Culture (since 1700).* Vol. 5 of *The Christian Tradition: A History of the Development of Doctrine.* Chicago: University of Chicago Press, 1989.

If the volumes are not individually titled and you are citing only one of them, add the volume number to the bibliography entry. (See below for citing a multivolume work as a whole.) In a note, put the volume number (without *vol.*) immediately before the page number, separated by a colon and no intervening spaces.

N: 36. Muriel St. Clare Byrne, ed., *The Lisle Letters* (Chicago: University of Chicago Press, 1981), 4:243.

B: Byrne, Muriel St. Clare, ed. *The Lisle Letters.* Vol. 4. Chicago: University of Chicago Press, 1981.

Some multivolume works have both a general editor and individual editors or authors for each volume. When citing parts of such works, put information about the individual editor or author of the volume (see 17.1.1) after the individual volume title and before the volume number and general title. The first example below also shows how to cite a volume published in more than one physical part (*vol. 2, bk. 3*).

N: 40. Barbara E. Mundy, "Mesoamerican Cartography," in *Cartography in the Traditional African, American, Arctic, Australian, and Pacific Societies,* ed. David Woodward and G. Malcolm Lewis, vol. 2, bk. 3 of *The History of Cartography,* ed. J. Brian Harley and David Woodward (Chicago: University of Chicago Press, 1998), 233.

B: Donne, John. *The "Anniversaries" and the "Epicedes and Obsequies."* Edited by Gary A. Stringer and Ted-Larry Pebworth. Vol. 6 of *The Variorum Edition of the Poetry of John Donne,* edited by Gary A. Stringer. Bloomington: Indiana University Press, 1995.

MULTIVOLUME WORK AS A WHOLE. If you cite more than one volume of a multivolume work in your notes, you may cite the work as a whole in your bibliography. (If the work involves both general and individual titles or volume editors, as described above, it is more precise to cite the volumes individually.) Give the title, the total number of volumes, and, if the volumes have been published over several years, the full span of publication dates.

B: Aristotle. *Complete Works of Aristotle: The Revised Oxford Translation.* Edited by J. Barnes. 2 vols. Princeton, NJ: Princeton University Press, 1983.
   Tillich, Paul. *Systematic Theology.* 3 vols. Chicago: University of Chicago Press, 1951–63.

17.1.5 Series

If a book cited is part of a formal series, you are not required to include information about the series, but you may include some or all of it to help readers locate or judge the credibility of the source. Insert this information after the title (and after, if any, edition and volume information) and before the facts of publication.

The most useful information about a series is its title. Present it in roman type with headline-style capitalization. If the volumes in the series are numbered, you may include the number of the work cited following the series title. The name of the series editor is often omitted, but you may include it after the series title.

N: 7. Gershon David Hundert, *The Jews in a Polish Private Town: The Case of Opatów in the Eighteenth Century,* Johns Hopkins Jewish Studies (Baltimore: Johns Hopkins University Press, 1992), 113.

B: Markman, Charles W. *Chicago before History: The Prehistoric Archaeology of a Modern Metropolitan Area.* Studies in Illinois Archaeology 7. Springfield: Illinois Historic Preservation Agency, 1991.

     Isenberg, Nancy. *Sex and Citizenship in Antebellum America.* Gender and American Culture, edited by Linda K. Kerber and Nell Irvin Painter. Chapel Hill: University of North Carolina Press, 1998.

Some numbered series have existed for so long that numbering has started over. Books in a new series are indicated by *n.s., 2nd ser.,* or some similar notation, usually enclosed in commas before the series number. Books in the old series are identified by *o.s., 1st ser.,* and so forth.

N: 3. Charles R. Boxer, ed., *South China in the Sixteenth Century,* Hakluyt Society Publications, 2nd ser., 106 (London, 1953), 44.

B: Palmatary, Helen C. *The Pottery of Marajó Island, Brazil.* Transactions of the American Philosophical Society, n.s., 39, pt. 3. Philadelphia, 1950.

17.1.6 Facts of Publication

The facts of publication usually include three elements: the place (city) of publication, the publisher's name, and the date (year) of publication. In notes, these elements are enclosed in parentheses; in bibliography entries, they are not.

N: 1. Jared Diamond, *Guns, Germs, and Steel: The Fates of Human Societies* (New York: W. W. Norton and Company, 1997), 47.

B: Diamond, Jared. *Guns, Germs, and Steel: The Fates of Human Societies.* New York: W. W. Norton and Company, 1997.

For books published before the twentieth century, or for which the information does not appear within the work, you may omit publishers' names as well as places of publication.

N: 32. Charles Lamb, *Essays of Elia* (1823), 5–6.

B: Lamb, Charles. *Essays of Elia.* 1823.

PLACE OF PUBLICATION. The place of publication is the city where the publisher's main editorial offices are located; it normally appears on the title page, but sometimes on the copyright page. Where two or more cities are given ("Chicago and London," for example), include only the first.

Los Angeles: J. Paul Getty Trust Publications

New York: Columbia University Press

If the city of publication might be unknown to readers or confused with another city of the same name, add the abbreviation of the state (see 24.3.1), province, or (if necessary) country. When the publisher's name includes the state name, no state abbreviation is needed.

Cheshire, CT: Graphics Press

Harmondsworth, UK: Penguin Books

Cambridge, MA: MIT Press

Chapel Hill: University of North Carolina Press

Use current, commonly used English names for foreign cities.

Belgrade (*not* Beograd)   Milan (*not* Milano)

When the place of publication is not known, you may use the abbreviation *n.p.* in a note (or *N.p.* in a bibliography entry) before the publisher's name. If the place can be surmised, include it with a question mark, in brackets.

(n.p.: Windsor, 1910)

[Lake Bluff, IL?]: Vliet & Edwards, 1890

PUBLISHER'S NAME. Give the publisher's name for each book exactly as it appears on the title page, even if you know that the name has since changed or is printed differently in different books in your bibliography.

Harcourt Brace and World
Harcourt Brace Jovanovich
Harcourt, Brace

To save space, however, you may omit an initial *The* and such abbreviations as *Inc., Ltd., S.A., Co., & Co.,* and *Publishing Co.*

University of Texas Press	*instead of*	The University of Texas Press
Houghton Mifflin	*instead of*	Houghton Mifflin Co.
Little, Brown	*instead of*	Little, Brown & Co.

For foreign publishers, do not translate or abbreviate any part of the publisher's name, but give the city name in its English form (as noted above). When the publisher is unknown, use just the place (if known) and date of publication.

DATE OF PUBLICATION The publication date for a book consists only of a year, not a month or day, and is usually identical to the copyright date. It generally appears on the copyright page and sometimes on the title page.

Revised editions and reprints may include more than one copyright date. In this case, the most recent indicates the publication date—for example, 2003 in the string "© 1982, 1992, 2003." See 17.1.3 for citing publication dates in such works.

If you cannot determine the publication date of a printed work, use the abbreviation *n.d.* in place of the year. If no date is provided but you believe you know it, you may add it in brackets, with a question mark to indicate uncertainty.

B: Smith, John. *A Book of Virtues.* Edinburgh, n.d.
   Miller, Samuel. *Another Book of Virtues.* Boston, [1750?].

If a book is under contract with a publisher and is already titled, but the date of publication is not yet known, use *forthcoming* in place of the date. Treat any book not yet under contract as an unpublished manuscript (see 17.6).

N: 91. Jane Q. Author, *Book Title* (Place of Publication: Publisher's Name, forthcoming).

17.1.7 Page Numbers and Other Locating Information

Page numbers and other information used to identify the location of a cited passage or element generally appear in notes but not in bibliographies.

For guidelines on expressing a span of numbers, see 23.2.4.

PAGE, CHAPTER, AND DIVISION NUMBERS. Page numbers are usually the last element in the citation of a book within a note. Do not include the word *page* or the abbreviation *p.* or *pp.* Use arabic numbers except for pages numbered with roman numerals in the original.

N: 14. Anne C. Rose, *Victorian America and the Civil War* (New York: Cambridge University Press, 1992), 145–46.

    17. Jerome Kagan, "Introduction to the Tenth-Anniversary Edition," in *The Nature of the Child* (New York: Basic Books, 1994), xxii–xxiv.

Sometimes a citation refers to a full chapter (abbreviated *chap.*), part (*pt.*), book (*bk.*), or section (*sec.*) instead of a span of page numbers.

N: 22. Donald L. Miller, *City of the Century: The Epic of Chicago and the Making of America* (New York: Simon and Schuster, 1996), pt. 2.

SPECIAL TYPES OF LOCATORS. Some parts of a book have special types of locators used in citations.

■ *Note numbers.* Use the abbreviation *n* (plural, *nn*) to cite notes. If the note cited is the only footnote on its page or is an unnumbered footnote, add *n* after the page number (with no intervening space or punctuation). If there are other notes on the same page as the note cited, list the page number followed by *n* or (if two or more consecutive notes are cited) *nn* and the note number(s).

N: 45. Anthony Grafton, *The Footnote: A Curious History* (Cambridge, MA: Harvard University Press, 1997), 72n.

    46. Dwight Bolinger, *Language: The Loaded Weapon* (London: Longman, 1980), 192n23, 192n30, 199n14, 201nn16–17.

■ *Illustration and table numbers.* Use the abbreviation *fig.* for *figure*, but spell out *table, map, plate,* and names of other types of illustrations. Give the page number before the illustration number.

N: 50. Richard Sobel, *Public Opinion in U.S. Foreign Policy: The Controversy over Contra Aid* (Boston: Rowman and Littlefield, 1993), 87, table 5.3.

■ *Line numbers.* For poetry and other works best identified by line number, avoid the abbreviations *l.* (line) and *ll.* (lines); they are too easily confused with the numerals 1 and 11. Use *line* or *lines,* or use numbers alone where you have made it clear that you are referring to lines.

N: 44. Ogden Nash, "Song for Ditherers," lines 1–4.

■ *Signature, leaf, and folio numbers.* Some books printed before 1800 do not carry page numbers but are divided into signatures and then into leaves or folios, each with a front side (*recto*, or *r*) and a back side (*verso*, or *v*). Locators for such works should consist of the relevant string of numbers and identifiers, run together without spaces or italics: for example, G6v, 176r, 232r–v, or (if you are citing entire folios) fol. 49.

URLS, PERMANENT SOURCE IDENTIFIERS, ACCESS DATES, AND DESCRIPTIVE LOCATORS. For a book published online (see 17.1.10), include the book's URL in both a note and a bibliography entry. Every URL begins with a lowercase abbreviation of the protocol used to deliver electronic material to readers, most commonly *http* (hypertext transfer protocol) and *ftp* (file transfer protocol). This abbreviation is invariably followed by a colon and a double slash, after which appears the publisher's domain name, followed by the path to the resource. Components following the domain name are separated from the domain name and from each other by single slashes.

http://www.jsri.msu.edu/museum/pubs/MexAmHist/chapter14.html#six

Capitalize the internal components of a URL exactly as they appear on the screen. If the URL has a "trailing slash" at the end, include it. Do not enclose the URL in brackets. It is best not to break a URL at the end of a line, but if you need to do so, see 20.4.2 for some guidelines.

Some online sources have permanent identifiers other than URLs. If a source uses digital object identifiers (DOIs) or a similar system, include information comparable to a URL in your citation.

doi:10.1006/jeth.2000.2694

When you cite any online source, provide the date you last accessed it, in case the content has since changed or been removed from the Web (see 15.4.1). Put the access date in parentheses after the URL or permanent identifier.

(accessed May 17, 2006)

Books published online might not include page numbers to help identify the location of a cited passage in a note. In this case, you may add a descriptive locator (such as a preceding subheading) before the URL and access date (see 17.1.10 for an example). You need not include such a locator in a bibliography entry.

17.1.8 Chapters and Other Titled Parts of a Book

In most cases, you should cite the main title of any book that offers a single, continuous argument or narrative, even if you actually use only a section of it. But if you consult only one part of a book that collects independent pieces on several topics, written by one or several authors, you may cite just the one chapter or part most relevant to your research. By doing so, you help readers see how the source fits into your project.

B: Demos, John. "Real Lives and Other Fictions: Reconsidering Wallace Stegner's *Angle of Repose.*" In *Novel History: Historians and Novelists Confront America's Past (and Each Other),* edited by Mark C. Carnes, 132–45. New York: Simon and Schuster, 2001.

instead of

Carnes, Mark C., ed. *Novel History: Historians and Novelists Confront America's Past (and Each Other).* New York: Simon and Schuster, 2001.

PARTS OF SINGLE-AUTHOR BOOKS. If you cite a titled part of a single-author book, include the title of the part first, in roman type and enclosed in quotation marks. After the designation *in,* give the book title. In a bibliography entry, include the full span of page numbers for that part following the book title; in a note, give the page number(s) for a specific reference as you would for any other quotation.

N: 1. John Charles Chasteen, "Neocolonialism," in *Born in Blood and Fire: A Concise History of Latin America* (New York: W. W. Norton & Company, 2001), 190–91.

B: Chasteen, John Charles. "Neocolonialism." In *Born in Blood and Fire: A Concise History of Latin America,* 179–206. New York: W. W. Norton & Company, 2001.

If you cite a part with a generic title such as *introduction, preface,* or *afterword,* add that term before the title of the book. List the generic title in roman type without quotation marks, and capitalize the first word only in a bibliography entry. If the part is written by someone other than the main author of the book, give the part author's name first and the book author's name after the title.

N: 7. Alfred W. Crosby, preface to the new edition of *Ecological Imperialism: The Biological Expansion of Europe, 900–1900,* new ed. (New York: Cambridge University Press, 2004), xv.
        16. Craig Calhoun, foreword to *Multicultural Politics: Racism, Ethnicity, and Muslims in Britain,* by Tariq Modood (Minneapolis: University of Minnesota Press, 2005), xvi.

B: Crosby, Alfred W. Preface to the new edition of *Ecological Imperialism: The Biological Expansion of Europe, 900–1900.* New ed. New York: Cambridge University Press, 2004.
    Calhoun, Craig. Foreword to *Multicultural Politics: Racism, Ethnicity, and Muslims in Britain,* by Tariq Modood. Minneapolis: University of Minnesota Press, 2005.

PARTS OF EDITED COLLECTIONS. If you cite part of an edited collection with contributions by multiple authors, list the part author and title (in roman type, enclosed in quotation marks) first. After the designation *in,* give the book title and the name of the editor. In a bibliography entry, include the full span of page numbers for that part following the book title; in a note, give the page number(s) for a specific reference as you would for any other quotation.

N: 3. Anne Carr and Douglas J. Schuurman, "Religion and Feminism: A Reformist Christian Analysis," in *Religion, Feminism, and the Family,* ed. Anne Carr and Mary Stewart Van Leeuwen (Louisville, KY: Westminster John Knox Press, 1996), 13–14.

B: Carr, Anne, and Douglas J. Schuurman. "Religion and Feminism: A Reformist Christian Analysis." In *Religion, Feminism, and the Family,* edited by Anne Carr and Mary Stewart Van Leeuwen, 11–32. Louisville, KY: Westminster John Knox Press, 1996.

If you cite two or more contributions to the same edited collection, you may treat them as separate sources, or you may use a space-saving shortened form like that discussed in 16.4.1. The first time you cite any part from the book in a note, give full bibliographical information about both the part and the book as a whole. Thereafter, if you cite another part from the book, provide the full author's name and title of the part, but give the information about the book in shortened form. Subsequent notes for individual parts follow the usual shortened note form.

N: 4. William H. Keating, "Fort Dearborn and Chicago," in *Prairie State: Impressions of Illinois, 1673–1967, by Travelers and Other Observers,* ed. Paul M. Angle (Chicago: University of Chicago Press, 1967), 84.
     12. Sara Clarke Lippincott, "Chicago," in Angle, 362.
     14. Keating, 85.
     15. Lippincott, 365.

In your bibliography, provide a full citation for the whole book and a variation on the shortened note form for individual parts.

B: Angle, Paul M., ed. *Prairie State: Impressions of Illinois, 1673–1967, by Travelers and Other Observers.* (Chicago: University of Chicago Press, 1967).
     Keating, William H. "Fort Dearborn and Chicago." In Angle, 84–87.
     Lippincott, Sara Clarke. "Chicago." In Angle, 362–70.

WORKS IN ANTHOLOGIES. Cite a short story, poem, essay, or other work published in an anthology in the same way you would a contribution to an edited collection with multiple authors. Give the titles of most works published in anthologies in roman type, enclosed in quotation marks. An exception is the title of an excerpt from a book-length poem or prose work, which should be italicized (see 22.3.2).

N: 2. Isabel Allende, "The Spirits Were Willing," in *The Oxford Book of Latin American Essays,* ed. Ilan Stavans (New York: Oxford University Press, 1997), 463–64.

B: Wigglesworth, Michael. Excerpt from *The Day of Doom.* In *The New Anthology of American Poetry: Traditions and Revolutions, Beginnings to 1900,* edited by Steven Gould Axelrod, Camille Roman, and Thomas Travisano, 68–74. New Brunswick, NJ: Rutgers University Press, 2003.

If the original publication date of a work is important in the context of your paper, include it after the title of the work and before the title of the anthology in both your notes and your bibliography.

N: 2. Isabel Allende, "The Spirits Were Willing" (1984), in *The Oxford Book . . .*

B: Wigglesworth, Michael. Excerpt from *The Day of Doom.* 1662. In *The New Anthology . . .*

17.1.9   Letters and Other Communications in Published Collections

You may cite specific parts of books that collect letters, memoranda, and other communications because a specific reference provides information not included in a whole book citation, such as the date and participants for an individual communication. (For unpublished personal communications, see 17.6.3; for unpublished letters in manuscript collections, see 17.6.4.)

To cite such an item, give the names of the sender and recipient, followed by a date and (if available and relevant) the place where the communication was prepared. The word *letter* is unnecessary, but label other forms, such as a report or memorandum. Give the title and other data for the collection in the usual form for an edited book. Notice the form for a shortened note, which differs from the usual pattern of elements.

N: 1. Adams to Charles Milnes Gaskell, London, March 30, 1896, in *Letters of Henry Adams, 1858–1891,* ed. Worthington Chauncey Ford (Boston: Houghton Mifflin, 1930), 141.

2. Adams to Gaskell, 142.

5. EBW to Harold Ross, memorandum, May 2, 1946, in *Letters of E. B. White,* ed. Dorothy Lobrano Guth (New York: Harper & Row, 1976), 273.

B: Jackson, Paulina. Paulina Jackson to John Pepys Junior, October 3, 1676. In *The Letters of Samuel Pepys and His Family Circle,* edited by Helen Truesdell Heath, no. 42. Oxford: Clarendon Press, 1955.

If you cite several letters or other communications from a single book in your notes, list just the book rather than the individual pieces in your bibliography.

B: Churchill, Winston, and Dwight D. Eisenhower. *The Churchill-Eisenhower Correspondence, 1953–1955,* edited by Peter G. Boyle. Chapel Hill: University of North Carolina Press, 1990.

17.1.10 Online and Other Electronic Books

For online books, follow the guidelines for print books. In addition to the usual elements, include the URL and the date you accessed the material (see 15.4.1, 17.1.7). Note that a URL alone is not sufficient; you must provide the full facts of publication, as far as they can be determined, so that a reader can search for the source even if the URL changes. If page numbers are not available, you may identify the location of a cited passage in a note by adding a descriptive locator (such as a preceding subheading) following the word *under* before the URL and access date.

N: 1. Julian Samora and Patricia Vandel Simon, *A History of the Mexican-American People,* rev. ed. (East Lansing, MI: Julian Samora Research Institute, Michigan State University, 2000), under "Civil War in Mexico," http://www.jsri.msu.edu/museum/pubs/MexAmHist/chapter14.html#six (accessed December 19, 2005).

B: Samora, Julian, and Patricia Vandel Simon. *A History of the Mexican-American People.* Rev. ed. East Lansing, MI: Julian Samora Research Institute, Michigan State University, 2000. http://www.jsri.msu.edu/museum/pubs/MexAmHist/chapter14.html#six (accessed December 19, 2005).

When you cite books published in other electronic formats, such as those available for download or other delivery from a bookseller or library, identify the format (CD-ROM, Microsoft Reader e-book).

N: 1. Thomas H. Davenport and John C. Beck, *The Attention Economy: Understanding the New Currency of Business* (Cambridge, MA: Harvard Business School Press, 2001), TK3 Reader e-book.

B: Hellman, Hal. *Great Feuds in Technology: Ten of the Liveliest Disputes Ever.* New York: John Wiley, 2004. Rocket e-book.

17.2 Journal Articles

Most of the periodicals you will consult for a paper are classified as journals, which are scholarly or professional periodicals available primarily in academic libraries and by subscription. Journals often include the word *journal* in their titles (*Journal of Modern History*), but not always (*Signs*). Magazines are usually not scholarly publications; they are more accessible to readers than journals, in both their content and their availability outside academic settings. This distinction is important because journal articles and magazine articles are cited differently. If you are unsure whether a periodical is a journal or a magazine, see whether its articles include citations; if so, treat it as a journal.

17.2.1 Author's Name

Give authors' names exactly as they appear at the heads of their articles. Follow the guidelines for book authors in 17.1.1.

17.2.2 Article Title

List complete article titles and subtitles. Use roman type, separate the title from the subtitle with a colon, and enclose both in quotation marks. Use headline-style capitalization (see 22.3.1).

N: 12. Nancy L. Green, "The Politics of Exit: Reversing the Immigration Paradigm," *Journal of Modern History* 77 (June 2005): 275.

B: Green, Nancy L. "The Politics of Exit: Reversing the Immigration Paradigm." *Journal of Modern History* 77 (June 2005): 263–89.

Terms normally italicized in text, such as species names and book titles, remain italicized within an article title; terms normally quoted in text are enclosed in single quotation marks because the title itself is within double quotation marks. Do not put a comma or period after an article title or subtitle that ends with a question mark or an exclamation point.

N: 23. Judith Lewis, "'Tis a Misfortune to Be a Great Ladie': Maternal Mortality in the British Aristocracy, 1558–1959," *Journal of British Studies* 37 (1998): 26.

B: Loften, Peter. "Reverberations between Wordplay and Swordplay in *Hamlet*." *Aeolian Studies* 2 (1989): 12–29.
Williamson, George S. "What Killed August von Kotzebue? The Temptations of Virtue and the Political Theology of German Nationalism, 1789–1819." *Journal of Modern History* 72 (December 2000): 890–943.

Foreign-language titles should generally be capitalized sentence style (see 22.3.1) according to the conventions of the particular language. If you add an English translation, enclose it in brackets, without quotation marks.

N: 22. Gérard Bouchard, "Un essai d'anthropologie régionale: L'histoire sociale du Saguenay aux XIXe et XXe siècles," *Annales: Économies, sociétés, civilisations* 34 (January 1979): 118.

B: Kern, W. "Waar verzamelde Pigafetta zijn Maleise woorden?" [Where did Pigafetta collect his Malaysian words?] *Tijdschrift voor Indische taal-, land- en volkenkunde* 78 (1938): 271–73.

17.2.3 Journal Title

After the article title, list the journal title in italics, with headline-style capitalization (see 22.3.1). Give the title exactly as it appears on the title

page or above the table of contents of the journal; do not use abbreviations, although you can omit an initial *The* (*Journal of Business*). If the
official title is an initialism such as *PMLA,* do not expand it. For foreign-
language journals, you may use either headline-style or sentence-style
capitalization, but retain all initial articles (*Der Spiegel*).

17.2.4 Issue Information

Most journal citations include volume number, issue number or month,
and year. Readers may not need all of these elements to locate an article,
but including them all guards against a possible error in one of them.

VOLUME AND ISSUE NUMBERS. The volume number follows the journal title
without intervening punctuation and is not italicized. Use arabic numerals even if the journal itself uses roman numerals. If there is an issue number, it follows the volume number, separated by a comma and preceded
by *no.*

N: 2. Christopher S. Mackay, "Lactantius and the Succession to Diocletian," *Classical
       Philology* 94, no. 2 (1999): 205.

B: Kumar, Rahul. "Reasonable Reasons in Contractualist Moral Argument." *Ethics* 114
     (October 2003): 6–37.

When a journal uses issue numbers only, without volume numbers, a
comma follows the journal title.

B: Beattie, J. M. "The Pattern of Crime in England, 1660–1800." *Past and Present,* no. 62
     (1974): 47–95.

DATE OF PUBLICATION. The date of publication appears in parentheses after
the volume number (or issue number, if given). For the form of the date,
follow the practice of the journal; it must include the year and may include a season, a month, or an exact day. Capitalize seasons in journal
citations, even though they are not capitalized in text.

N: 27. Sarah Burns, "Ordering the Artist's Body: Thomas Eakins's Acts of Self-
       portrayal," *American Art* 19, no. 1 (Spring 2005): 95.

B: Jenkins, J. Craig, David Jacobs, and Jon Agnone. "Political Opportunities and African-
     American Protest, 1948–1997." *American Journal of Sociology* 109, no. 2 (Septem-
     ber 2003): 277–303.

If an article has been accepted for publication but has not yet appeared,
use *forthcoming* in place of the date and page numbers. Treat any article
not yet accepted for publication as an unpublished manuscript (see 17.6).

N: 4. Margaret M. Author, "Article Title," *Journal Name* 98 (forthcoming).

B: Author, Margaret M. "Article Title." *Journal Name* 98 (forthcoming).

17.2.5 Page Numbers and Other Locating Information

If you cite a particular passage in a note, give only the specific page(s) cited. For a bibliography entry or a note that cites the entire article, give ⌐ the full span of page numbers for the article (see 23.2.4). By convention, page numbers of journal articles follow colons rather than commas.

N: 4. Tim Hitchcock, "Begging on the Streets of Eighteenth-century London," *Journal of British Studies* 44 (July 2005): 478.

B: Gold, Ann Grodzins. "Grains of Truth: Shifting Hierarchies of Food and Grace in Three Rajasthani Tales." *History of Religions* 38, no. 2 (1998): 150–71.

For journal articles published online, include page numbers (if available) as well as the URL (or permanent identifier) and the date you accessed the article. For details and examples, see 17.2.7. For general principles of punctuation and capitalization in URLs, see 17.1.7.

17.2.6 Special Issues and Supplements

A journal issue devoted to a single theme is known as a *special issue*. It carries a normal volume and issue number. If a special issue has a title and an editor of its own, include both in the citations. The title is given in roman type and enclosed in quotation marks.

N: 67. Matthew L. Jones, "Descartes's Geometry as a Spiritual Exercise," in "Things," ed. Bill Brown, special issue, *Critical Inquiry* 28, no. 1 (Autumn 2001): 43–44.

B: Jones, Matthew L. "Descartes's Geometry as a Spiritual Exercise." In "Things," ed. Bill Brown. Special issue, *Critical Inquiry* 28, no. 1 (Autumn 2001): 40–71.

If you need to cite the issue as a whole, omit the article information.

B: Brown, Bill, ed. "Things." Special issue, *Critical Inquiry* 28, no. 1 (Autumn 2001).

A journal *supplement* may also have a title and an author or editor of its own. Unlike a special issue, it is numbered separately from the regular issues of the journal, often with *S* as part of its page numbers. Use a comma between the volume number and the supplement number.

N: 4. Ivar Ekeland, James J. Heckman, and Lars Nesheim, "Identification and Estimation of Hedonic Models," in "Papers in Honor of Sherwin Rosen," *Journal of Political Economy* 112, S1 (February 2004): S72.

B: Ekeland, Ivar, James J. Heckman, and Lars Nesheim. "Identification and Estimation of Hedonic Models." In "Papers in Honor of Sherwin Rosen," *Journal of Political Economy* 112, S1 (February 2004): S60–S109.

17.2.7 Articles Published Online

For online journals, follow the guidelines for articles in print journals. In addition, include the URL and the date you accessed the material (see 15.4.1). Note that a URL alone is not sufficient; you must provide the full facts of publication, as far as they can be determined, so that a reader can search for the source even if the URL changes. Articles in online journals might not include page numbers, especially if they are not published in parallel print journals. If page numbers are not available, you may identify the location of a cited passage in a note by adding a descriptive locator (such as a preceding subheading) following the word *under* before the URL and access date.

N: 4. Brian Uzzi and Jarrett Spiro, "Collaboration and Creativity: The Small World Problem," *American Journal of Sociology* 111, no. 2 (September 2005), under "Milgram's Small World Theory," http://www.journals.uchicago.edu/AJS/journal/issues/v111n2/090090/090090.html (accessed December 19, 2005).

B: Uzzi, Brian, and Jarrett Spiro. "Collaboration and Creativity: The Small World Problem." *American Journal of Sociology* 111, no. 2 (September 2005). http://www.journals.uchicago.edu/AJS/journal/issues/v111n2/090090/090090.html (accessed December 19, 2005).

Online databases of articles generally list all the elements necessary for citations. Include the stable URL listed, which also identifies the database in which you consulted the article.

N: 6. Lawrence A. Shapiro, "Multiple Realizations," *Journal of Philosophy* 97, no. 12 (December 2000): 642, http://links.jstor.org/sici?sici=0022–362X%28200012%2997%3A12%3C635%3AMR%3E2.0.CO%3B2-Q (accessed June 27, 2006).

B: Shapiro, Lawrence A. "Multiple Realizations." *Journal of Philosophy* 97, no. 12 (December 2000): 635–54. http://links.jstor.org/sici?sici=0022–362X%28200012%2997%3A12%3C635%3AMR%3E2.0.CO%3B2-Q (accessed June 27, 2006).

17.3 Magazine Articles

Many guidelines for citing journal articles (see 17.2) apply equally to magazine articles.

In most cases, cite weekly or monthly magazines by date only, even if they are numbered by volume and issue. Do not enclose the date in parentheses. If you cite a specific passage in a note, include its page number. But you may omit the article's inclusive page numbers in a bibliography entry, since magazine articles often span many pages that include extraneous material. If you include page numbers, use a comma rather than a colon to separate them from the date of issue.

N: 11. Mark Schapiro, "New Power for 'Old Europe,'" *The Nation,* December 27, 2004, 12–13.

B: Schapiro, Mark. "New Power for 'Old Europe.'" *The Nation,* December 27, 2004.

If you cite a department or column that appears regularly, capitalize it headline style and do not enclose it in quotation marks. For a department without a named author, use the name of the magazine in place of the author in a bibliography entry.

N: 2. Barbara Wallraff, Word Court, *Atlantic Monthly,* June 2005, 128.

B: *New Yorker.* Talk of the Town. April 10, 2000.

For online magazines, follow the guidelines for articles in print magazines. In addition, include the URL and the date you accessed the material (see 15.4.1). Note that a URL alone is not sufficient; you must provide the full facts of publication, as far as they can be determined, so that a reader can search for the source even if the URL changes. Articles in online magazines might not include page numbers, but you may identify the location of a cited passage in a note by adding a descriptive locator (such as a preceding subheading) following the word *under* before the URL and access date.

N: 7. Stephan Faris, "'Freedom': No Documents Found," *Salon.com,* December 16, 2005, under "The Internet Has No Memory in China,"http://www.salon.com/tech/feature/2005/12/16/censorship/index1.html (accessed December 19, 2005).

B: Faris, Stephan. "'Freedom': No Documents Found." *Salon.com,* December 16, 2005. http://www.salon.com/tech/feature/2005/12/16/censorship/index1.html (accessed December 19, 2005).

17.4 Newspaper Articles

In most cases, cite articles and other pieces from daily newspapers only in notes. You generally need not include them in your bibliography, although you may choose to include a specific article that is critical to your argument or frequently cited.

Follow the general pattern for citation of articles in magazines (see 17.3). Omit page numbers, because a newspaper may have several editions in which items may appear on different pages or may even be dropped. You may clarify which edition you consulted by adding *final edition, Midwest edition,* or some such identifier.

N: 4. Editorial, *Milwaukee Journal-Sentinel,* June 1, 1998.

       6. Obituary of Jacques Derrida, *New York Times,* October 10, 2004, national edition.

If you cite an article by its headline, you can use either headline- or sentence-style capitalization (see 22.3.1), but be consistent. Newspapers use both, so change all headlines to conform to the style you choose.

N: 9. Blair Kamin, "Wrigley Building Clearly a Landmark," *Chicago Tribune,* July 1, 2005.

or

       9. Blair Kamin, "Wrigley Building clearly a landmark," *Chicago Tribune,* July 1, 2005.

Instead of using a note, you can sometimes cite articles by weaving several key elements into your text; at a minimum, include the name and date of the paper and the author of the article (if any). Some of this information can appear in parentheses, even if it does not follow the form for parenthetical notes described in 16.4.3.

In a *New York Times* article on the transitions within the Supreme Court (September 30, 2005), Linda Greenhouse discusses these trends.

or

In an article published on September 30, 2005, in the *New York Times,* Linda Greenhouse discusses the transitions within the Supreme Court.

17.4.1   Special Format Issues

For American newspapers, omit an initial *The* in the name of the newspaper. If the name does not include a city, add it to the official title, except for well-known national papers such as the *Wall Street Journal* or the *Christian Science Monitor.* If a name is shared by many cities or is obscure, you may add the state or province in parentheses (usually abbreviated; see 24.3.1). For foreign newspapers, retain initial articles, and add city names after titles.

Chicago Tribune   *Le Monde*

Saint Paul (Alberta or AB) Journal   *Times* (London)

The names of news services should be capitalized headline style but not italicized when treated as the author of an article.

N: 6. Associated Press, "Iraq Constitution Distributed amid Attacks," *Los Angeles Times,* October 6, 2005.

17.4.2 Special Types of Newspaper Citations

In addition to individual, signed articles, newspapers include many other types of pieces, some of which require special treatment in citations.

■ *Regular columns.* Many regular columns carry headlines as well as column titles. You may use either both or, to save space, the column title alone (in roman type, not enclosed in quotation marks).

N: 5. Gretchen Morgenson, "Applying a Discount to Good Earnings News," Market Watch, *New York Times,* April 23, 2000.

or

    5. Gretchen Morgenson, Market Watch, *New York Times,* April 23, 2000.

■ *Letters to the editor.* Cite published letters to the editor generically, without headlines.

N: 6. Virginia J. Davis, letter to the editor, *Chicago Tribune,* July 29, 2005.

■ *Articles in supplements.* Treat articles from Sunday "magazine" supplements or other special sections as you would magazine articles (see 17.3).
■ *Articles published online.* For online newspapers, follow the guidelines for articles in print newspapers. In addition, include the URL and the date you accessed the material (see 15.4.1). Note that a URL alone is not sufficient; you must provide the full facts of publication, as far as they can be determined, so that a reader can search for the source even if the URL changes. You may identify the location of a cited passage in a note by adding a descriptive locator (such as a preceding subheading) following the word *under.*

N: 12. Dave Hoekstra, "Restoring a Legacy," *Chicago Sun-Times,* December 19, 2005, under "Home Away from Home," http://www.suntimes.com/output/hurricane/cst-ftr-nola19.html (accessed December 19, 2005).

17.5 Additional Types of Published Sources

There are several additional types of published material that have special requirements for citations.

17.5.1 Classical, Medieval, and Early English Literary Works

Literary works produced in classical Greece and Rome, medieval Europe, and Renaissance England are cited differently from modern literary works. These sources are often organized into numbered sections (books, lines, stanzas, and so forth) that are generally cited in place of page numbers. Because such works have been published in so many versions and translations over the centuries, the facts of publication for modern editions are generally less important than in other types of citations.

For this reason, classical, medieval, and early English literary works should usually be cited only in footnotes or even in parenthetical notes (see 16.4.3), as in the first example below. Include the author's name, the title, and the section number (given in arabic numerals). See below regarding differences in punctuation, abbreviations, and numbers among different types of works.

The eighty days of inactivity reported by Thucydides (8.44.4) for the Peloponnesian fleet at Rhodes, terminating before the end of winter (8.60.2–3), suggests . . .

N: 3. Ovid *Amores* 1.7.27.
      8. *Beowulf,* lines 2401–7.
      11. Spenser, *The Faerie Queene,* bk. 2, canto 8, st. 14.

If your paper is in literary studies or another field concerned with close analysis of texts, or if differences in translations are relevant, include such works in your bibliography. Follow the rules for other translated and edited books in 17.1.1.

N: 35. Propertius, *Elegies,* ed. and trans. G. P. Goold, Loeb Classical Library 18 (Cambridge, MA: Harvard University Press, 1990), 45.

B: Aristotle. *Complete Works of Aristotle: The Revised Oxford Translation.* Edited by J. Barnes. 2 vols. Princeton, NJ: Princeton University Press, 1983.

CLASSICAL WORKS. In addition to the general principles listed above, the following rules apply to citations of classical works.

Use no punctuation between author and title of work, or between title and section number. Numerical divisions are separated by periods without spaces. Use arabic numerals (and lowercase letters, if needed) for section numbers. Put commas between two or more citations of the same source and semicolons between citations of different sources.

N: 5. Aristophanes *Frogs* 1019–30.
      6. Cicero *Verr.* 1.3.21, 2.3.120; Tacitus *Germ.* 10.2–3.
      10. Aristotle *Metaphysics* 3.2.996b5–8; Plato *Republic* 360e–361b.

You can also abbreviate the names of authors, works, collections, and so forth. The most widely accepted abbreviations appear in the *Oxford Classical Dictionary*. Use these abbreviations rather than *ibid.* in succeeding references to the same work.

N: 9. Thuc. 2.40.2–3.
         14. Pindar *Isthm.* 7.43–45.

MEDIEVAL WORKS. The form for classical references works equally well for medieval works written in languages other than English.

N: 27. Augustine *De civitate Dei* 20.2.
         31. Abelard *Epistle 17 to Heloïse* (Migne *PL* 180.375c–378a).

EARLY ENGLISH WORKS. In addition to the general principles listed above, the following rules apply to citations of early English literary works.

Cite poems and plays by book, canto, and stanza; stanza and line; act, scene, and line; or similar divisions.

N: 1. Chaucer, "Wife of Bath's Prologue," *Canterbury Tales*, lines 105–14.
         3. Milton, *Paradise Lost*, book 1, lines 83–86.

You may shorten numbered divisions by omitting *act, line,* and such and using a system similar to that in classical references (see above). Be sure to explain your system in a note.

N: 3. Milton, *Paradise Lost*, 1.83–86.

If editions differ in wording, line numbering, and even scene division—especially works of Shakespeare—include the work in your bibliography, with edition specified. If you do not have a bibliography, specify the edition in the first note.

B: Shakespeare, William. *Hamlet.* Arden edition. Edited by Harold Jenkins. London: Methuen, 1982.

17.5.2 The Bible and Other Sacred Works

Cite the Bible and sacred works of other religious traditions in footnotes, endnotes, or parenthetical notes (see 16.4.3). You do not need to include these works in your bibliography.

For citations from the Bible, include the abbreviated name of the book, the chapter number, and the verse number—never a page number. Depending on the context, you may use either traditional or shorter abbreviations for the names of books (see 24.6); consult your instructor if you are unsure which form is appropriate. Use arabic numerals for chapter and verse numbers (with a colon between them) and for numbered books.

Traditional abbreviations:

N: 4. 1 Thess. 4:11, 5:2–5, 5:14.

Shorter abbreviations:

N: 5. 2 Sm 11:1–17, 11:26–27; 1 Chr 10:13–14.

Since books and numbering differ among versions of the scriptures, identify the version you are using in your first citation, either with the spelled-out name or an accepted abbreviation (see 24.6.4).

N: 6. 2 Kings 11:8 (New Revised Standard Version).
          7. 1 Cor. 6:1–10 (NAB).

For citations from the sacred works of other religious traditions, adapt the general pattern for biblical citations as appropriate (see 24.6.5).

17.5.3 Reference Works

Well-known reference works, such as major dictionaries and encyclopedias, should usually be cited only in notes. You generally need not include them in your bibliography, although you may choose to include a specific work that is critical to your argument or frequently cited. Within the note, you may omit the facts of publication, but you must specify the edition (if not the first). For an alphabetically arranged work such as an encyclopedia, cite the item (not the volume or page number) preceded by *s.v. (sub verbo,* "under the word"; pl. *s.vv.*)

N: 1. *Encyclopaedia Britannica,* 15th ed., s.v. "Salvation."
          2. *Dictionary of American Biography,* s.v. "Wadsworth, Jeremiah."

For reference works that are less well known, include the publication details in your notes, and list the work in your bibliography.

N: 3. *The Times Guide to English Style and Usage,* rev. ed. (London: Times Books, 1999), s.vv. "police ranks," "postal addresses."

B: Aulestia, Gorka. *Basque English Dictionary.* Reno: University of Nevada Press, 1989.

Online versions of encyclopedias are regularly updated, so include both the URL and the date you accessed the material (see 15.4.1). Note that some reference works will indicate the appropriate URL to cite for a specific entry; use this rather than the less stable URL generated by search engines.

N: 1. *Encyclopaedia Britannica Online*, s.v. "Sibelius, Jean," http://www.britannica
.com/ebc/article?tocId=9378608 (accessed June 1, 2005).

17.5.4 Reviews

Reviews of books, performances, and so forth may appear in a variety of periodicals and should usually be cited only in a note. You generally need not include them in your bibliography, although you may choose to include a specific review that is critical to your argument or frequently cited.

Include the name of the reviewer; the words *review of,* followed by the name of the work reviewed and its author (or composer, director, and so forth); location and date (in the case of a performance); and finally the periodical in which the review appeared.

N: 7. Richard P. Taub, review of *Reclaiming Public Housing: A Half-century of Struggle in Three Public Neighborhoods,* by Lawrence J. Vale, *American Journal of Sociology* 110, no. 3 (November 2004): 797.

    15. Charles Isherwood, review of *Birdie Blue,* by Cheryl L. West, directed by Seret Scott, Second Stage Theater, New York, *New York Times,* June 24, 2005.

B: Kozinn, Allan. Review of concert performance by Timothy Fain (violin) and Steven Beck (piano), 92nd Street Y, New York. *New York Times,* April 21, 2000.

17.5.5 Abstracts

Abstracts of journal articles, conference proceedings, dissertations, and so forth may appear along with the work being abstracted or in special publications (usually journals) that consist entirely of abstracts. In either case, abstracts should usually be cited only in a note. You generally need not include them in your bibliography, although you may choose to include a specific abstract that is critical to your argument or frequently cited.

Include the full citation of the work being abstracted. If the abstract appears next to the work itself, insert the word *abstract* within the citation, following the title. If the abstract appears in a different publication, insert the words *abstract in* following the initial citation, and then cite the location of the abstract.

N: 13. Joseph Luders, "The Economics of Movement Success: Business Responses to Civil Rights Mobilization," abstract, *American Journal of Sociology* 111, no. 4 (January 2006): 963.

    18. Cecilia Albin, "Negotiating International Cooperation: Global Public Goods and Fairness," *Review of International Studies* 29 (July 2003): 365–85, abstract in *Peace Research Abstracts Journal* 42, publ. nr. 236625 (February 2005): 6.

17.5.6 Pamphlets and Reports

Cite pamphlets, corporate reports, brochures, and other freestanding publications as you would a book. If you lack data for some of the usual elements, such as author and publisher, give enough other information to identify the document. Such sources should usually be cited only in notes. You generally need not include them in your bibliography, although you may choose to include a specific work that is critical to your argument or frequently cited.

N: 34. Hazel V. Clark, *Mesopotamia: Between Two Rivers* (Mesopotamia, OH: End of the Commons General Store, 1957).

35. TIAA-CREF, *2005 Annual Report: College Retirement Equities Fund* (New York: TIAA-CREF, 2005), 62.

17.5.7 Microform Editions

Cite works that you have consulted in microform editions, including dissertations, as you would a book. (For dissertations consulted in print form or online, see 17.6.1.) Specify the form of publication (fiche, microfilm, and so forth) after the facts of publication. In a note, include a locator if possible. In the first example below, the page number (identified with the abbreviation *p.* for clarity) appears within the printed text on the fiche; the other numbers indicate the fiche and frame, and the letter indicates the row.

N: 5. Beatrice Farwell, *French Popular Lithographic Imagery,* vol. 12, *Lithography in Art and Commerce* (Chicago: University of Chicago Press, 1995), text-fiche, p. 67, 3C12.

B: Tauber, Abraham. *Spelling Reform in the United States.* Ann Arbor, MI: University Microfilms, 1958. Microfilm.

17.5.8 CD-ROMs or DVD-ROMs

Cite works published on CD- or DVD-ROM as you would analogous printed works, most often books.

N: 11. *Complete National Geographic: 110 Years of "National Geographic" Magazine,* CD-ROM (Mindscape, 2000).

B: *Oxford English Dictionary.* 2nd ed. CD-ROM, version 2.0. New York: Oxford University Press, 1999.

17.5.9 Online Databases

For citation of journal articles published in online databases, see 17.2.7. To cite documents or records from other types of online databases in a note, give the author and title of the document (if available), the name of the database (in roman type), the URL, and the date you accessed the material. In your bibliography entry, list the database as a whole, with the URL for the main page and without an access date. Note that a URL alone is not sufficient; you must provide the full facts of publication, as far as they can be determined, so that a reader can search for the source even if the URL changes. For dissertations in online databases, see 17.6.1.

N: 1. Pliny the Elder, *The Natural History*, ed. John Bostock and H. T. Riley, in the Perseus Digital Library, http://www.perseus.tufts.edu/cgi-bin/ptext?lookup=Plin.+Nat.+1.dedication (accessed March 31, 2006).

B: Perseus Digital Library. http://www.perseus.tufts.edu/

17.6   Unpublished Sources

Sources that have never been published can be more difficult for readers to locate than published ones, because they exist in only one place and lack official publication information. When citing such sources, it is especially important to include *all* of the information listed below to give readers as much help as possible.

Titles of unpublished works are given in roman type, enclosed in quotation marks, and not italicized. This format difference distinguishes them from similar but published works. Capitalize titles headline style.

17.6.1   Theses and Dissertations

If you consult an unpublished thesis or dissertation in print form, treat it as an unpublished manuscript. After the author and title, list the kind of thesis, the academic institution, and the date. Like the publication data of a book, these are enclosed in parentheses in a note but not in a bibliography. Abbreviate *dissertation* as *diss.* The word *unpublished* is unnecessary.

N: 1. Karen Leigh Culcasi, "Cartographic Representations of Kurdistan in the Print Media" (master's thesis, Syracuse University, 2003), 15.

B: Murphy, Priscilla Coit. "What a Book Can Do: *Silent Spring* and Media-Borne Public Debate." PhD diss., University of North Carolina, 2000.

To cite a dissertation consulted in an online database, add the name of the database, the URL, and the access date following the institutional information. (For microform editions, see 17.5.7.)

B: Murphy, Priscilla Coit. "What a Book Can Do: *Silent Spring* and Media-Borne Public Debate." PhD diss., University of North Carolina, 2000. In ProQuest Dissertations and Theses, http://proquest.umi.com/pqdweb?did=727710781&sid=2&Fmt=2& clientId=13392&RQT=309&VName=PQD (accessed April 1, 2006).

17.6.2 Lectures and Papers Presented at Meetings

After the author and title of the speech or paper, list the sponsorship, location, and date of the meeting at which it was given. Enclose this information in parentheses in a note but not in a bibliography. The word *unpublished* is unnecessary.

N: 2. John Troutman, "Indian Blues: American Indians and the Politics of Music, 1890–1935" (lecture, Newberry Library, Chicago, IL, February 2, 2005).

7. Karene Grad, "When High Culture Was Popular Culture" (paper presented at the annual meeting of the Organization of American Historians, Boston, MA, March 26, 2004).

B: Skocpol, Theda. "Voice and Inequality: The Transformation of American Civic Democracy." Presidential address, annual meeting of the American Political Science Association, Philadelphia, PA, August 28, 2003.

17.6.3 Interviews and Personal Communications

Unpublished interviews (including those you have conducted yourself) should usually be cited only in notes. You generally need not include them in your bibliography, although you may choose to include a specific interview that is critical to your argument or frequently cited. Begin the note with the names of the person interviewed and the interviewer; also include the place and date of the interview (if known) and the location of any tapes or transcripts (if available). Notice the form for a shortened note, which differs from the usual pattern. (For broadcast interviews, see 17.8.3.)

N: 7. Andrew Macmillan, interview by author, San Diego, CA, March 2, 2007.

14. Benjamin Spock, interview by Milton J. E. Senn, November 20, 1974, interview 67A, transcript, Senn Oral History Collection, National Library of Medicine, Bethesda, MD.

17. Macmillan, interview; Spock, interview.

If you cannot reveal the name of the person interviewed, cite it in a form appropriate to the context. Explain the absence of a name ("All interviews were confidential; the names of interviewees are withheld by mutual agreement") in a note or a preface.

N: 10. Interview with a health care worker, August 10, 2006.

Cite conversations, letters, e-mail messages, and the like only in notes. You generally need not include them in your bibliography, although you may choose to include a specific communication that is critical to your argument or frequently cited. The key elements are the name of the other person, the type of communication, and the date of the communication. In many cases, you may be able to use a parenthetical note (see 16.4.3) or include some or all of this information in the text. Omit e-mail addresses. To cite postings to electronic mailing lists, see 17.7.3.

N: 2. Maxine Greene, e-mail message to author, September 29, 2005.

In a telephone conversation with the author on October 12, 2006, Colonel William Rich revealed that . . .

17.6.4 Manuscript Collections

Documents from collections of unpublished manuscripts involve more complicated and varied elements than published sources. In your citations, include as much identifying information as you can, format the elements consistently, and adapt the general patterns outlined here as needed.

ELEMENTS TO INCLUDE AND THEIR ORDER. If possible, identify the author and date of each item, the title or type of document, the name of the collection, and the name of the depository. In a note, begin with the author's name; if a document has a title but no author, or the title is more important than the author, list the title first.

N: 5. George Creel to Colonel House, September 25, 1918, Edward M. House Papers, Yale University Library, New Haven, CT.
        23. James Oglethorpe to the Trustees, January 13, 1733, Phillipps Collection of Egmont Manuscripts, 14200:13, University of Georgia Library, Athens (hereafter cited as Egmont MSS).
        24. Burton to Merriam, telegram, January 26, 1923, Charles E. Merriam Papers, University of Chicago Library.
        31. Minutes of the Committee for Improving the Condition of Free Blacks, Pennsylvania Abolition Society, 1790–1803, Papers of the Pennsylvania Society for the Abolition of Slavery, Historical Society of Pennsylvania, Philadelphia (hereafter cited as Minutes, Pennsylvania Society).
        44. Memorandum by Alvin Johnson, 1937, file 36, Horace Kallen Papers, YIVO Institute, New York.
        45. Joseph Purcell, "A Map of the Southern Indian District of North America" [ca. 1772], MS 228, Ayer Collection, Newberry Library, Chicago.

For shortened notes, adapt the usual pattern of elements (see 16.4.1) to accommodate the available information and identify the document unambiguously.

N: 46. R. S. Baker to House, November 1, 1919, House Papers.
        47. Minutes, April 15, 1795, Pennsylvania Society.

If you cite only one document from a collection and it is critical to your argument or frequently cited within your paper, you may choose to include it in your bibliography. Begin the entry with the author's name; if a document has a title but no author, or the title is more important than the author, list the title first.

B: Dinkel, Joseph. Description of Louis Agassiz written at the request of Elizabeth Cary
    Agassiz. Agassiz Papers. Houghton Library, Harvard University, Cambridge, MA.

If you cite multiple documents from a collection, list the collection as a whole in your bibliography, under the name of the collection, the author(s) of the items in the collection, or the depository. For similar types of unpublished material that have not been placed in archives, replace information about the collection with such wording as "in the author's possession" or "private collection," and do not mention the location.

B: Egmont Manuscripts. Phillipps Collection. University of Georgia Library, Athens.
    House, Edward M., Papers. Yale University Library, New Haven, CT.
    Pennsylvania Society for the Abolition of Slavery. Papers. Historical Society of Penn-
    sylvania, Philadelphia.
    Strother, French, and Edward Lowry. Undated correspondence. Herbert Hoover Pres-
    idential Library, West Branch, IA.
    Women's Organization for National Prohibition Reform Papers. Alice Belin du Pont
    files, Pierre S. du Pont Papers. Eleutherian Mills Historical Library, Wilmington, DE.

HOW TO FORMAT THE ELEMENTS. Here are some special formatting recommendations for documents in manuscript collections.

- *Specific versus generic titles.* Use quotation marks for specific titles of documents but not for generic names such as *report* or *minutes.* Capitalize generic names of this kind only if they are part of a formal heading in the manuscript, not if they are merely descriptive.
- *Locating information.* Although some manuscripts may include page numbers that can be included in notes, many will have other types of locators, or none at all. Older manuscripts are usually numbered by signatures only or by folios (*fol., fols.*) rather than by page. Some manuscript collections have identifying series or file numbers that you can include in a citation.
- *Papers and manuscripts.* In titles of manuscript collections the terms *papers* and *manuscripts* are synonymous. Both are acceptable, as are the abbreviations *MS* and *MSS* (plural).
- *Letters.* To cite a letter in a note, start with the name of the letter writer, followed by *to* and the name of the recipient. You may omit first names if the identities of the sender and the recipient are clear from the text. Omit

the word *letter,* which is understood, but for other forms of communication, specify the type (telegram, memorandum).

17.7   Informally Published Electronic Sources

Material that is informally published, or "posted," online will often lack the standard facts of publication—author, title, publisher, or date. Even if you can determine few or no facts of publication, you must still include information beyond the URL in your citations. If you cite only a URL and that URL changes or becomes obsolete, your citation becomes useless to readers. The URL tells where the material was located when you consulted it; a complete citation must also indicate what a source is and the date on which you last accessed it (see 15.4.1).

17.7.1   Web Sites

For original content from online sources other than books or periodicals, include as much of the following as you can: author, title of the page (in roman type, enclosed in quotation marks), title or owner of the site (in roman type), URL, and access date.

N: 14. Evanston Public Library Board of Trustees, "Evanston Public Library Strategic Plan, 2000–2010: A Decade of Outreach," Evanston Public Library, http://www.epl.org/library/strategic-plan-00.html (accessed June 1, 2005).

B: Evanston Public Library Board of Trustees. "Evanston Public Library Strategic Plan, 2000–2010: A Decade of Outreach." Evanston Public Library. http://www.epl.org/library/strategic-plan-00.html (accessed June 1, 2005).

If there is no named author, give the name of the owner of the site.

N: 19. The Bahá'ís of the United States, "Education," The Bahá'í Faith, http://www.bahai.us/content/section/7/36/ (accessed March 28, 2006).
      25. Federation of American Scientists, "Resolution Comparison: Reading License Plates and Headlines," http://www.fas.org/irp/imint/resolve5.html (accessed June 1, 2005).

B: The Bahá'ís of the United States. "Education." The Bahá'í Faith. http://www.bahai.us/content/section/7/36/ (accessed March 28, 2006).

Use descriptive phrases for content from informal sites, such as personal home pages and fan sites, where titles may be lacking.

N: 1. Camp Taconic Alumni, 1955 photo gallery, http://www.taconicalumni.org/1955.html (accessed June 1, 2005).

17.7.2 Weblog Entries and Comments

To cite an entry posted on a Weblog (or blog) by the author of the site, follow the basic pattern for Web sites. Include the author's name and the date of the posting. Such items should usually be cited only in a note. You generally need not include them in your bibliography, although you may choose to include a specific item that is critical to your argument or frequently cited.

N: 7. Gary Becker, "The New American Dilemma: Illegal Immigration," The Becker-Posner Blog, entry posted March 6, 2006, http://www.becker-posner-blog.com/archives/2006/03/the_new_america.html (accessed March 28, 2006).

To cite a comment posted on a Weblog by someone other than the author of the site, follow the basic pattern for Weblog entries. Identify the material as a comment, and include the date when the comment (not the entry itself) was posted. If the comment author's name is incomplete or a pseudonym, add *pseud.* in brackets after the posted name.

N: 8. Peter Pearson, comment on "The New American Dilemma: Illegal Immigration," The Becker-Posner Blog, comment posted March 6, 2006, http://www.becker-posner-blog.com/archives/2006/03/the_new_america.html#c080052 (accessed March 28, 2006).
       11. Bill [pseud.], comment on "The New American Dilemma: Illegal Immigration," The Becker-Posner Blog, comment posted March 10, 2006, http://www.becker-posner-blog.com/archives/2006/03/the_new_america.html#c080149 (accessed March 28, 2006).

17.7.3 Electronic Mailing Lists

To cite material from an electronic mailing list, include the name of the author, the name of the list, and the date of the posting. Omit e-mail addresses. If the material is archived, also include the URL and the date you accessed the material. Such items should usually be cited only in a note. You generally need not include them in your bibliography, although you may choose to include a specific item that is critical to your argument or frequently cited.

N: 17. John Powell, e-mail to Grapevine mailing list, October 30, 2004, http://www.electriceditors.net/grapevine/issues/83.txt (accessed October 12, 2005).

17.8 Sources in the Visual and Performing Arts

The visual and performing arts generate a variety of sources, including visual images, live performances, broadcasts, recordings in various media, and texts. Citing some of these sources can be difficult when they lack the types of identifying information common to published sources. Include as much identifying information as you can, format the elements consistently, and adapt the general patterns outlined here as needed.

You should cite most of the sources covered in this section only in notes or by weaving the key elements into your text. Unless otherwise noted, you generally need not include these sources in your bibliography, although you may choose to include a specific item that is critical to your argument or frequently cited. If your paper is for a course in the arts, media studies, or a similar field, consult your instructor.

17.8.1 Visual Sources

PAINTINGS, SCULPTURES, PHOTOGRAPHS, AND OTHER ARTWORKS. Cite paintings, sculptures, photographs, and other artworks only in notes. Include the name of the artist, the title of the artwork and date of its creation (preceded by *ca.* [*circa*] if approximate), and the name of the institution that houses it (if any), including location. Italicize the titles of paintings and sculptures, but set the titles of photographs in roman type, enclosed in quotation marks.

N: 7. Georgia O'Keeffe, *The Cliff Chimneys,* 1938, Milwaukee Art Museum.

       11. Michelangelo, *David,* 1501–4, Galleria dell'Accademia, Florence.

       24. Ansel Adams, "North Dome, Basket Dome, Mount Hoffman, Yosemite," ca. 1935, Smithsonian American Art Museum, Washington, DC.

Instead of using a note, you can sometimes cite artworks by weaving the elements into your text. Some of the elements can appear in parentheses, even if they do not follow the form for parenthetical notes described in 16.4.3.

O'Keeffe first demonstrated this technique in *The Cliff Chimneys* (1938; Milwaukee Art Museum).

If you viewed the artwork in a published source and your local guidelines require you to identify this source, give the publication information in place of the institutional name and location. For online images, see 17.8.6.

N: 7. Georgia O'Keeffe, *The Cliff Chimneys,* 1938, in Barbara Buhler Lynes, Lesley Poling-Kempes, and Frederick W. Turner, *Georgia O'Keeffe and New Mexico: A Sense of Place* (Princeton: Princeton University Press, 2004), 25.

OTHER GRAPHIC SOURCES. You may need to cite other graphic sources, such as print advertisements, maps, cartoons, and so forth. Cite such items only in notes, adapting the basic patterns for artworks and giving as much information as possible. Give the titles in roman type, enclosed in quotation marks, and identify the type of graphic if it is unclear from the title. For online graphics, see 17.8.6.

N: 12. National Center for Family Literacy, "Because I Can Read," advertisement, *Atlantic Monthly,* April 2006, 59.

17.8.2 Live Performances

THEATER, MUSIC, AND DANCE. Cite live theatrical, musical, or dance performances only in notes. Include the title of the work performed, the names of any key performers and an indication of their roles, the venue and its location, and the date. Italicize the titles of plays and long musical compositions, but set the titles of shorter works in roman type, enclosed in quotation marks. If the citation is focused on an individual's performance, list that person's name before the title of the work.

N: 14. *Birdie Blue,* by Cheryl L. West, directed by Seret Scott, Second Stage Theater, New York, June 22, 2005.
        16. Yuja Wang, pianist, "La Valse," by Maurice Ravel, Orchestra Hall, Chicago, March 26, 2006.

Instead of using a note, you can sometimes cite live performances by weaving the elements into your text. Some of the elements can appear in parentheses, even if they do not follow the form for parenthetical notes described in 16.4.3.

Yuja Wang's performance of Maurice Ravel's "La Valse" (March 26, 2006, at Orchestra Hall, Chicago) demonstrated her understanding . . .

If you viewed or listened to a live performance in a recorded medium, cite the recording. For sound recordings, see 17.8.4; for video recordings, see 17.8.5; for online files, see 17.8.6.

MOVIES. If you viewed a movie in a theater, cite it similarly to a live performance in a note or by weaving the elements into your text. (For movies viewed as video recordings, see 17.8.5; for movies viewed online, see 17.8.6.) Include the title of the movie (in italics), the director, the name of the production company or distributor, and the year in which the movie was released. If relevant, describe the scene you are citing.

N: 3. *Capote,* directed by Bennett Miller, Sony Pictures Classics, 2005, opening scene.

17.8.3 Television Programs and Other Broadcast Sources

PROGRAMS. Cite television programs, radio programs, and other broadcast sources only in notes. Include at least the title of the program and the date on which you watched or listened to it. You may also include the episode title and number (if available), the names of any key performers (if relevant to your discussion), the broadcast venue, and the date of original broadcast (if different from the date you watched or listened to it). Italicize the titles of programs, but set the titles of episodes or segments in roman type, enclosed in quotation marks.

N: 16. *Seinfeld*, "The Opposite," episode 86, September 22, 2005 (originally aired May 19, 1994).
      23. *All Things Considered*, NPR, April 20, 2006.

Instead of using a note, you can often cite such programs by weaving the key elements into your text, especially if some or all of the additional elements are not available or relevant to the citation.

The *Seinfeld* episode titled "The Opposite" (aired September 22, 2005) perfectly illustrates this story structure.

If you viewed or listened to a broadcast program in a recorded medium, cite the recording. For video recordings, see 17.8.5; for online files, see 17.8.6.

INTERVIEWS. Cite broadcast interviews only in notes or by weaving the elements into your text. Treat the person interviewed as the author, and identify the interviewer in the context of the citation. Also include the forum and date of the broadcast. For unpublished interviews, see 17.6.3.

N: 10. Condoleezza Rice, interview by Jim Lehrer, *News Hour*, PBS, July 28, 2005.

ADVERTISEMENTS. Cite broadcast advertisements only in notes or by weaving the elements into your text. Give as much information as possible.

N: 18. Federal Express, "Caveman" advertisement, aired during *Super Bowl XL*, February 5, 2006.

17.8.4 Sound Recordings

If you listened to a musical or spoken performance on a sound recording, cite the recording. Like published works, such recordings generally have stable and available identifying information and should be listed in your bibliography.

List recordings either under the title of the recording or under the name of the composer or performer, depending on which is more relevant to your discussion. Include as much information about the recording as you can to distinguish it from similar recordings, including the name of the recording company, the identifying number of the recording, the medium, and the copyright date or date of production (or both). Abbreviate *compact disc* as *CD*.

N: 11. *The Fireside Treasury of Folk Songs,* vol. 1, orchestra and chorus dir. Mitch Miller, Golden Record A198:17A–B, 33 rpm, 1972.
       14. Ludwig van Beethoven, *Piano Sonata no. 29 "Hammerklavier,"* Rudolf Serkin, ProArte Digital CDD 270, 1992.

B: Anderson, Doug. *Frostwork.* OAR 1001, Dolby HX PRO. Audiocassette. 2001.
    Bernstein, Leonard, dir. *Symphony no. 5,* by Dmitri Shostakovich. New York Philharmonic. CBS IM 35854. 1985.

Treat recordings of drama, prose or poetry readings, lectures, and the like as you would musical recordings.

N: 6. Dylan Thomas, *Under Milk Wood,* performed by Dylan Thomas and others, Caedmon TC–2005 (audiocassette), CDLS–2005 (CD), 1950.

B: Auden, W. H. *Poems.* Read by the author. Spoken Arts 7137. CD. 1955.

17.8.5 Video Recordings

If you viewed a live performance, a movie, or a television program or other broadcast source on a video recording, cite the recording. Like published works, such recordings generally have stable and available identifying information and should be listed in your bibliography.

Citations of video recordings generally follow the pattern for books, with the addition of the medium (VHS, DVD). Note that in the second example, the citation is to material original to the 2001 edition, so the original release date of the film is omitted.

N: 7. George Frederic Handel, *Messiah,* VHS, Atlanta Symphony Orchestra and Chamber Chorus, conducted by Robert Shaw (Batavia, OH: Video Treasures, 1988).

B: Cleese, John, Terry Gilliam, Eric Idle, Terry Jones, and Michael Palin. "Commentaries." Disc 2. *Monty Python and the Holy Grail,* special ed. DVD. Directed by Terry Gilliam and Terry Jones. Culver City, CA: Columbia TriStar Home Entertainment, 2001.

17.8.6 Online Multimedia Files

If you viewed an image, a live performance, a movie, or a television program or other broadcast source online (including podcasts), cite the online file. Like published works, online multimedia files generally have stable and available identifying information and should be included in your bibliography.

Follow the citation principles for the relevant type of source described above. Some elements, such as file dates, may be difficult to identify, but provide as much information as you can. In addition, list the title of the online site, the type of file, and (in notes, if relevant) the time at which the cited material appears in the file. Include the URL and an access date. Note that a URL alone is not sufficient; you must provide additional information so that a reader can search for the source even if the URL changes. If a file lacks an individual URL (as in the second example below), cite the site as a whole.

N: 12. BBC, "Blair Announces New Africa Panel," BBC News Web site, Windows Media Player video file, 3:43, http://news.bbc.co.uk/nolavconsole/ifs_news/hi/newsid_5110000/newsid_5119200/nb_wm_5119262.stm (accessed June 27, 2006).

18. Wolfgang Amadeus Mozart, "Allegro Moderato," *Piano Sonata no. 10 in C Major* (1778), Kunst der Fuge, MIDI file, 1:02, http://www.kunstderfuge.com/mozart.htm (accessed November 19, 2005).

B: BBC. "Blair Announces New Africa Panel." BBC News Web site. Windows Media Player video file. http://news.bbc.co.uk/nolavconsole/ifs_news/hi/newsid_5110000/newsid_5119200/nb_wm_5119262.stm (accessed June 27, 2006).

Mozart, Wolfgang Amadeus. "Allegro Moderato," *Piano Sonata no. 10 in C Major.* 1778. Kunst der Fuge. MIDI file. http://www.kunstderfuge.com/mozart.htm (accessed November 19, 2005).

17.8.7 Texts in the Visual and Performing Arts

ART EXHIBITION CATALOGS. Cite an art exhibition catalog as you would a book. In the bibliography entry only, include the name and location(s) of the exhibition following the publication data.

N: 6. Judith A. Barter, ed., *Mary Cassatt: Modern Woman* (Chicago: Art Institute of Chicago, in association with Harry N. Abrams, 1998), 5.

B: Barter, Judith A., ed. *Mary Cassatt: Modern Woman.* Chicago: Art Institute of Chicago, in association with Harry N. Abrams, 1998. Published in conjunction with the exhibition "Mary Cassatt: Modern Woman" shown at the Boston Museum of Fine Arts, the National Gallery in Washington, DC, and the Art Institute of Chicago.

PLAYS. In some cases, you can cite well-known English-language plays in notes only. (See also 17.5.1.). Omit publication data, and cite passages by act and scene (or other division) instead of by page number.

N: 22. Eugene O'Neill, *Long Day's Journey into Night,* act 2, scene 1.

If your paper is in literary studies or another field concerned with close analysis of texts, or if you are citing a translation or an obscure work, cite every play as you would a book, and include it in your bibliography. Cite passages either by division or by page, according to your local guidelines.

N: 25. Enid Bagnold, *The Chalk Garden* (New York: Random House, 1953), 8–9.

B: Anouilh, Jean. *Becket, or the Honor of God.* Translated by Lucienne Hill. New York: Riverhead Books, 1996.

MUSICAL SCORES. Cite a published musical score as you would a book.

N: 1. Giuseppe Verdi, *Il corsaro* (*melodramma tragico* in three acts), libretto by Francesco Maria Piave, ed. Elizabeth Hudson, 2 vols., The Works of Giuseppe Verdi, ser. 1, Operas (Chicago: University of Chicago Press; Milan: G. Ricordi, 1998).

B: Mozart, Wolfgang Amadeus. *Sonatas and Fantasies for the Piano.* Prepared from the autographs and earliest printed sources by Nathan Broder. Rev. ed. Bryn Mawr, PA: Theodore Presser, 1960.

Cite an unpublished score as you would unpublished material in manuscript collections.

N: 2. Ralph Shapey, "Partita for Violin and Thirteen Players," score, 1966, Special Collections, Joseph Regenstein Library, University of Chicago.

17.9 Public Documents

Public documents include a wide array of sources produced by governments at all levels throughout the world. This section presents basic principles for some common types of public documents available in English; if you need to cite other types, adapt the closest model.

Such documents involve more complicated and varied elements than published sources. In your citations, include as much identifying information as you can, format the elements consistently, and adapt the general patterns outlined here as needed.

The bulk of this section is concerned with documents published by U.S. governmental bodies and agencies. For documents published by the governments of Canada and the United Kingdom and by international bodies, see 17.9.9–17.9.11. For unpublished government documents, see 17.9.12.

17.9.1 Elements to Include, Their Order, and How to Format Them

In your citations, include as many of the following elements as you can:

- name of the government (country, state, city, county, or other division) and government body (legislative body, executive department, court bureau, board, commission, or committee) that issued the document
- title, if any, of the document or collection (generally italicized)
- name of individual author, editor, or compiler, if given
- report number or other identifying information
- facts of publication: place of publication and publisher's name, if different from the issuing body (for all publications of the U.S. federal government, covered in 17.9.2–17.9.4, use *Washington, DC,* and *Government Printing Office,* respectively); date of publication
- page numbers or other locators, if relevant

In general, list the relevant elements in the order given above. Exceptions for certain types of documents are explained in the following sections of 17.9.

N: 1. Senate Committee on Foreign Relations, *The Mutual Security Act of 1956,* 84th Cong., 2d sess., 1956, S. Rep. 2273, 9–10.

B: U.S. Congress. Senate. Committee on Foreign Relations. *The Mutual Security Act of 1956.* 84th Cong., 2d sess., 1956. S. Rep. 2273.

Note that some shortened forms and abbreviations used in citing public documents are different from those used elsewhere, such as *2d* instead of *2nd* and *3d* instead of *3rd.* Other examples are noted in the relevant sections of 17.9.

17.9.2 Congressional Publications
For congressional publications, bibliography entries usually begin with the designation *U.S. Congress,* followed by *Senate* or *House.* (You may also simplify this to *U.S. Senate* or *U.S. House.*) In notes, *U.S.* is usually omitted. Other common elements include committee and subcommittee, if any; title of document; number of the Congress and session (abbreviated *Cong.* and *sess.* respectively in this position); date of publication; and number and description of the document (for example, H. Doc. 487), if available.

DEBATES. Since 1873, congressional debates have been published by the government in the *Congressional Record* (in notes, often abbreviated as *Cong. Rec.*). Whenever possible, cite the permanent volumes, which often reflect changes from the daily issues of the *Record.*

N: 16. *Cong. Rec.,* 71st Cong., 2d sess., 1930, 72, pt. 10: 10828–30.

B: U.S. Congress. *Congressional Record.* 71st Cong., 2d sess., 1930. Vol. 72, pt. 10.

Occasionally you may need to identify a speaker in a debate, the subject, and a date in a note.

N: 4. Senator Kennedy of Massachusetts, speaking for the Joint Resolution on Nuclear Weapons Freeze and Reductions, on March 10, 1982, to the Committee on Foreign Relations, S.J. Res. 163, 97th Cong., 1st sess., *Cong. Rec.* 128, pt. 3: 3832–34.

Before 1874, congressional debates were published in *Annals of the
Congress of the United States* (also known by other names and covering
the years 1789–1824), *Congressional Debates* (1824–37), and *Congressional
Globe* (1833–73). Cite these works similarly to the *Congressional Record.*

REPORTS AND DOCUMENTS. When you cite reports and documents of the
Senate (abbreviated *S.*) and the House (*H.*), include both the Congress
and session numbers and, if possible, the series number. Notice the form
for a shortened note, which differs from the usual pattern (see 16.4.1).

N: 9. Senate Committee on Foreign Relations, *The Mutual Security Act of 1956,* 84th
Cong., 2d sess., 1956, S. Rep. 2273, 9–10.
       14. *Declarations of a State of War with Japan, Germany, and Italy,* 77th Cong., 1st
sess., 1941, S. Doc. 148, serial 10575, 2–5.
       15. Senate Committee, *Mutual Security Act,* 9.
       22. *Reorganization of the Federal Judiciary,* 75th Cong., 1st sess., 1937, S. Rep. 711.

B: U.S. Congress. House. *Report of Activities of the National Advisory Council on International Monetary and Financial Problems to March 31, 1947.* 80th Cong., 1st sess.,
1947. H. Doc. 365.

HEARINGS. Records of testimony given before congressional committees
are usually published with titles, which should be included in citations.
List the relevant committee as author. Notice the form for a shortened
note, which differs from the usual pattern (see 16.4.1).

N: 13. House Committee on Banking and Currency, *Bretton Woods Agreements Act:
Hearings on H.R. 3314,* 79th Cong., 1st sess., 1945, 12–14.
       14. House Committee, *Bretton Woods,* 13.

B: U.S. Congress. Senate. Committee on Foreign Relations. *Famine in Africa: Hearing before the Committee on Foreign Relations.* 99th Cong., 1st sess., January 17, 1985.

BILLS AND RESOLUTIONS. Congressional bills (proposed laws) and resolutions are published in pamphlet form. In citations, bills and resolutions
originating in the House of Representatives are abbreviated *HR* and those
originating in the Senate, *S.* Include publication details in the *Congressional Record* (if available).

N: 16. *Food Security Act of 1985*, HR 2100, 99th Cong., 1st sess., *Congressional Record* 131, no. 132, daily ed. (October 8, 1985): H 8461.

B: U.S. Congress. House. *Food Security Act of 1985*. HR 2100. 99th Cong., 1st sess. *Congressional Record* 131, no. 132, daily ed. (October 8, 1985): H 8353–8486.

STATUTES. Statutes, which are bills or resolutions that have been passed into law, are first published separately and then collected in the annual bound volumes of the *United States Statutes at Large,* which began publication in 1874. Later they are incorporated into the *United States Code.* Cite *U.S. Statutes,* the *U.S. Code,* or both; cite specific provisions by section (preceded by a section symbol and a space) and, in *Statutes,* by page.

Cite statutes in notes only; you do not need to include them in your bibliography. Notice the form for a shortened note, which differs from the usual pattern (see 16.4.1).

N: 18. *Atomic Energy Act of 1946,* Public Law 585, 79th Cong., 2d sess. (August 1, 1946), 12, 19.
      19. *Telecommunications Act of 1996,* Public Law 104–104, *U.S. Statutes at Large* 110 (1996): 56.
      25. *National Environmental Policy Act of 1969,* Public Law 91–190, § 102, *U.S. Statutes at Large* 83 (1970): 853, codified at *U.S. Code* 42 (2000), § 4332.
      27. *National Environmental Policy Act,* § 103.

Before 1874, laws were published in the seventeen-volume *Statutes at Large of the United States of America, 1789–1873.* Citations to this collection include the volume number and its publication date.

17.9.3 Presidential Publications

Presidential proclamations, executive orders, vetoes, addresses, and the like are published in the *Weekly Compilation of Presidential Documents* and in *Public Papers of the Presidents of the United States.* Proclamations and executive orders are also carried in the daily *Federal Register* and then published in title 3 of the *Code of Federal Regulations.* Once they have been published in the *Code,* use that as your source.

N: 2. President, Proclamation, "Caribbean Basin Economic Recovery Act, Proclamation 5142, Amending Proclamation 5133," *Federal Register* 49, no. 2 (January 4, 1984): 341.
      21. Executive Order no. 11,609, *Code of Federal Regulations,* title 3, p. 586 (1971–75).

B: U.S. President. Proclamation. "Caribbean Basin Economic Recovery Act, Proclamation 5142, Amending Proclamation 5133." *Federal Register* 49, no. 2 (January 4, 1984): 341.

The public papers of U.S. presidents are collected in two multivolume works: *Compilation of the Messages and Papers of the Presidents, 1789–1897*, and, for subsequent administrations, *Public Papers of the Presidents of the United States*. Notice the form for a shortened note, which differs from the usual pattern (see 16.4.1).

N: 27. *House Miscellaneous Document no. 210*, 53d Cong., 2d sess., in *Compilation of the Messages and Papers of the Presidents, 1789–1897*, ed. J. D. Richardson (Washington, DC: Government Printing Office, 1907], 4:16.
       32. *House Misc. Doc. no. 210*, 17.

B: Hoover, Herbert. *Public Papers of the Presidents of the United States: Herbert Hoover, 1929–33.* 4 vols. Washington, DC: Government Printing Office, 1974–77.

17.9.4   Publications of Government Departments and Agencies

Executive departments, bureaus, and agencies issue reports, bulletins, circulars, and other materials. Include the name of an identified author after the title.

N: 30. U.S. Department of the Treasury, *Report of the Secretary of the Treasury Transmitting a Report from the Register of the Treasury of the Commerce and Navigation of the United States for the Year Ending the 30th of June, 1850*, 31st Cong., 2d sess., House Executive Document 8 (Washington, DC, 1850–51).

B: U.S. Department of the Interior. Minerals Management Service. *An Oilspill Risk Analysis for the Central Gulf (April 1984) and Western Gulf of Mexico (July 1984)*, by Robert P. LaBelle. Open-file report, U.S. Geological Survey. Denver, 1984.

      U.S. Bureau of the Census. *Median Gross Rent by Counties of the United States, 1970.* Prepared by the Geography Division in cooperation with the Housing Division, Bureau of the Census. Washington, DC: Government Printing Office, 1975.

Cite bulletins, circulars, reports, and study papers issued by government commissions such as the Federal Communications Commission or the Securities and Exchange Commission much like legislative reports. They are often classified as House (*H*) or Senate (*S*) documents.

N: 32. Senate, *Report of the Federal Trade Commission on Utility Corporations*, 70th Cong., 1st sess., 1935, S. Doc. 91, pt. 71A.

B: U.S. Securities and Exchange Commission. *Annual Report of the Securities and Exchange Commission for the Fiscal Year.* Washington, DC: Government Printing Office, 1983.

17.9.5   U.S. Constitution

The U.S. Constitution should be cited only in notes; you need not include it in your bibliography. Include the article or amendment, section, and, if relevant, clause. Use arabic numerals and, if you prefer, abbreviations for terms such as *amendment* and *section*.

N: 32. U.S. Constitution, art. 2, sec. 1, cl. 3.
      33. U.S. Constitution, amend. 14, sec. 2.

In many cases, you can use a parenthetical note (see 16.4.3) or even include the identifying information in your text. Spell out the names of parts in text. Capitalize the names of specific amendments when used in place of numbers.

The U.S. Constitution, in article 1, section 9, forbids suspension of the writ "unless when in Cases of Rebellion or Invasion the public Safety may require it."

The First Amendment protects the right of free speech.

17.9.6 Treaties

The texts of treaties signed before 1949 are published in *United States Statutes at Large;* the unofficial citation is to the *Treaty Series* or the *Executive Agreement Series.* Those signed in 1949 or later appear in *United States Treaties and Other International Agreements (UST,* 1950–), or *Treaties and Other International Acts Series (TIAS,* 1946–). Treaties involving more than two nations may be found in the United Nations *Treaty Series: Treaties and International Agreements Registered or Filed or Recorded with the Secretariat of the United Nations* or, from 1920 to 1946, in the League of Nations *Treaty Series.*

Put titles of treaties in roman type, enclosed in quotation marks. Italicize the names of the publications, even if they are multivolume works or series. An exact date indicates the date of signing and is therefore preferable to a year alone, which may differ from the year the treaty was published. Notice the form for a shortened note, which differs from the usual pattern (see 16.4.1).

N: 4. "Nuclear Weapons Test Ban," August 5, 1963, *United States Treaties and Other International Agreements* 14, pt. 2.
      15. "Denmark and Italy: Convention concerning Military Service," July 15, 1954, *Treaties and Other International Acts Series* 250, no. 3516 (1956): 45.
      39. "Nuclear Weapons Test Ban."

B: United States. "Naval Armament Limitation Treaty." February 26, 1922. *U.S. Statutes at Large* 43, pt. 2 (1922).

17.9.7 Legal Cases

Citations of legal cases generally take the same form for courts at all levels. In notes, give the full case name (including the abbreviation *v.*) in roman type, not enclosed in parentheses. Include the volume number (arabic), name of the reporter (abbreviated; see below), ordinal series number (if applicable), abbreviated name of the court and date (together in parentheses), and other relevant information, such as the publisher for a loose-leaf service or the name of a state or local court (if not identified by the series title). A single page number designates the opening page of a decision; an additional number designates an actual page cited.

Cite statutes in notes only; you do not need to include them in your bibliography.

N: 18. United States v. Christmas, 222 F.3d 141, 145 (4th Cir. 2000).
       21. Profit Sharing Plan v. MBank Dallas, N.A., 683 F. Supp. 592 (N.D. Tex. 1988).

A shortened note may consist of the case name and, if needed, a page number.

N: 35. United States v. Christmas, 146.
       42. Georgia v. Brailsford, 2.

The one element that depends on the level of the court is the name of the reporter. The most common ones are as follows.

- *U.S. Supreme Court.* For Supreme Court decisions, cite *United States Supreme Court Reports* (abbreviated *U.S.*) or, if not yet published there, *Supreme Court Reporter* (abbreviated *S. Ct.*).

N: 21. AT&T Corp. v. Iowa Utilities Bd., 525 U.S. 366 (1999).
       39. Arthur Andersen LLP v. United States. 125 S. Ct. 2129 (2005).

- *Lower federal courts.* For lower federal-court decisions, cite *Federal Reporter* (F.) or *Federal Supplement* (F. Supp.).

N: 3. United States v. Dennis, 183 F. 201 (2d Cir. 1950).
       15. Eaton v. IBM Corp., 925 F. Supp. 487 (S.D. Tex. 1996).

- *State and local courts.* For state and local court decisions, cite official state reporters whenever possible. If you use a commercial reporter, cite it as in the second example below. If the reporter does not identify the court's name, include it before the date, within the parentheses.

N: 6. Williams v. Davis, 27 Cal. 2d 746 (1946).
       8. Bivens v. Mobley, 724 So. 2d 458, 465 (Miss. Ct. App. 1998).

17.9.8 State and Local Government Documents

Cite state and local government documents as you would federal documents. Use roman type (no quotation marks) for state laws and municipal ordinances; use italics for codes (compilations). Include a name where necessary to indicate the version of the code being cited, followed by the date of the code edition, in parentheses.

N: 39. Illinois General Assembly, Law Revision Commission, *Report to the 80th General Assembly of the State of Illinois* (Chicago, 1977), 14–18.

     41. New Mexico Constitution, art. 4, sec. 7.

     44. *Ohio Revised Code Annotated,* sec. 3599.01 (West 2000).

     52. Methamphetamine Control and Community Protection Act, *Illinois Compiled Statutes,* ch. 720, sec. 646/10 (2005).

B: Illinois Institute for Environmental Quality (IIEQ). *Review and Synopsis of Public Participation regarding Sulfur Dioxide and Particulate Emissions,* by Sidney M. Marder. IIEQ Document no. 77/21. Chicago, 1977.

17.9.9   Canadian Government Documents

Cite Canadian government documents similarly to U.S. public documents. Begin citations with the word *Canada* unless it is obvious from the context. Generally abbreviate *chapter* and *section* as *c.* and *s.,* but if you cite only a few Canadian documents, use *chap.* and *sec.*

Canadian government documents are issued by both houses of the federal Parliament (the Senate and the House of Commons), by the provincial and territorial legislatures, and by various executive departments.

Parliamentary debates are published in separate series, *House of Commons Debates* and *Senate Debates.* Include the name of the person speaking, where relevant. Provincial and territorial legislatures publish their own debates.

N: 2. Canada, *House of Commons Debates* (June 3, 2000), p. 7904 (Mrs. Lalonde, MP).

B: Canada. Manitoba. Legislative Assembly. *Debates and Proceedings.* August 17, 2000.

Cite parliamentary bills by bill number, title, session number, Parliament number, year, and additional information as needed.

N: 3. Bill C-40 , *Extradition Act,* 2d sess., 36th Parliament, 1998, cl. 1 (assented to June 17, 1999), *Statutes of Canada* 1999, c. 18.

Canadian statutes are first published in the annual *Statutes of Canada* and were most recently consolidated in 1985 in the *Revised Statutes of Canada.* Wherever possible, use the latter source and identify the statute by title, reporter, year of compilation, chapter, and section.

N: 4. *Canada Wildlife Act, Revised Statutes of Canada* 1985, c. W-9, s. 1.

     5. *Assisted Human Reproduction Act, Statutes of Canada* 2004, c. 2, s. 2.

17.9.10 British Government Documents

Cite British government documents similarly to U.S. public documents. Begin citations with the phrase *United Kingdom* unless it is obvious from the context. The publisher of most British government material is Her (or His) Majesty's Stationery Office (HMSO) in London.

Parliamentary debates have been published in several series and, since 1909, in separate series for the House of Lords and the House of Commons. Citations include series, volume number, date, and (if relevant) column or occasionally page number. In some cases, you may cite a specific document within a volume. Notice the form for a shortened note, which differs from the usual pattern (see 16.4.1).

N: 1. *Hansard Parliamentary Debates,* 3d ser., vol. 249 [1879], cols. 611–27.

5. *Hansard,* 3d ser., vol. 249, col. 628.

21. Churchill, Speech to the House of Commons, January 18, 1945, *Parliamentary Debates,* Commons, 5th ser., vol. 407 (1944–45), cols. 425–46.

B: United Kingdom. *Hansard Parliamentary Debates,* 3d ser., vol. 249 [1879].

Churchill, Winston. Speech to the House of Commons, January 18, 1945. *Parliamentary Debates,* Commons, 5th ser., vol. 407 (1944–45), cols. 425–46.

The bills, reports, and papers issued separately by Parliament are published together at the end of each session in volumes referred to as *Sessional Papers.* Each volume includes a divisional title.

N: 8. House of Commons, "Present and Future Role of the Assistant Chief Education Officer," *Sessional Papers, 1982–83, Prison Education,* April 25, 1983, vol. 2, par. 9.14, p. 102.

B: United Kingdom. House of Commons. "Present and Future Role of the Assistant Chief Education Officer." *Sessional Papers, 1982–83, Prison Education,* April 25, 1983, vol. 2, par. 9.14, p. 102.

Acts of Parliament should usually be cited only in a note. You generally need not include them in your bibliography, although you may choose to include a specific act that is critical to your argument or frequently cited. Identify acts by title (in roman type, not enclosed in quotation marks), date, and chapter number (*c.* for chapter; arabic numeral for national number, lowercase roman for local). Acts from before 1963 are cited by regnal year and monarch's name (abbreviated) and ordinal (arabic numeral).

N: 8. Act of Settlement, 1701, 12 & 13 Will. 3, c. 2.

15. Consolidated Fund Act, 1963, c. 1.

16. Manchester Corporation Act, 1967, c. xl.

There are many compilations of British historical records, some of them transcriptions of the documents preserved in the Public Record Office. In notes, use abbreviations for frequently cited items.

N: 19. *Rot. parl.,* vol. 2 (1341) (n.p., n.d.).

B: United Kingdom. *Acts of the Privy Council of England.* Edited by J. R. Dasent. 32 vols. London, 1890–1907.
United Kingdom. *Rotuli parliamentorum . . .* (1278–1504). 6 vols. N.p., n.d.
United Kingdom. *Statutes of the Realm.* Edited by A. Luders and others. 11 vols. London, 1810–28.

17.9.11 Publications of International Bodies

If you cite documents of international bodies such as the United Nations, identify the authorizing body (and the author or editor where appropriate), the topic or title of the document, and the date. Also include series and publication numbers, place of publication, and a page reference. You may use abbreviations in both notes and bibliography entries for major bodies (*UN* for *United Nations, WTO* for *World Trade Organization,* and so forth) where the reference is clear.

N: 1. League of Nations, *Position of Women of Russian Origin in the Far East,* ser. LoNP (Geneva, 1935), IV.3.
3. UN General Assembly, Ninth Session, Official Records, Supplement 19, *Special United Nations Fund for Economic Development: Final Report,* prepared by Raymond Scheyven in pursuance of UN General Assembly Resolution 724B (VIII), A/2728, 1954.

B: General Agreement on Tariffs and Trade. *The Results of the Uruguay Round of Multilateral Trade Negotiations: The Legal Texts.* Geneva: GATT Secretariat, 1994.
World Trade Organization. *International Trade: Trends and Statistics.* Geneva: WTO, 1995.

17.9.12 Unpublished Government Documents

If you cite unpublished government documents, follow the patterns described in 17.6.4.

Most unpublished documents of the U.S. government are housed in the National Archives (NA) in Washington, DC, or in one of its branches. Cite them all, including films, photographs, and sound recordings as well as written materials, by record group (RG) number.

The comparable institution for unpublished Canadian government documents is the National Archives of Canada (NAC), in Ottawa, Ontario. The United Kingdom has a number of depositories of unpublished government documents, most notably the Public Record Office (PRO) and the British Library (BL), both in London.

17.9.13 Online Public Documents

To cite online public documents, follow the relevant examples presented elsewhere in 17.9. In addition, include the URL and the date you accessed the material (see 15.4.1). Note that a URL alone is not sufficient; you must provide the full facts of publication, as far as they can be determined, so that a reader can search for the source if the URL changes. If page numbers are not available, you may identify the location of a cited passage in a note by adding a descriptive locator (such as a preceding subheading) following the word *under* before the URL and access date.

N: 39. U.S. Bureau of the Census, "Income, Poverty, and Health Insurance Coverage in the United States, 2004," under "Ratio of Income to Poverty Level," http://www.census.gov/prod/2005pubs/p60–229.pdf (accessed December 19, 2005).

B: U.S. Bureau of the Census. "Income, Poverty, and Health Insurance Coverage in the United States, 2004." http://www.census.gov/prod/2005pubs/p60–229.pdf (accessed December 19, 2005).

17.10 One Source Quoted in Another

Responsible researchers avoid repeating quotations that they have not actually seen in the original. If one source includes a useful quotation from another source, readers expect you to obtain the original to verify not only that the quotation is accurate, but also that it fairly represents what the original meant.

If the original source is unavailable, however, cite it as "quoted in" the secondary source in your note. For the bibliography entry, adapt the "quoted in" format as needed.

N: 8. Louis Zukofsky, "Sincerity and Objectification," *Poetry* 37 (February 1931): 269, quoted in Bonnie Costello, *Marianne Moore: Imaginary Possessions* (Cambridge, MA: Harvard University Press, 1981), 78.

B: Zukofsky, Louis. "Sincerity and Objectification." *Poetry* 37 (February 1931): 269. Quoted in Bonnie Costello, *Marianne Moore: Imaginary Possessions*. Cambridge, MA: Harvard University Press, 1981.

The same situation may arise with a quotation you find in a secondary source drawn from a primary source (see 3.1.1). Often, you will not be able to consult the primary source, especially if it is in an unpublished manuscript collection. In this case, follow the principles outlined above.

18 Parenthetical Citations–Reference List Style: The Basic Form

A citation style used widely in most social sciences and in the natural and physical sciences is the *parenthetical citations–reference list style,* or *reference list style* for short. It is also known as *author-date style,* because the author's name and the date of publication are the critical elements for identifying sources. This chapter presents an overview of the basic pattern for citations in reference list style, including both reference list entries and parenthetical citations. Examples of parenthetical citations are identified with a P; examples of reference list entries are identified with an R.

In reference list style, you signal that you have used a source by placing a *parenthetical citation* (including author, date, and relevant page numbers) next to your reference to that source:

According to one scholar, "The railroads had made Chicago the most important meeting place between East and West" (Cronon 1991, 92–93).

At the end of the paper, you list all sources in a *reference list.* That list normally includes every source you cited in a parenthetical citation and sometimes others you consulted but did not cite. Since parenthetical citations do not include complete bibliographical information for a source, you must include that information in your reference list. All reference list entries have the same general form:

R: Cronon, William. 1991. *Nature's metropolis: Chicago and the Great West.* New York: W. W. Norton & Company.

Readers expect you to follow the rules for correct citations exactly. These rules cover not only what data you must include and their order, but also punctuation, capitalization, italicizing, and so on. To get your citations right, you must pay close attention to many minute details that few researchers can easily remember. The next chapter provides a ready reference guide to those details.

18.1 Basic Patterns

Although sources and their citations come in almost endless variety, you are likely to use only a few kinds. While you may need to look up details to cite some unusual sources, you can easily learn the basic patterns for the few kinds you will use most often. You can then create templates that will help you record bibliographical data quickly and reliably as you read.

The rest of this section describes the basic patterns, and figure 18.1 provides templates for examples of several common types of sources. Chapter 19 includes examples of a wide range of sources, including exceptions to the patterns discussed here.

18.1.1 Order of Elements

The order of elements in reference list entries follows the same general pattern for all types of sources: author, date (year) of publication, title, other facts of publication. Parenthetical citations include only the first two of these elements. If they cite specific passages, they also include page numbers or other locating information; reference list entries do not, though they do include a full span of page numbers for a source that is part of a larger whole, such as an article or a chapter.

18.1.2 Punctuation

In reference list entries, separate most elements with periods; in parenthetical citations, do not use a punctuation mark between the author and the date, but separate the date from a page number with a comma.

18.1.3 Capitalization

Capitalize most titles sentence style, but capitalize the titles of journals, magazines, and newspapers headline style. (See 22.3.1 for both styles.)

Figure 18.1. Templates for reference list entries and parenthetical citations

The following templates show what elements should be included in what order when citing several common types of sources in reference lists (R) and parenthetical citations (P). They also show punctuation, capitalization of titles, and typography of the elements. Gray shading shows abbreviations and other terms as they would actually appear in a citation. *XX* stands in for page numbers actually cited, *YY* for a full span of page numbers for an article or a chapter.

    For further examples, explanations, and variations, see chapter 19.

Books

1. Single Author or Editor

R: Author's Last Name, Author's First Name. Date of Publication. *Title of book: Subtitle of book.* Place of Publication: Publisher's Name.

    Diamond, Jared. 1997. *Guns, germs, and steel: The fates of human societies.* New York: W. W. Norton and Company.

P: (Author's Last Name Date of Publication, XX–XX)

    (Diamond 1997, 47–48)

For a book with an editor instead of an author, adapt the pattern as follows:

R: Editor's Last Name, Editor's First Name, ed. Date of Publication . . .

    Noll, Mark A., ed. 1990 . . .

P: (Editor's Last Name Date of Publication, XX–XX)

    (Noll 1990, 75–80)

2. Multiple Authors

For a book with two authors, use the following pattern:

R: Author #1's Last Name, Author #1's First Name, and Author #2's First and Last Names. Date of Publication. *Title of book: Subtitle of book.* Place of Publication: Publisher's Name.

    Bird, Kai, and Martin J. Sherwin. 2005. *American Prometheus: The triumph and tragedy of J. Robert Oppenheimer.* New York: Alfred A. Knopf.

P: (Author #1's Last Name and Author #2's Last Name Date of Publication, XX–XX)

    (Bird and Sherwin 2005, 52)

For a book with three authors, adapt the pattern as follows:

R: Author #1's Last Name, Author #1's First Name, Author #2's First and Last Names, and Author #3's First and Last Names. Date of Publication . . .

    Appleby, Joyce, Lynn Hunt, and Margaret Jacob. 1994 . . .

P: (Author #1's Last Name, Author #2's Last Name, ▨▨▨ Author #3's Last Name Date of Publication, XX–XX)

(Appleby, Hunt, and Jacob 1994, 135–36)

For a book with four or more authors, adapt the parenthetical citation pattern only as follows:

P: (Author #1's Last Name ▨▨▨ Date of Publication, XX–XX)

(Hall et al. 1987, 114–15)

3. Author(s) Plus Editor or Translator

For a book with an author plus an editor, use the following pattern:

R: Author's Last Name, Author's First Name. Date of Publication. *Title of book: Subtitle of book.* ▨▨▨ Editor's First and Last Names. Place of Publication: Publisher's Name.

Harley, J. B. 2002. *The new nature of maps: Essays in the history of cartography.* Ed. Paul Laxton. Baltimore: Johns Hopkins University Press.

P: (Author's Last Name Date of Publication, XX–XX)

(Harley 2002, 132–33)

If a book has a translator instead of an editor, substitute the word *Trans.* and the translator's name for the editor data in the reference list entry.

4. Edition Number

R: Author's Last Name, Author's First Name. Date of Publication. *Title of book: Subtitle of book.* Edition Number ▨▨▨ Place of Publication: Publisher's Name.

Daniels, Roger. 2002. *Coming to America: A history of immigration and ethnicity in American life.* 2nd ed. New York: Harper Perennial.

P: (Author's Last Name Date of Publication, XX–XX)

(Daniels 2002, 84)

5. Single Chapter in an Edited Book

R: Chapter Author's Last Name, Chapter Author's First Name. Date of Publication. Title of chapter: Subtitle of chapter. ▨▨▨ *Title of book: Subtitle of book,* ▨▨▨ Editor's First and Last Names, YY–YY. Place of Publication: Publisher's Name.

Spirn, Anne Whiston. 1996. Constructing nature: The legacy of Frederick Law Olmsted. In *Uncommon ground: Rethinking the human place in nature,* ed. William Cronon, 91–113. New York: W. W. Norton and Company.

P: (Chapter Author's Last Name Date of Publication, XX–XX)

(Spirn 1996, 101)

Figure 18.1. Templates for reference list entries and parenthetical citations *(continued)*

Journal Articles

6. Journal Article in Print

R: Author's Last Name, Author's First Name. Date of Publication. Title of article: Subtitle of article. *Title of Journal* Volume Number (Additional Date Information): YY–YY.

Nayar, Pramod K. 2005. Marvelous excesses: English travel writing and India, 1680–1727. *Journal of British Studies* 44, no. 2 (April): 213–38.

P: (Author's Last Name Date of Publication, XX–XX)

[Nayar 2005, 213]

For an article with multiple authors, follow the relevant pattern for authors' names in template 2.

7. Journal Article Online

R: Author's Last Name, Author's First Name. Date of Publication. Title of article: Subtitle of article. *Title of Journal* Volume Number (Additional Date Information). URL (accessed Date of Access).

McFarland, Daniel A. 2004. Resistance as a social drama: A study of change-oriented encounters. *American Journal of Sociology* 109, no. 6 (May). http://www.journals.uchicago.edu/AJS/journal/issues/v109n6/050199/050199.html [accessed May 3, 2006].

P: (Author's Last Name Date of Publication)

[McFarland 2004]

Capitalize proper nouns in the usual way (see chapter 22). In some fields, you may use headline-style capitalization throughout the reference list; check your local guidelines.

18.1.4 Typography of Titles

Titles of larger entities (books, journals) are printed in italics; titles of smaller entities (chapters, articles) are printed in roman type and not enclosed in quotation marks. Titles of unpublished works (such as dissertations) are printed in roman type and not enclosed in quotation marks, even if they are book length.

18.1.5 Numbers

In titles, numbers are spelled out or given in numerals exactly as they are in the original. Page numbers that are in roman numerals in the original are presented in lowercase roman numerals. All other numbers (such as chapter numbers or figure numbers) are given in arabic numerals, even if they are in roman numerals or spelled out in the original.

18.1.6 Abbreviations

Abbreviate terms such as *editor, translator,* and *volume* (*ed., trans.,* and *vol.*). The plural is usually formed by adding *s* (*eds.*) unless the abbreviation ends in an *s* (use *trans.* for both singular and plural). Your local guidelines may allow you to use additional abbreviations such as *Univ.* for *University.*

18.1.7 Indentation

Reference list entries have a hanging indentation: the first line is flush left and all following lines are indented the same space as paragraphs. Parenthetical citations are placed within the text and are not indented.

18.2 Reference Lists

In papers that use parenthetical citations–reference list style, the reference list presents full bibliographical information for all the sources cited in parenthetical citations (other than a few special types of sources; see 18.2.2). You may also include works that were important to your thinking but that you did not specifically mention in the text. In addition to providing bibliographical information, reference lists show readers the extent of your research and its relationship to prior work, and they help readers use your sources in their own research. If you use this citation style, you must include a reference list in your paper.

Label the list *References.* See figure A.16 in the appendix for a sample page of a reference list.

18.2.1 Arrangement of Entries

ALPHABETICAL AND CHRONOLOGICAL BY AUTHOR. A reference list is normally a single list of all sources arranged alphabetically by the last name of the author, editor, or whoever is first in each entry. (For alphabetizing foreign names, compound names, and other special cases, see 19.1.1.) Most word processors provide an alphabetical sorting function; if you use it, be sure each entry is followed by a hard return. If you are writing a thesis or dissertation, your department or university may specify that you should alphabetize the entries letter by letter or word by word; see 18.56–59 of the *Chicago Manual of Style,* 15th edition (2003), for an explanation of these two systems.

If your reference list includes two or more works written, edited, or translated by the same individual, arrange the entries chronologically by publication date. For all entries after the first, replace the individual's name with a long dash called a 3-em dash (see 21.7.3). For edited or translated works, put a comma and the appropriate designation (*ed., trans.,* and so on) after the dash. List all such works before any that the individual coauthored or coedited.

R: Gates, Henry Louis Jr. 1989. *The signifying monkey: A theory of African-American liter-ary criticism.* New York: Oxford University Press.
———, ed. 2002. *The classic slave narratives.* New York: Penguin Putnam.
———. 2004. *America behind the color line: Dialogues with African Americans.* New York: Warner Books.
Gates, Henry Louis Jr., and Cornel West. 2000. *The African American century: How black Americans have shaped our country.* New York: Free Press.

The same principles apply to works by a single group of authors named in the same order.

R: Marty, Martin E., and R. Scott Appleby. 1992. *The glory and the power: The fundamen-talist challenge to the modern world.* Boston: Beacon Press.
———, eds. 2004. *Accounting for fundamentalisms.* Chicago: University of Chicago Press.
Marty, Martin E., and Micah Marty. 1998. *When true simplicity is gained: Finding spiri-tual clarity in a complex world.* Grand Rapids, MI: William B. Eerdmans Publishing Company.

If your reference list includes more than one work published in the same year by an author or group of authors named in the same order, arrange the entries alphabetically by title (ignoring articles such as *a* or *the*). Add the letters *a, b, c,* and so forth to the year, set in roman type without an intervening space. Your parenthetical citations to these works should include the letters (see 18.3.2).

R: Davis, Natalie Zemon. 1983a. Beyond the market: Books as gifts in sixteenth-century France. *Transactions of the Royal Historical Society* 33: 69–88.
———. 1983b. *The return of Martin Guerre.* Cambridge, MA: Harvard University Press.

If a book or journal article does not have an author or editor (or other named compiler, such as a translator), put the title first in your reference list entry and alphabetize based on it, ignoring articles such as *a* or *the*.

R: *Account of the operations of the Great Trigonometrical Survey of India.* 1870–1910. 22 vols. Dehra Dun: Survey of India.
The Great Trigonometrical Survey of India. 1863. *The Calcutta Review* 38: 26–62.
State and prospects of Asia. 1839. *The Quarterly Review* 63, no. 126 (March): 369–402.

For magazine and newspaper articles without authors, use the title of the magazine or newspaper in place of the author (see 19.3 and 19.4). For other types of sources, see the relevant section in chapter 19 for guidance; if not stated otherwise, use a title in this position.

CATEGORIZED LISTINGS. Because readers following a parenthetical citation will have only an author and a date to help them identify the relevant reference list entry, organize the list as described above except in rare cases. Under the following circumstances, you may consider dividing the list into separate categories:

- If you have more than three or four entries for a special type of source, such as manuscripts, archival collections, recordings, and so on, list them separately from the rest of your entries.
- If it is critical to distinguish primary sources from secondary and tertiary ones, list the entries in separate sections.

If you categorize sources, introduce each separate section with a subheading and, if necessary, a headnote. Order the entries within each section according to the principles described above, and do not list a source in more than one section unless it clearly could be categorized in two or more ways.

18.2.2 Sources That May Be Omitted

By convention, you may omit the following types of sources from a reference list:

- classical, medieval, and early English literary works (19.5.1) and (in some cases) well-known English-language plays (19.8.7)
- the Bible and other sacred works (19.5.2)
- well-known reference works, such as major dictionaries and encyclopedias (19.5.3)
- anonymous unpublished interviews and personal communications (19.6.3), individual Weblog entries and comments (19.7.2), and postings to electronic mailing lists (19.7.3)
- many sources in the visual and performing arts, including artworks and other visual sources (19.8.1), live performances (19.8.2), and television and other broadcast programs (19.8.3)
- the U.S. Constitution (19.9.5) and some other public documents (19.9)

You may choose to include in your reference list a specific work from one of these categories that is critical to your argument or frequently cited.

18.3 Parenthetical Citations

Parenthetical citations include enough information for readers to find the full citation in your reference list—usually the author's name, the date of publication, and (if you are citing a specific passage), a page number or other locating information. The name and date must match those in the relevant reference list entry exactly. (Note that both the elements and the punctuation in parenthetical citations are slightly different from those used in bibliography-style parenthetical notes, which are described in 16.4.3; do not confuse or combine the two styles.)

18.3.1 Placement in Text

Whenever you refer to or otherwise use material from a source, you must insert into your text a parenthetical citation with basic identifying information about that source. For a quotation, put the parenthetical citation immediately following, whether the quotation is run into the text or set off as a block quotation (see 25.2.2). Otherwise, put parenthetical citations at the end of a sentence or clause. The closing parenthesis precedes a comma, period, or other punctuation mark when the quotation is run into the text.

"What on introspection seems to happen immediately and without effort is often a complex symphony of processes that take time to complete" (LeDoux 2003, 116).

While one school claims that "material culture may be the most objective source of information we have concerning America's past" (Deetz 1996, 259), others disagree.

The color blue became more prominent in the eighteenth century (Pastoureau 2001, 124).

With a block quotation, however, the parenthetical citation follows the terminal punctuation mark.

He concludes with the following observation:

> The new society that I sought to depict and that I wish to judge is only being born. Time has not yet fixed its form; the great revolution that created it still endures, and in what is happening in our day it is almost impossible to discern what will pass away with the revolution itself and what will remain after it. (Tocqueville 2000, 673)

See figure A.11 for a sample page of text with parenthetical citations.

18.3.2 Special Elements and Format Issues

The basic pattern for parenthetical citations is described in 18.1, and templates for several common types of sources appear in figure 18.1. This section covers special elements that may need to be included and special format issues that may arise in parenthetical citations of all types.

In the following situations, treat the name of an editor, translator, or other compiler of a work as you would an author's name, unless otherwise specified.

AUTHORS WITH SAME LAST NAME. If you cite works by more than one author with the same last name, add the author's first initial to each parenthetical citation, even if the dates are different. If the initials are the same, spell out the first names.

(J. Smith 2001, 140)	(Adele Gottfried 1988, 15)
(T. Smith 1998, 25–26)	(Allen Gottfried 1994, 270)

WORKS WITH SAME AUTHOR AND DATE. If you cite more than one work published in the same year by an author or group of authors named in the same order, arrange the entries alphabetically by title in your reference list and add the letters *a*, *b*, *c*, and so forth to the year (see 18.2.1). Use the same designations in your parenthetical citations (letters set in roman type, without an intervening space after the date).

(Davis 1983a, 74)

(Davis 1983b, 59–60)

NO AUTHOR. If you cite a book or journal article without an author, use the title in place of the author in your reference list (see 18.2.1). In parenthetical citations, use a shortened title composed of up to four distinctive words from the full title, and print the title in italics or roman as in the reference list.

(*Account of operations* 1870–1910)

(Great Trigonometrical Survey 1863, 26)

For magazine and newspaper articles without authors, use the title of the magazine or newspaper in place of the author in both locations (see 19.3 and 19.4). For other types of sources, see the relevant section in chapter 19 for guidance; if not stated otherwise, use a shortened title in this position.

NO DATE. If you cite a published work without a date, use the designation *n.d.* ("no date") in place of the date in both your reference list and parenthetical citations. Use roman type and lowercase letters.

(Smith n.d., 5)

For other types of sources, see the relevant section in chapter 19 for guidance.

AUTHOR MENTIONED IN TEXT. If the author's name is mentioned in the text, you may omit this element from the parenthetical citation. If necessary for clarity, put the remainder of the citation immediately following the author's name, even if it does not come at the end of a sentence or clause.

Chang then describes the occupation of Nanking in great detail (1997, 159–67).

The arguments made by Ariès (1965) have been modified by further research.

MORE THAN ONE WORK CITED. If you cite several sources to make a single point, group them into a single parenthetical citation. List them alphabetically, chronologically, or in order of importance (depending on the context), and separate them with semicolons.

Several theorists disagreed strongly with this position (Armstrong and Malacinski 1989; Pickett and White 1995; Beigl 2004).

18.3.3 Footnotes and Parenthetical Citations

If you wish to make substantive comments on the text, use footnotes instead of parenthetical citations. See 16.3.2–16.3.4 for note placement, numbering, and format. To cite a source within a footnote, use the normal parenthetical citation form.

N: 10. James Wilson has noted that "no politician ever lost votes by denouncing the bureaucracy" (1989, 235).

19 Parenthetical Citations–Reference List Style: Citing Specific Types of Sources

Chapter 18 presents an overview of the basic pattern for citations in the parenthetical citations–reference list style, including both reference list entries and parenthetical citations. If you are not familiar with this citation style, read that chapter before consulting this one.

This chapter provides detailed information on the form of reference list entries (and, to a lesser extent, parenthetical citations) for a wide range of sources. It is organized by type of source. It begins with the most common—books and journal articles—and then addresses other published, unpublished, and recorded sources. The sections on books (19.1) and journal articles (19.2) discuss variations in such elements as authors' names, titles, and URLs in greater depth than sections on less common sources.

Online and other electronic sources that are analogous to print sources (online journal articles, for example) are included under the relevant type of source. Other online sources, considered "informally published" (see 15.4.1), are discussed in 19.7.

Most sections include guidelines and examples for reference list entries (identified with an R). Since most parenthetical citations follow the basic pattern described in chapter 18, they are discussed here (P) only for clarification or if unusual elements might cause confusion in preparing a parenthetical citation (for example, when a work has both an author and an editor).

To cite a type of source that is not covered in this chapter, consult chapter 17 of the *Chicago Manual of Style*, 15th edition (2003). You may also create your own style, adapted from the principles and examples given here. Most instructors, departments, and universities accept such adaptations, as long as you use them consistently.

19.1 Books

Books reflect a wider range of elements than most other types of published sources. Many of the variations in elements discussed in this section are also relevant to other types of sources.

19.1.1 Author's Name

In your reference list, give each author's name exactly as it appears on the title page. If the name includes more than one initial, use spaces between them (see 24.2.1). List authors' names in inverted order (last name first), except for some non-English names and other cases explained in "Special Types of Names" below (p. 233).

R: Ball, Philip. 2001. *Bright earth: Art and the invention of color.* New York: Farrar, Straus and Giroux.

Breen, T. H. 2004. *The marketplace of revolution: How consumer politics shaped American independence.* New York: Oxford University Press.

Elizabeth I. 2000. *Collected works.* Ed. Leah S. Marcus, Janel Mueller, and Mary Beth Rose. Chicago: University of Chicago Press.

In parenthetical citations, use only the author's last name, exactly as given in the reference list. If the author is known by a single name, use it instead of a last name.

P: (Ball 2001, 140)
(Breen 2004, 48)
(Elizabeth I 2000, 102–4)

MULTIPLE AUTHORS. In a reference list entry for a book with more than one author, list the first author's name in inverted order, followed by a comma, and list the rest of the authors in standard order. Use a comma before the *and* in a series of three or more. Include all authors, no matter how many; do not use *et al.*

R: Bird, Kai, and Martin J. Sherwin. 2005. *American Prometheus: The triumph and tragedy of J. Robert Oppenheimer.* New York: Alfred A. Knopf.
Appleby, Joyce, Lynn Hunt, and Margaret Jacob. 1994. *Telling the truth about history.* New York: W. W. Norton & Company.
Hall, Jacquelyn Dowd, James Leloudis, Robert Korstad, Mary Murphy, Lu Ann Jones, and Christopher B. Daly. 1987. *Like a family: The making of a Southern cotton mill world.* Chapel Hill: University of North Carolina Press.

In a parenthetical citation, use the authors' last names, exactly as given in the reference list. If there are four or more authors, list only the first author's name followed by *et al.* (with no intervening comma). Put a period after *al.* (an abbreviation for *alii,* "others") but not after *et* (not an abbreviation; the Latin word for "and").

P: (Bird and Sherwin 2005, 52)
(Appleby, Hunt, and Jacob 1994, 135–36)
(Hall et al. 1987, 114–15)

EDITOR OR TRANSLATOR IN ADDITION TO AN AUTHOR. If a title page lists an editor or a translator in addition to an author, treat the author's name as described above. Add the editor or translator's name after the book's title. If there is a translator as well as an editor, list the names in the same order as on the title page of the original.

In reference list entries, insert the abbreviation *Ed.* (never *Eds.,* because in this context it means "edited by" rather than "editor") or *Trans.* before the editor's or translator's name.

R: Bonnefoy, Yves. 1995. *New and selected poems.* Ed. John Naughton and Anthony Rudolf. Chicago: University of Chicago Press.

Menchú, Rigoberta. 1999. *Crossing borders.* Trans. and ed. Ann Wright. New York: Verso.
Adorno, Theodor W., and Walter Benjamin. 1999. *The complete correspondence, 1928–1940.* Ed. Henri Lonitz. Trans. Nicholas Walker. Cambridge, MA: Harvard University Press.

When a title page identifies an editor or translator with a complicated description, such as "Edited with an Introduction and Notes by" or "Translated with a Foreword by," you can simplify this phrase to *ed.* or *trans.* and follow the above examples. In general, if a foreword or an introduction is written by someone other than the author, you need not mention that person unless you cite that part specifically (see 19.1.9). For cases in which the author's name appears in the book's title and the editor's name appears on the title page instead, see "Additional Authorial Situations" below.

In parenthetical citations, do not include the name of an editor or translator if the work appears in your reference list under the author's name.

P: (Bonnefoy 1995, 35)
(Menchú 1999, 50–51)
(Adorno and Benjamin 1999, 212)

EDITOR OR TRANSLATOR IN PLACE OF AN AUTHOR. When an editor or a translator is listed on a book's title page instead of an author, use that person's name in the author's slot. Treat it as you would an author's name (see above), but in the reference list, add the abbreviation *ed.* (plural, *eds.*) or *trans.* (singular or plural) following the name. If there are multiple editors or translators, follow the principles in "Multiple Authors" (see p. 230, above).

R: Silverstein, Theodore, trans. 1974. *Sir Gawain and the green knight.* Chicago: University of Chicago Press.
Fulop, Timothy E., and Albert J. Raboteau, eds. 1997. *African-American religion: Interpretive essays in history and culture.* New York: Routledge.

P: (Silverstein 1974, 34)
(Fulop and Raboteau 1997, 412–14)

ADDITIONAL AUTHORIAL SITUATIONS. Following are some additional ways authors might be identified in your sources. If you encounter situations not covered here, adapt the pattern that seems most closely related.

■ *Author's name in title.* If an author's name appears in the title or subtitle of a book such as an autobiography, include it in its usual position in a reference list entry (despite the repetition) and also in a parenthetical citation.

Although many such works also have editors, do not list the works under the editor's name except in special cases (for example, in a study of works edited by that individual).

R: Sherman, W. T. 1990. *Memoirs of General W. T. Sherman.* Ed. Charles Royster. New York: Library of America.

McCullers, Carson. 1999. *Illumination and night glare: The unfinished autobiography of Carson McCullers.* Ed. Carlos L. Dews. Madison: University of Wisconsin Press.

P: (Sherman 1990, 836)

(McCullers 1999, 54)

■ *Organization as author.* If a publication issued by an organization, association, commission, or corporation has no personal author's name on the title page, list the organization itself as author, even if it is also given as publisher.

R: World Health Organization. 2003. *Organization of services for mental health.* Geneva: World Health Organization.

P: (World Health Organization 2003, 50)

■ *Pseudonym.* Treat a widely used pseudonym as if it were the author's real name. If the real name is unknown, add *pseud.* in brackets after the pseudonym in a reference list entry, though not in a parenthetical citation.

R: Twain, Mark. 1899. *The prince and the pauper: A tale for young people of all ages.* New York: Harper & Brothers.

Centinel [pseud.]. 1981. Letters. In *The complete anti-Federalist,* ed. Herbert J. Storing. Chicago: University of Chicago Press.

P: (Twain 1899, 34)

(Centinel 1981, 2)

■ *Anonymous author.* If the authorship is known or guessed at but omitted from the book's title page, include the name in brackets (with a question mark to indicate uncertainty). If the author or editor is unknown, avoid the use of *Anonymous* in place of a name and begin the reference list entry with the title. In parenthetical citations, use a shortened title (see 18.3.2).

R: [Cook, Ebenezer?]. 1730. *Sotweed redivivus, or the planter's looking-glass.* Annapolis.

A true and sincere declaration of the purpose and ends of the plantation begun in Virginia, of the degrees which it hath received, and means by which it hath been advanced. 1610.

P: ([Ebenezer Cook?] 1730, 5–6)

(*True and sincere declaration* 1610, 17)

SPECIAL TYPES OF NAMES. Some authors' names consist of more than a readily identifiable "first name" and "last name." For names of well-known historical authors, consult *Merriam-Webster's Biographical Dictionary;* for contemporary authors, consult your library's online catalog. Following are some general principles for alphabetizing such names. In parenthetical citations, use the last name exactly as inverted (shown below in boldface).

- *Compound names.* Alphabetize compound last names, including hyphenated names, by the first part of the compound. If a woman uses both her own family name and her husband's but does not hyphenate them, generally alphabetize by the second name. While many foreign languages have predictable patterns for compound names (see below), others—such as French and German—do not.

Kessler-Harris, Alice	**Mies van der Rohe,** Ludwig
Hine, Darlene Clark	**Teilhard de Chardin,** Pierre

- *Names with particles.* Depending on the language, particles such as *de, di, D',* and *van* may or may not be considered the first part of a last name for alphabetizing. Consult one of the resources noted above if you are unsure about a particular name. Note that particles may be either lowercased or capitalized, and some are followed by an apostrophe.

de Gaulle, Charles	**Beauvoir,** Simone de
di Leonardo, Micaela	**Kooning,** Willem de
Van Rensselaer, Stephen	**Medici,** Lorenzo de'

- *Names beginning with "Mac," "Saint," or "O'."* Names that begin with *Mac, Saint,* or *O'* can have many variations in abbreviations (*Mc, St.*), spelling (*Sainte, San*), capitalization (*Macmillan, McAllister*), and hyphenation or apostrophes (*O'Neill* or *Odell; Saint-Gaudens* or *St. Denis*). Alphabetize all such names based on the letters actually present; do not group them because they are similar.

- *Names in languages other than English.* Naming conventions in many languages are different from those in English. If your paper involves many names from a particular language, study these conventions for the relevant language.

   Many Spanish last names are compound names, consisting of an individual's paternal and maternal family names and usually joined by the conjunction *y.* Alphabetize such names under the first part.

Ortega y Gasset, José	**Sánchez Mendoza,** Juana

Alphabetize Arabic last names that begin with the particle *al-* or *el-* ("the") under the element following the particle. Names that begin with *Abu, Abd,* and *Ibn* are similar to English names beginning with *Mac* or *Saint* and should be alphabetized under these terms.

Hakim, Tawfiq al-	Abu Zafar Nadvi, Syed
Jamal, Muhammad Hamid al-	Ibn Saud, Aziz

If an author with a Chinese or Japanese name follows traditional usage (family name followed by given name), do not invert the name or insert a comma between the "first" and "last" names. If the author follows westernized usage (given name followed by family name), treat the name as you would an English name.

Traditional usage	Westernized usage
Chao Wu-chi	Tsou, Tang
Yoshida Shigeru	Kurosawa, Noriaki

19.1.2   Date of Publication

The publication date for a book consists only of a year, not a month or day, and is usually identical to the copyright date. It generally appears on the copyright page and sometimes on the title page.

In a reference list entry, set off the date as its own element with periods. In a parenthetical citation, put it after the author's name without intervening punctuation.

R: Ginsborg, Paul. 2005. *The politics of everyday life: Making choices, changing lives.* New Haven: Yale University Press.

P: (Ginsborg 2005, 53)

Revised editions and reprints may include more than one copyright date. In this case, the most recent indicates the publication date—for example, 2003 in the string "© 1982, 1992, 2003." See 19.1.4 for citing publication dates in such works.

If you cannot determine the publication date of a printed work, use the abbreviation *n.d.* in place of the year. If no date is provided but you believe you know it, you may add it in brackets, with a question mark to indicate uncertainty.

R: Smith, John. n.d. *A book of virtues.* Edinburgh.
     Miller, Samuel. [1750?]. *Another book of virtues.* Boston.

P: (Smith n.d., 5)
     (Miller [1750?], 5)

If a book is under contract with a publisher and is already titled, but the date of publication is not yet known, use *forthcoming* in place of the date. To avoid confusion, include a comma after the author's name in a parenthetical citation of this type. Treat any book not yet under contract as an unpublished manuscript (see 19.6).

R: Author, Jane Q. Forthcoming. *Book title.* Place of Publication: Publisher's Name.

P: (Author, forthcoming, 16)

19.1.3 Title

List complete book titles and subtitles in reference list entries. Italicize both, and separate the title from the subtitle with a colon. If there are two subtitles, use a colon before the first and a semicolon before the second.

R: Kalicki, Jan H., and David L. Goldwyn, eds. 2005. *Energy and security: Toward a new foreign policy strategy.* Baltimore: Johns Hopkins University Press.
Ahmed, Leila. 1999. *A border passage: From Cairo to America; A woman's journey.* New York: Farrar, Straus & Giroux.

Capitalize all titles and subtitles sentence style; that is, capitalize only the first letter of the first word of the title and subtitle and any proper nouns and proper adjectives thereafter (see 22.3.1). Preserve the spelling, hyphenation, and punctuation of the original title, although you may change an ampersand (&) to *and.* Spell out numbers or give them as numerals according to the original (*twelfth century* or *12th century*) unless there is a good reason to make them consistent with other titles in the list.

For titles of chapters and other parts of a book, see 19.1.9.

SPECIAL ELEMENTS IN TITLES. Several elements in titles require special typography.

■ *Dates.* Use a comma to set off dates in a title or subtitle, even if there is no punctuation in the original source. If the source introduces the dates with a preposition ("from 1920 to 1945") or a colon, follow the usage in the source.

R: McDougall, Walter A. 2004. *Freedom just around the corner: A new American history, 1525–1828.* New York: HarperCollins.
Jellicoe, Geoffrey, and Susan Jellicoe. 1995. *The landscape of man: Shaping the environment from prehistory to the present day.* 3rd ed. New York: Thames & Hudson.

■ *Titles and quotations within titles.* When the title of a work that would normally be italicized appears *within* the italicized title of another, enclose the quoted title in quotation marks. If the title-within-a-title would normally be enclosed in quotation marks, keep the quotation marks. Use sentence-style capitalization (see above) within the quoted titles.

R: Applegate, Celia. 2005. *Bach in Berlin: Nation and culture in Mendelssohn's revival of the "St. Matthew Passion."* Ithaca: Cornell University Press.

McHugh, Roland. 1991. *Annotations to "Finnegans wake."* 2nd ed. Baltimore: Johns Hopkins University Press.

However, when a quotation is used as the entire main title of a book, do not enclose it in quotation marks.

R: Swope, Sam. 2004. *I am a pencil: A teacher, his kids, and their world of stories.* New York: Henry Holt and Company.

Chernoff, John M. 2003. *Hustling is not stealing: Stories of an African bar girl.* Chicago: University of Chicago Press.

- *Italicized terms.* When an italicized title includes terms normally italicized in text, such as species names or names of ships, set the terms in roman type.

R: Pennington, T. Hugh. 2003. *When food kills: BSE,* E. coli, *and disaster science.* New York: Oxford University Press.

Lech, Raymond B. 2001. *The tragic fate of the* U.S.S. Indianapolis: *The U.S. Navy's worst disaster at sea.* New York: Cooper Square Press.

- *Question marks and exclamation points.* When a title or a subtitle ends with a question mark or an exclamation point, no other punctuation follows.

R: Frank, Thomas. 2004. *What's the matter with Kansas? How conservatives won the heart of America.* New York: Metropolitan Books.

Aaron, Henry. 1973. *Why is welfare so hard to reform?* Washington, DC: Brookings Institution Press.

OLDER TITLES. For titles of works published in the eighteenth century or earlier, retain the original punctuation and spelling, but change the capitalization to sentence style (see above). If the title is very long, you may shorten it, giving enough information for readers to find the full title in a library or publisher's catalog. Indicate omissions in such titles by three ellipsis dots within a title. If the omission comes at the end of a title, use four dots (three ellipsis dots and a period; see 25.3.2).

R: Ray, John. 1673. *Observations topographical, moral, and physiological: Made in a journey through part of the Low-Countries, Germany, Italy, and France: with a catalogue of plants not native of England . . . whereunto is added a brief account of Francis Willughby, Esq., his voyage through a great part of Spain.* (London).

Escalante, Bernardino. 1579. *A discourse of the navigation which the Portugales doe make to the realmes and provinces of the east partes of the worlde. . . .* Trans. John Frampton. London.

NON-ENGLISH TITLES. For non-English titles, follow the capitalization principles for proper nouns and adjectives within the relevant language. If you are unfamiliar with these principles, consult a reliable source.

R: Maisonneuve, Danielle, Jean-François Lamarche, and Yves St-Amand. 1998. *Les relations publiques: Dans une société en mouvance.* Sainte-Foy, QC: Presses de l'Université de Québec.

Stojanovic, Ljiljana Piletic, ed. 1971. *Gutfreund i ceski kubizam.* Belgrade: Muzej savremene umetnosti.

Krone-Schmalz, Gabriele. 1992. *In Wahrheit sind wir stärker: Frauenalltag in der Sowjetunion.* Frankfurt am Main: Fischer Taschenbuch Verlag.

If you add the English translation of a title, place it after the original. Enclose it in brackets, without italics or quotation marks.

R: Wereszycki, Henryk. 1977. *Koniec sojuszu trzech cesarzy* [The end of the Three Emperors' League]. Warsaw: PWN.

Zhongguo renkou tongji nianjian 1996 [China population statistics yearbook 1996]. 1996. Beijing: Zhongguo tongji chubanshe.

If you need to cite both the original and a translation, use one of the following forms, depending on whether you want to focus readers on the original or the translation.

R: Furet, François. 1995. *Le passé d'une illusion.* Paris: Éditions Robert Laffont. Trans. Deborah Furet as *The passing of an illusion* (Chicago: University of Chicago Press, 1999).

or

Furet, François. 1999. *The passing of an illusion.* Trans. Deborah Furet. Chicago: University of Chicago Press. Originally published as *Le passé d'une illusion* (Paris: Éditions Robert Laffont, 1995).

19.1.4 Edition

The term *edition* has several meanings, all based on the fact that some works are published more than once with changes in content and/or format. If you cite a book published in more than one edition, always indicate in your reference list which edition you consulted because editions may differ. (If none of the markers described below apply to a book, you can assume it is a first edition, a fact that is not cited.)

REVISED EDITIONS. When a book is reissued with significant content changes, it may be called a "revised" edition or a "second" (or subsequent) edition. This information usually appears on the book's title page and is repeated, along with the date of the edition, on the copyright page.

When you cite an edition other than the first, include the number or description of the edition after the title. Abbreviate such wording as "Second Edition, Revised and Enlarged" as *2nd ed.;* abbreviate "Revised Edition" as *Rev. ed.* Include the publication date only of the edition you are citing, not of any previous editions (see 19.1.2).

R: Daniels, Roger. 2002. *Coming to America: A history of immigration and ethnicity in American life.* 2nd ed. New York: Harper Perennial.
   Babb, Florence. 1989. *Between field and cooking pot: The political economy of market-women in Peru.* Rev. ed. Austin: University of Texas Press.

REPRINT EDITIONS. A book may also be reissued in a new format—for example, in a paperback edition (by the original publisher or a different publisher), or in electronic form (see 19.1.10). Even though the contents of the book might be minimally changed from the original, cite the reprint edition if you consulted it. You may wish to indicate in your reference list that it is a reprint, especially if it was published more than a year or two after the original edition. In this case, treat the date of the reprint as the publication date, and include the date of the original (see 19.1.2) in parentheses in the reference list entry.

R: Fay, Peter Ward. 1997. *The Opium War, 1840–1842.* Chapel Hill: University of North Carolina Press. (Orig. pub. 1975.)

P: (Fay 1997, 67–68)

If the reprint is a modern printing of a classic work, you should still cite the reprint edition, but if the original publication date is important in the context of your paper, include it in brackets before the reprint date in both your reference list and your parenthetical citations.

R: Emerson, Ralph Waldo. 1985. *Nature.* Boston: Beacon. (Orig. pub. 1836.)

P: (Emerson 1985, 10)

   or

R: Emerson, Ralph Waldo. [1836] 1985. *Nature.* Boston: Beacon.

P: (Emerson [1836] 1985, 10)

19.1.5 Volume

If a book is part of a multivolume work, include this information in your citations.

SPECIFIC VOLUME. How you cite a specific volume in a multivolume work depends on whether the volume has a title different from the work as a whole. If so, list the title of the specific volume, followed by both the volume number and the general title. Abbreviate *vol.* and use arabic numbers for volume numbers.

R: Pelikan, Jaroslav. 1989. *Christian doctrine and modern culture (since 1700).* Vol. 5 of *The Christian tradition: A history of the development of doctrine.* Chicago: University of Chicago Press.

If the volumes are not individually titled and you are citing only one of them, add the volume number to the reference list entry. (See below for citing a multivolume work as a whole.) In a parenthetical citation, put the volume number immediately before the page number, separated by a colon and no intervening spaces.

R: Byrne, Muriel St. Clare, ed. 1981. *The Lisle letters.* Vol. 4. Chicago: University of Chicago Press.

P: (Byrne 1981, 4:243)

Some multivolume works have both a general editor and individual editors or authors for each volume. When citing parts of such works, put information about the individual editor or author of the volume (see 19.1.1) after the individual volume title and before the volume number and general title in a reference list entry. This example also shows how to cite a volume published in more than one physical part (*vol. 2, bk. 3*). In a parenthetical citation, list only the author of the part cited.

R: Mundy, Barbara E. 1998. Mesoamerican cartography. In *Cartography in the traditional African, American, Arctic, Australian, and Pacific societies,* ed. David Woodward and G. Malcolm Lewis, vol. 2, bk. 3 of *The history of cartography,* ed. J. Brian Harley and David Woodward, 183–256. Chicago: University of Chicago Press.

P: (Mundy 1998, 233)

MULTIVOLUME WORK AS A WHOLE. If you cite more than one volume of a multivolume work in your parenthetical citations, cite the work as a whole in your reference list. (If the work involves both general and individual volume titles or editors, as described above, it is more precise to cite the volumes individually.) Give the title and the total number of volumes. If the volumes have been published over several years, list the full span of publication dates in both your reference list and your parenthetical citations.

R: Aristotle. 1983. *Complete works of Aristotle: The revised Oxford translation.* Ed. J. Barnes. 2 vols. Princeton, NJ: Princeton University Press.

Tillich, Paul. 1951–63. *Systematic theology.* 3 vols. Chicago: University of Chicago Press.

P: (Tillich 1951–63, 2:41)

19.1.6 Series

If a book cited is part of a formal series, you are not required to include information about the series, but you may include some or all of it to help readers locate or judge the credibility of the source. Insert this information after the title (and, if any, edition and volume information) and before the facts of publication.

The most useful information about a series is its title. Present it in roman type with headline-style capitalization; that is, capitalize the first letter of the first and last words of the title and subtitle and all major words (see 22.3.1). If the volumes in the series are numbered, you may include the number of the work cited following the series title. The name of the series editor is often omitted, but you may include it after the series title.

R: Markman, Charles W. 1991. *Chicago before history: The prehistoric archaeology of a modern metropolitan area.* Studies in Illinois Archaeology 7. Springfield: Illinois Historic Preservation Agency.

Isenberg, Nancy. 1998. *Sex and citizenship in antebellum America.* Gender and American Culture, ed. Linda K. Kerber and Nell Irvin Painter. Chapel Hill: University of North Carolina Press.

Some numbered series have existed for so long that numbering has started over. Books in a new series are indicated by *n.s., 2nd ser.,* or some similar notation, usually enclosed in commas before the series number. Books in the old series are identified by *o.s., 1st ser.,* and so forth.

R: Boxer, Charles R., ed. 1953. *South China in the sixteenth century.* Hakluyt Society Publications, 2nd ser., 106. London.

Palmatary, Helen C. 1950. *The pottery of Marajó Island, Brazil.* Transactions of the American Philosophical Society, n.s., 39, pt. 3. Philadelphia.

19.1.7 Facts of Publication

The facts of publication usually include two elements: the place (city) of publication and the publisher's name. (A third fact of publication, the date, appears as a separate element following the author's name in this citation style; see 19.1.2.)

R: Diamond, Jared. 1997. *Guns, germs, and steel: The fates of human societies.* New York: W. W. Norton and Company.

For books published before the twentieth century, or for which the information does not appear within the work, you may omit these facts of publication.

R: Lamb, Charles. 1823. *Essays of Elia.*

PLACE OF PUBLICATION. The place of publication is the city where the publisher's main editorial offices are located; it normally appears on the title page, but sometimes on the copyright page. Where two or more cities are given ("Chicago and London," for example), include only the first.

Los Angeles: J. Paul Getty Trust Publications

New York: Columbia University Press

If the city of publication might be unknown to readers or confused with another city of the same name, add the abbreviation of the state (see 24.3.1), province, or (if necessary) country. When the publisher's name includes the state name, no state abbreviation is needed.

Cheshire, CT: Graphics Press

Harmondsworth, UK: Penguin Books

Cambridge, MA: MIT Press

Chapel Hill: University of North Carolina Press

Use current, commonly used English names for foreign cities.

Belgrade (*not* Beograd)   Milan (*not* Milano)

When the place of publication is not known, you may use the abbreviation *N.p.* before the publisher's name. If the place can be surmised, include it with a question mark, in brackets.

N.p.: Windsor.

[Lake Bluff, IL?]: Vliet & Edwards.

PUBLISHER'S NAME. Give the publisher's name for each book exactly as it appears on the title page, even if you know that the name has since changed or is printed differently in different books in your reference list.

Harcourt Brace and World
Harcourt Brace Jovanovich
Harcourt, Brace

To save space, however, you may omit an initial *The* and such abbrevia-
·tions as *Inc., Ltd, S.A., Co., & Co.,* and *Publishing Co.*

University of Texas Press	*instead of*	The University of Texas Press
Houghton Mifflin	*instead of*	Houghton Mifflin Co.
Little, Brown	*instead of*	Little, Brown & Co.

For foreign publishers, do not translate or abbreviate any part of the
publisher's name, but give the city name in its English form (as noted
above). When the publisher is unknown, use just the place (if known) and
date of publication.

19.1.8   Page Numbers and Other Locating Information

Page numbers and other information used to identify the location of a
cited passage or element generally appear in parenthetical citations but
not in reference lists.

For guidelines for expressing a span of numbers, see 23.2.4.

PAGE, CHAPTER, AND DIVISION NUMBERS. Page numbers are usually the last element in the citation of a book within a parenthetical citation. Do not
include the word *page* or the abbreviation *p.* or *pp.* Use arabic numbers
except for pages numbered with roman numerals in the original.

P: (Rose 1992, 145–46)
(Kagan 1994, xxii–xxiv)

Sometimes a citation refers to a full chapter (abbreviated *chap.*), part
(*pt.*), book (*bk.*), or section (*sec.*) instead of a span of page numbers.

P: (Miller 1996, pt. 2)

SPECIAL TYPES OF LOCATORS. Some parts of a book have special types of locators used in citations.

■ *Note numbers.* Use the abbreviation *n* (plural, *nn*) to cite notes. If the note
cited is the only footnote on its page or is an unnumbered footnote, add
n after the page number (with no intervening space or punctuation). If
there are other notes on the same page as the note cited, list the page
.   number followed by *n* or (if two or more consecutive notes are cited) *nn*
and the note number(s).

P: (Grafton 1997, 72n)
   (Bolinger 1980, 192n23, 192n30, 199n14, 201nn16–17)

■ *Illustration and table numbers.* Use the abbreviation *fig.* for *figure,* but spell out *table, map, plate,* and names of other types of illustrations. Give the page number before the illustration number.

P: (Sobel 1993, 87, table 5.3)

■ *Line numbers.* For poetry and other works best identified by line number, avoid the abbreviations *l.* (line) and *ll.* (lines); they are too easily confused with the numerals 1 and 11. Use *line* or *lines,* or use numbers alone where you have made it clear that you are referring to lines.

P: (Nash 1945, lines 1–4)

■ *Signature, leaf, and folio numbers.* Some books printed before 1800 do not carry page numbers but are divided into signatures and then into leaves or folios, each with a front side (*recto,* or *r*) and a back side (*verso,* or *v*). Locators for such works should consist of the relevant string of numbers and identifiers, run together without spaces or italics: for example, G6v, 176r, 232r–v, or (if you are citing entire folios) fol. 49.

URLS, PERMANENT SOURCE IDENTIFIERS, ACCESS DATES, AND DESCRIPTIVE LOCATORS. For a book published online (see 19.1.10), include the book's URL in a reference list entry only. Every URL begins with a lowercase abbreviation of the protocol used to deliver electronic material to readers, most commonly *http* (hypertext transfer protocol) and *ftp* (file transfer protocol). This abbreviation is invariably followed by a colon and a double slash, after which appears the publisher's domain name, followed by the path to the resource. Components following the domain name are separated from the domain name and from each other by single slashes.

http://www.jsri.msu.edu/museum/pubs/MexAmHist/chapter14.html#six

Capitalize the internal components of a URL exactly as they appear on the screen. If the URL has a "trailing slash" at the end, include it. Do not enclose the URL in brackets. It is best not to break a URL at the end of a line, but if you need to do so, see 20.4.2 for some guidelines.

Some online sources have permanent identifiers other than URLs. If a source uses digital object identifiers (DOIs) or a similar system, include information comparable to a URL in your citation.

doi:10.1006/jeth.2000.2694

When you cite any online source, provide the date you last accessed it, in case the content has since changed or been removed from the Web (see 15.4.1). Put the access date in parentheses after the URL or permanent identifier.

(accessed May 17, 2006)

Books published online might not include page numbers to help identify the location of a cited passage in a parenthetical citation. In this case, you may add a descriptive locator (such as a preceding subheading) before the URL and access date (see 19.1.10 for an example). You need not include such a locator in a reference list entry.

19.1.9 Chapters and Other Titled Parts of a Book

In most cases, you should cite the main title of any book that offers a single, continuous argument or narrative, even if you actually use only a section of it. But if you consult only one part of a book that collects independent pieces on several topics, written by one or several authors, you may cite just the one chapter or part most relevant to your research. By doing so, you help readers see how the source fits into your project.

R: Demos, John. 2001. Real lives and other fictions: Reconsidering Wallace Stegner's "Angle of repose." In *Novel history: Historians and novelists confront America's past (and each other)*, ed. Mark C. Carnes, 132–45. New York: Simon and Schuster.

P: (Demos 2001, 137)

   instead of

R: Carnes, Mark C., ed. 2001. *Novel history: Historians and novelists confront America's past (and each other)*. New York: Simon and Schuster.

P: (Carnes 2001, 137)

PARTS OF SINGLE-AUTHOR BOOKS. If you cite a titled part of a single-author book, the reference list should include the title of the part first, in roman type without quotation marks, followed by a period. After the designation *In,* give the book title, followed by the full span of page numbers for that part.

R: Chasteen, John Charles. 2001. Neocolonialism. In *Born in blood and fire: A concise history of Latin America*, 179–206. New York: W. W. Norton & Company.

If you cite a part with a generic title such as *introduction, preface,* or *afterword,* add that term before the title of the book. List the generic title in roman type without quotation marks, and capitalize the first word only.

If the part is written by someone other than the main author of the book, give the part author's name first and the book author's name after the title; parenthetical citations mention only the part author's name.

R: Crosby, Alfred W. 2004. Preface to the new edition of *Ecological imperialism: The biological expansion of Europe, 900–1900.* New ed. New York: Cambridge University Press.
   Calhoun, Craig. 2005. Foreword to *Multicultural politics: Racism, ethnicity, and Muslims in Britain,* by Tariq Modood. Minneapolis: University of Minnesota Press.

P: (Calhoun 2005, xv)

PARTS OF EDITED COLLECTIONS. In a reference list, if you cite part of an edited collection with contributions by multiple authors, first list the part author, the date, and the part title (in roman type without quotation marks). After the designation *In,* give the book title, the name of the editor, and the full span of page numbers for that part. Parenthetical citations mention only the part author's name.

R: Carr, Anne, and Douglas J. Schuurman. 1996. Religion and feminism: A reformist Christian analysis. In *Religion, feminism, and the family,* ed. Anne Carr and Mary Stewart Van Leeuwen, 11–32. Louisville, KY: Westminster John Knox Press.

P: (Carr and Schuurman 1996, 13–14)

If you cite two or more contributions to the same edited collection, you may treat them as separate sources, or you may use a space-saving shortened form. In your reference list, provide a full citation for the whole book and shortened citations for each individual part. For the latter, provide the full author's name, the publication date, and the full title of the part; after the designation *In,* add the shortened name of the book's editor, the publication date, and the full span of page numbers for that part.

R: Angle, Paul M., ed. 1967. *Prairie state: Impressions of Illinois, 1673–1967, by travelers and other observers.* Chicago: University of Chicago Press.
   Keating, William H. 1967. Fort Dearborn and Chicago. In Angle 1967, 84–87.
   Lippincott, Sara Clarke. 1967. Chicago. In Angle 1967, 362–70.

If you use this form, your parenthetical citations should refer to the parts only, not to the book as a whole.

P: (Keating 1967, 84), *not* (Angle 1967, 84)
   (Lippincott 1967, 362), *not* (Angle 1967, 362)

WORKS IN ANTHOLOGIES. Cite a short story, poem, essay, or other work published in an anthology in the same way you would a contribution to an edited collection with multiple authors. Give the titles of most works published in anthologies in roman type. An exception is the title of an excerpt from a book-length poem or prose work, which should be italicized (see 22.3.2).

R: Allende, Isabel. 1997. The spirits were willing. In *The Oxford book of Latin American essays,* ed. Ilan Stavans, 461–67. New York: Oxford University Press.
Wigglesworth, Michael. 2003. Excerpt from *The day of doom.* In *The new anthology of American poetry: Traditions and revolutions, beginnings to 1900,* ed. Steven Gould Axelrod, Camille Roman, and Thomas Travisano, 68–74. New Brunswick, NJ: Rutgers University Press.

P: (Allende 1997, 463–64)
(Wigglesworth 2003, 68)

If the original publication date of a work is important in the context of your paper, include it in brackets before the anthology's publication date in both your reference list and your parenthetical citations.

R: Wigglesworth, Michael. [1662] 2003. Excerpt from . . .

P: (Wigglesworth [1662] 2003, 68)

19.1.10 Online and Other Electronic Books

For online books, follow the guidelines for print books. In addition to the usual elements, include the URL and the date you accessed the material in your reference list (see 15.4.1, 19.1.8). Note that a URL alone is not sufficient; you must provide the full facts of publication, as far as they can be determined, so that a reader can search for the source even if the URL changes. If page numbers are not available, you may identify the location of a cited passage in a parenthetical citation by adding a descriptive locator (such as a preceding subheading) following the word *under.*

R: Samora, Julian, and Patricia Vandel Simon. 2000. *A history of the Mexican-American people.* Rev. ed. East Lansing, MI: Julian Samora Research Institute, Michigan State University. http://www.jsri.msu.edu/museum/pubs/MexAmHist/chapter14.html#six (accessed December 19, 2005).

P: (Samora and Vandel Simon 2000, under "Civil War in Mexico")

or

(Samora and Vandel Simon 2000)

When you cite books published in other electronic formats, such as those available for download or other delivery from a bookseller or library, identify the format (CD-ROM, Microsoft Reader e-book).

R: Davenport, Thomas H., and John C. Beck. 2001. *The attention economy: Understanding the new currency of business.* Cambridge, MA: Harvard Business School Press. TK3 Reader e-book.

Hellman, Hal. 2004. *Great feuds in technology: Ten of the liveliest disputes ever.* New York: John Wiley. Rocket e-book.

19.2 Journal Articles

Most of the periodicals you will consult for a paper are classified as jour-nals, which are scholarly or professional periodicals available primarily in academic libraries and by subscription. Journals often include the word *journal* in their titles (*Journal of Modern History*), but not always (*Signs*). Magazines are usually not scholarly publications; they are more accessible to readers than journals, in both their content and their availability out-side academic settings. This distinction is important because journal ar-ticles and magazine articles are cited differently. If you are unsure whether a periodical is a journal or a magazine, see whether its articles include citations; if so, treat it as a journal.

19.2.1 Author's Name

Give authors' names exactly as they appear at the heads of their articles. Follow the guidelines for book authors in 19.1.1.

19.2.2 Date of Publication

The main date of publication for a journal article consists only of a year. In a reference list entry, set it off as its own element with periods follow-ing the author's name. In a parenthetical citation, put it after the author's name without intervening punctuation.

R: Burns, Sarah. 2005. Ordering the artist's body: Thomas Eakins's acts of self-portrayal. *American Art* 19, no. 1 (Spring): 82–107.

Jenkins, J. Craig, David Jacobs, and Jon Agnone. 2003. Political opportunities and African-American protest, 1948–1997. *American Journal of Sociology* 109, no. 2 (September): 277–303.

P: (Burns 2005, 95)

(Jenkins, Jacobs, and Agnone 2003, 298–99)

Notice that additional date information may appear in parentheses later in a reference list entry, after the volume number (or issue number, if given; see 19.2.5).

If an article has been accepted for publication but has not yet appeared, use *forthcoming* in place of the date (and page numbers). To avoid confu-sion, include a comma after the author's name in a parenthetical citation of this type. Treat any article not yet accepted for publication as an unpublished manuscript (see 19.6).

R: Author, Margaret M. Forthcoming. Article title. *Journal Name* 98.

P: (Author, forthcoming)

19.2.3 Article Title

List complete article titles and subtitles. Use roman type, separate the title from the subtitle with a colon, and do not use quotation marks. Use sentence-style capitalization (see 22.3.1).

R: Green, Nancy L. 2005. The politics of exit: Reversing the immigration paradigm. *Journal of Modern History* 77 (June): 263–89.

Terms normally italicized in text, such as species names and book titles, remain italicized within an article title; terms normally quoted in text remain in double quotation marks. Do not put a comma or period after an article title or subtitle that ends with a question mark or an exclamation point.

R: Lewis, Judith. 1998. "'Tis a misfortune to be a great ladie": Maternal mortality in the British aristocracy, 1558–1959. *Journal of British Studies* 37:26–40.
Loften, Peter. 1989. Reverberations between wordplay and swordplay in *Hamlet. Aeolian Studies* 2:12–29.
Williamson, George S. 2000. What killed August von Kotzebue? The temptations of virtue and the political theology of German nationalism, 1789–1819. *Journal of Modern History* 72 (December): 890–943.

Foreign-language titles should also be capitalized sentence style according to the conventions of the particular language. If you add an English translation, enclose it in brackets, without quotation marks.

R: Bouchard, Gérard. 1979. Un essai d'anthropologie régionale: L'histoire sociale du Saguenay aux XIXe et XXe siècles. *Annales: Économies, sociétés, civilisations* 34 (January): 118–34.
Kern, W. 1938. Waar verzamelde Pigafetta zijn Maleise woorden? [Where did Pigafetta collect his Malaysian words?] *Tijdschrift voor Indische taal-, land- en volkenkunde* 78:271–73.

19.2.4 Journal Title

After the article title, list the journal title in italics, with headline-style capitalization (see 22.3.1). Give the title exactly as it appears on the title page or above the table of contents of the journal; do not use abbreviations, although you can omit an initial *The* (*Journal of Business*). If the official title is an initialism such as *PMLA,* do not expand it. For foreign-language journals, you may use either headline-style or sentence-style capitalization, but retain all initial articles (*Der Spiegel*).

19.2.5 Issue Information

In addition to a date of publication, most reference list entries include volume number and issue number. Readers may not need all of these elements to locate an article, but including them all guards against a possible error in one of them.

The volume number follows the journal title without intervening punctuation and is not italicized. Use arabic numerals even if the journal itself uses roman numerals. If there is an issue number, it follows the volume number, separated by a comma and preceded by *no.* If you have any additional date information beyond the year of publication (see 19.2.2), include it in parentheses after the volume and issue number. For such information, follow the practice of the journal; it may include a season, a month, or an exact day. Capitalize seasons in journal citations, even though they are not capitalized in text.

R: Mackay, Christopher S. 1999. Lactantius and the succession to Diocletian. *Classical Philology* 94, no. 2:198–209.

Kumar, Rahul. 2003. Reasonable reasons in contractualist moral argument. *Ethics* 114 (October): 6–37.

When a journal uses issue numbers only, without volume numbers, a comma follows the journal title.

R: Beattie, J. M. 1974. The pattern of crime in England, 1660–1800. *Past and Present,* no. 62:47–95.

19.2.6 Page Numbers and Other Locating Information

For a reference list entry, give the full span of page numbers for the article (see 23.2.4). By convention, page numbers of journal articles in reference lists follow colons rather than commas. When additional date information in parentheses immediately precedes the colon, leave a space after the colon; when the volume or issue number immediately precedes the colon, do not leave a space after it.

R: Hitchcock, Tim. 2005. Begging on the streets of eighteenth-century London. *Journal of British Studies* 44, no. 3 (July): 478–98.

Gold, Ann Grodzins. 1998. Grains of truth: Shifting hierarchies of food and grace in three Rajasthani tales. *History of Religions* 38, no. 2:150–71.

If you cite a particular passage in a parenthetical citation, give only the specific page(s) cited, preceded by a comma (not a colon).

P: (Hitchcock 2005, 478)
(Gold 1998, 152–53)

For journal articles published online, include page numbers (if available) as well as the URL (or permanent identifier) and the date you accessed the article. For details and examples, see 19.2.8. For general principles of punctuation and capitalization in URLs, see 19.1.8.

19.2.7 Special Issues and Supplements

A journal issue devoted to a single theme is known as a *special issue.* It carries a normal volume and issue number. If a special issue has a title and an editor of its own, include both in a reference list entry. The title is given in roman type and enclosed in quotation marks. In a parenthetical citation, give only the author of the part cited.

R: Jones, Matthew L. 2001. Descartes's geometry as a spiritual exercise. In "Things," ed. Bill Brown. Special issue, *Critical Inquiry* 28, no. 1 (Autumn): 40–71.

P: (Jones 2001, 43–44)

If you need to cite the issue as a whole, omit the article information.

R: Brown, Bill, ed. 2001. "Things." Special issue, *Critical Inquiry* 28, no. 1 (Autumn).

A journal *supplement* may also have a title and an author or editor of its own. Unlike a special issue, it is numbered separately from the regular issues of the journal, often with S as part of its page numbers. Use a comma between the volume number and the supplement number.

R: Ekeland, Ivar, James J. Heckman, and Lars Nesheim. 2004. Identification and estimation of hedonic models. In "Papers in Honor of Sherwin Rosen," *Journal of Political Economy* 112, S1 (February): S60–S109.

19.2.8 Articles Published Online

For online journals, follow the guidelines for articles in print journals. In addition, include the URL and the date you accessed the material in your reference list (see 15.4.1). Note that a URL alone is not sufficient; you must provide the full facts of publication, as far as they can be determined, so that a reader can search for the source even if the URL changes. Articles in online journals might not include page numbers, especially if they are not published in parallel print journals. If page numbers are not available, you may identify the location of a cited passage in a parenthetical citation by adding a descriptive locator (such as a preceding subheading) following the word *under.*

R: Uzzi, Brian, and Jarrett Spiro. 2005. Collaboration and creativity: The small world problem. *American Journal of Sociology* 111, no. 2 (September). http://www.journals.uchicago.edu/AJS/journal/issues/v111n2/090090/090090.html (accessed December 19, 2005).

P: (Uzzi and Spiro 2005, under "Milgram's small world theory")

or

(Uzzi and Spiro 2005)

Online databases of articles generally list all the elements necessary for citations. Include the stable URL listed, which also identifies the database in which you consulted the article.

R: Shapiro, Lawrence A. 2000. Multiple realizations. *Journal of Philosophy* 97, no. 12 (December): 635–54. http://links.jstor.org/sici?sici=0022–362X%28200012%2997%3A12%3C635%3AMR%3E2.0.CO%3B2-Q (accessed June 27, 2006).

P: (Shapiro 2000, 642)

19.3 Magazine Articles

Many guidelines for citing journal articles (see 19.2) apply equally to magazine articles. Put article titles in roman type without quotation marks, capitalized sentence style; put magazine titles in italics, capitalized headline style (see 22.3.1).

In most cases, cite weekly or monthly magazines by date only, even if they are numbered by volume and issue. In reference list entries, put the year in the usual position and any additional date information (such as month or exact day) after the magazine title but not enclosed in parentheses. If you cite a specific passage in a parenthetical citation, include its page number. But you may omit the article's inclusive page numbers in a reference list entry, since magazine articles often span many pages that include extraneous material. If you include page numbers in a reference list entry, use a comma rather than a colon to separate them from the date of issue.

R: Schapiro, Mark. 2004. New power for "Old Europe." *The Nation*, December 27.

P: (Schapiro 2004, 12–13)

If you cite a department or column that appears regularly, capitalize it headline style and do not enclose it in quotation marks. For a department without a named author, use the name of the magazine in place of the author.

R: Walraff, Barbara. 2005. Word Court, *Atlantic Monthly,* June, 128.
New Yorker. 2000. Talk of the Town. April 10.

P: (Walraff 2005, 128)
(*New Yorker* 2000, 15)

For online magazines, follow the guidelines for articles in print magazines. In addition, include the URL and the date you accessed the material in your reference list (see 15.4.1). Note that a URL alone is not sufficient; you must provide the full facts of publication, as far as they can
be determined, so that a reader can search for the source even if the URL
changes. Articles in online magazines might not include page numbers,
but you may identify the location of a cited passage in a parenthetical
citation by adding a descriptive locator (such as a preceding subheading)
following the word *under.*

R: Faris, Stephan. 2005. "Freedom": No documents found. *Salon.com,* December 16.
http://www.salon.com/tech/feature/2005/12/16/censorship/index1.html (accessed
December 19, 2005).

P: (Faris 2005, under "The Internet has no memory in China")

or

(Faris 2005)

19.4 Newspaper Articles

In your reference list, cite articles and other pieces from daily newspapers
generally as you would articles in magazines (see 19.3). For an unsigned
article, use the name of the newspaper in place of the author. Because a
newspaper may have several editions with slightly different contents, you
may clarify which edition you consulted by adding *final edition, Midwest
edition,* or some such identifier.

R: Kamin, Blair. 2005. Wrigley Building clearly a landmark. *Chicago Tribune.* July 1.
Milwaukee Journal-Sentinel. 1998. Editorial. June 1.
New York Times, national edition. 2004. Obituary of Jacques Derrida. October 10.

Omit page numbers in parenthetical citations because the item may
appear on different pages or may even be dropped in different editions of
the newspaper. Also omit descriptions of the edition from the name of the
newspaper if it is cited as the author.

P: (Kamin 2005)
(*Milwaukee Journal-Sentinel* 1998)
(*New York Times* 2004)

Instead of using a parenthetical citation, you can include some of the elements of the citation in your text. You should still give a full citation to the article in your reference list.

In a *New York Times* article on the transitions within the Supreme Court (2005), Greenhouse discusses these trends.

or

In an article published on September 30, 2005, in the *New York Times*, Linda Greenhouse discusses the transitions within the Supreme Court.

19.4.1 Special Format Issues

For American newspapers, omit an initial *The* in the name of the newspaper. If the name does not include a city, add it to the official title, except for well-known national papers such as the *Wall Street Journal* or the *Christian Science Monitor*. If a name is shared by many cities or is obscure, you may add the state or province in parentheses (usually abbreviated; see 24.3.1). For foreign newspapers, retain initial articles, and add city names after titles.

Chicago Tribune	*Le Monde*
Saint Paul (Alberta or AB) Journal	*Times* (London)

The names of news services should be capitalized headline style but not italicized when treated as the author of an article.

R: Associated Press. 2005. Iraq constitution distributed amid attacks. *Los Angeles Times.* October 6.

P: (Associated Press 2005)

19.4.2 Special Types of Newspaper Citations

In addition to individual, signed articles, newspapers include many other types of pieces, some of which require special treatment in citations.

■ *Regular columns.* Many regular columns carry headlines as well as column titles. You may use either both or, to save space, the column title alone (in roman type, not enclosed in quotation marks, and capitalized headline style).

R: Morgenson, Gretchen. 2000. Applying a discount to good earnings news. Market Watch. *New York Times.* April 23.

or

Morgenson, Gretchen. 2000. Market Watch. *New York Times.* April 23.

■ *Letters to the editor.* Cite published letters to the editor generically, without headlines.

R: Davis, Virginia J. 2005. Letter to the editor. *Chicago Tribune.* July 29.

■ *Articles in supplements.* Treat articles from Sunday "magazine" supplements or other special sections as you would magazine articles (see 19.3).

■ *Articles published online.* For online newspapers, follow the guidelines for articles in print newspapers. In addition, include the URL and the date you accessed the material (see 15.4.1). Note that a URL alone is not sufficient; you must provide the full facts of publication, as far as they can be determined, so that a reader can search for the source even if the URL changes.

R: Hoekstra, Dave. 2005. Restoring a legacy. *Chicago Sun-Times.* December 19. http://www.suntimes.com/output/hurricane/cst-ftr-nola19.html (accessed December 19, 2005).

19.5 Additional Types of Published Sources

There are several additional types of published material that have special requirements for citations.

19.5.1 Classical, Medieval, and Early English Literary Works

Literary works produced in classical Greece and Rome, medieval Europe, and Renaissance England are cited differently from modern literary works. These sources are often organized into numbered sections (books, lines, stanzas, and so forth) that are generally cited in place of page numbers. Because such works have been published in so many versions and translations over the centuries, the date and other facts of publication for modern editions are generally less important than in other types of citations.

For this reason, classical, medieval, and early English literary works should usually be cited only in parenthetical citations. If the author's name and the title are not already mentioned in the surrounding text, include them along with the section number upon first reference. If subsequent citations clearly refer to the same work, list only the section number. See below regarding differences in punctuation, abbreviations, and numbers among different types of works.

The eighty days of inactivity for the Peloponnesian fleet at Rhodes (Thucydides *The history of the Peloponnesian War* 8.44.4), terminating before the end of winter (8.60.2–3), suggests . . .

or

The eighty days of inactivity reported by Thucydides for the Peloponnesian fleet at Rhodes (*The history of the Peloponnesian War* 8.44.4), terminating before the end of winter (8.60.2–3), suggests . . .

If your paper is in literary studies or another field concerned with close analysis of texts, or if differences in translations are relevant, include such works in your reference list. Follow the rules for other translated and edited books in 19.1.1.

R: Propertius. 1990. *Elegies.* Ed. and trans. G. P. Goold. Loeb Classical Library 18. Cambridge, MA: Harvard University Press.
Aristotle. 1983. *Complete works of Aristotle: The revised Oxford translation.* Ed. J. Barnes. 2 vols. Princeton, NJ: Princeton University Press.

CLASSICAL WORKS. In addition to the general principles listed above, the following rules apply to citations of classical works.

Use no punctuation between author and title of work, or between title and section number. Numerical divisions are separated by periods without spaces. Use arabic numerals (and lowercase letters, if needed) for section numbers. Put commas between two or more citations of the same source and semicolons between citations of different sources.

P: (Aristophanes *Frogs* 1019–30)
(Cicero *Verr.* 1.3.21, 2.3.120; Tacitus *Germ.* 10.2–3)
(Aristotle *Metaphysics* 3.2.996b5–8; Plato *Republic* 360e–361b)

You can also abbreviate the names of authors, works, collections, and so forth. The most widely accepted abbreviations appear in the *Oxford Classical Dictionary.* Use these abbreviations rather than *ibid.* in succeeding references to the same work.

P: (Thuc. 2.40.2–3)
(Pindar *Isthm.* 7.43–45)

MEDIEVAL WORKS. The form for classical references works equally well for medieval works written in languages other than English. If the section number is preceded by a descriptive term, separate it from the title of the work with a comma for clarity.

P: (Augustine *De civitate Dei* 20.2)
(Abelard *Epistle 17 to Heloïse,* Migne *PL* 180.375c–378a)

EARLY ENGLISH WORKS. In addition to the general principles listed above, the following rules apply to citations of early English literary works.

Cite poems and plays by book, canto, and stanza; stanza and line; act, scene, and line; or similar divisions. Separate the elements with commas for clarity.

P: [Chaucer, Wife of Bath's prologue, *Canterbury tales*, lines 105–14]
[Milton, *Paradise lost*, book 1, lines 83–86]

You may shorten numbered divisions by omitting *act*, *line*, and such and using a system similar to that in classical references (see above). Be sure to explain your system in a footnote.

P: [Milton, *Paradise lost*, 1.83–86]

If editions differ in wording, line numbering, and even scene division—especially works of Shakespeare—include the work in your reference list, with edition specified.

R: Shakespeare, William. 1982. *Hamlet*. Arden edition. Ed. Harold Jenkins. London: Methuen.

19.5.2   The Bible and Other Sacred Works

Cite the Bible and sacred works of other religious traditions in parenthetical citations. You do not need to include them in your reference list.

For citations from the Bible, include the abbreviated name of the book, the chapter number, and the verse number—never a page number. Depending on the context, you may use either traditional or shorter abbreviations for the names of books (see 24.6); consult your instructor if you are unsure which form is appropriate. Use arabic numerals for chapter and verse numbers (with a colon between them) and for numbered books.

Traditional abbreviations:

P: [1 Thess. 4:11, 5:2–5, 5:14]

Shorter abbreviations:

P: [2 Sm 11:1–17, 11:26–27; 1 Chr 10:13–14]

Since books and numbering differ among versions of the scriptures, identify the version you are using in brackets in your first citation, either with the spelled-out name or an accepted abbreviation (see 24.6.4).

P: [2 Kings 11:8 [New Revised Standard Version]]
[1 Cor. 6:1–10 [NAB]]

For citations from the sacred works of other religious traditions, adapt the general pattern for biblical citations as appropriate (see 24.6.5).

19.5.3 Reference Works

Well-known reference works, such as major dictionaries and encyclopedias, should usually be cited only in parenthetical citations. You generally need not include them in your reference list, although you may choose to include a specific work that is critical to your argument or frequently cited. Omit the date, but specify the edition (if not the first). For an alphabetically arranged work such as an encyclopedia, cite the item (not the volume or page number) preceded by *s.v.* (*sub verbo*, "under the word"; pl. *s.vv.*)

P: (*Encyclopaedia Britannica* 15th ed., s.v. "Salvation")
    (*Dictionary of American biography*, s.v. "Wadsworth, Jeremiah")

Treat reference works that are less well known as you would a book (see 19.1).

R: *The Times guide to English style and usage.* 1999. Rev. ed. London: Times Books.
    Aulestia, Gorka. 1989. *Basque English dictionary.* Reno: University of Nevada Press.

P: (*Times guide* 1999, s.vv. "police ranks," "postal addresses")
    (Aulestia 1989, 509)

Online versions of encyclopedias are regularly updated, so include both the URL and the date you accessed the material (see 15.4.1). Note that some reference works will indicate the appropriate URL to cite for a specific entry; use this rather than the less stable URL generated by search engines.

P: (*Encyclopaedia Britannica online*, s.v. "Sibelius, Jean," http://www.britannica.com/ebc/article?tocId=9378608 [accessed June 1, 2005])

19.5.4 Reviews

Reviews of books, performances, and so forth may appear in a variety of periodicals. In your reference list, include the name of the reviewer; the words *review of*, followed by the name of the work reviewed and its author (or composer, director, and so forth); location and date (in the case of a performance); and finally the periodical in which the review appeared.

R: Taub, Richard P. 2004. Review of *Reclaiming public housing: A half-century of struggle in three public neighborhoods,* by Lawrence J. Vale. *American Journal of Sociology* 110, no. 3 (November): 797–99.

Isherwood, Charles. 2005. Review of *Birdie blue,* by Cheryl L. West, directed by Seret Scott. Second Stage Theater, New York. *New York Times.* June 24.

Kozinn, Allan. 2000. Review of concert performance by Timothy Fain (violin) and Steven Beck (piano). 92nd Street Y, New York. *New York Times.* April 21.

19.5.5   Abstracts

Abstracts of journal articles, conference proceedings, dissertations, and so forth may appear along with the work being abstracted or in special publications (usually journals) that consist entirely of abstracts.

Include the full citation of the work being abstracted. If the abstract appears next to the work itself, insert the word *abstract* within the citation, following the title. If the abstract appears in a different publication, insert the words *Abstract in* following the initial citation, and then cite the location of the abstract. Use the date of the work itself, not the abstract, following the author's name.

R: Luders, Joseph. 2006. The economics of movement success: Business responses to civil rights mobilization. Abstract. *American Journal of Sociology* 111, no. 4 (January): 963.

Albin, Cecilia. 2003. Negotiating international cooperation: Global public goods and fairness. *Review of International Studies* 29 (July): 365–85. Abstract in *Peace Research Abstracts Journal* 42, publ. nr. 236625 (February 2005): 6.

19.5.6   Pamphlets and Reports

Cite pamphlets, corporate reports, brochures, and other freestanding publications as you would a book. If you lack data for some of the usual elements, such as author and publisher, give enough other information to identify the document.

R: Clark, Hazel V. 1957. *Mesopotamia: Between two rivers.* Mesopotamia, OH: End of the Commons General Store.

TIAA-CREF. 2005. 2005 *Annual report: College Retirement Equities Fund.* New York: TIAA-CREF.

19.5.7   Microform Editions

In your reference list, cite works that you have consulted in microform editions, including dissertations, as you would a book. (For dissertations consulted in print form or online, see 19.6.1.) Specify the form of publication (fiche, microfilm, and so forth) after the facts of publication.

R: Farwell, Beatrice. 1995. *French popular lithographic imagery.* Vol. 12, *Lithography in art and commerce.* Chicago: University of Chicago Press. Text-fiche.

Tauber, Abraham. 1958. *Spelling reform in the United States.* Ann Arbor, MI: University Microfilms. Microfilm.

In a parenthetical citation, include a locator if possible. In the following example, the page number (identified with the abbreviation *p.* for clarity) appears within the printed text on the fiche; the other numbers indicate the fiche and frame, and the letter indicates the row.

P: (Farwell 1995, p. 67, 3C12)

19.5.8 CD-ROMs or DVD-ROMs

Cite works issued on CD- or DVD-ROM as you would analogous printed works, most often books.

R: *Complete National Geographic: 110 years of "National Geographic" magazine.* 2000. CD-ROM. Mindscape.
Oxford English dictionary. 1999. 2nd ed. CD-ROM, version 2.0. New York: Oxford University Press.

19.5.9 Online Databases

For citation of journal articles published in online databases, see 19.2.8. For other types of online databases, list the database as a whole in your reference list if you cite multiple documents or records from it. Give the name of the database (in roman type), the URL for the main page, and the date (or range of dates) you accessed the material. Note that a URL alone is not sufficient; you must provide the full facts of publication, as far as they can be determined, so that a reader can search for the source even if the URL changes.

R: Perseus Digital Library. http://www.perseus.tufts.edu/ (accessed February 1–March 31, 2006).

If you cite only one document or record from such a database, list it individually in your reference list. Give the author and title of the document (if available), the name of the database (in roman type), the URL for the specific page, and the date you accessed the material. For dissertations in online databases, see 19.6.1.

R: Pliny the Elder. *The natural history,* ed. John Bostock and H. T. Riley. In the Perseus Digital Library, http://www.perseus.tufts.edu/cgi-bin/ptext?lookup=Plin.+Nat.+1 .dedication (accessed March 31, 2006).

To cite a document or record in your text, include as much information as possible to link the citation to the reference list entry. Place this information either in a parenthetical citation (with the elements separated by commas) or in the text.

P: (Pliny the Elder, Perseus Digital Library)

. . . as illustrated in Pliny the Elder's treatise *The Natural History* (Perseus Digital Library).

19.6   Unpublished Sources

Sources that have never been published can be more difficult for readers to locate than published ones, because they exist in only one place and lack official publication information. When citing such sources in your reference list, it is especially important to include *all* of the information listed below to give readers as much help as possible.

Titles of unpublished works are given in roman type and not enclosed in quotation marks or italicized. This format difference distinguishes them from similar but published works.

19.6.1   Theses and Dissertations

If you consult an unpublished thesis or dissertation in print form, treat it as an unpublished manuscript. After the author, date (if available), and title, list the kind of thesis and the academic institution. Abbreviate *dissertation* as *diss.* The word *unpublished* is unnecessary.

R: Murphy, Priscilla Coit. 2000. What a book can do: *Silent Spring* and media-borne public debate. PhD diss., University of North Carolina.

Culcasi, Karen Leigh. 2003. Cartographic representations of Kurdistan in the print media. Master's thesis, Syracuse University.

To cite a dissertation consulted in an online database, add the name of the database, the URL, and the access date following the institutional information in your reference list. (For microform editions, see 19.5.7.)

R: Murphy, Priscilla Coit. 2000. What a book can do: *Silent Spring* and media-borne public debate. PhD diss., University of North Carolina. In ProQuest Dissertations and Theses, http://proquest.umi.com/pqdweb?did=727710781&sid=2&Fmt=2&clientId=13392&RQT=309&VName=PQD (accessed April 1, 2006).

19.6.2   Lectures and Papers Presented at Meetings

After the author, date, and title of the speech or paper, list the sponsorship, location, and (if available) specific day of the meeting at which it was given. The word *unpublished* is unnecessary.

R: Troutman, John. 2005. Indian blues: American Indians and the politics of music, 1890–1935. Lecture, Newberry Library, Chicago, IL. February 2.

Grad, Karene. 2004. When high culture was popular culture. Paper presented at the annual meeting of the Organization of American Historians, Boston, MA. March 26.

Skocpol, Theda. 2003. Voice and inequality: The transformation of American civic democracy. Presidential address, annual meeting of the American Political Science Association, Philadelphia, PA. August 28.

19.6.3 Interviews and Personal Communications

To cite an unpublished interview (including one you have conducted yourself), begin a reference list entry with the names of the person interviewed and the interviewer; also include the place and date of the interview (if known) and the location of any tapes or transcripts (if available). (For broadcast interviews, see 19.8.3.)

R: Macmillan, Andrew. 2007. Interview by author. San Diego, CA. March 2.
Spock, Benjamin. 1974. Interview by Milton J. E. Senn. November 20. Interview 67A, transcript, Senn Oral History Collection, National Library of Medicine, Bethesda, MD.

In parenthetical citations, use the name of the person interviewed, not that of the interviewer.

P: (Macmillan 2007)
(Spock 1974)

If you cannot reveal the name of the person interviewed, use only a parenthetical citation, with information appropriate to the context. You can also weave some or all of this information into the text, but you do not need to include the interview in your reference list. Explain the absence of a name ("All interviews were confidential; the names of interviewees are withheld by mutual agreement") in a footnote or a preface.

P: (interview with a health care worker, August 10, 2006)

Cite conversations, letters, e-mail messages, and the like only in parenthetical citations. You generally need not include them in your reference list, although you may choose to include a specific communication that is critical to your argument or frequently cited. The key elements, which should be separated with commas, are the name of the other person, the date, and the type of communication. In many cases, you may be able to include some or all of this information in the text. Omit e-mail addresses. To cite postings to electronic mailing lists, see 19.7.3.

P: (Maxine Greene, September 29, 2005, e-mail message to author)

In a telephone conversation with the author on October 12, 2006, Colonel William Rich revealed that . . .

19.6.4 Manuscript Collections

Documents from collections of unpublished manuscripts involve more complicated and varied elements than published sources. In your citations, include as much identifying information as you can, format the elements consistently, and adapt the general patterns outlined here as needed.

ELEMENTS TO INCLUDE AND THEIR ORDER. If you cite multiple documents from a collection, list the collection as a whole in your reference list, under the name of the collection, the author(s) of the items in the collection, or the depository. For similar types of unpublished material that have not been placed in archives, replace information about the collection with such wording as "in the author's possession" or "private collection," and do not mention the location. Do not include a date, since most collections contain items from various dates.

R: Egmont Manuscripts. Phillipps Collection. University of Georgia Library, Athens.
House, Edward M., Papers. Yale University Library, New Haven, CT.
Pennsylvania Society for the Abolition of Slavery. Papers. Historical Society of Pennsylvania, Philadelphia.
Strother, French, and Edward Lowry. Undated correspondence. Herbert Hoover Presidential Library, West Branch, IA.
Women's Organization for National Prohibition Reform Papers. Alice Belin du Pont files, Pierre S. du Pont Papers. Eleutherian Mills Historical Library, Wilmington, DE.

To cite an individual document from such a collection in your text, identify the author and date, the title or type of document, and the name of the collection or the depository used in the reference list entry. Separate the elements with commas. In many cases, you may be able to include some or all of this information in the text.

P: (James Oglethorpe to the trustees, January 13, 1733, Egmont Manuscripts)

In his letter of January 13, 1733, to the trustees (Egmont Manuscripts), James Oglethorpe declared . . .

If you cite only one document from a collection, list it individually in your reference list, and follow the usual pattern for parenthetical citations.

R: Dinkel, Joseph. 1869. Description of Louis Agassiz written at the request of Elizabeth Cary Agassiz. Agassiz Papers. Houghton Library, Harvard University, Cambridge, MA.

P: (Dinkel 1869)

HOW TO FORMAT THE ELEMENTS. Here are some special formatting recommendations for documents in manuscript collections.

- *Specific versus generic titles.* Give both specific titles and generic names such as *report* or *minutes* in roman type, not enclosed in quotation marks or italicized. Capitalize generic names of this kind only if they are part of a formal heading in the manuscript, not if they are merely descriptive.
- *Locating information.* Although some manuscripts may include page numbers that can be included in parenthetical citations, many will have other types of locators, or none at all. Older manuscripts are usually numbered by signatures only or by folios (*fol., fols.*) rather than by page. Some manuscript collections have identifying series or file numbers that you can include in a citation.
- *Papers and manuscripts.* In titles of manuscript collections the terms *papers* and *manuscripts* are synonymous. Both are acceptable, as are the abbreviations *MS* and *MSS* (plural).
- *Letters.* To cite a letter in a parenthetical citation, start with the name of the letter writer, followed by *to* and the name of the recipient. Omit the word *letter,* which is understood, but for other forms of communication, specify the type (telegram, memorandum).

19.7 Informally Published Electronic Sources

Material that is informally published, or "posted," online will often lack the standard facts of publication—author, title, publisher, or date. Even if you can determine few or no facts of publication, you must still include information beyond the URL in your reference list. If you cite only a URL and that URL changes or becomes obsolete, your citation becomes useless to readers. The URL tells where the material was located when you consulted it; a complete citation must also indicate what a source is and the date on which you last accessed it (see 15.4.1).

19.7.1 Web Sites

For original content from online sources other than books or periodicals, include as much of the following as you can in your reference list: author, title of the page (in roman type, not enclosed in quotation marks), title or owner of the site, URL, and access date (or range of access dates).

R: Evanston Public Library Board of Trustees. Evanston Public Library strategic plan, 2000–2010: A decade of outreach. Evanston Public Library. http://www.epl.org/library/strategic-plan-00.html (accessed June 1–August 15, 2005).

If there is no named author, give the name of the owner of the site.

R: Federation of American Scientists. Resolution comparison: Reading license plates and
   headlines. http://www.fas.org/irp/imint/resolve5.html (accessed June 1, 2005).

Use descriptive phrases for content from informal sites, such as personal home pages and fan sites, where titles may be lacking.

R: Camp Taconic Alumni. 1955 photo gallery. http://www.taconicalumni.org/1955.html
   (accessed June 1, 2005).

To cite a Web site without a formal publication date in your text, give
the name of the author or site owner or the descriptive phrase used in the
reference list entry. Include this information either in parentheses or in
the text.

As indicated on the Federation of American Scientists' Web site . . .

19.7.2 Weblog Entries and Comments

If you cite entries or comments posted on a Weblog (or blog), include the
Weblog in your reference list, following the basic pattern for Web sites.
Give the URL for the main page of the site.

R: The Becker-Posner blog. http://www.becker-posner-blog.com/ (accessed March 28,
   2006).

Cite individual entries and comments posted to a Weblog only in parenthetical citations. The key elements, which should be separated with
commas, are the name of the author, the title of the Weblog, an indication
whether the item is an entry (posted by the author of the site) or a comment (posted by someone else), and the date of the posting. If an author's
name is incomplete or a pseudonym, cite it as given. In many cases, you
may be able to include some or all of this information in the text.

P: (Peter Pearson, The Becker-Posner Blog, comment posted March 6, 2006)

   . . . according to Gary Becker (entry posted March 6, 2006, on the Becker-Posner
   Blog). Comments by Peter Pearson (posted March 6) and Bill (posted March 10)
   responded . . .

19.7.3 Electronic Mailing Lists

To cite material from an electronic mailing list, include the name of the
author, the date of the posting, and the name of the list. Omit e-mail
addresses. Such items should usually be cited only in a parenthetical cita-

tion, with the elements separated with commas. You generally need not include them in your reference list, although you may choose to include a specific item that is critical to your argument or frequently cited. In many cases, you may be able to include some or all of this information in the text.

P: (John Powell, October 30, 2004, e-mail to Grapevine mailing list)

In an e-mail to the Grapevine mailing list on October 30, 2004, John Powell declares . . .

19.8　Sources in the Visual and Performing Arts

The visual and performing arts generate a variety of sources, including visual images, live performances, broadcasts, recordings in various media, and texts. Citing some of these sources can be difficult when they lack the types of identifying information common to published sources. Include as much identifying information as you can, format the elements consistently, and adapt the general patterns outlined here as needed.

You should cite most of the sources covered in this section only in parenthetical citations or even by weaving the key elements into your text. Unless otherwise noted, you generally need not include these sources in your reference list, although you may choose to include a specific item that is critical to your argument or frequently cited. If your paper is for a course in the arts, media studies, or a similar field, consult your instructor.

19.8.1　Visual Sources

PAINTINGS, SCULPTURES, PHOTOGRAPHS, AND OTHER ARTWORKS. Cite paintings, sculptures, photographs, and other artworks only in parenthetical citations. Include the name of the artist, the title of the artwork and date of its creation (preceded by *ca.* [*circa*] if approximate), and the name of the institution that houses it (if any), including location. Italicize the titles of paintings and sculptures, but set the titles of photographs in roman type, enclosed in quotation marks. Use headline-style capitalization for titles. Separate the elements with commas.

P: (Georgia O'Keeffe, *The Cliff Chimneys*, 1938, Milwaukee Art Museum)
(Michelangelo, *David*, 1501–4, Galleria dell'Accademia, Florence)
(Ansel Adams, "North Dome, Basket Dome, Mount Hoffman, Yosemite," ca. 1935, Smithsonian American Art Museum, Washington, DC)

Instead of using a parenthetical citation, you can sometimes cite artworks by weaving the elements into your text.

O'Keeffe first demonstrated this technique in *The Cliff Chimneys* (1938; Milwaukee Art Museum).

If you viewed the artwork in a published source and your local guidelines require you to identify this source, list the published source in your reference list. In your parenthetical citation, give the usual author-date citation in place of the institutional name and location. For online images, see 19.8.6.

R: Lynes, Barbara Buhler, Lesley Poling-Kempes, and Frederick W. Turner. 2004. *Georgia O'Keeffe and New Mexico: A sense of place.* Princeton: Princeton University Press.

P: (Georgia O'Keeffe, *The Cliff Chimneys,* 1938, in Lynes, Poling-Kempes, and Turner 2004, 25)

OTHER GRAPHIC SOURCES. You may need to cite other graphic sources, such as print advertisements, maps, cartoons, and so forth. Cite such items only in parenthetical citations, adapting the basic patterns for artworks and giving as much information as possible. Give the titles in roman type, enclosed in quotation marks, and identify the type of graphic if it is unclear from the title. For online graphics, see 19.8.6.

P: (National Center for Family Literacy, "Because I Can Read," advertisement, *Atlantic Monthly,* April 2006, 59)

19.8.2 Live Performances

THEATER, MUSIC, AND DANCE. Cite live theatrical, musical, or dance performances only in parenthetical citations. Include the title of the work performed, the names of any key performers and an indication of their roles, the venue and its location, and the date. Italicize the titles of plays and long musical compositions, but set the titles of shorter works in roman type, enclosed in quotation marks. Use headline-style capitalization for titles. If the citation is focused on an individual's performance, list that person's name before the title of the work. Separate the elements with commas.

P: (*Birdie Blue,* by Cheryl L. West, directed by Seret Scott, Second Stage Theater, New York, June 22, 2005)
(Yuja Wang, pianist, "La Valse," by Maurice Ravel, Orchestra Hall, Chicago, March 26, 2006)

Instead of using a parenthetical citation, you can sometimes cite live performances by weaving the elements into your text.

Yuja Wang's performance of Maurice Ravel's "La Valse" (March 26, 2006, at Orchestra Hall, Chicago) demonstrated her understanding . . .

If you viewed or listened to a live performance in a recorded medium, cite the recording. For sound recordings, see 19.8.4; for video recordings, see 19.8.5; for online files, see 19.8.6.

MOVIES. If you viewed a movie in a theater, cite it similarly to a live performance in a parenthetical citation or by weaving the elements into your text. (For movies viewed as video recordings, see 19.8.5; for movies viewed online, see 19.8.6.) Include the title of the movie (in italics), the director, the name of the production company or distributor, and the year in which the movie was released. Use headline-style capitalization for titles. Separate the elements with commas. If relevant, describe the scene you are citing.

P: (*Capote*, directed by Bennett Miller, Sony Pictures Classics, 2005, opening scene)

19.8.3 Television Programs and Other Broadcast Sources

PROGRAMS. Cite television programs, radio programs, and other broadcast sources only in parenthetical citations. Include at least the title of the program and the date on which you watched or listened to it. You may also include the episode title and number (if available), the names of any key performers (if relevant to your discussion), the broadcast venue, and the date of original broadcast (if different from the date you watched or listened to it). Italicize the titles of programs, but set the titles of episodes or segments in roman type, enclosed in quotation marks. Use headline-style capitalization for titles. Separate the elements with commas.

P: (*Seinfeld*, "The Opposite," episode 86, September 22, 2005 [originally aired May 19, 1994])
    (*All Things Considered*, NPR, April 20, 2006)

Instead of using a parenthetical citation, you can often cite such programs by weaving the key elements into your text, especially if some or all of the additional elements are not available or relevant to the citation.

The *Seinfeld* episode titled "The Opposite" (aired September 22, 2005) perfectly illustrates this story structure.

If you viewed or listened to a broadcast program in a recorded medium, cite the recording. For video recordings, see 19.8.5; for online files, see 19.8.6.

INTERVIEWS. Cite broadcast interviews only in parenthetical citations or by weaving the elements into your text. Treat the person interviewed as the author, and identify the interviewer in the context of the citation. Also include the forum and date of the broadcast. Use headline-style capitalization for titles. Separate the elements with commas. For unpublished interviews, see 19.6.3.

P: (Condoleezza Rice, interview by Jim Lehrer, *News Hour*, PBS, July 28, 2005)

ADVERTISEMENTS. Cite broadcast advertisements only in parenthetical citations or by weaving the elements into your text. Give as much information as possible.

P: (Federal Express, "Caveman" advertisement, aired during *Super Bowl XL*, February 5, 2006)

19.8.4   Sound Recordings

If you listened to a musical or spoken performance on a sound recording, cite the recording. Like published works, such recordings generally have stable and available identifying information and should be listed in your reference list. Parenthetical citations follow the usual author-date form.

List recordings in your reference list under the name of either the composer or performer, depending on which is more relevant to your discussion. Include as much information about the recording as you can to distinguish it from similar recordings, including the name of the recording company, the identifying number of the recording, the medium, and the copyright date or date of production (or both). Abbreviate *compact disc* as *CD*.

R: ·Beethoven, Ludwig van. 1992. *Piano sonata no. 29 "Hammerklavier."* Rudolf Serkin. ProArte Digital CDD 270.
Anderson, Doug. 2001. *Frostwork*. OAR 1001, Dolby HX PRO. Audiocassette.
Bernstein, Leonard, dir. 1985. *Symphony no. 5*, by Dmitri Shostakovich. New York Philharmonic. CBS IM 35854.

Treat recordings of drama, prose or poetry readings, lectures, and the like as you would musical recordings.

R: Thomas, Dylan. 1950. *Under Milk Wood*. Performed by Dylan Thomas and others. Caedmon TC–2005 (audiocassette), CDLS–2005 (CD).

To cite an item without a formal recording date in your text, give the name of the composer or performer used in the reference list entry and the title of the work. Include this information either in parentheses or in the text.

19.8.5   Video Recordings

If you viewed a live performance, a movie, or a television program or other broadcast source on a video recording, cite the recording. Like published works, such recordings generally have stable and available identifying information and should be listed in your reference list. Parenthetical citations follow the usual author-date form.

Citations of video recordings generally follow the pattern for books, with the addition of the medium (VHS, DVD). Note that in the second example, the citation is to material original to the 2001 edition, so the original release date of the film is omitted.

R: Handel,. George Frederic. 1988. *Messiah.* VHS. Atlanta Symphony Orchestra and Chamber Chorus, conducted by Robert Shaw. Batavia, OH: Video Treasures.

Cleese, John, Terry Gilliam, Eric Idle, Terry Jones, and Michael Palin. 2001. Commentaries. Disc 2. *Monty Python and the Holy Grail,* special ed. DVD. Directed by Terry Gilliam and Terry Jones. Culver City, CA: Columbia TriStar Home Entertainment.

19.8.6 Online Multimedia Files

If you viewed an image, a live performance, a movie, or a television program or other broadcast source online (including podcasts), cite the online file. Like published works, online multimedia files generally have stable and available identifying information and should be included in your reference list.

Follow the citation principles for the relevant type of source described above. If a file date is difficult to identify, use the abbreviation *n.d.* or give a date that is otherwise relevant. In addition, list the title of the online site and the type of file. Include the URL and an access date. Note that a URL alone is not sufficient; you must provide additional information so that a reader can search for the source even if the URL changes. If a file lacks an individual URL (as in the second example below), cite the site as a whole.

R: BBC. n.d. "Blair announces new Africa panel." BBC News Web site. Windows Media Player video file. http://news.bbc.co.uk/nolavconsole/ifs_news/hi/newsid_5110000/newsid_5119200/nb_wm_5119262.stm (accessed June 27, 2006).

Mozart, Wolfgang Amadeus. 1778. "Allegro moderato," *Piano sonata no. 10 in C Major.* Kunst der Fuge. MIDI file. http://www.kunstderfuge.com/mozart.htm (accessed November 19, 2005).

To cite a file without a formal date in your text, give the name of the author used in the reference list entry and the title of the work. Include this information either in parentheses or in the text. If relevant, also include the time at which the cited material appears in the file.

P: (BBC n.d., 3:43)

19.8.7 Texts in the Visual and Performing Arts

Texts in the visual and performing arts generally have stable and available identifying information and should be listed in your reference list. Parenthetical citations follow the usual author-date form.

ART EXHIBITION CATALOGS. Cite an art exhibition catalog as you would a book. In your reference list, include the name and location(s) of the exhibition following the publication data.

R: Barter, Judith A., ed. 1998. *Mary Cassatt: Modern woman.* Chicago: Art Institute of Chicago, in association with Harry N. Abrams. Published in conjunction with the exhibition "Mary Cassatt: Modern Woman" shown at the Boston Museum of Fine Arts, the National Gallery in Washington, DC, and the Art Institute of Chicago.

PLAYS. In some cases, you can cite well-known English-language plays in parenthetical citations only. (See also 19.5.1.) Use headline-style capitalization for titles. Separate the elements with commas. Omit publication data, and cite passages by act and scene (or other division) instead of by page number.

P: (Eugene O'Neill, *Long Day's Journey into Night,* act 2, scene 1)

If your paper is in literary studies or another field concerned with close analysis of texts, or if you are citing a translation or an obscure work, cite every play as you would a book, and include it in your reference list. Cite passages either by division or by page, according to your local guidelines.

R: Bagnold, Enid. 1953. *The chalk garden.* New York: Random House.
Anouilh, Jean. 1996. *Becket, or the honor of God.* Trans. Lucienne Hill. New York: Riverhead Books.

P: (Bagnold 1953, 8–9)
(Anouilh 1996, act 1, scene 1)

MUSICAL SCORES. Cite a published musical score as you would a book.

R: Verdi, Giuseppe. 1998. *Il corsaro (melodramma tragico* in three acts). Libretto by Francesco Maria Piave. Ed. Elizabeth Hudson. 2 vols. The Works of Giuseppe Verdi, ser. 1, Operas. Chicago: University of Chicago Press; Milan: G. Ricordi.
Mozart, Wolfgang Amadeus. 1960. *Sonatas and fantasies for the piano.* Prepared from the autographs and earliest printed sources by Nathan Broder. Rev. ed. Bryn Mawr, PA: Theodore Presser.

Cite an unpublished score as you would unpublished material in manuscript collections.

R: Shapey, Ralph. 1966. Partita for violin and thirteen players. Score. Special Collections, Joseph Regenstein Library. University of Chicago.

19.9 Public Documents

Public documents include a wide array of sources produced by governments at all levels throughout the world. This section presents basic principles for some common types of public documents available in English; if you need to cite other types, adapt the closest model.

Such documents involve more complicated and varied elements than published sources. In your citations, include as much identifying information as you can, format the elements consistently, and adapt the general patterns outlined here as needed.

The bulk of this section is concerned with documents published by U.S. governmental bodies and agencies. For documents published by the governments of Canada and the United Kingdom and by international bodies, see 19.9.9–19.9.11. For unpublished government documents generally, see 19.9.12.

19.9.1 Elements to Include, Their Order, and How to Format Them

In your reference list, include as many of the following elements as you can:

- name of the government (country, state, city, county, or other division) and government body (legislative body, executive department, court bureau, board, commission, or committee) that issued the document
- date of publication
- title, if any, of the document or collection (capitalized headline style and generally italicized)
- name of individual author, editor,·or compiler, if given
- report number or other identifying information
- facts of publication: place of publication and publisher's name, if different from the issuing body (for all publications of the U.S. federal government, covered in 19.9.2–19.9.4, use *Washington, DC,* and *Government Printing Office* respectively)
- page numbers or other locators, if relevant

In general, list the relevant elements in the order given above. Exceptions for certain types of documents are explained in the following sections of 19.9.

R: U.S. Congress. Senate. Committee on Foreign Relations. 1956. *The Mutual Security Act of 1956.* 84th Cong., 2d sess. S. Rep. 2273.

For parenthetical citations, treat the information listed before the date in your reference list as the author. If this information is lengthy, you may shorten it, as long as you do so logically and consistently in your citations. In many cases, you may be able to include some or all of this information in the text instead of a parenthetical citation.

P: (U.S. Senate 1956, 9–10)

> . . . as the Senate Committee on Foreign Relations decreed in its report accompany-
> ing the *Mutual Security Act* of 1956 (9–10).

Note that some shortened forms and abbreviations used in citing public documents are different from those used elsewhere, such as *2d* instead of *2nd* and *3d* instead of *3rd*. Other examples are noted in the relevant sections of 19.9.

19.9.2 Congressional Publications

For congressional publications, reference list entries usually begin with the designation *U.S. Congress,* followed by *Senate* or *House.* (You may also simplify this to *U.S. Senate* or *U.S. House.*) Other common elements include committee and subcommittee, if any; date of publication; title of document; number of the Congress and session (abbreviated *Cong.* and *sess.* respectively in this position); and number and description of the document (for example, H. Doc. 487), if available.

DEBATES. Since 1873, congressional debates have been published by the government in the *Congressional Record.* Whenever possible, cite the permanent volumes, which often reflect changes from the daily issues of the *Record.* Begin parenthetical citations with the abbreviation *Cong. Rec.,* and identify the volume and part numbers as well as the page numbers.

R: U.S. Congress. *Congressional Record.* 1930. 71st Cong., 2d sess. Vol. 72, pt. 10.

P: (*Cong. Rec.* 1930, 72, pt. 10: 10828–30)

If you need to identify a speaker and the subject in a debate, do so in text, and include a parenthetical citation for the publication only.

> Senator Kennedy of Massachusetts spoke for the Joint Resolution on Nuclear Weap-
> ons Freeze and Reductions (*Cong. Rec.* 1982, 128, pt. 3: 3832–34).

Before 1874, congressional debates were published in *Annals of the Congress of the United States* (also known by other names and covering the years 1789–1824), *Congressional Debates* (1824–37), and *Congressional Globe* (1833–73). Cite these works similarly to the *Congressional Record.*

REPORTS AND DOCUMENTS. When you cite reports and documents of the Senate (abbreviated *S.*) and the House (*H.*), include both the Congress and session numbers and, if possible, the series number.

R: U.S. Congress. House. 1947. *Report of Activities of the National Advisory Council on International Monetary and Financial Problems to March 31, 1947.* 80th Cong., 1st sess.
H. Doc. 365.

P: (U.S. House 1947, 4)

HEARINGS. Records of testimony given before congressional committees are usually published with titles, which should be included in reference list entries. List the relevant committee as author.

R: U.S. Congress. Senate. Committee on Foreign Relations. 1985. *Famine in Africa: Hearing before the Committee on Foreign Relations.* 99th Cong., 1st sess., January 17.

P: (U.S. Senate 1985, 53)

BILLS AND RESOLUTIONS. Congressional bills (proposed laws) and resolutions are published in pamphlet form. In citations, bills and resolutions originating in the House of Representatives are abbreviated *HR* and those originating in the Senate, *S.* Include publication details in the *Congressional Record* (if available).

R: U.S. Congress. House. 1985. *Food Security Act of 1985.* HR 2100. 99th Cong., 1st sess., *Congressional Record* 131, no. 132, daily ed. (October 8): H 8353–8486.

P: (U.S. House 1985, H 8461)

STATUTES. Statutes, which are bills or resolutions that have been passed into law, are first published separately and then collected in the annual bound volumes of the *United States Statutes at Large,* which began publication in 1874. Later they are incorporated into the *United States Code.* Cite *U.S. Statutes,* the *U.S. Code,* or both; cite specific provisions by section (preceded by a section symbol and a space) and, in *Statutes,* by page.

In a parenthetical citation, indicate the year the act was passed; in your reference list, also include the publication date of the statutory compilation, which may differ from the year of passage.

R: *Atomic Energy Act of 1946.* Public Law 585. 79th Cong., 2d sess. August 1.
Fair Credit Reporting Act. 1970. *U.S. Code* 15 (2000), §§ 1681 et seq.
National Environmental Policy Act of 1969. Public Law 91–190. *U.S. Statutes at Large* 83 (1970): 852. Codified at *U.S. Code* 42 (2000), §§ 4321 et seq.

P: (*Atomic Energy Act of 1946*)
(*Fair Credit Reporting Act 1970*)
(*National Environmental Policy Act of 1969,* sec. 102)

Before 1874, laws were published in the seventeen-volume *Statutes at Large of the United States of America, 1789–1873.* Citations to this collection include the volume number and its publication date.

19.9.3   Presidential Publications

Presidential proclamations, executive orders, vetoes, addresses, and the like are published in the *Weekly Compilation of Presidential Documents* and in *Public Papers of the Presidents of the United States.* Proclamations and executive orders are also carried in the daily *Federal Register* and then published in title 3 of the *Code of Federal Regulations.* Once they have been published in the *Code,* use that as your source.

R: U.S. President. 1984. Proclamation. Caribbean Basin Economic Recovery Act, Proclamation 5142, Amending Proclamation 5133. *Federal Register* 49, no. 2, p. 341
   (January 4).
   U.S. President. 1971. Executive Order no. 11,609. *Code of Federal Regulations,* title 3,
   p. 586 (1971–75).

P: (U.S. President 1984, 341)
   (U.S. President 1971)

The public papers of U.S. presidents are collected in two multivolume works: *Compilation of the Messages and Papers of the Presidents, 1789–1897,* and, for subsequent administrations, *Public Papers of the Presidents of the United States.*

R: Hoover, Herbert. 1977. *Public Papers of the Presidents of the United States: Herbert
   Hoover, 1929–33.* Vol. 4. Washington, DC: Government Printing Office.

P: (Hoover 1977, 178–83)

19.9.4   Publications of Government Departments and Agencies

Executive departments, bureaus, and agencies issue reports, bulletins, circulars, and other materials. Include the name of an identified author after the title.

R: U.S. Department of the Interior. Minerals Management Service. 1984. *An Oilspill Risk
   Analysis for the Central Gulf (April 1984) and Western Gulf of Mexico (July 1984),* by
   Robert P. LaBelle. Open-file report, U.S. Geological Survey. Denver.
   U.S. Bureau of the Census. 1975. *Median Gross Rent by Counties of the United States,
   1970.* Prepared by the Geography Division in cooperation with the Housing Divi-
   sion, Bureau of the Census. Washington, DC: Government Printing Office.

P: (U.S. Department of the Interior 1984, 3)
   (U.S. Bureau of the Census 1975, 15–16)

Cite bulletins, circulars, reports, and study papers issued by government commissions such as the Federal Communications Commission or the Securities and Exchange Commission much like legislative reports. They are often classified as House (*H*) or Senate (*S*) documents.

R: U.S. Congress. Senate. 1935. *Report of the Federal Trade Commission on Utility Corpo-rations.* 70th Cong., 1st sess. S. Doc. 91, pt. 71A.

U.S. Securities and Exchange Commission. 1983. *Annual Report of the Securities and Exchange Commission for the Fiscal Year.* Washington, DC: Government Printing Office.

P: (U.S. Senate 1935, 1)

(U.S. Securities and Exchange Commission 1983, 42)

19.9.5 U.S. Constitution

The U.S. Constitution should be cited only in parenthetical citations; you need not include it in your reference list. Include the article or amendment, section, and, if relevant, clause. Use arabic numerals and, if you prefer, abbreviations for terms such as *amendment* and *section*.

P: (U.S. Constitution, art. 2, sec. 1, cl. 3)

(U.S. Constitution, amend. 14, sec. 2)

In many cases, you can include the identifying information in your text, but spell out the names of parts. Capitalize the names of specific amendments when used in place of numbers.

The U.S. Constitution, in article 1, section 9, forbids suspension of the writ "unless when in Cases of Rebellion or Invasion the public Safety may require it."

The First Amendment protects the right of free speech.

19.9.6 Treaties

The texts of treaties signed before 1949 are published in *United States Statutes at Large;* the unofficial citation is to the *Treaty Series* or the *Executive Agreement Series.* Those signed in 1949 or later appear in *United States Treaties and Other International Agreements (UST,* 1950–), or *Treaties and Other International Acts Series (TIAS,* 1946–). Treaties involving more than two nations may be found in the United Nations *Treaty Series: Treaties and International Agreements Registered or Filed or Recorded with the Secretariat of the United Nations* or, from 1920 to 1946, in the League of Nations *Treaty Series.*

Put titles of treaties in roman type, not enclosed in quotation marks. Italicize the names of the publications, even if they are multivolume works or series. An exact date indicates the date of signing and may be included in addition to the year the treaty was published.

R: U.S. Department of State. 1963. Nuclear Weapons Test Ban, August 5, 1963. *United States Treaties and Other International Agreements* 14, pt. 2.

United States. 1922. Naval Armament Limitation Treaty. February 26, 1922. *United States Statutes at Large* 43, pt. 2.

P: [U.S. Department of State 1963]
    [United States 1922]

19.9.7 Legal Cases

Citations of legal cases generally take the same form for courts at all levels. In your reference list, italicize the full case name (including the abbreviation *v*.). Include the volume number (arabic), name of the reporter (abbreviated; see below), ordinal series number (if applicable), opening page number of the decision, abbreviated name of the court and date, and other relevant information, such as the publisher for a loose-leaf service or the name of a state or local court (if not identified by the reporter title).

R: *United States v. Christmas.* 222 F.3d 141 [4th Cir. 2000].
    Profit Sharing Plan v. Mbank Dallas, N.A. 683 F. Supp. 592 [N.D. Tex. 1988].

The one element that depends on the level of the court is the name of the reporter. The most common ones are as follows.

■ *U.S. Supreme Court.* For Supreme Court decisions, cite *United States Supreme Court Reports* (abbreviated *U.S.*) or, if not yet published there, *Supreme Court Reporter* (abbreviated *S. Ct.*).

R: *AT&T Corp. v. Iowa Utilities Bd.* 525 U.S. 366 [1999].
    Arthur Andersen LLP v. United States. 125 S. Ct. 2129 [2005].

■ *Lower federal courts.* For lower federal-court decisions, cite *Federal Reporter* (F.) or *Federal Supplement* (F. Supp.).

R: *United States v. Dennis.* 183 F. 201 [2d Cir. 1950].
    Eaton v. IBM Corp. 925 F. Supp. 487 [S.D. Tex. 1996].

■ *State and local courts.* For state and local court decisions, cite official state reporters whenever possible. If you use a commercial reporter, cite it as in the second example below. If the reporter does not identify the court's name, include it before the date, within parentheses.

R: *Williams v. Davis.* 27 Cal. 2d 746 [1946].
    Bivens v. Mobley. 724 So. 2d 458. [Miss. Ct. App. 1998].

To cite a legal case in your text, give the name of the case and the date (if citing specific language, provide the page number as well). In many instances, you may be able to include either or both elements in the text.

P: [*United States v. Christmas* 2000]

    . . . his principle was best exemplified by *United States v. Christmas* [2000].

19.9.8 State and Local Government Documents

Cite state and local government documents as you would federal documents. Use roman type (no quotation marks) for state laws and municipal ordinances; use italics for codes (compilations). Include a name where necessary to indicate the version of the code being cited, followed by the date of the code edition, in parentheses.

R: *Methamphetamine Control and Community Protection Act.* 2005. *Illinois Compiled Statutes,* ch. 720, sec. 646/10 (2005).

Illinois Institute for Environmental Quality (IIEQ). 1977. *Review and Synopsis of Public Participation Regarding Sulfur Dioxide and Particulate Emissions.* By Sidney M. Marder. IIEQ Document no. 77/21. Chicago.

P: (New Mexico Constitution, art. 4, sec. 7)

(*Methamphetamine Control and Community Protection Act* 2005)

19.9.9 Canadian Government Documents

Cite Canadian government documents similarly to U.S. public documents. Begin citations with the word *Canada* unless it is obvious from the context. Generally abbreviate *chapter* and *section* as *c.* and *s.,* but if you cite only a few Canadian documents, use *chap.* and *sec.*

Canadian government documents are issued by both houses of the federal Parliament (the Senate and the House of Commons), by the provincial and territorial legislatures, and by various executive departments.

Parliamentary debates are published in separate series, *House of Commons Debates* and *Senate Debates.* Include the name of the person speaking, where relevant. Provincial and territorial legislatures publish their own debates.

R: Canada. Manitoba. Legislative Assembly. 2000. *Debates and Proceedings.* August 17.

P: (Canada 2000, 5326)

Cite parliamentary bills by bill number, title, year of passage where relevant, session number, Parliament number, and additional information as needed.

R: Bill C-40, *Extradition Act.* 1999. 2d sess., 36th Parliament, 1998, cl. 1. *Statutes of Canada,* c. 18.

P: (Bill C-40, Extradition Act 1999)

Canadian statutes are first published in the annual *Statutes of Canada* and were most recently consolidated in 1985 in the *Revised Statutes of Canada.* Wherever possible, use the latter source and identify the statute by title, reporter, year of compilation, chapter, and section.

R: *Canada Wildlife Act, Revised Statutes of Canada* 1985, c. W-9, s. 1.
   Assisted Human Reproduction Act, Statutes of Canada 2004, c. 2, s. 2.

P: (*Canada Wildlife Act* 1985)

19.9.10   British Government Documents

Cite British government documents similarly to U.S. public documents. Begin citations with the phrase *United Kingdom* unless it is obvious from the context. The publisher of most British government material is Her (or His) Majesty's Stationery Office (HMSO) in London.

Parliamentary debates have been published in several series and, since 1909, in separate series for the House of Lords and the House of Commons. Citations include date, series, volume number, and (if relevant) column or occasionally page number. In some cases, you may cite a specific document within a volume.

R: United Kingdom. 1879. *Hansard Parliamentary Debates.* 3d ser., vol. 249.
   Churchill, Winston. 1945. Speech to the House of Commons, January 18. *Parliamentary Debates*, Commons, 5th ser., vol. 407 (1944–45), cols. 425–46.

P: (United Kingdom 1879, cols. 611–27)
   (Churchill 1945, cols. 425–46)

The bills, reports, and papers issued separately by Parliament are published together at the end of each session in volumes referred to as *Sessional Papers.* Each volume includes a divisional title.

R: United Kingdom. House of Commons. 1983. Present and Future Role of the Assistant Chief Education Officer. *Sessional Papers, 1982–83, Prison Education.* April 25. Vol. 2.

P: (United Kingdom 1983, vol. 2, par. 9.14, p. 102)

Acts of Parliament should usually be cited only in parenthetical citations or in the text. You generally need not include them in your reference list, although you may choose to include a specific work that is critical to your argument or frequently cited. Identify acts by title (in roman type, not enclosed in quotation marks), date, and chapter number (*c.* for chapter; arabic numeral for national number, lowercase roman for local). Acts from before 1963 are cited by regnal year and monarch's name (abbreviated) and ordinal (arabic numeral).

P: (Act of Settlement 1701, 12 & 13 Will. 3, c. 2)
   (Consolidated Fund Act 1963, c. 1)
   (Manchester Corporation Act 1967, c. xl)

There are many compilations of British historical records, some of them transcriptions of the documents preserved in the Public Record Office.

R: United Kingdom. 1890–1907. *Acts of the Privy Council of England.* Ed. J. R. Dasent. 32 vols. London.
   United Kingdom. n.d. *Rotuli parliamentorum . . .* (1278–1504). 6 vols. N.p.
   United Kingdom. 1810–28. *Statutes of the Realm.* Ed. A. Luders and others. 11 vols. London.

P: (United Kingdom, 1810–28)

19.9.11 Publications of International Bodies

If you cite documents of international bodies such as the United Nations, identify the authorizing body (and the author or editor where appropriate), the date, and the topic or title of the document. Also include series and publication numbers, place of publication, and publisher. You may use abbreviations for major bodies (*UN* for *United Nations, WTO* for *World Trade Organization,* and so forth) where the reference is clear.

R: League of Nations. 1935. *Position of Women of Russian Origin in the Far East.* Ser. LoNP, IV.3. Geneva: League of Nations.
   General Agreement on Tariffs and Trade. 1994. *The Results of the Uruguay Round of Multilateral Trade Negotiations: The Legal Texts.* Geneva: GATT Secretariat.

P: (League of Nations 1935)
   (GATT 1994)

19.9.12 Unpublished Government Documents

If you cite unpublished government documents, follow the patterns described in 19.6.4.

Most unpublished documents of the U.S. government are housed in the National Archives (NA) in Washington, DC, or in one of its branches. Cite them all, including films, photographs, and sound recordings as well as written materials, by record group (RG) number.

The comparable institution for unpublished Canadian government documents is the National Archives of Canada (NAC) in Ottawa, Ontario. The United Kingdom has a number of depositories of unpublished government documents, most notably the Public Record Office (PRO) and the British Library (BL), both in London.

19.9.13 Online Public Documents

To cite online public documents, follow the relevant examples presented elsewhere in 19.9. In addition, include the URL and the date you accessed the material (see 15.4.1). Note that a URL alone is not sufficient; you must provide the full facts of publication, as far as they can be determined, so that a reader can search for the source if the URL changes. If page numbers are not available, you may identify the location of a cited passage in a parenthetical citation by adding a descriptive locator (such as a preceding subheading) following the word *under.*

R: U.S. Bureau of the Census. 2004. Income, Poverty, and Health Insurance Coverage in the United States, 2004. http://www.census.gov/prod/2005pubs/p60–229.pdf (accessed December 19, 2005).

P: (U.S. Bureau of the Census 2004, under "Ratio of Income to Poverty Level")

or

(U.S. Bureau of the Census 2004)

19.10 One Source Quoted in Another

Responsible researchers avoid repeating quotations that they have not actually seen in the original. If one source includes a useful quotation from another source, readers expect you to obtain the original to verify not only that the quotation is accurate, but also that it fairly represents what the original meant.

If the original source is unavailable, however, cite it as "quoted in" the secondary source in your reference list. In a parenthetical citation, give only the name of the original author.

R: Zukofsky, Louis. 1931. Sincerity and objectification. *Poetry* 37 (February): 269. Quoted in Bonnie Costello, *Marianne Moore: Imaginary possessions* (Cambridge, MA: Harvard University Press, 1981).

P: (Zukofsky 1931, 269)

The same situation may arise with a quotation you find in a secondary source drawn from a primary source (see 3.1.1). Often, you will not be able to consult the primary source, especially if it is in an unpublished manuscript collection. In this case, follow the principles outlined above.

PART III

Style

20 Spelling

Model your spelling on American usage and be consistent, except in quotations, where you should usually follow the original spelling exactly (see chapter 25). When in doubt, consult a dictionary. Be aware, however, that dictionaries often differ on how to spell the same word and that some are more accurate and up-to-date than others.

The most reliable authority for spelling is *Webster's Third New International Dictionary* or its abridgment, the eleventh edition of *Merriam-Webster's Collegiate Dictionary.* The abridgment is available in book, CD-ROM, and Web-based formats. For the names of people and places, see the listings at the end of Webster's or the separate publications *Merriam-Webster's Biographical Dictionary* and *Merriam-Webster's Geographical Dictionary.*

Where Webster's offers a choice between spellings, use the following principles to select one: where variants are separated by *or,* choose either one and use it consistently; where variants are separated by *also,* use the first. If the preferred spelling in Webster's differs from the conventional one in your discipline, follow the spelling of the discipline. For style guides in various disciplines, see the bibliography.

The spell-checking feature in most word processors can catch certain spelling errors but not others. It will not recognize, for example, that you typed *and* when you meant *an,* or *quite* instead of *quiet.* It will probably not help with proper nouns or foreign terms, and it may lead you to make global spelling changes that in some cases are inaccurate. A spell-checker is not a substitute for a good dictionary or careful proofreading.

This chapter offers general guidelines for spellings not found in most dictionaries. If you are writing a thesis or dissertation, your department or university may have specific requirements for spelling (including use of particular dictionaries). Those requirements are usually available from the office of theses and dissertations. If you are writing a class paper, your instructor may also ask you to follow certain principles of spelling. Review these requirements before you prepare your paper. They take precedence over the guidelines suggested here.

20.1 Plurals

20.1.1 General Rule

For most common nouns, form the plural by adding *s* (or *es,* for words ending in *ch, j, s, sh, x,* or *z*). Most dictionaries give plural forms only for words that do not follow the general rule.

The general rule applies to the names of persons and to other proper nouns, including Native American tribes. If such a noun ends in *y,* do not change the *y* to *ie,* as required for common nouns. (Do not confuse plural forms with possessives, which are described in 20.2).

the Costellos   the two Germanys
the Frys (*not* the Fries)   the Hopis of Arizona (*not* the Hopi)
the Rodriguezes

20.1.2 Special Cases

COMPOUND WORDS. For compound words consisting of two nouns, add *s* or *es* to the last noun.

bookkeepers   district attorneys   actor-singers

When a prepositional phrase or adjective follows, add *s* or *es* to the main noun.

sisters-in-law   attorneys general   men-of-war

LETTERS AND NUMERALS. In most cases, form the plurals of capital letters and numerals by adding *s* alone (not *'s*).

the three Rs   the 1950s   767s

With lowercase letters and some single capital letters, however, an *s* without an apostrophe can seem to create a different word (*is*, *As*) or an abbreviation (*ms*). If the *s* might create confusion, add an apostrophe. The apostrophe and *s* are roman even if the letter is italic (see 22.2.2).

dotting all the i's   x's and y's   three A's and two B's

ABBREVIATIONS. Form plurals of abbreviations without internal periods by adding *s* alone. If the singular form of the abbreviation ends in a period, put the *s* before the period. (See 24.1.3 on the punctuation of abbreviations.)

URLs   vols.
DVDs   eds.

Add an apostrophe before the *s* only when an abbreviation contains internal periods or both capital and lowercase letters.

PhD's (or Ph.D.'s; see 24.2.3)

A few abbreviations have irregular plurals (see also 24.7).

pp. (plural of p., page)   nn. (plural of n., note)

If you are writing in the sciences and using abbreviations for units of measure (see 24.5), use the same abbreviation for both the singular and the plural.

6 kg   37 m²

TERMS IN ITALICS AND QUOTATION MARKS. Form the plural of a term in italics by adding *s* alone (not *'s*) in roman type. Do not form the plural of a term in quotation marks by adding *'s*; rephrase the sentence.

two *Chicago Tribunes*

. . . included "To be continued" many times

not

. . . included many "To be continued's"

20.2 Possessives

20.2.1 General Rule

Form the possessive of most singular common and proper nouns, including those that end in *s*, *x*, or *z*, by adding an apostrophe and *s*. This rule
also applies to letters and numerals used as singular nouns, and to abbreviations. (Do not confuse possessives with plural forms, which are described in 20.1). For special cases, see 20.2.2.

an argument's effects	Stevens's poems	2009's economic outlook
the phalanx's advance	Diaz's revolt	JFK's speech

Inanimate nouns—except for references to time—rarely take the possessive form.

a day's length	*but not*	the house's door

Form the possessive of most plural common and proper nouns by adding only an apostrophe. For special cases, see 20.2.2.

politicians' votes	*not*	politicians's votes
the Rodriguezes' house	*not*	the Rodriguezes's house

For irregular plurals that do not end in *s*, add *s* after the apostrophe.

the mice's nest	children's literature

20.2.2 Special Cases

SINGULAR NOUNS ENDING IN S. Form the possessive of the following types of
nouns with only an apostrophe:

- nouns that name a group or collective entity but are treated as grammatically singular

politics' true meaning	the United States' role

- names that end in an unpronounced *s*

Descartes' *Discourse on Method*	Albert Camus' novels

- names of more than one syllable with an unaccented ending pronounced
eez, including many Greek and hellenized names

Aristophanes' plays	the Ganges' source	Charles Yerkes' ideas

- nouns in *For . . . sake* expressions that end in an *s* or an *s* sound

for conscience' sake	for appearance' sake

You might instead rephrase a sentence that contains one of these exceptions. (For use of the abbreviation *U.S.* in this situation, see 24.3.1.)

the role of the United States	*instead of*	the United States' role
for the sake of appearance	*instead of*	for appearance' sake

COMPOUND WORDS. Form the possessives of singular compound words by
adding an apostrophe and *s* to the last word, even if the main noun is
first.

his sister-in-law's business	the attorney general's decision

Avoid using the possessive for plural compounds in which the noun is
followed by a prepositional phrase or adjective; rephrase instead.

decisions of the attorneys general	*not*	attorneys' general decisions

MULTIPLE NOUNS. If a possessive indicates that two or more entities each
possess something separately, make all the nouns possessive.

New York's and Chicago's teams	historians' and economists' methods

If a possessive indicates that two or more entities possess something
jointly, make only the last noun possessive.

Minneapolis and St. Paul's teams	historians and economists' data

TERMS IN ITALICS AND QUOTATION MARKS. If a term in italics is possessive, both
the apostrophe and the *s* should be in roman type. Do not add a possessive to a term in quotation marks; rephrase the sentence.

the *Atlantic Monthly*'s editor	admirers of "Ode on a Grecian Urn"

20.3 Compounds and Words Formed with Prefixes

It is difficult to predict when a compound word, or a compound modifier,
should be hyphenated, left open (with a space, not a hyphen, between
elements), or closed (spelled as one word). The best authority is your dictionary. If you cannot find a compound there, follow the principles in the
following paragraphs to decide whether or not to hyphenate. If you cannot find the form in either place, leave the compound open.

The patterns outlined below are not hard-and-fast rules. You will have
to decide many individual cases on the basis of context, personal taste, or
common usage in your discipline. Although much of the suggested hyphenation is logical and aids readability, some is only traditional.

20.3.1 Compounds Used as Adjectives

Some compounds are used only as adjectives. In most cases, hyphenate such a compound when it precedes the noun it modifies; otherwise leave it open.

Before noun	After noun
open-ended question	most of the questions were *open ended*
full-length treatment	treatment is *full length*
duty-free goods	goods brought in *duty free*
thought-provoking commentary	commentary was *thought provoking*
over-the-counter drug	drug sold *over the counter*
a frequently *referred-to* book	this book is frequently *referred to*
spelled-out numbers	numbers that are *spelled out*

There are a few exceptions:

- If a compound that would normally be hyphenated is preceded and modified by an adverb (such as *very*), omit the hyphen, because the grouping of the words will be clear to the reader.

Before noun with modifier	After noun with modifier
a *well-known* author	a very *well known* author
an *ill-advised* step	a somewhat *ill advised* step

- Hyphenate compounds that begin with *all* and *cross,* except for a few words that are conventionally closed, such as *crossover* (check your dictionary when in doubt).

Before noun	After noun
all-encompassing treatment	text that includes *cross-references*

- Close up compounds that end with the terms *borne, like,* and *wide,* unless the first part of the compound has three or more syllables, is a proper noun, or ends with the same letter with which the second term begins.

General pattern	Exceptions
foodborne	mosquito-borne
childlike	bell-like
worldwide	Chicago-wide

- Comparative constructions beginning with such terms as *more/most, less/least,* and *better/best* should be hyphenated only when there may be confusion about whether the comparative term is modifying the adjective that follows within the compound or the noun after the compound.

Modifying adjective	Modifying noun
colleges produce *more-skilled* workers	we hired *more skilled* workers for the holidays

■ Constructions that consist of an adverb ending in *-ly* followed by an adjective are not compounds and should not be hyphenated in any context.

Before noun	After noun
highly developed species	the species was *highly developed*
widely disseminated literature	literature has been *widely disseminated*

20.3.2 Compounds Used as Both Nouns and Adjectives

Some compounds are primarily nouns but can also function as adjectives when they precede and modify another noun. (Unlike the examples in 20.3.1, these compounds are rarely used as adjectives after a noun, and then only with a verb such as *was* or *are,* as in the third example below.) In most cases, hyphenate such a compound when it precedes a noun that it modifies; otherwise leave it open.

Adjective before noun	Noun, or adjective after noun
the *decision-making* process	*decision making* became her specialty
a *continuing-education* course	a program of *continuing education*
a *middle-class* neighborhood	her neighborhood was *middle class*

There are a few exceptions:

■ For a compound that begins with *e* (short for *electronic*), *ex,* or *self,* use a hyphen in all contexts. One exception: if *self* is preceded by *un,* the compound should be closed (as in *unselfconscious*).

ex–husband	self-destructive	e-mail

■ For a compound that ends with *elect,* use a hyphen in all contexts when the name of the office is only one word, but leave it open when the name is two or more words.

president-elect	district attorney elect

- For a compound formed by two coordinated nouns that could be joined by *and,* use a hyphen in all contexts.

actor-singer	*mother-daughter* relationship
city-state	*parent-teacher* conference

- For a compound composed of directional words, use a closed compound when the term describes a single direction. Use a hyphen if the compound consists of coordinated nouns that could be joined with *and* or *by.*

northeast	a street running *north-south*
southwest	*east-southeast* winds

- Compounds that describe family relationships vary in whether they are closed up or hyphenated. When in doubt, consult your dictionary. (For the plural and possessive forms of *in-law* compounds, see 20.1.2 and 20.2.2, respectively.)

grandfather	stepdaughter	great-grandmother	son-in-law

- Some familiar phrases are always hyphenated.

stick-in-the-mud	jack-of-all-trades

COMPOUNDS INCLUDING PROPER NOUNS. Leave open most compounds that include proper nouns, including names of ethnic groups.

Adjective before noun	*Noun, or adjective after noun*
African American culture	an *African American* has written
French Canadian explorer	the explorer was *French Canadian*
Middle Eastern geography	the geography of the *Middle East*
State Department employees	employed by the *State Department*
Korean War veterans	veterans of the *Korean War*

If, however, the first term is shortened, use a hyphen.

Afro-American culture	an *Afro-American* has written

If coordinated terms could be joined by *and,* hyphenate them.

Israel-Egypt peace treaty	*Spanish-English* dictionary

COMPOUNDS INCLUDING NUMBERS. If a compound includes a number, hyphenate it if it precedes a noun that it modifies; otherwise leave it open. (For the use of numerals versus spelled-out numbers, see chapter 23.)

Adjective before noun	Noun, or adjective after noun
fifty-year project	the project took *fifty years*
four-year-old child	the child was *four years* old
twentieth-century literature	studied the literature of the *twentieth century*
third-floor apartment	she lived on the *third floor*
214-day standoff	standoff that lasted *214 days*

There are a few exceptions:

■ Always leave open a compound including the word *percent,* and give the number in arabic numerals (see 23.1.3).

a *15 percent* increase   increased by *15 percent*

■ Always use a hyphen to spell a fraction with words. (See 23.1.3 for use of numerals versus spelled-out numbers in fractions.)

a *two-thirds* majority   a majority of *two-thirds*

■ For a fraction beginning with *half* or *quarter,* use a hyphen when it precedes a noun that it modifies; otherwise leave it open.

Adjective before noun	Noun, or adjective after noun
a *half-hour* session	after a *half hour* had passed
a *quarter-mile* run	ran a *quarter mile*

■ For a compound indicating a span of numbers, use a hyphen in both terms, but omit the second part of the compound in the first term.

five- to *ten-minute* intervals   *eight-* to *ten-year-olds*

20.3.3 Words Formed with Prefixes

Words formed with prefixes are normally closed, whether they are nouns (*postmodernism*), verbs (*misrepresent*), adjectives (*antebellum*), or adverbs (*prematurely*). Use a hyphen, however, in these cases:

■ when the prefix is combined with a capitalized word

sub-Saharan	*but*	subdivision
pro-Asian	*but*	pronuclear

- when the prefix is combined with a numeral

| pre-1950 | *but* | predisposed |
| mid-80s | *but* | midlife |

- to separate two *i*'s, two *a*'s, or other combinations of letters or syllables that might cause misreading

| anti-intellectual | *but* | antidepressant |
| semi-invalid | *but* | semiopaque |

- when the prefix precedes a compound word that is hyphenated or open

| non-coffee-drinking | *but* | nonbelief |
| post-high school | *but* | postgame |

- to separate repeated terms in a double prefix

sub-subentry

- when a prefix stands alone

pre- and postwar   macro- and microeconomics

These patterns apply to words formed with the following prefixes, among others.

ante	cyber	macro	multi	proto	super
anti	extra	mega	neo	pseudo	supra
bi	hyper	meta	non	re	trans
bio	infra	micro	post	semi	ultra
co	inter	mid	pre	socio	un
counter	intra	mini	pro	sub	

The patterns also apply to prepositions such as *over* and *under* that can be attached to words in the same position as prefixes.

overachiever   underhanded   over- and underused

20.4 Line Breaks

20.4.1 Breaks within Words

For most papers, the only words that should be hyphenated at the ends of lines are those you have deliberately hyphenated, such as compounds (see 20.3). Set your word processor to left justify (with a "ragged" right margin), and do not use its automated hyphenation feature.

If, however, you are required to justify both the left and right margins, you may have to hyphenate lines to avoid large gaps between words. Do not end four or more consecutive lines with hyphens (resulting in a "hyphen block" along the margin), and do not leave the hyphenation entirely to the automated function of your word processor. It will be generally reliable but will also make errors. So review word breaks after your word processor inserts them. When in doubt, consult your dictionary, which indicates acceptable breaks with centered dots or similar devices in the main word entry.

One special type of problem concerns words with the same spelling but different pronunciations. Such words may have different syllable breaks, such as *rec-ord* and *re-cord*. Your word processor may break such words identically, regardless of context.

20.4.2 Breaks over Spaces and Punctuation

Your word processor may also allow certain types of unacceptable line breaks to occur over spaces or punctuation. Always review your paper for such breaks.

■ *Initials.* If initials are used in place of both a person's first and middle names, include a space between them but do not divide them over a line. If necessary, you can break the name before the last name. See also 24.2.1.

M. F. K. Fisher   M. F. K. / Fisher   *but not*   M. / F. K. Fisher

■ *Numbers and dates.* Never put a line break within numbers expressed as numerals (25,000) or any terms consisting of numerals plus symbols, abbreviations, or units of measure (10%; £6 4s. 6d.; 6:40 p.m.; AD 1895; 245 ml). In dates, do not divide a day of the month from the name of the month (February 15). See chapter 23 for more on numbers and date systems.

■ *Abbreviations.* Do not break abbreviations over lines, regardless of their internal capitalization, punctuation, and spacing (BA, U.S., NATO, p.m., kg, PhD, Gov. Gen.). The only exception is that an abbreviation that already includes a hyphen, such as AFL-CIO, may be divided on the hyphen. See chapter 24 for more on abbreviations.

■ *Punctuation.* Never begin a line with a closing quotation mark, parenthesis, or bracket. Never end a line with an opening quotation mark, parenthesis, or bracket or with (*a*) or (1), as at the beginning of a list. See chapter 21 for more on punctuation and 23.4.2 for lists. Avoid breaking an ellipsis (see 25.3.2) over a line; use your word processor's ellipsis character to prevent this problem.

■ *URLs and e-mail addresses.* Avoid breaking URLs and e-mail addresses over lines. If you have to break one, insert the break after a colon, a slash (or double slash), or the symbol @ but before a period or any other punctuation or symbols. Hyphens are frequently included as part of a URL or e-mail address, so to avoid confusion, never add a hyphen to indicate the break, or break a URL or address at an existing hyphen.

```
http://
www.press.uchicago.edu
```

```
http://www
.press.uchicago.edu
```

```
http://www.press.uchicago.edu/
cgi-bin/hfs.cgi/00/12917.ctl
```

If your word processor automatically formats URLs and e-mail addresses as hyperlinks, it may break these items contrary to the guidelines above. In many settings, such breaks are acceptable as long as the full URL or address is clearly identified as a hyperlink (through underlining or a second color) and no extra hyphens are added to indicate the line breaks.

21 Punctuation

This chapter offers general guidelines for punctuation in the text of your paper. Some rules are clear-cut, but others are not, so you often have to depend on sound judgment and a good ear.

Special elements such as abbreviations, quotations, and citations have their own guidelines for punctuation, which are treated in relevant chapters in this book.

If you are writing a thesis or dissertation, your department or university may have specific requirements for punctuation, which are usually available from the office of theses and dissertations. If you are writing a class paper, your instructor may also ask you to follow certain principles for punctuation. Review these requirements before you prepare your paper. They take precedence over the guidelines suggested here. For style guides in various disciplines, see the bibliography.

21.1 Period

A period ends a sentence that is a declarative statement, an imperative statement, or an indirect question. A period can also end a sentence fragment, if the context makes its rhetorical function clear. But this usage is rare in academic writing. In all these cases, the period is a *terminal period* and should be followed by a single space.

Consider the advantages of this method.

The question was whether these differences could be reconciled.

Put a period at the end of items in a vertical list only if the items are complete sentences (see 23.4.2). Otherwise, omit terminal periods, even for the last item, and do not capitalize the first words.

The report covers three areas:

1. the securities markets

2. the securities industry

3. the securities industry in the economy

Individual periods can also be used in other contexts, including abbreviations (see especially 24.1.3) and citations (16.1.2 and 18.1.2), and also in URLs (20.4.2, 17.1.7, and 19.1.8), where they are often called *dots*. Strings of periods, or dots, can be used in quotations (see 25.3.2), where they are called *ellipses,* and in tables (26.2.6) and front matter pages (A.2.1), where they are called *leaders*.

Do not use periods after chapter and part titles and most subheadings (see A.2.2) or after table titles (26.2.2). For periods in figure captions, see 26.3.2.

21.2 Comma

Commas separate items within a sentence, including clauses, phrases, and individual words. They are especially important when a reader might mistake where a clause or phrase ends and another begins:

Before leaving the members of the committee met in the assembly room.

Before leaving, the members of the committee met in the assembly room.

For use of commas in numbers, see 23.2.2. For use of commas in citations, see 16.1.2 and 18.1.2.

21.2.1 Independent Clauses

In a sentence containing two or more independent clauses joined by a coordinating conjunction (*and, but, or, nor, for, so, yet*), put a comma before the conjunction. This is not a hard-and-fast rule; no comma is needed between two short independent clauses with no internal punctuation.

Students around the world want to learn English, and many young Americans are eager to teach them.

The senator arrived at noon and the president left at one.

In a sentence containing three or more short and simple independent clauses with no internal punctuation, separate the clauses with commas and add a coordinating conjunction before the last one. (Always include a comma before the coordinating conjunction.) If the clauses are longer and more complex, separate them with semicolons (see 21.3)—or, better, rewrite the sentence.

The committee designed the questionnaire, the field workers collected responses, and the statistician analyzed the results.

The committee designed the questionnaire, which was short; the field workers, who did not participate, collected responses; and the statistician analyzed the results, though not until several days later.

Ordinarily, do not insert a comma before a conjunction joining two subjects or two predicates.

The agencies that design the surveys and the analysts who evaluate the results should work together.

They do not condone such practices but attempt to refute them theoretically.

When a sentence opens with a phrase or dependent clause that modifies following two independent coordinate clauses, put a comma after the introductory element but not between the two independent clauses.

Within ten years, interest rates surged and the housing market declined.

21.2.2 Series

In a series consisting of three or more words, phrases, or clauses with no internal punctuation of their own, separate the elements with commas. Always use a comma before the conjunction that introduces the last item.

The governor wrote his senators, the president, and the vice president.

Attending the conference were Fernandez, Sullivan, and Kendrick.

The public approved, the committee agreed, but the measure failed.

Do not use commas when all the elements in a series are joined by conjunctions.

The palette consisted of blue and green and orange.

If a series of three or more words, phrases, or clauses ends with an expression indicating continuation (*and so forth, and so on, and the like,* or *etc.*), punctuate that final expression as though it were the final item in the series. You may, however, add a comma after the continuation expression to prevent confusion after a long series.

They discussed movies, books, plays, and the like until late in the night.

Management can improve not just productivity, but hours, working conditions, training, benefits, and so on, without reducing wages.

Use semicolons to separate the items in a series if one or more includes commas, or if the items are long and complex (see 21.3). If such a series comes before the main verb of a sentence, however, rephrase the sentence.

The three cities that we compare are Hartford, Connecticut; Kalamazoo, Michigan; and Pasadena, California.

but not

Hartford, Connecticut; Kalamazoo, Michigan; and Pasadena, California, are three cities worth comparing.

21.2.3 Nonrestrictive Clauses and Phrases

Use paired commas to set off a nonrestrictive clause. A clause is nonrestrictive if it is not necessary to uniquely identify the noun it modifies.

These five books, which are on reserve in the library, are required reading.

Here, the noun phrase *These five books* uniquely identifies the books that the writer has in mind; the nonrestrictive clause is not necessary to identify the books further. On the other hand, in the following sentence, the dependent clause (*that are required reading*) is restrictive, because it identifies the specific books that are required reading. Commas are therefore not used around the clause.

The books that are required reading are on reserve in the library.

Although *which* is often used with restrictive clauses, careful writers preserve the distinction between restrictive *that* (no comma) and nonrestrictive *which* (comma).

The same principles apply to restrictive and nonrestrictive phrases.

The president, wearing a red dress, attended the conference.

The woman wearing a red dress is the president.

21.2.4 Other Uses

Commas are used in a variety of other situations. (For use of commas in dates, see 23.3.1.)

■ *Introductory words and phrases.* When you begin a sentence with an introductory element of more than a few words, follow it with a comma, especially if a slight pause normally occurs in speech. A comma is not necessary after a short prepositional phrase unless the sentence could be misread without one.

If the insurrection is to succeed, the army and police must stand side by side.

Having accomplished her mission, she returned to headquarters.

To Anthony, Blake remained an enigma.

After this week the commission will be able to write its report.

■ *Two or more adjectives preceding a noun.* Separate two or more adjectives preceding a noun with commas when they could, without affecting meaning, be joined by *and.* Do not use a comma if the first adjective modifies the second and cannot be omitted without affecting meaning.

It was a large, well-placed, beautiful house.

They strolled out into the warm, luminous night.

She refused to be identified with a traditional political label.

■ *Clarifying comments.* Words and phrases such as *namely, that is,* and *for example* usually introduce a clarifying comment, so all take a comma after them, and may need a semicolon or period before them. Also, when you use *or* in the sense of "in other words," put a comma before it. (These and similar expressions may also be set off by dashes or parentheses; see 21.7.2 and 21.8.1.)

Many people resent accidents of fate; that is, they look on illness or bereavement as undeserved.

The compass stand, or binnacle, must be visible to the helmsman.

■ *Appositives.* A word or phrase is in apposition to a noun when it follows the noun and acts like a nonrestrictive clause (see 21.2.3). Such an element is set off by commas. When the appositive is necessary to identify the noun it modifies, however, commas are not used.

Smith, a Reed College graduate, taught at Harvard for several years.

Kierkegaard, the Danish philosopher, asked, "What is anxiety?"

but

The Danish philosopher Kierkegaard asked, "What is anxiety?"

■ *Place-names.* Use commas to set off multiple individual elements in names of places. (For commas in addresses, see 23.1.7.)

Cincinnati, Ohio, is on the Ohio River.

The next leg of the trip was to Florence, Italy.

■ *Interjections and conjunctive adverbs.* Set off interjections, conjunctive adverbs, and the like to suggest a break in the flow of thought or the rhythm of the sentence. But omit commas when such elements do not break the continuity and do not require a pause in reading.

Nevertheless, it is a matter of great importance.

It is, perhaps, the best that could be expected.

Perhaps it is therefore clear that no deposits were made.

■ *Contrasted elements.* Put commas around an interjected phrase beginning with *not, not only,* or similar expressions only if you intend the reader to pause before the phrase. Use a comma between clauses of *the more . . . the more* type unless they are very short or might be misread.

The idea, not its expression, is significant.

She was delighted with, but also disturbed by, her new freedom.

The more it stays the same, the less it changes.

- *Parenthetical elements.* Use paired commas when you set off a parenthetical element between a subject and a verb or a verb and its object. If you find yourself setting off more than one such interrupting element in a sentence, consider rewriting the sentence.

The Quinn Report was, to say the least, a bombshell.

Wolinski, after receiving instructions, left for Algiers.

- *Repeated words.* Use a comma to separate identical words. An exception is the word *that.*

They marched in, in twos.

Whatever is, is right.

but

He gave his life so that that cause might prevail.

21.3   Semicolon

A semicolon marks a greater break in the continuity of a sentence than does a comma. Use a semicolon in a compound sentence to separate independent clauses that are not connected by a coordinating conjunction (*and, but, or, nor, yet, for, so*).

One hundred communities are in various stages of completion; more are on the drawing board.

You can also use a semicolon with a coordinating conjunction if the clauses are long and have commas or other punctuation within them. In such cases, you probably should replace the semicolon with a period.

Although productivity per capita in U.S. industry is much more than that in China, China has an increasingly well educated young labor force; but the crucial point is that knowledge—which is transferable between peoples—has become the most important world economic resource.

Use a semicolon before the words *then, however, thus, hence, indeed, accordingly, besides,* and *therefore* when those words are used transitionally between two independent clauses.

Some think freedom always comes with democracy; however, many voters in many countries have voted for governments that they know will restrict their rights.

When items in a series have internal punctuation, separate them with semicolons (see also 21.2.2).

Green indicates vegetation that remained stable; red, vegetation that disappeared; yellow, new vegetation.

21.4 Colon

A colon introduces a clause, phrase, or series of elements that expands, clarifies, or exemplifies the meaning of what precedes it. Between independent clauses, it functions much like a semicolon, though more strongly emphasizing balance or consequence.

People expect three things of government: peace, prosperity, and respect for civil rights.

Chinese culture is unrivaled in its depth and antiquity: it is unmatched in its rich artistic and philosophical records.

Use a colon to introduce illustrative material or a list. Do not place a colon directly after a verb; instead, use an introductory element such as *the following* or *as follows*. (See also 23.4.2.)

The qualifications are as follows: a doctorate in economics and an ability to communicate statistical data to a lay audience.

but not

The qualifications are: a doctorate in economics . . .

Note that the first word following a colon within a sentence is generally not capitalized unless it is a proper noun. For capitalization in quotations introduced by a colon, see chapter 25.

Colons are also used in titles (see 17.1.2 and 19.1.3), in notations of time (23.1.5), in URLs (17.1.7 and 19.1.8), and in various ways in citations.

21.5 Question Mark

Put a question mark at the end of a complete sentence phrased as a question. If the question mark is the terminal punctuation, it should be followed by a single space.

Who would lead the nation in its hour of need?

Put a question mark after a clause phrased as a question and included as part of a sentence. Do not use quotation marks unless the question is a quotation and the rest of the sentence is not.

Would the union agree? was the critical question.

If the included question is at the end of the sentence, do not add a period after the question mark. You are not required to capitalize the first word of the included question, but an initial capital helps readers identify the question, especially if it includes internal punctuation. If the sentence becomes awkward, you may instead rephrase the question as a declarative statement followed by a period.

Several legislators raised the question, Can the fund be used in an emergency, or must it remain dedicated to its original purpose?

Several legislators raised the question of using the fund in an emergency, which was not its original purpose.

A question mark may also indicate doubt or uncertainty, as in a date.

The painter Niccolò dell'Abbate (1512?–71) assisted in the decorations at Fontainebleau.

21.6 Exclamation Point

Exclamation points are rarely appropriate for academic writing, except where they are part of quoted material. In this case, if an exclamation point is the terminal punctuation in a sentence, it should be followed by a single space.

21.7 Hyphen and Dashes

21.7.1 Hyphen

Hyphens are used in a variety of contexts, including compound words (see 20.3) and inclusive numbers (23.2.4).

21.7.2 Dash

A dash is an elongated hyphen used to set off text in a way similar to but more prominent than commas (see 21.2) or parentheses (21.8.1). Technically called an *em dash* (before the introduction of computerized fonts, it was exactly the width of the capital letter *m*), this character is available in most word processors.[1] It can be represented with two consecutive hy-

---

1. There is a second type of dash, called an *en dash* (a dash that used to be exactly the width of the capital letter *n*), that is used in published works to mean "through," usually in connection with numbers or dates (1998–2008). It can also be used in other contexts, as discussed in 6.83–86 of the *Chicago Manual of Style*, 15th edition (2003). If your local guidelines require it, this character is available in most word processors; otherwise use a hyphen in these contexts. Note that this book uses en dashes where they are appropriate, as in the preceding reference to the *Chicago Manual.*

phens, but most word processors can be set to convert double hyphens to em dashes automatically. Do not leave space on either side of the dash.

When you use dashes to set off a parenthetical element, pair them as you would commas or parentheses. Since they are rather intrusive, however, do not use more than one pair in any one sentence; instead, use parentheses for the second layer of parenthetical information.

The influence of three impressionists—Monet (1840–1926), Sisley (1839–99), and Degas (1834–1917)—is obvious in her work.

You can also use a single dash to set off an amplifying or explanatory element.

It was a revival of a most potent image—the revolutionary idea.

Use a dash or a pair of dashes enclosing a phrase to indicate a strong break in thought that also disrupts the sentence structure.

Rutherford—how could he have misinterpreted the evidence?

Some characters in *Tom Jones* are "flat"—if you do not object to this borrowing of E. M. Forster's somewhat discredited term—because they are caricatures of their names.

A dash may also introduce a summarizing subject after a list of several elements.

The statue of the discus thrower, the charioteer at Delphi, the poetry of Pindar—all represent the great ideal.

21.7.3 Multiple Dashes

When you quote from a mutilated or illegible text or represent an obscenity, indicate a missing word or missing letters with a 2-em dash (formed with two consecutive em dashes, or four hyphens). For a missing word, leave a space on either side of the dash; for missing letters, leave no space between the dash and the existing part of the word.

The vessel left the —— of July.

H——h? [Hirsch?]

It was a d—— shame.

A 3-em dash (formed with three consecutive em dashes, or six hyphens) is used in bibliographies and reference lists to represent the repeated name of an author or editor (see 16.2.2 and 18.2.1).

21.8 Parentheses and Brackets

21.8.1 Parentheses

Parentheses usually set off explanatory or interrupting elements of a sentence, much like paired commas (see 21.2) and dashes (21.7.2). In general, use commas for material closely related to the main clause, dashes and parentheses for material less closely connected. The abbreviations *e.g.* and *i.e.,* which may introduce a clarifying comment (see 24.7), are used only in parentheses or in notes.

The conference has (with some malice) divided into four groups.

Each painting depicts a public occasion; in each—a banquet, a parade, a coronation (though the person crowned is obscured)—crowds of people are pictured as swarming ants.

There are tax incentives for "clean cars" (e.g., gasoline-electric hybrids and vehicles powered by compressed natural gas and liquefied propane).

Parentheses can also be used with citations (see chapters 16 and 18) and to set off the numbers or letters in a list or an outline (see 23.4.2).

21.8.2 Brackets

Brackets are most often used in quotations, to indicate changes made to a quoted passage (see 25.3 for examples). They can also be used to enclose a second layer of parenthetical material within parentheses.

He agrees with the idea that childhood has a history (first advanced by Philippe Ariès [1914–84] in his book *Centuries of Childhood* [1962]).

21.9 Slashes

The forward slash is used in a few contexts, such as fractions (see 23.1.3) and quotations of poetry (see 25.2.1). Single and double slashes, as well as backward slashes, appear in URLs and other electronic identifiers (see 20.4.2).

21.10 Quotation Marks

For the use of quotation marks in quoted material, see 25.2.1. For use in titles and other special situations, see 22.3.2. For use in citations, see 16.1.4 and 18.1.4.

Some fields—linguistics, philosophy, and theology, for example—use single quotation marks to set off words and concepts. The closing quotation mark should precede a comma or period in this case (see 21.11.1).

kami 'hair, beard'

The variables of quantification, 'something', 'nothing', . . .

In most other fields, follow the guidelines in 22.2.2 for using quotation marks and italics with definitions of terms.

21.11 Multiple Punctuation Marks

The guidelines given throughout this chapter sometimes call for the use of two punctuation marks together—for example, a period and a closing parenthesis. The guidelines below govern the omission of one of the marks and the order of the marks when both are used.

21.11.1 Omission of Punctuation Marks

Except for ellipses, never use two periods together, as when a period in an abbreviation ends a sentence. Keep the abbreviation period when a sentence ends with a question mark or an exclamation point.

The exchange occurred at 5:30 p.m.

Could anyone match the productivity of Rogers Inc.?

If a situation calls for both a comma and a stronger punctuation mark, such as a question mark or a dash, omit the comma.

If he had read "What Do Dogs Think?" he would have known the answer.

While the senator couldn't endorse the proposal—and he certainly had doubts about it—he didn't condemn it.

21.11.2 Order of Punctuation Marks

The most likely cases of adjacent marks of punctuation involve terminal punctuation marks with quotation marks, parentheses, or brackets. American usage follows a few reliable guidelines for ordering multiple marks.

WITH QUOTATION MARKS. A final comma or period nearly always precedes a closing quotation mark, whether it is part of the quoted matter or not.

In support of the effort "to bring justice to our people," she joined the strike.

She made the argument in an article titled "On 'Managing Public Debt.'"

One exception: when single quotation marks are used to set off special terms in certain fields, such as linguistics, philosophy, and theology (see 21.10), put a period or comma after the closing quotation mark.

Some contemporary theologians, who favored 'religionless Christianity', were proclaiming the 'death of God'.

Question marks and exclamation points precede a closing quotation mark if they are part of the quoted matter. They follow the quotation mark if they apply to the entire sentence in which the quotation appears.

Her poem is titled "What Did the Crow Know?"

Do we accept Jefferson's concept of "a natural aristocracy"?

Semicolons and colons always follow quotation marks. If the quotation ends with a semicolon or a colon, change it to a period or a comma to fit the structure of the main sentence (see 25.3.1).

He claimed that "every choice reflects an attitude toward Everyman"; his speech then enlarged on the point in a telling way.

The Emergency Center is "almost its own city": it has its own services and governance.

WITH PARENTHESES AND BRACKETS. When you enclose a complete sentence in parentheses, put the terminal period (or other terminal punctuation mark) for that sentence before the last parenthesis. However, put the period outside when material in parentheses, even a grammatically complete sentence, is included within another sentence. The same principles apply to material in brackets.

We have noted similar motifs in Japan. (They can also be found in Korean folktales.)

Use periods in all these situations (your readers will expect them).

Myths have been accepted as allegorically true (by the Stoics) and as priestly lies (by the Enlightenment).

(The director promised completion "on time and *under budget*" [italics mine].)

For terminal punctuation with citations given parenthetically, see 25.2.

22 | Names, Special Terms, and Titles of Works

This chapter offers general guidelines for presenting names, special terms, and titles of works, including when to use capital or lowercase letters at the beginnings of words and when to use quotation marks or italic type (as opposed to regular, roman type) to set off words, phrases, or titles.

In some cases, you may need to adapt these guidelines to situations not described here. If so, be consistent. If you cannot use an italic font, underline instead.

If you are writing a thesis or dissertation, your department or university may have specific requirements for presenting names, special terms, and titles. Those requirements are usually available from the office of theses and dissertations. If you are writing a class paper, your instructor may also ask you follow certain principles for presenting such items. Review these requirements before you prepare your paper. They take precedence over the guidelines suggested here. For style guides in various disciplines, see the bibliography.

22.1 Names

Proper nouns, or names, are always capitalized, but it is sometimes difficult to distinguish a name from a generic term. This section covers the most common cases. For more detailed information, see chapter 8 of the *Chicago Manual of Style,* 15th edition (2003).

In text, names are normally presented in roman type, but there are a few exceptions noted in 22.1.3.

22.1.1 People, Places, and Organizations

In general, capitalize the first letter in each element of the names of specific people, places, and organizations. However, personal names that contain particles (such as *de* and *van*) or compound last names may vary in capitalization. When in doubt, consult *Webster's Biographical Dictionary* or another reliable authority. Prepositions (*of*) and conjunctions (*and*) that are parts of names are usually lowercase, as is *the* when it precedes a name. For possessive forms of names, see 20.2. For abbreviations with names, see 24.2. For names with numbers, see 23.1.6.

Eleanor Roosevelt	the United States Congress
W. E. B. Du Bois	the State Department
Ludwig van Beethoven	the European Union
Victoria Sackville-West	the University of North Carolina
Chiang Kai-shek	the Honda Motor Company
Sierra Leone	Skidmore, Owings & Merrill
Central America	the University of Chicago Press
New York City	the National Conference of Christians and Jews
the Atlantic Ocean	the Roman Catholic Church
the Republic of Lithuania	the Allied Expeditionary Force

A professional title that immediately precedes a personal name is treated as part of the name and should be capitalized. If you use the title alone or after the personal name, it becomes a generic term and should be lowercased. The same principle applies to other generic terms that are part of place or organization names.

President Harry Truman announced	the president announced
Professors Harris and Wilson wrote	the professors wrote
next to the Indian Ocean	next to the ocean
students at Albion College	students at the college

Names of ethnic and national groups are also capitalized. Terms denoting socioeconomic level, however, are not. (For hyphenation of compounds of both types, see 20.3.2. For plurals of tribal names, such as *Hopi,* see 20.1.1.)

Arab Americans	the middle class
Latinos	blue-collar workers

Capitalize adjectives derived from names, unless they have lost their literal associations with particular persons or places and have become part of everyday language.

Machiavellian scheme	french fries
Roman and Arabic art	roman and arabic numerals

22.1.2 Historical Events, Cultural Terms, and Designations of Time

The names of many historical periods and events are traditionally capitalized; more generic terms usually are not, unless they include names. Follow the conventions of your discipline.

the Bronze Age	ancient Rome
the Depression	the nineteenth century
the Industrial Revolution	the Shang dynasty
Prohibition	the colonial period
the Seven Years' War	the baby boom

Nouns and adjectives designating cultural styles, movements, and schools are generally capitalized only when derived from names or when they need to be distinguished from generic terms (as in *Stoicism*). Again, follow the conventions of your discipline.

classical	Aristotelian reasoning
impressionism	Dadaism
modernism	Hudson River school
deconstruction	Romanesque architecture

Names of days of the week, months, and holidays are capitalized, but names of seasons are not. For more on date systems, see 23.3.

Tuesday	September	Independence Day	spring

22.1.3 Other Types of Names

Other types of names also follow specific patterns for capitalization, and some require italics.

■ *Academic courses and subjects.* Capitalize the names of specific courses but not of general subjects or fields of study, except for the names of languages.

Introduction to Asian Art	art history
Topics in Victorian Literature	English literature

■ *Acts, treaties, and government programs.* Capitalize the formal or accepted titles of acts, treaties, government programs, and similar documents or entities, but lowercase informal or generic titles.

the United States (or U.S.) Constitution   the due process clause
the Treaty of Versailles   the treaty
Head Start

■ *Brand names.* Capitalize the brand names of products, but do not use the symbols ® or ™ after the names. Unless you are discussing a specific product, however, use a generic term instead of a brand name.

Coca-Cola   cola
Xerox   photocopy

■ *Electronic technology.* Capitalize names of computer hardware and software, networks, browsers, systems, and languages as well as shortened forms of these names.

Windows XP   the Internet; the Net
Internet Explorer   the World Wide Web; the Web

■ *Legal cases.* Capitalize and italicize the names of legal cases; italicize the *v.* (versus). You may shorten the case name after a full reference to it. For citations of legal cases, see 17.9.7 and 19.9.7.

First reference	Subsequent references
Miranda v. Arizona	*Miranda*
United States v. Carlisle	*Carlisle*

■ *Ships, aircraft, and other vessels.* Capitalize and italicize the names of ships, aircraft, and the like. If the names are preceded by such abbreviations as USS (United States ship) or HMS (Her [or His] Majesty's ship), do not italicize these abbreviations or use the word *ship* in addition to the name.

USS *Constitution*   *Spirit of St. Louis*
HMS *Saranac*   the space shuttle *Endeavor*

■ *Plants and animals.* For papers in the humanities and social sciences, do not capitalize the names of plants and animals unless they include other proper nouns, such as geographical names. Binomial Latin species names should be italicized, with the genus name capitalized and the species name (or specific epithet) lowercase. The names of phyla, orders, and such should be in roman type. For papers in the sciences, follow the conventions of your discipline.

rhesus monkey   Rocky Mountain sheep   *Rosa caroliniana*   Chordata

22.2   Special Terms

Some special terms require use of italics, quotation marks, and capitalization.

22.2.1   Foreign Language Terms

Italicize isolated words and phrases in foreign languages likely to be unfamiliar to readers of English, and capitalize them as in their language. (If you are unfamiliar with the capitalization principles of a language, consult a reliable authority such as chapter 10 of the *Chicago Manual of Style*, 15th edition [2003].) For titles of works in foreign languages, see 22.3.1.

This leads to the idea of *bermensch* and to the theory of the *acte gratuit* and surrealism.

Do not italicize foreign terms familiar enough to appear in *Merriam-Webster's Collegiate Dictionary*.

de facto   vis-à-vis   pasha   eros

Do not italicize foreign names or personal titles that accompany them.

Padre Pio
the Académie Française
the Puerto del Sol

If you define a foreign term, put the definition in parentheses or quotation marks, either following the term in the text or in a note.

The usual phrase was *ena tuainu-iai*, "I wanted to eat."

According to Sartrean ontology, man is always *de trop* (in excess).

For longer quotations from a foreign language, use roman type. Italicize the quotation as a whole or any words within it only if they are italicized in the original. Enclose the quotation in quotation marks within the text or use a block quotation following the principles in 25.2.

The confusion of *le pragmatisme* is traced to the supposed failure to distinguish "les propriétés de la valeur en général" from the incidental.

22.2.2   Words Defined as Terms

To emphasize key terms that you define, italicize them on their first use; thereafter use roman type. You can use quotation marks (called "scare quotes") to alert readers that you are using a term in a nonstandard or ironic way. When overused, both techniques become less effective.

The two chief tactics of this group, *obstructionism* and *misinformation,* require careful analysis.

Government "efficiency" resulted in a huge deficit.

Italicize a term when you refer to it as a term.

The term *critical mass* is more often used metaphorically than literally.

How did she define the word *existential?*

but

A critical mass of students took existential philosophy.

Italicize letters referred to as letters, and present them in lowercase. Letters used to denote grades and to identify exemplars should be roman and capitalized. For plural forms of letters used in these ways, see 20.1.2.

Many of the place-names there begin with the letters *h* and *k.*

In her senior year, she received an A and six B's.

Imagine a group of interconnected persons: A knows B, B knows C, and C knows D.

22.3 Titles of Works

When you cite a written, artistic, or broadcast work, present its title exactly as it appears in the original work or, if the original is unavailable, in a reliable authority.

Always preserve the original spelling (including hyphenation) in such titles, even if it does not conform to current American usage as described in chapter 20. See 17.1.2 for some permissible changes to the punctuation of titles, such as the use of a colon between a title and a subtitle, and the addition of a comma before dates.

Academic convention prescribes that titles follow specific patterns of capitalization and typography (italics, quotation marks, or neither), regardless of how they appear in the original. The principles vary somewhat for titles used in text and those used in citations.

22.3.1 Capitalization

Titles have two patterns of capitalization: headline style and sentence style. Present most titles mentioned in the text in headline style. For foreign language titles, use sentence style.

In citations, the choice depends on the citation style you are using: generally, headline style for bibliography-style citations, and sentence style for reference list–style citations. (There are some exceptions; see chapters 17 and 19 respectively.)

Use headline-style capitalization for the title of your paper and the titles of any parts or chapters within it unless your discipline prefers sentence style (see A.1.5).

HEADLINE-STYLE CAPITALIZATION. Headline-style capitalization is intended to distinguish titles clearly from surrounding text. In this style, capitalize the first letter of the first and last words of the title and subtitle and all other words, except as follows:

- Do not capitalize articles (*a, an, the*), coordinating conjunctions (*and, but, or, nor, for, so, yet*), or the words *to* and *as* unless such a word is the first or last word in the title or subtitle.
- Do not capitalize prepositions (*of, in, at, above, under,* and so forth) unless they are emphasized (*through* in *A River Runs Through It*) or used as adverbs (*up* in *Look Up*), adjectives (*on* in *The On Button*), or conjunctions (*before* in *Look Before You Leap*).
- Do not capitalize the second part (or subsequent parts) of a hyphenated compound unless it is a proper noun or adjective. (Remember to follow the original hyphenation of titles even if it differs from the principles discussed in 20.3.)
- Do not capitalize parts of proper nouns that are normally in lowercase, as described in 22.1.1 (*van* in *Ludwig van Beethoven*).

The Economic Effects of the Civil War in the Mid-Atlantic States

To Have and to Hold: A Twenty-first-century View of Marriage

All That Is True: The Life of Vincent van Gogh, 1853–90

Four Readings of the Gospel according to Matthew

Self-government and the Re-establishment of a New World Order

Global Warming: What We Are Doing about It Today

Still Life with Oranges

E-flat Concerto

Although many short words are lowercase in this style, length does not determine capitalization. You must capitalize short verbs (*is, are*), adjectives (*new*), personal pronouns (*it, we*), and relative pronouns (*that*), because they are not among the exceptions listed above. Use lowercase for long prepositions (*according*) since they are among the exceptions.

Two kinds of titles should not be presented in headline style even if you use it for all other titles:

- For titles in languages other than English, use sentence-style capitalization (see below).
- For titles of works published in the eighteenth century or earlier, retain the original capitalization (and spelling), except that words spelled out in all capital letters should be given with an initial capital only.

A Treatise of morall philosophy Contaynyge the sayings of the wyse

SENTENCE-STYLE CAPITALIZATION. Sentence-style capitalization is a simpler, though less distinct, way of presenting titles than headline style. In this style, capitalize only the first letter of the first word of the title and subtitle and any proper nouns and proper adjectives thereafter.

Seeing and selling late-nineteenth-century Japan

Natural crisis: Symbol and imagination in the mid-American farm crisis

Religious feminism: A challenge from the National Organization for Women

The last supper

Sentence style is also used for titles of works in foreign languages. Foreign languages have capitalization principles different from English, so if you are uncertain about these principles in a particular language, consult a reliable authority.

Speculum Romanae magnificentiae

Historia de la Orden de San Gerónimo

Reallexikon zur deutschen Kunstgeschichte

Phénoménologie et religion: Structures de l'institution chrétienne

22.3.2 Typography

Special typography—italics and quotation marks—also helps set off the titles of works from surrounding text. The guidelines listed here apply to titles used in text. They also apply to most titles in bibliography-style citations (see chapter 17), but not to those in reference list–style citations (see chapter 19).

The examples below are presented with headline-style capitalization, but the guidelines also apply to titles with sentence-style capitalization (see 22.3.1).

ITALICS. Italicize the titles of longer works that have been published (in print or electronic form) or otherwise made public, including the following types. In text (but not citations), the word *the* should be roman and lowercase at the beginning of most titles, even when it is part of the official title. For parts of these works and shorter works of the same type, see below.

- books (*Culture and Anarchy*, the *Chicago Manual of Style*)
- plays (*A Winter's Tale*) and very long poems, especially those of book length (Dante's *Inferno*)
- journals (*Signs*), magazines (*Time*), newspapers (the *Washington Post*), and other periodicals
- long musical compositions (the *Marriage of Figaro*)
- paintings (*Mona Lisa*), sculptures (Michelangelo's *David*), and other works of art, except for photographs
- movies (*Citizen Kane*) and television (*Sesame Street*) and radio programs (*All Things Considered*)

QUOTATION MARKS. Enclose in quotation marks, but do not italicize, the title of a shorter work, which may or may not be part of a longer work (such as those listed above).

- chapters ("The Later Years") or other titled parts of books
- short stories ("The Dead"), short poems ("The Housekeeper"), and essays ("Of Books")
- articles or other features in journals ("The Function of Fashion in Eighteenth-century America"), magazines ("Who Should Lead the Supreme Court?"), newspapers ("Election Comes Down to the Wire"), and other periodicals
- individual episodes of television programs ("The Opposite")
- short musical compositions ("The Star-Spangled Banner")
- photographs (Ansel Adams's "North Dome")

Also use quotation marks and roman type for titles of whole works that have not been formally published, including the following:

- theses and dissertations ("A Study of Kant's Early Works")
- lectures and papers presented at meetings ("Voice and Inequality: The Transformation of American Civic Democracy")

- titled documents in manuscript collections ("A Map of the Southern Indian District of North America")

  NO SPECIAL TYPOGRAPHY. Capitalize but do not use italics or quotation marks with these special types of titles:

- book series (Studies in Legal History)
- manuscript collections (Egmont Manuscripts)
- scriptures (the Bible) and other revered works (the Upanishads), as well as versions of the Bible (the King James Version) and its books (Genesis; see 24.6 for a complete list)
- musical works referred to by their genre (Symphony no. 41, Cantata BWV 80), though the popular titles for such works should be italicized (the *Jupiter Symphony*) or placed in quotation marks ("Ein feste Burg ist unser Gott") depending on their length, as noted above
- Web sites referred to generally (MSNBC.com), though in citations the titles of Web sites should be italicized (*Salon.com*), and the titles of individual articles or pages should be set in roman type and enclosed in quotation marks ("The Fix")

  Treat generic terms for parts of books or other works as you would any other word. Do not capitalize them or use italics or quotation marks unless you would do the same for an ordinary word (as at the beginning of a sentence). If a part includes a number, give it in arabic numerals, regardless of its appearance in the original work (see 23.1.8).

in Lionel Trilling's preface	as discussed in chapters 4 and 5
a comprehensive bibliography	killed off in act 3, scene 2

22.3.3 Punctuation

Follow standard guidelines for placing a comma, period, or other punctuation mark at the end of a title in text. If a title ends in dates, set them off with paired commas except at the end of a sentence, where the terminal punctuation mark supersedes the second comma (see also 17.1.2). For titles in quotation marks, place a comma or period before the closing punctuation mark (see also 21.11.2).

Have you ever read *The Creation of the American Republic, 1776–1787?*

Her article, "Continuity and Change, 1500–1800," argues in favor of continuity.

23 Numbers

This chapter offers general guidelines for presenting numbers. These guidelines are appropriate for most humanities and social science disciplines, but disciplines that rely heavily on numerical data may have more specific guidelines. If you are writing a paper in the natural or physical sciences, mathematics, or any other very technical field, follow the conventions of the discipline. For style guides in various disciplines, see the bibliography.

In some cases, you may need to adapt these guidelines to situations not described here. If so, be consistent.

If you are writing a thesis or a dissertation, your department or university may have specific requirements for presenting numbers, which are usually available from the office of theses and dissertations. If you are writing a class paper, your instructor may also ask you to follow certain principles for presenting numbers. Review these requirements before you prepare your paper. They take precedence over the guidelines suggested here.

23.1 Words or Numerals?

The most common question in presenting numbers is whether to spell them out in words (twenty-two) or give them in numerals (22). When the number is followed by a unit of measure, you must also decide whether to give that unit in words (percent) or as a symbol (%) or an abbreviation.

The guidelines presented in 23.1–23.3 pertain to numbers used in the text of your paper. For numbers used in tables, figures, and citations and in the structure of your paper, see 23.4.

Unless otherwise specified, *numerals* here means arabic numerals (1, 2, 3, etc.). For roman numerals (i, ii, iii, etc.), see table 23.1.

23.1.1 General Rule

Before you draft your paper, you should decide on a general rule for presenting numbers and follow it consistently. Which rule you choose depends on how many numerical data you are presenting and the conventions of your discipline. For situations in which you might modify this rule, see 23.1.2–23.1.8.

In the humanities and social sciences, if you use only a few numerical data, spell out numbers from one through one hundred. If the number

Table 23.1. Roman numerals

Arabic	Roman	Arabic	Roman	Arabic	Roman
1	I	11	XI	30	XXX
2	II	12	XII	40	XL
3	III	13	XIII	50	L
4	IV	14	XIV	60	LX
5	V	15	XV	70	LXX
6	VI	16	XVI	80	LXXX
7	VII	17	XVII	90	XC
8	VIII	18	XVIII	100	C
9	IX	19	XIX	500	D
10	X	20	XX	1,000	M

Note: Roman numerals are shown capitalized; for lowercase, use the same forms as in letters (*i* for *I*, *v* for *V*, etc.). For numbers not listed, follow the patterns shown.

has two words, use a hyphen (fifty-five). Also spell out round numbers followed by *hundred, thousand, hundred thousand, million,* and so on. For all other numbers, use arabic numerals. Follow this pattern for numbers that are part of physical quantities (distances, lengths, temperatures, and so on), and do not use abbreviations for the units in such quantities (see 24.5).

After seven years of war came sixty-four years of peace.

The population of the three states was approximately twelve million.

He catalogued more than 527 works of art.

Within fifteen minutes the temperature dropped twenty degrees.

If your topic relies heavily on numerical data, follow a different rule: spell out only single-digit numbers and use numerals for all others.

This study of 14 electoral districts over seven years included 142 participants.

He hit the wall at 65 miles per hour, leaving skid marks for nine feet.

In the sciences, your general rule may be to use numerals for all numbers, except when they begin a sentence (see 23.1.2). You may also use abbreviations for quantities (see 24.5).

The mean weight proved to be 7 g, far less than predicted.

With any of these rules, use the same principles for ordinal numbers (*first, second,* etc.) that you use for standard ones. Add *st, nd, rd,* or *th* as appropriate.

On the 122nd and 123rd days of his trip, he received his eighteenth and nineteenth letters from home.

23.1.2 Special Cases

In a few common situations, the general rule discussed in 23.1.1 requires modification.

INITIAL NUMBERS. Never begin a sentence with a numeral. Either spell out the number or recast the sentence, especially when there are other numerals of a similar type in the sentence.

Two hundred fifty soldiers in the unit escaped injury; 175 sustained minor injuries.

or, better,

Of the soldiers in the unit, 250 escaped injury and 175 sustained minor injuries.

When spelling out numbers over one hundred, omit the word *and* within the term (not *two hundred and fifty*).

SERIES OF NUMBERS. Ignore the general rule when you have a series of numbers in the same sentence that are above *and* below the threshold, especially when those numbers are being compared. In these examples, all are expressed in numerals.

Of the group surveyed, 78 students had studied French and 142 had studied Spanish for three years or more.

We analyzed 62 cases; of these, 59 had occurred in adults and 3 in children.

If you are discussing two sets of items in close proximity, ignore the general rule and, for clarity, spell out all numbers in one set and use numerals for all numbers in the other.

Within the program, 9 children showed some improvement after six months and 37 showed significant improvement after eighteen months.

ROUND NUMBERS. Spell out a round number (a whole number followed by *hundred, thousand, hundred thousand, million,* and so on) in isolation (see 23.1.1), but give several round numbers close together in numerals. You may also express large round numbers in a combination of numerals and words. (See also 23.1.4.)

They sold 1,500 copies in the first year and 8,000 in the second.

These changes will affect about 7.8 million people in New York alone.

23.1.3 Percentages and Decimal Fractions

Use numerals to express percentages and decimal fractions, except at the beginning of a sentence (see 23.1.2). Spell out the word *percent,* except when you use many percentage figures and in the sciences, where the symbol % is usually preferred (with no intervening space after the number). Notice that the noun *percentage* should not be used with a number.

Scores for students who skipped summer school improved only 9 percent. The percentage of students who failed was about 2.4 times the usual rate.

Within this system, the subject scored 3.8, or 95%.

but not

The average rose 9 percentage points.

When you use fractional and whole numbers for the same type of item in the same sentence or paragraph, give both as numerals.

The average number of children born to college graduates dropped from 2.4 to 2.

Put a zero in front of a decimal fraction of less than 1.00 if the quantity expressed is capable of equaling or exceeding 1.00; otherwise, omit the initial zero.

a mean of 0.73   a loss of 0.08 $p < .05$

For fractions standing alone, follow the general rule (see 23.1.1) for spelling out the parts. If you spell the parts, include a hyphen between them. Express in numerals a unit composed of a whole number and a fraction, with no intervening space between these items.

Trade and commodity services accounted for nine-tenths of all international receipts and payments.

One year during the Dust Bowl era, the town received only 15/16 of an inch of rain.

The main carving implement used in this society measured 2½ feet.

23.1.4 Money

U.S. CURRENCY. If you refer only occasionally to U.S. currency, follow the general rule (see 23.1.1), and spell out the words *dollars* and *cents*. Otherwise use numerals along with the symbol $ or ¢. Omit the decimal point and following zeros for whole-dollar amounts, unless you refer to fractional amounts as well.

Rarely do they spend more than five dollars a week on recreation.

The report showed $135 collected in fines.

After peaking at $200.00, shares of the stock plummeted to $36.75.

Express large round numbers in a combination of numerals and words.

The deficit that year was $420 billion.

OTHER CURRENCIES. For currencies other than that of the United States, follow the pattern for the U.S. dollar. Most currencies put unit symbols before numerals. Even though European nations represent decimal points with commas instead of periods, you may use periods, except in direct quotations from sources.

When she returned, she had barely fifty euros to her name.

The household records show that it cost only £36.50.

Its current estimated worth is ¥377 million.

Most European nations now use the unified currency called the euro (€), but if you are writing about topics from the period before 2002, you may encounter such currencies as the French franc (F), German deutsche mark (DM), and Italian lira (Lit). British currency is still expressed in pounds (£) and pence (p.), though before decimalization in 1971, it was expressed in pounds, shillings, and pence (for example, £12 17s. 6d.). Note that *billion* in traditional British usage means a million million, not a thousand million; to avoid confusion, do not use *billion* for British sums.

If you are unfamiliar with the conventions of a particular currency, consult a reliable authority.

23.1.5 Time

For references to times of day in even increments of an hour, half hour, or quarter hour, spell out the times, with a hyphen between parts. If necessary, specify *in the morning* or *in the evening.* You may use *o'clock,* although it is now rare in research writing.

The participants planned to meet every Thursday around ten-thirty in the morning.

When emphasizing exact times, use numerals and, if necessary, *a.m.* or *p.m.* (lowercase, roman, no intervening space; see also 24.4.1). Always include zeros after the colon for even hours.

Although scheduled to end at 11:00 a.m., the council meeting ran until 1:37 p.m.

In either situation, use the words *noon* and *midnight* (rather than numerals) to express these specific times of day.

For use of words or numerals in dates, see 23.3.

23.1.6 Names with Numbers

Some types of personal, governmental, and organizational names include numbers given in either words or numerals. See also 22.1 for capitalization of proper names generally.

■ *Leaders.* Emperors, sovereigns, or popes with the same first name are differentiated by capitalized roman numerals (see table 23.1).

Charles V   Napoleon III   Elizabeth II   Benedict XVI

■ *Family members.* Male family members with identical full names are often differentiated with roman or arabic numerals (see also 24.2.1). Note that there are no commas between the name and the numeral.

Adlai E. Stevenson III   Michael F. Johnson 2nd

■ *Governments and political divisions.* Certain dynasties, governments, governing bodies, political and judicial divisions, and military units are commonly designated by an ordinal number before the noun. Spell out and capitalize numbers through one hundred (with a hyphen between the parts of the number, if relevant); use numerals for those over one hundred.

Nineteenth Dynasty   Fourteenth Congressional District
Fifth Republic   Forty-seventh Ward
Eighty-first Congress   Tenth Circuit
109th Congress   101st Airborne Division

■ *Churches and religious organizations.* Spell out and capitalize numbers before the names of churches or religious organizations in ordinal form (with a hyphen between the parts of the number, if relevant).

Twenty-first Church of Christ, Scientist

■ *Secular organizations.* Express local branches of fraternal lodges and unions in numerals following the name.

American Legion, Department of Illinois, Crispus Attucks Post no. 1268

United Auto Workers, Local 890

23.1.7 Addresses and Thoroughfares

Follow the general rule (see 23.1.1) for the names of local numbered streets. State, federal, and interstate highways are always designated with numerals, as are street or building addresses and telephone and fax numbers. Note that in text the elements of a full address are separated by commas, except before a zip code. See 24.3.2 for abbreviations in addresses.

The National Park Service maintains as a museum the house where Lincoln died (516 10th Street NW, Washington, DC 20004; 202-426-6924).

Ludwig Mies van der Rohe designed the apartments at 860–880 North Lake Shore Drive.

Interstate 95 serves as a critical transportation line from Boston to Miami.

23.1.8 Parts of Published Works

Numbers in parts of published works are given in arabic numerals, regardless of the general rule (see 23.1.1) or their appearance in the work
itself. See also 22.3.2.

chapter 14   part 2   act 1, scene 3

23.1.9 Equations and Formulas

Numbers in equations and formulas are always given as numerals, regardless of the general rule (see 23.1.1). For detailed guidance on presenting
mathematical expressions, see chapter 14 of the *Chicago Manual of Style*,
15th edition (2003).

23.2 Plurals and Punctuation

23.2.1 Plurals

Form the plurals of spelled-out numbers like the plurals of other nouns
(see 20.1).

Half the men surveyed were in their thirties or forties.

Form the plurals of numbers expressed in numerals by adding *s* alone
(not *'s*).

The pattern changed in the late 1990s as more taxpayers submitted 1040s online.

To fly 767s, the pilots required special training.

23.2.2 Commas within Numbers

In most numbers of four or more digits, set off thousands, hundreds of
thousands, millions, and so on with commas. In the sciences, commas are
often omitted from four-digit numbers.

1,500   12,275,500   1,475,525,000

Do not use a comma within a four-digit year; do use one for years with
five or more digits (see also 23.3).

2007   10,000 BC

Do not use a comma in four-digit page numbers, street addresses, telephone or fax numbers, zip codes, decimal fractions of less than one, or organization names.

page 1012   0.1911 centimeters   Committee of 1000

23.2.3 Other Punctuation within Numbers

Numbers sometimes include other internal punctuation. For periods (decimals), see 23.1.3 and 23.1.4; for colons, see 23.1.5; for hyphens, see 23.1.1 and 23.1.3; for dashes, see 23.2.4.

23.2.4 Inclusive Numbers

To express a range of numbers, such as pages or years, give the first and last (or *inclusive*) numbers of the sequence. If the numbers are spelled out, express the range with the words *from* and *to;* if they are expressed in numerals, use either these words or a connecting hyphen with no space on either side. In some settings, such as citations, always use hyphens (see chapters 16–19). Do not combine words and hyphens in expressing inclusive numbers.

from 45 to 50   *but not*   from 45–50
45–50   *but not*   forty-five–fifty

For inclusive numbers of one hundred or greater, you may either use full numbers on either side of a hyphen (245–280, or 1929–1994) or abbreviate the second number. Table 23.2 shows one system of abbreviation.

This system works well for both page numbers and years, which include commas only after they reach five digits, which rarely happens (see 23.2.2). For numbers that include one or more commas, repeat numerals to the right of the commas as necessary for clarity. Never abbreviate roman numerals (see table 23.1).

6,000–6,018   12,473–479   xxv–xxviii

For years, give all digits for a span that includes more than one century. Also give full dates in a system in which dates are counted backward from a specific point (most notably BC, "before Christ," and BCE, "before the common era"). Otherwise, use the system shown in table 23.2. See 23.3 for more on date systems.

the years 1933–36   15,000–14,000 BCE
the winter of 1999–2000   115 BC–AD 10

Table 23.2. Abbreviation system for inclusive numbers

First number	Second number	Examples
1–99	Use all digits	3–10, 71–72, 96–117
100 or multiples of 100	Use all digits	100–104, 1100–1113
101 through 109, 201 through 209, etc.	Use changed part only	101–8, 1103–4
110 through 199, 210 through 299, etc.	Use two or more digits as needed	245–48, 498–532, 1929–94
	But if three digits change in a four-digit number, use all four	1894–1986, 2787–2816

23.3 Date Systems

Presenting dates in text involves many of the same concerns as in 23.1 and 23.2 but also some conventions for ordering and naming elements.

23.3.1 Month, Day, and Year

Spell out the names of months when they occur in text, whether alone or in dates. Express days and years in numerals, and avoid using them at the beginning of a sentence, where they would have to be spelled out (see 23.1.2). Do not abbreviate references to the year ("the great flood of '05"). For abbreviations acceptable in tables, figures, and citations, see 24.4.2.

Every September, we recall the events of 2001.

but not

Two thousand one was a memorable year.

For full references to dates, give the month, the day (followed by a comma), and the year, in accordance with U.S. practices. If you omit the day, omit the comma. Also omit the comma for dates given with seasons instead of months; do not capitalize the names of seasons (see 22.1.2). If material you are quoting uses British-style dates (15 March 2007), do not alter them.

President John F. Kennedy was assassinated on November 22, 1963.

By March 1865, the war was nearly over.

The research was conducted over several weeks in spring 2006.

Note that, within complete dates, days are generally not given as ordinals—that is, the numerals are not followed by *st, nd, rd,* or *th.* Use these endings only with spelled-out numbers when you specify the day without the month or year.

The date chosen for the raid was the twenty-ninth.

but not

The events occurred on June 11th, 1968.

23.3.2 Decades, Centuries, and Eras

In general, refer to decades using numerals, including the century (see 23.2.1 for plurals). If the century is clear, do not abbreviate numerals (for example, "the '90s"); instead, spell out the name of the decade. The first two decades of any century do not lend themselves to either style and should be described fully for clarity.

The 1920s brought unheralded financial prosperity.

During the fifties, the Cold War dominated the headlines.

Many of these discoveries were announced during the first decade of the twenty-first century.

Refer to centuries using either numerals or lowercase spelled-out names (see 23.2.1 for plurals). If the century is spelled out and used as an adjective preceding a noun that it modifies, as in the second example, use a hyphen; otherwise, do not (see 20.3.2).

The Ottoman Empire reached its apex in the 1600s.

She teaches nineteenth-century novels but would rather teach poetry from the twentieth century.

The most common designations for eras use the abbreviations BC ("before Christ") and AD (*anno Domini,* "in the year of the Lord"). Some disciplines use different designations, such as BCE and CE (see 24.4.3). AD precedes the year number; the other designations follow it. For inclusive numbers with eras, see 23.2.4.

Solomon's Temple was destroyed by the Babylonians in 586 BC and again by the Romans in AD 70.

23.4 Numbers Used outside the Text

The preceding sections provide guidelines for presenting numbers in the text of your paper. For numbers used elsewhere within the paper or in the structure of the paper itself, follow the specific guidelines for the relevant sections or divisions of the paper.

23.4.1 Numbers in Tables, Figures, and Citations

Numerical data in tables and figures are almost always presented in arabic numerals. For a discussion of numbers in tables, including table titles, see 26.2; for numbers in figures, including figure captions, see 26.3.

With a few exceptions, arabic numerals are used to cite volume numbers, edition numbers, and page numbers and other locators. For a discussion of numbers in bibliography-style citations, see 16.1.5 and chapter 17; for numbers in reference list–style citations, see 18.1.5 and chapter 19.

23.4.2 Enumerations

You may use numbers to enumerate points discussed in the text, in appendixes, or in materials related to drafting your paper.

LISTS. Your text may contain lists of items that you choose to enumerate for emphasis. When such lists are very short and simple, include them in one grammatical sentence. Be sure that all the items are grammatically parallel (all noun phrases, adjectives, and so forth). Each item should be preceded by an arabic numeral in parentheses. If there are more than two items, each should be followed by a comma (or, if the item is complex in structure, a semicolon; see 21.3). If the list is an appositive, use a colon to introduce it; otherwise, do not use punctuation in this position.

Wilson's secretary gave three reasons for his resignation: (1) advancing age, (2) gradually failing eyesight, and (3) opposition to the war.

The committee strongly endorsed the policies of (1) complete executive power, except as constitutionally limited; (2) strong legislative prerogatives; (3) limited judicial authority, especially when it interfered with their own role.

If you are already using arabic numerals in parentheses for other purposes, substitute lowercase italic letters for the numbers.

Haskin's latest theory has several drawbacks: (a) it is not based on current evidence and (b) it has a weak theoretical grounding.

If the items in the list are longer or you wish to give them greater emphasis, arrange them in a vertical list. Introduce the list with a complete sentence followed by a colon. Again, be sure that all the items are grammatically parallel, and begin each one with a bullet or an arabic numeral followed by a period, without parentheses. If the items are complete sentences, capitalize the first letter in each item, and use terminal periods; otherwise use lowercase letters and no periods (see 21.1). Align the numerals on the periods and the runovers with the first word in the first line.

My research therefore suggests the following conclusions:

1.   The painting could not have been a genuine Picasso, regardless of the claims of earlier scholars.
2.   It is impossible to identify the true artist without further technical analysis.

OUTLINES. In some situations, you may include an outline or a similar enumeration in an appendix to your paper, or in a draft stage of the paper (see 6.2.1). Use the following system of notation, consisting of letters and roman and arabic numerals, and indent each level by one further tab (usually a half inch). You should have at least two items to list at each level; if you do not, reconsider the structure of the outline. If the items are phrases, capitalize them sentence style (see 22.3.1) and do not use terminal punctuation. If they are complete sentences, capitalize and punctuate them as you would any other sentence (see 6.2.1 for an example).

I. Wars of the nineteenth century
    A. United States
        1. Civil War, 1861–65
            a) Cause
                (1) Slavery
                    (a) Compromise
                        i)   Missouri Compromise
                        ii) Compromise of 1850 . . .
            b) Result
. . . .
II. Wars of the twentieth century
    A. United States
        1. First World War . . .

23.4.3 Paper Structure

The structure of your paper itself requires the use of numbers in many contexts, including pagination and part and chapter titles. For a detailed discussion of numbers in paper structure, see the appendix.

24 Abbreviations

24.1 General Principles

24.1.1 Types of Abbreviations
24.1.2 When to Use Abbreviations
24.1.3 How to Format Abbreviations

24.2 Names and Titles

24.2.1 Personal Names
24.2.2 Professional Titles
24.2.3 Academic Degrees
24.2.4 Agencies, Companies, and Other Organizations

24.3 Geographical Terms

24.3.1 Place-Names
24.3.2 Addresses

24.4 Time and Dates

24.4.1 Time
24.4.2 Days and Months
24.4.3 Eras

24.5 Units of Measure

24.6 The Bible and Other Sacred Works

24.6.1 Jewish Bible/Old Testament
24.6.2 Apocrypha
24.6.3 New Testament
24.6.4 Versions of the Bible
24.6.5 Other Sacred Works

24.7 Abbreviations in Citations and Other Scholarly Contexts

This chapter offers general guidelines for using abbreviations. Abbreviations in formal writing were once limited to a few special circumstances, but they are now widely used in writing of all kinds. Even so, their use must reflect the conventions of specific disciplines. The guidelines presented here are appropriate for most humanities and social science disciplines. If you are writing a paper in the natural or physical sciences, mathematics, or any other technical field, follow the conventions of the discipline.

In some disciplines, you may need to use abbreviations not covered here. *Merriam-Webster's Collegiate Dictionary* gives many abbreviations from many fields. Another resource is chapter 15 of the *Chicago Manual of Style*, 15th edition (2003). For style guides in various disciplines, see the bibliography.

If you are writing a thesis or dissertation, your department or university may have specific requirements for using abbreviations, which are usually available from the office of theses and dissertations. If you are writing a class paper, your instructor may also ask you to follow certain principles for using abbreviations. Review these requirements before you prepare your paper. They take precedence over the guidelines suggested here.

24.1 General Principles

24.1.1 Types of Abbreviations

Terms can be shortened, or abbreviated, in several ways. When a term is shortened to only the first letters of each word and pronounced as a single word (NATO, AIDS), it is called an *acronym;* if the letters are pronounced as a series of letters (EU, PBS), it is called an *initialism.* Other terms are shortened through *contraction:* just the first and last letters of the term are retained (Mr., Dr.), or the last letters are dropped (ed., Tues.). This chapter treats all of these forms under the general term *abbreviations,* with distinctions between types noted as relevant.

24.1.2 When to Use Abbreviations

In most papers, use abbreviations sparingly in text because they can make your writing seem either too informal or too technical. This chapter covers types of abbreviations that are preferred over spelled-out terms and others that are considered acceptable in academic writing if used consistently.

If your local guidelines allow it, you may use abbreviations for names, titles, and other terms used frequently in your paper. Give the full term on first reference, followed by the abbreviation in parentheses. For subsequent references, use the abbreviation consistently. If you use more than a few such abbreviations, consider adding a list of abbreviations to the front matter of the paper to aid readers who might miss your first reference to an abbreviation (see A.2.1).

Abbreviations are more common, and are often required, outside the text of the paper. This chapter discusses some abbreviations that may be used in tables, figures, and citations. For additional discussion of abbreviations in tables and figures, see chapter 26; for abbreviations in bibliography-style citations, see 16.1.6 and chapter 17; for abbreviations in reference list–style citations, see 18.1.6 and chapter 19.

24.1.3 How to Format Abbreviations

Although abbreviations follow the general principles discussed here, there are many exceptions.

- *Capitalization.* Abbreviations are given in all capital letters, all lowercase letters, or a combination.

BC	p.	Gov.
CEO	a.m.	Dist. Atty.
U.S.	kg	PhD

- *Punctuation.* In general, abbreviations given in all capital letters do not include periods, while those given in lowercase or a combination of capital and lowercase letters have a period after each abbreviated element. However, as you can see from the examples above, there are exceptions: the abbreviation *U.S.* includes periods (see 24.3.1); metric units of measure (see 24.5) are in lowercase without periods; and the abbreviation *PhD* has no periods. Other exceptions are noted throughout this chapter.
- *Spacing.* In general, do not leave a space between letters in acronyms (NATO) and initialisms (PBS), but do leave a space between elements in abbreviations formed through shortening (Dist. Atty.). If an abbreviation contains an ampersand (&), do not leave spaces around it (Texas A&M). For spaces in personal names, see 24.2.1.
- *Typography.* Do not italicize abbreviations.
- *Indefinite articles.* When an abbreviation follows an indefinite article, choose between *a* and *an* depending on how the abbreviation is read aloud. Acronyms (NATO, AIDS) are pronounced as words; initialisms (EU) are read as a series of letters.

member nation of NATO	a NATO member
person with AIDS	an AIDS patient
member nation of the EU	an EU member

24.2 Names and Titles

24.2.1 Personal Names

In general, do not abbreviate a person's first (Benj. Franklin) or last name. Once you have used a full name in text, use just the person's last name in subsequent references. However, if you are referring to more than one person with that last name, spell out their names fully on each use to avoid confusion (Alice James, William James). If you refer to these names very frequently in your paper, you may instead use abbreviations that you devise (AJ, WJ), but be sure to treat these abbreviations as described in 24.1.2.

Some individuals are known primarily by initials in place of a first and/ or middle name. Such initials should be followed by a period and a space. If you abbreviate an entire name, however, omit periods and spaces.

G. K. Chesterton	*but*	JFK
M. F. K. Fisher	*but*	FDR

Social titles such as *Ms.* and *Mr.* should always be abbreviated and cap-italized, followed by a period. In most papers, however, you need not use such titles unless there is a possibility of confusion, such as referring to either a husband or wife.

Write abbreviations such as *Sr., Jr., III* (or *3rd*), and *IV* (or *4th*) with-out commas before them. Use them only after a full name, not with a surname alone, although royal and religious figures may be known only by a first name. Do not spell out the term when it is part of a name (for example, not *John Smith Junior*).

Oliver Wendell Holmes Jr.   William J. Kaufmann III   Mary II

24.2.2 Professional Titles

Some individuals have civil, military, or religious titles such as the follow-ing along with their personal names. Many of these titles are convention-ally abbreviated rather than spelled out in text when they precede and are treated as part of a personal name. Since they are all shortened forms of official (proper) titles, only the first letter is capitalized, and they are fol-lowed by periods.

Adm.	Admiral		Lt.	Lieutenant
Ald.	Alderman, Alderwoman		Lt. Col.	Lieutenant Colonel
Atty. Gen.	Attorney General		Maj.	Major
Capt.	Captain		Pres.	President
Col.	Colonel		Rep.	Representative
Dist. Atty.	District Attorney		Rev.	Reverend
Dr.	Doctor		Sen.	Senator
Fr.	Father		Sgt.	Sergeant
Gen.	General		Sr.	Sister
Gov.	Governor		St.	Saint
Hon.	Honorable			

On first reference to an individual with such a title, use the abbreviation with the person's full name. (If you prefer, you may always spell out the titles, but do so consistently.) For subsequent references, you may usually give just the person's last name, but if you need to repeat the title (to distinguish two people with similar names, or as a disciplinary sign of respect), give the spelled-out title with the last name. Never use *Reverend* or *Honorable* except with a full name, in which case the title should be preceded by the word *the*.

Sen. Barack Obama	Senator Obama
Gen. Richard Myers	General Myers
Rev. Jane Schaefer	the Reverend Jane Schaefer

If you use one of these titles alone or after a personal name, it becomes a generic term and should be lowercased and spelled out.

the senator from Illinois	Myers served as a general

An exception to the general pattern is *Dr.* Use either the abbreviation *Dr.* before the name, or the official abbreviation for the degree (see 24.2.3), set off with two commas, after the name. Do not use both together.

Dr. Lauren Shapiro discovered the cause of the outbreak.

Lauren Shapiro, MD, discovered . . .

Dr. Shapiro discovered . . .

The doctor discovered . . .

In addition to academic degrees, here are a few other professional titles that may be abbreviated following a personal name. Such titles should be set off with commas, as in the examples above.

JP	justice of the peace
LPN	licensed practical nurse
MP	member of Parliament
SJ	Society of Jesus

24.2.3 Academic Degrees

You may use abbreviations in text and elsewhere for the common academic degrees noted in the following list. Some are initialisms (see 24.1.1), which are written in capital letters, without periods or spaces. Others contain both initials and shortened terms and therefore both capital and lowercase letters, usually without periods or spaces. If you are writing a thesis or a dissertation, however, your department or university guidelines may require that you format these degrees (and possibly also the initialisms) with internal periods, as shown in parentheses.

AB	Artium Baccalaureus (Bachelor of Arts)
AM	Artium Magister (Master of Arts)
BA	Bachelor of Arts
BD	Bachelor of Divinity
BFA	Bachelor of Fine Arts
BM	Bachelor of Music
BS	Bachelor of Science
DB	Divinitatis Baccalaureus (Bachelor of Divinity)
DD	Divinitatis Doctor (Doctor of Divinity)
DMin (D.Min.)	Doctor of Ministry
EdD	Doctor of Education
JD	Juris Doctor (Doctor of Law)
LHD	Litterarum Humaniorum Doctor (Doctor of Humanities)
LittD (Litt.D.)	Litterarum Doctor (Doctor of Letters)
LLB (LL.B.)	Legum Baccalaureus (Bachelor of Laws)
LLD (LL.D.)	Legum Doctor (Doctor of Laws)
MA	Master of Arts
MBA	Master of Business Administration
MD	Medicinae Doctor (Doctor of Medicine)
MFA	Master of Fine Arts
MS	Master of Science
PhB (Ph.B.)	Philosophiae Baccalaureus (Bachelor of Philosophy)
PhD (Ph.D.)	Philosophiae Doctor (Doctor of Philosophy)
SB	Scientiae Baccalaureus (Bachelor of Science)
SM	Scientiae Magister (Master of Science)
STB	Sacrae Theologiae Baccalaureus (Bachelor of Sacred Theology)

24.2.4 Agencies, Companies, and Other Organizations

You may use abbreviations in text and elsewhere for the names of government agencies, broadcasting companies, associations, fraternal and service organizations, unions, and other groups that are commonly known by acronyms or initialisms (see 24.1.1). Spell out the full name on first reference, followed by the abbreviation in parentheses (see 24.1.2). Such abbreviations are in full capitals with no periods. Here is a representative list of such abbreviations; other names within these categories (for example, ABA, CBS, and NEH) should be treated similarly.

AAAS	CNN	NAFTA	TVA	YMCA
AFL-CIO	EU	NFL	UN	
AMA	FTC	NIMH	UNESCO	
AT&T	HMO	NSF	VA	
CDC	NAACP	OPEC	WHO	

If a company is not commonly known by an abbreviation, spell out and capitalize its name in the text. You may omit the terms *Inc.* or *Ltd.* from the name, and do not capitalize the word *the* at the beginning of the name.

Merck and Company   the University of Chicago Press

In tables, figures, and citations, you may also use the following abbreviations in company names. Note the differences in capitalization and punctuation.

Assoc.	Ltd.
Bros.	Mfg.
Co.	PLC (public limited company)
Corp.	RR (railroad)
Inc.	Ry. (railway)
LP (limited partnership)	

24.3 Geographical Terms

24.3.1 Place-Names

In text, always spell out and capitalize the names of countries, states, counties, provinces, territories, bodies of water, mountains, and the like (see 22.1.1). One exception is the former Union of Soviet Socialist Republics, commonly referred to as *the former USSR.*

Always spell out *United States* when using it as a noun. When using it as an adjective, you may either abbreviate it to *U.S.* or spell it out (for a more formal tone). By convention, it includes periods, even though it is an acronym.

She was ineligible for the presidency because she was not born in the United States.

His U.S. citizenship was revoked later that year.

In tables, figures, citations, and mailing addresses, abbreviate the names of U.S. states using the two-letter, no-period postal codes created by the U.S. Postal Service.

AK	Alaska	DE	Delaware
AL	Alabama	FL	Florida
AR	Arkansas	GA	Georgia
AZ	Arizona	HI	Hawaii
CA	California	IA	Iowa
CO	Colorado	ID	Idaho
CT	Connecticut	IL	Illinois
DC	District of Columbia	IN	Indiana

KS	Kansas	NY	New York
KY	Kentucky	OH	Ohio
LA	Louisiana	OK	Oklahoma
MA	Massachusetts	OR	Oregon
MD	Maryland	PA	Pennsylvania
ME	Maine	RI	Rhode Island
MI	Michigan	SC	South Carolina
MN	Minnesota	SD	South Dakota
MO	Missouri	TN	Tennessee
MS	Mississippi	TX	Texas
MT	Montana	UT	Utah
NC	North Carolina	VA	Virginia
ND	North Dakota	VT.	Vermont
NE	Nebraska	WA	Washington
NH	New Hampshire	WI	Wisconsin
NJ	New Jersey	WV	West Virginia
NM	New Mexico	WY	Wyoming
NV	Nevada		

You may also abbreviate the names of Canadian provinces and territories where state names would be abbreviated.

AB	Alberta	NU	Nunavut
BC	British Columbia	ON	Ontario
MB	Manitoba	PE	Prince Edward Island
NB	New Brunswick	QC	Quebec
NL	Newfoundland and Labrador	SK	Saskatchewan
NS	Nova Scotia	YT	Yukon
NT	Northwest Territories		

24.3.2 Addresses

In text, spell out and capitalize terms that are part of addresses, including those listed below and similar ones (other synonyms for *street,* for example). In tables, figures, citations, and mailing addresses, use the abbreviations. Note that all the abbreviations use periods except for the acronyms (*Northeast* and such). See 23.1.7 for an example of an address in text.

Ave.	Avenue	St.	Street
Blvd.	Boulevard	N.	North
Ct.	Court	S.	South
Dr.	Drive	E.	East
Expy.	Expressway	W.	West
Pkwy.	Parkway	NE	Northeast
Rd.	Road	NW	Northwest
Sq.	Square	SE	Southeast
		SW	Southwest

If you use one of these terms alone, it becomes a generic term and should be lowercased and spelled out.

He drove down the street.

The storm came in from the west.

24.4 Time and Dates

24.4.1 Time

You may use the abbreviations *a.m.* (*ante meridiem,* or before noon) and *p.m.* (*post meridiem,* or after noon) in text and elsewhere to designate specific times. The abbreviations should be lowercase, in roman type, with no intervening space. Do not combine them with *in the morning, in the evening,* or *o'clock;* see also 23.1.5.

24.4.2 Days and Months

In text, spell out and capitalize the names of days of the week and months of the year; see also 23.3.1. In tables, figures, and citations, you may abbreviate them if you do so consistently. Use periods with the abbreviations.

Sun.	Wed.	Sat.		Jan.	Apr.	July	Oct.
Mon.	Thur.			Feb.	May	Aug.	Nov.
Tues.	Fri.			Mar.	June	Sept.	Dec.

24.4.3 Eras

There are various systems for designating eras, all of which use abbreviations with numerical dates. The most common system uses the terms *BC* and *AD,* but some disciplines use different designations, such as those listed below. Use the relevant abbreviations throughout your paper; put them in all capitals, without periods. *AD* precedes the year number; the other designations follow it (see also 23.2.4 and 23.3.2).

BC	before Christ
and	
AD	*anno Domini* (in the year of the Lord)
BCE	before the common era
and	
CE	common era
BP	before the present
MYA (*or* mya)	million years ago

24.5 Units of Measure

In the humanities and social sciences, spell out the names of units of measure such as dimensions, distances, volumes, weights, degrees, and so on. Spell out the numbers or use numerals according to the general rule you are following (see 23.1.1).

five miles   150 kilograms   14.5 meters

In the sciences, use standard abbreviations for units of measure when the amount is given in numerals. (You may use abbreviations in other disciplines, depending on your local guidelines.) Leave a space between the numeral and the unit, except where convention dictates otherwise (36°; 512K), and note that abbreviations are the same in singular and plural. Spell out units of measure when they are not preceded by a number or when the number is spelled out (as at the beginning of a sentence; see 23.1.1).

We injected 10 μL of virus near the implants.

Results are given in microliters.

Twelve microliters of virus was considered a safe amount.

For a list of abbreviations including common units of measure, see 15.55 of the *Chicago Manual of Style,* 15th edition (2003).

24.6 The Bible and Other Sacred Works

When you refer in text to whole chapters or books of the Bible or the Apocrypha, spell out the names of the books, but do not italicize them.

Jeremiah 42–44 records the flight of the Jews to Egypt.

The Revelation of St. John the Divine, known as "Revelation," closes the New Testament.

When you cite biblical passages by verse (see 17.5.2 and 19.5.2), abbreviate the names of the books, using arabic numerals if they are numbered (1 Kings). Also use arabic numerals for chapter and verse numbers, with a colon between them. Since different versions of the scriptures use different names and numbers for books, identify the version you are citing. Depending on the context, you may either spell out the name of the version, at least on first occurrence, or use abbreviations (see 24.6.4), without preceding or internal punctuation.

1 Song of Sol. 2:1–5 NRSV   Ruth 3:14 NAB

The following sections list both traditional and shorter abbreviations for the books of the Bible, arranged in alphabetical order. If you are unsure which form of abbreviation is appropriate, consult your instructor. Where no abbreviation is given, use the full form.

24.6.1 Jewish Bible/Old Testament

Note that the abbreviation for Old Testament is OT.

Traditional	Shorter	Full name
Amos	Am	Amos
1 Chron.	1 Chr	1 Chronicles
2 Chron.	2 Chr	2 Chronicles
Dan.	Dn	Daniel
Deut.	Dt	Deuteronomy
Eccles.	Eccl	Ecclesiastes
Esther	Est	Esther
Exod.	Ex	Exodus
Ezek.	Ez	Ezekiel
Ezra	Ezr	Ezra
Gen.	Gn	Genesis
Hab.	Hb	Habakkuk
Hag.	Hg	Haggai
Hosea	Hos	Hosea
Isa.	Is	Isaiah
Jer.	Jer	Jeremiah
Job	Jb	Job
Joel	Jl	Joel
Jon.	Jon	Jonah
Josh.	Jo	Joshua
Judg.	Jgs	Judges
1 Kings	1 Kgs	1 Kings
2 Kings	2 Kgs	2 Kings
Lam.	Lam	Lamentations
Lev.	Lv	Leviticus
Mal.	Mal	Malachi
Mic.	Mi	Micah
Nah.	Na	Nahum
Neh.	Neh	Nehemiah
Num.	Nm	Numbers
Obad.	Ob	Obadiah
Prov.	Prv	Proverbs
Ps. (plural, Pss.)	Ps (plural, Pss)	Psalms
Ruth	Ru	Ruth

1 Sam.	1 Sm	1 Samuel
2 Sam.	2 Sm	2 Samuel
Song of Sol.	Sg	Song of Solomon (Song of Songs)
Zech.	Zec	Zechariah
Zeph.	Zep	Zephaniah

24.6.2 Apocrypha

The books of the Apocrypha are included in Roman Catholic but not Jewish or Protestant versions of the Bible. Note that the traditional abbreviation for Apocrypha is Apoc. (no shorter abbreviation).

Traditional	Shorter	Full name
Bar.	Bar	Baruch
Bel and Dragon	—	Bel and the Dragon
Ecclus.	Sir	Ecclesiasticus (Sirach)
1 Esd.	—	1 Esdras
2 Esd.	—	2 Esdras
Jth.	Jdt	Judith
1 Macc.	1 Mc	1 Maccabees
2 Macc.	2 Mc	2 Maccabees
Pr. of Man.	—	Prayer of Manasses (Manasseh)
Song of Three Children	—	Song of the Three Holy Children
Sus.	—	Susanna
Tob.	Tb	Tobit
Wisd. of Sol.	Ws	Wisdom of Solomon
—	—	Additions to Esther (Rest of Esther)

24.6.3 New Testament

Note that the abbreviation for New Testament is NT.

Traditional	Shorter	Full name
Acts	—	Acts of the Apostles
Apoc.	—	Apocalypse (Revelation)
Col.	Col	Colossians
1 Cor.	1 Cor	1 Corinthians
2 Cor.	2 Cor	2 Corinthians
Eph.	Eph	Ephesians
Gal.	Gal	Galatians
Heb.	Heb	Hebrews
James	Jas	James
John	Jn	John (Gospel)
1 John	1 Jn	1 John (Epistle)
2 John	2 Jn	2 John (Epistle)
3 John	3 Jn	3 John (Epistle)

Jude	—	Jude
Luke	Lk	Luke
Mark	Mk	Mark
Matt.	Mt	Matthew
1 Pet.	1 Pt	1 Peter
2 Pet.	2 Pt	2 Peter
Phil.	Phil	Philippians
Philem.	Phlm	Philemon
Rev.	Rv	Revelation (Apocalypse)
Rom.	Rom	Romans
1 Thess.	1 Thes	1 Thessalonians
2 Thess.	2 Thes	2 Thessalonians
1 Tim.	1 Tm	1 Timothy
2 Tim.	2 Tm	2 Timothy
Titus	Ti	Titus

24.6.4 Versions of the Bible

These abbreviations cover many standard versions of the Bible. If the version you are citing is not listed here, consult your instructor.

ARV	American Revised Version
ASV	American Standard Version
AT	American Translation
AV	Authorized (King James) Version
CEV	Contemporary English Version
DV	Douay Version
ERV	English Revised Version
EV	English version(s)
JB	Jerusalem Bible
NAB	New American Bible
NEB	New English Bible
NRSV	New Revised Standard Version
RSV	Revised Standard Version
RV	Revised Version
Vulg.	Vulgate

24.6.5 Other Sacred Works

Many sacred works of other religious traditions are divided into parts similar to those of the Bible. Capitalize and set in roman type the names of the works themselves (Qur'an, Vedas), but italicize the names of their parts (*al-Baqarah, Rig-Veda*). Although there is no widely accepted method for abbreviating the names of these works or their parts, you may punctuate citations from them similarly to those from the Bible (see also 17.5.2 and 19.5.2). If a work has multiple numbered divisions, you may substitute periods or commas for colons or make other adaptations to clarify the location of the cited passage.

Qur'an 2:257 *or* Qur'an 2 (*al-Baqarah*): 257

Mahabharata 1.2.3

If your paper is in religious studies, consult your instructor for more specific guidance.

24.7 Abbreviations in Citations and Other Scholarly Contexts

Abbreviations are commonly used and even preferred in citations, especially for identifying the roles of individuals other than authors (ed., trans.), the parts of works (vol., bk., sec.), and locating information (p., n). In text and in some citations, however, you should use words instead of abbreviations. For guidelines on using abbreviations in bibliography-style citations, see 16.1.6 and chapter 17; for abbreviations in reference list–style citations, see 18.1.6 and chapter 19.

Some disciplines allow the use of scholarly abbreviations, such as *e.g.* and *i.e.,* within parenthetical statements in the text of a paper. Consult your local guidelines on the use of such abbreviations.

Following is a list of the most common abbreviations used in citations and other scholarly contexts. For most abbreviations, add *s* or *es* for plural forms, unless otherwise shown. Do not italicize abbreviations of Latin terms. If you are not sure how to use a particular abbreviation appropriately, consult a reliable authority.

abbr.	abbreviated, abbreviation
abr.	abridged, abridgment
anon.	anonymous
app.	appendix
assn.	association
b.	born
bib.	Bible, biblical
bibliog.	bibliography, bibliographer
biog.	biography, biographer
bk.	book
ca.	*circa*, about, approximately
cap.	capital, capitalize
CD	compact disc
cf.	*confer*, compare
chap.	chapter
col.	column
comp.	compiler, compiled by

cont.	continued
d.	died
dept.	department
dict.	dictionary
diss.	dissertation
div.	division
DOI	digital object identifier
DVD	digital versatile (or video) disc
ed.	editor, edition, edited by
e.g.	*exempli gratia*, for example
esp.	especially
et al.	*et alii* or *et alia*, and others
etc.	*et cetera*, and so forth
ex.	example
fig.	figure
ff.	and following
fol.	folio
ftp	file transfer protocol
http	hypertext transfer protocol
ibid.	*ibidem*, in the same place
id.	*idem*, the same
i.e.	*id est*, that is
intl.	international
intro.	introduction
l. (*pl.* ll.)	line
loc. cit.	*loco citato*, in the place cited
misc.	miscellaneous
MS (*pl.* MSS)	manuscript
n (*pl.* nn)	note
natl.	national
n.b. or NB	*nota bene*, take careful note
n.d.	no date
no.	number
n.p.	no place; no publisher; no page
NS	New Style (dates)
n.s.	new series
op. cit.	*opera citato*, in the work cited
org.	organization
OS	Old Style (dates)
o.s.	old series
p. (*pl.* pp.)	page
par.	paragraph
pl.	plate; plural
PS	*postscriptum*, postscript
pseud.	pseudonym

pt.	part
pub.	publication, publisher, published by
q.v.	*quod vide*, which see
r.	*recto*, right
repr.	reprint
rev.	revised, revised by, revision; review, reviewed by
ROM	read-only memory
sec.	section
ser.	series
sing.	singular
soc.	society
sup.	*supra*, above
supp.	supplement
s.v. (*pl.* s.vv.)	*sub verbo, sub voce*, under the word
syn.	synonym, synonymous
trans.	translated by, translator
univ.	university
URL	uniform resource locator
usu.	usually
v. (*pl.* vv.)	verse; *verso*, right
viz.	*videlicet*, namely
vol.	volume
vs. *or* v.	versus (in legal contexts, use *v.*)

25 Quotations

This chapter offers general guidelines for presenting quotations. Although all of the examples are in English, the guidelines also apply to quotations from other languages (see also 22.2.1).

Quoting directly from a source is just one of several options for representing the work of others in your paper; for a discussion of the alternatives and when to use them, see 7.4. Whichever option you choose, you must cite the source of the words or ideas. Chapter 15 provides an introduction to citation practices, and the following chapters describe two common citation styles (chapters 16 and 17, bibliography style; chapters 18 and 19, reference list style).

If you are writing a thesis or a dissertation, your department or university may have specific requirements for presenting quotations, which are usually available from the office of theses and dissertations. If you are writing a class paper, your instructor may also ask you to follow certain principles for presenting quotations. Review these requirements before you prepare your paper. They take precedence over the guidelines suggested here. For style guides in various disciplines, see the bibliography.

If your dissertation will be submitted to an external dissertation repository, you may need to obtain formal permission from copyright holders for certain types of quotations. See chapter 4 of the *Chicago Manual of Style,* 15th edition (2003).

25.1 Quoting Accurately and Avoiding Plagiarism

Accurate quotation is crucial to the scholarly enterprise, so you must

- use the most reliable edition available
- transcribe the words exactly as they are in the original, or modify them only as described in 25.3
- accurately report the source in your bibliography or reference list (see chapters 16 and 18) so that readers can consult it for themselves

The ethics of scholarship also require that whenever you quote words, tables, graphics, or data from a source, you clearly indicate what you borrowed and from where, using the appropriate citation style (see chapter 15). If you do not, you risk a charge of plagiarism. But even if you do cite a source accurately, you still risk a charge of plagiarism if you use the exact words of the source but fail to identify them as a quotation in one of the ways described in 25.2. For a fuller discussion of plagiarism, see 7.9.

25.2 Incorporating Quotations into Your Text

You can incorporate a quotation into your text in one of two ways, depending on its length. If the quotation is four lines or fewer, run it into your text and enclose it in quotation marks. If it is five lines or longer, set it off as a block quotation, without quotation marks. Follow the same principles for quotations within footnotes or endnotes (see 16.3.5).

You may use a block quotation for a quotation shorter than five lines if you want to emphasize it or compare it to a longer quotation.

25.2.1 Run-in Quotations

When quoting a passage of fewer than five lines, enclose the exact words quoted in double quotation marks. There are several ways to integrate a quotation into the flow of your text; see 7.5. You may introduce it with the name of the author accompanied by a term such as *notes, claims, argues,* or *according to.* (Note that these terms are usually in the present tense, rather than *noted, claimed,* and so forth, but some disciplines follow different practices.) In this case, put a comma before the quotation.

Ricoeur writes, "The boundary between plot and argument is no easier to trace."

As Ricoeur notes, "The boundary between plot and argument is no easier to trace."

If you weave a quotation more tightly into the syntax of your sentence, as with the word *that,* do not put a comma before it.

Ricoeur warns us that "the boundary between plot and argument is no easier to trace."

If you put the attributing phrase in the middle of a quotation, set it off with commas.

"The boundary between plot and argument," says Ricoeur, "is no easier to trace."

For use of commas, periods, and other punctuation marks within the quotation, see 21.11.2 and 25.3.1; for capitalization within the quotation, see 25.3.1.

PLACEMENT OF CITATIONS. If you cite the source of a quotation in a footnote or endnote, where you place the superscript note number (see 16.3.2) depends on where the quotation falls within a sentence. If the quotation is at the end of the sentence, put the number after the closing quotation mark.

According to Litwack, "Scores of newly freed slaves viewed movement as a vital expression of their emancipation."[4]

If the quotation ends in the middle of a sentence, put the number at the end of the clause that includes the quotation, which often is the end of the sentence.

"Scores of newly freed slaves viewed movement as a vital expression of their emancipation," according to Litwack.[4]

Litwack argues that "scores of newly freed slaves viewed movement as a vital expression of their emancipation,"[4] and he proceeds to prove this assertion.

The same placement options apply to citations given parenthetically with either bibliography-style (16.4.3) or reference list–style citations (see 18.3.1), with one critical difference: if a period or comma would normally precede the closing quotation mark, place it outside the quotation, following the closing parenthesis.

The authors seek to understand "how people categorize the objects they encounter in everyday situations" (Bowker and Star 1999, 59).

To determine "how people categorize the objects they encounter in everyday situations" (Bowker and Star 1999, 59), the authors devised a study.

Understanding "how people categorize the objects they encounter in everyday situations" is the key for Bowker and Star (1999, 59).

SPECIAL PUNCTUATION. For a quotation within a quotation, use single quotation marks for the inner set of quoted words.

Rothko, argues Ball, "wanted to make works that wrought a transcendent effect, that dealt with spiritual concerns: 'Paintings must be like miracles,' he once said."

If you run two or more lines of poetry into your text, separate them with a slash (/), with a space before and after it. In most cases, however, use block quotations for poetry.

They reduce life to a simple proposition, "All things have rest, and ripen toward the grave; / In silence, ripen, fall, and cease."

25.2.2 Block Quotations

PROSE. Present a prose quotation of five or more lines as a block quotation. Introduce the quotation in your own words in the text; see 7.5. If you introduce the quotation with a complete sentence, end the sentence with a colon. If you use only an attribution phrase such as *notes, claims, argues,* or *according to* along with the author's name, end the phrase with a comma. If you weave the quotation into the syntax of your sentence, do not use any punctuation before the quotation if no punctuation would ordinarily appear there (see the second example below).

Single-space a block quotation, and leave a blank line before and after it. Do not add quotation marks at the beginning or end, but preserve any quotation marks in the original. Indent the entire quotation as far as you indent the first line of a paragraph. (In literary studies and other fields concerned with close analysis of texts, you should indent the first line of a block quotation further than the rest of the quotation if the text is indented in the original; see also 25.3.) For other punctuation and capitalization within the quotation, see 25.3.1.

Jackson begins by evoking the importance of home:

Housing is an outward expression of the inner human nature; no society can be fully understood apart from the residences of its members. A nineteenth-century melody declares, "There's no place like home," and even though she had Emerald City at her feet, Dorothy could think of no place she would rather be than at home in Kansas. Our homes are our havens from the world.[1]

In the rest of his introduction, he discusses . . .

If you quote more than one paragraph, do not add extra lines between them, but indent the first line of the second and subsequent paragraphs further than the rest of the quotation.

He observed that

governments ordinarily perish by powerlessness or by tyranny. In the first case, power escapes them; in the other, it is torn from them.

Many people, on seeing democratic states fall into anarchy, have thought that government in these states was naturally weak and powerless. The truth is that

> when war among their parties has once been set aflame, government loses its
> action on society. (Tocqueville, 248)

If you cite the source in a footnote or endnote, place the note number as a superscript at the end of the block quotation, as in the first example above (see also 16.3.2). If you cite the source parenthetically, put the citation after the terminal punctuation of a block quotation, as in the second example above. (Note that this differs from its placement with a run-in quotation, as described in 25.2.1.)

POETRY AND DRAMA. Present a quotation of two or more lines from poetry as a block quotation. Begin each line of the poem on a new line, with punctuation at the ends of lines as in the original. For most papers, indent a block of poetry as you would a prose quotation; if a line is too long to fit on a single line, indent the runover further than the rest of the quotation. But in a dissertation or other longer paper that includes many poetry quotations, center each quotation on the page.

> Whitman's poem includes some memorable passages:
>
> > My tongue, every atom of my blood, form'd from this soil, this air,
> > Born here of parents born here from parents the same, and their parents
> >   the same
> > I, now thirty-seven years old in perfect health begin,
> > Hoping to cease not till death.

If you are quoting a poem with an unusual alignment, reproduce the alignment of the original.

> This is what Herbert captured so beautifully:
>
> > Sure there was wine
> > Before my sighs did drie it: there was corn
> >   Before my tears did drown it.
> >   Is the yeare onely lost to me?
> >   Have I no bayes to crown it?
> > No flowers, no garlands gay? all blasted?
> >   All wasted?

If you quote two or more lines of dialogue from a dramatic work, set the quotation apart in a block quotation formatted as you would prose. Present each speaker's name so that it is distinct from the dialogue, such as in all capital letters or in a different font. Begin each speech on a new line, and indent runovers further than the rest of the quotation.

> Then the play takes an unusual turn:

R. ROISTER DOISTER. Except I have her to my wife, I shall run mad.

M. MERYGREEKE. Nay, "unwise" perhaps, but I warrant you for
  "mad."

EPIGRAPHS. An epigraph is a quotation that establishes a theme of your paper. For epigraphs used in the front matter of a thesis or dissertation, see A.2.1. Treat an epigraph at the beginning of a chapter or section as a block quotation. On the line below it, give the author and the title, flush right and preceded by an em dash (or two hyphens; see 21.7.2). You do not need a more formal citation for an epigraph. Leave two blank lines between the source line and the beginning of text. See also figure A.9.

The city, however, does not tell its past, but contains it like the lines of a hand.

—Italo Calvino, *Invisible Cities*

25.3 | Modifying Quotations

Whenever you quote, you must record the exact wording, spelling, capitalization, and punctuation of the source, even if they do not follow the guidelines in this manual. When you incorporate the quotation, however, you may modify it to fit the syntax of the surrounding text or to focus on certain parts of it.

Note that disciplines have different standards for issues discussed in this section, such as modifying initial capital and lowercase letters and using ellipses for omissions. For papers in most disciplines, follow the general guidelines. For papers in literary studies and other fields concerned with close analysis of texts, follow the stricter guidelines given under some topics. If you are not sure which set to follow, consult your local guidelines or your instructor.

25.3.1 Permissible Changes

SPELLING. If the original source contains an obvious typographic error, correct it without comment.

Original: These conclusions are not definate, but they are certainly suggestive.

Clayton admits that his conclusions are "not definite."

If, however, such an error reveals something significant about the source or is relevant to your argument, preserve it in your quotation. Immediately following the error, insert the Latin word *sic* ("so"), italicized and enclosed in brackets, to identify it as the author's error. It is considered bad manners to call out errors just to embarrass a source.

Original: The average American does not know how to spell and cannot use a coma properly.

Russell exemplifies her own argument by claiming that the average American "cannot use a coma [*sic*] properly."

When quoting from an older source or one that represents dialect with nonstandard spelling, preserve idiosyncrasies of spelling, and do not use *sic.* If you modernize or alter all of the spelling and punctuation for clarity, inform your readers in a note or preface.

CAPITALIZATION AND PUNCTUATION. In most disciplines, you may change the initial letter of a quoted passage from capital to lowercase or from lowercase to capital without noting the change. If you weave the quotation into the syntax of your sentence, begin it with a lowercase letter. Otherwise, begin it with a capital letter if it begins with a complete sentence, with a lowercase letter if it does not. You may also make similar changes when you use ellipses; see 25.3.2.

Original: As a result of these factors, the Mexican people were bound to benefit from the change.

Fernandez claims, "The Mexican people were bound to benefit from the change."

Fernandez claims that "the Mexican people were bound to benefit from the change."

Fernandez points out that "as a result of these factors, the Mexican people were bound to benefit from the change."

"The Mexican people," notes Fernandez, "were bound to benefit from the change."

Depending on how you work the quotation in the text, you may also omit a final period or change it to a comma.

Fernandez notes that the Mexicans were "bound to benefit from the change" as a result of the factors he discusses.

"The Mexican people were bound to benefit from the change," argues Fernandez.

In literary studies and other fields concerned with close analysis of texts, indicate any change in capitalization by putting the altered letter in brackets.

"[T]he Mexican people were bound to benefit from the change," argues Fernandez.

Fernandez points out that "[a]s a result of these factors, the Mexican people were bound to benefit from the change."

In any discipline, if you put double quotation marks around a passage that already includes double quotation marks, change the internal marks to single quotation marks for clarity (see 25.2.1). If the original passage ends with a semicolon or a colon, change it to a period or a comma to fit the structure of your sentence (see 21.11.2).

ITALICS. You may italicize for emphasis words that are not italicized in the original, but you must indicate the change with the notation *italics mine* or *emphasis added,* placed either in the quotation or in its citation. Within the quotation, add the notation in square brackets immediately after the italicized words. In a citation, add the notation after the page number, preceded by a semicolon (see also 16.3.5). If you add italics at two or more points in a quotation, use a note rather than a parenthetical comment. See also 22.2.2.

According to Schultz, "By the end of 2010, *every democracy* [emphasis added] will face the challenge of nuclear terrorism."[1]

Brown notes simply that the destruction of the tribes "had all happened in *less than ten years*" (271; italics mine).

INSERTIONS. If you need to insert a word or more of explanation, clarification, or correction into a quotation, enclose the insertion in brackets. If you find yourself making many such insertions, consider paraphrasing or weaving smaller quotations into your text instead.

As she observes, "These masters [Picasso, Braque, Matisse] rebelled against academic training."

She observes that Picasso, Braque, and Matisse "rebelled against academic training."

NOTES. If you quote a passage that includes a superscript note number but do not quote the note itself, you may omit the note number.

25.3.2 Omissions

If you omit words, phrases, sentences, or even paragraphs in a quotation because they are irrelevant, do not change or misrepresent the meaning of the original quotation. Not only must you preserve words that might change the entire meaning of the quotation (such as *not, never,* or *always*), but you must also preserve important qualifications. The quotation shown in the following example would be a misrepresentation of the author's meaning. (See also 4.2.3.)

Original: The change was sure to be beneficial once the immediate troubles subsided.

Yang claims, "The change was sure to be beneficial."

To indicate the omission of a word, phrase, or sentence, use ellipsis dots—three periods with spaces between them. (Many word processors have a special character that represents an ellipsis.) Since the dots stand for words omitted, they always go inside the quotation marks or block quotation. Leave a space between the last quoted word or punctuation mark and the first ellipsis dot and another space after the last dot before the next word or punctuation mark.

"We are fighting for truth; . . . for freedom . . . ; and . . . for survival."

How you use ellipses in certain situations depends on your discipline. For most disciplines, follow the general method; for literary studies and other fields concerned with close analysis of texts, follow the textual studies method (see below). If you are not sure which method to follow, consult your local guidelines or your instructor. See 25.3.1 for adjustments to capitalization and punctuation with omissions.

GENERAL METHOD. You may shorten a quotation such as the following in several different ways.

Original: When a nation is wrong, it should say so and apologize to the wronged party. It should conduct itself according to the standards of international diplomacy. It should also take steps to change the situation.

If you omit words within a sentence, use three ellipsis dots as described above.

"When a nation is wrong, it should . . . apologize to the wronged party."

If you omit material between sentences and the material preceding the omission is a grammatically complete sentence, use a terminal punctuation mark immediately following that sentence. Leave a space between that punctuation mark and the first ellipsis dot. Follow this practice even if the omission includes the end of the preceding sentence as long as what is left is grammatically complete (as in the second example here).

"When a nation is wrong, it should say so and apologize to the wronged party. . . . It should also take steps to change the situation."

"When a nation is wrong, it should say so. . . . It should also take steps to change the situation."

If you omit material between sentences so that the material preceding and following the omission combines to form a grammatically complete sentence, do not include terminal punctuation before the ellipsis. To avoid misrepresenting the author's meaning, however, it is generally better to use one of the shortening options above or to use two separate quotations in this situation.

"When a nation is wrong, it should say so and . . . take steps to change the situation."

The same principles apply with other types of punctuation marks, which precede or follow an ellipsis depending on where the words are omitted. In some situations, such as the second example below, consider using a more selective quotation.

"How cold was it? . . . No one could function in that climate."

"The merchant's stock included dry goods and sundry other items . . . , all for purchase by the women of the town."

or

The merchant stocked "dry goods and sundry other items" for the town's women.

Since in many contexts it is obvious when a quotation has been shortened, you need not use ellipsis points in the following situations:

- before or after a quoted phrase, incomplete sentence, or other fragment from the original that is clearly not a complete sentence. If you omit anything within the fragment, however, use ellipsis points at the appropriate place:

  Smith wrote that the president had been "very much impressed" by the paper that stressed "using the economic resources . . . of all the major powers."

- at the beginning of a quotation, even if the beginning of the sentence from the original has been omitted
- at the end of a quotation, even if the end of the sentence from the original has been omitted

TEXTUAL STUDIES METHOD. The textual studies method uses ellipses more strictly than the general method to represent omissions of material at the beginning and end of quoted sentences. If you use this method, follow the principles of the general method except as noted below.

Original: When a nation is wrong, it should say so and apologize to the wronged party. It should conduct itself according to the standards of international diplomacy. It should also take steps to change the situation.

- If you omit material between sentences but quote the sentence preceding the omission in full, use a terminal punctuation mark immediately following that sentence. Leave a space between that punctuation mark and the first ellipsis dot, as in the general method, shown in the first example below. However, if the omission includes the end of the preceding sentence (even if what is left is a grammatically complete sentence), put a space instead of a punctuation mark immediately following that sentence. After the space, use four ellipsis dots to represent the omission (as in the second example here).

  "When a nation is wrong, it should say so and apologize to the wronged party. . . . It should also take steps to change the situation."

  but

  "When a nation is wrong, it should say so . . . . It should also take steps to change the situation."

- If you begin a quotation with a sentence that is grammatically complete despite an omission at the beginning of the sentence, indicate the omission with an ellipsis. If the first word is capitalized in the quotation but not in the original, indicate the changed letter in brackets (see 25.3.1).

  . . . [I]t should say so and apologize to the wronged party."

- If you end a quotation with a sentence that is grammatically complete despite an omission at the end of the sentence, indicate the omission with a four-dot ellipsis, as you would for an omitted ending between sentences.

  "When a nation is wrong, it should say so. . . ."

SPECIAL TYPES OF OMISSIONS. The following practices apply to both the general and textual studies methods of handling omissions.

If you omit a full paragraph or more within a block quotation, indicate that omission with a period and three ellipsis dots at the end of the paragraph before the omission. If the quotation includes another paragraph after the omission, indent the first line of the new paragraph. If it starts in the middle of a paragraph, begin with three ellipsis points after the indentation.

Merton writes:

  A brand-new conscience was just coming into existence as an actual, operating function of a soul. My choices were just about to become responsible. . . .

  . . . Since no man ever can, or could, live by himself and for himself alone, the destinies of thousands of other people were bound to be affected.

Show the omission of one or more complete lines of a poem quoted in a block quotation by a line of ellipsis points about as long as the line above it.

The key passage reads as follows:

> Weep no more, woeful shepherds, weep no more,
> For Lycidas your sorrow is not dead,
> . . . .
> To all that wander in that perilous flood.

26 Tables and Figures

Many research papers use tables and figures to present data. *Tables* are grids consisting of columns and rows that present numerical or verbal facts by categories. *Figures* include charts, graphs, diagrams, photographs, maps, musical examples, drawings, and other images. All these types of nontextual material are collectively referred to as *illustrations* (a term sometimes used interchangeably with *figures*) or *graphics*.

When you have data that could be conveyed in a table or figure, your first task is to choose the most effective of these formats; some kinds of data are better represented in a table, some in a chart, others in a graph. Your choice will affect how your readers respond to your data. These are rhetorical issues, discussed in chapter 8. This chapter focuses on how to construct the particular form you choose, looking specifically at tables and at two types of figures—charts and graphs.

Most tables, charts, and graphs are now generated with software. You cannot, however, rely on software to select the most effective format or to generate such items in the correct style, nor will software assure logical or

formal consistency. Expect to change some default settings before gener-
ating tables, charts, and graphs and to fine-tune these items once they are
produced. For information about inserting tables and all types of figures
into your paper, especially if they are not created in your word processor,
see A.3.1 in the appendix.

If you are writing a thesis or dissertation that includes tables and figures, your department or university may have specific format requirements,
which are usually available from the office of theses and dissertations. If
you are writing a class paper, your instructor may also ask you to prepare
tables and figures in a certain way. Review these requirements before you
prepare your paper. They take precedence over the guidelines suggested
here. For style guides in various disciplines, see the bibliography.

26.1 General Issues

There are several issues common to the presentation of tables and figures
in papers.

26.1.1 Position in the Text

A table or figure should follow as closely as possible the paragraph in
which you first mention it. If the table or figure does not fit on the rest of
the page but is smaller than a full page, continue the text to complete the
page and place the table or figure at the top of the next page. (See A.3.1
for information about inserting tables and figures into your paper, and
figs. A.12 and A.13 for examples of tables and figures as they should appear on a page.)

You may group smaller tables or figures on a page, as long as they are
clearly distinct from one another. Grouped tables generally retain their
own titles (see 26.2.2). If grouped figures are closely related, give them a
single number and a general caption; otherwise use separate numbers and
captions (see 26.3.2).

If a table or figure is marginally relevant or too large to put in the text,
put it in an appendix or a section labeled *Illustrations* in the back matter
of your paper (see A.2.3).

26.1.2 Size

Whenever you can, format tables and figures to fit on one page in normal, or *portrait,* orientation. If they do not fit, try shortening long column
heads or abbreviating repeated terms.

If you cannot make a table or figure fit on a page, you have several
options.

- *Landscape.* If a table or figure is too wide for a page, turn it ninety degrees so that the left side is at the bottom of the page; this orientation is called *landscape* or *broadside.* Do not put any text on a page containing a landscape table or figure. Set the table title or figure caption in either landscape or portrait orientation. See figure A.13 for an example.
- *Side by side.* If a table is longer than a page but less than half a page wide, divide it in half and position the two parts side by side on the same page. Include the column heads on both parts.
- *Multiple pages.* If a table or figure is too long to fit on a single page in portrait orientation or too wide to fit in landscape, divide it between two (or more) pages. For tables, repeat the stub column and all column heads (see 26.2) on every page. Put the table number on a "continued" line at the top left of every page after the first, flush left, in italic letters (*Table 2 continued*). Omit the bottom rule on all pages except the last.
- *Reduction.* If the figure is a photograph or other image, consider reducing it. Consult your local guidelines for information about resolution and related characteristics.
- *Separate items.* If none of the above solutions is appropriate, consider presenting the data in two or more separate tables or figures.
- *Supplement.* If the table or figure consists of material that cannot be presented in print form, such as a large data set or a multimedia file, treat it as an appendix, as described in A.2.3.

26.1.3 Source Lines

You must acknowledge the sources of any data you use in tables and figures that you did not collect yourself. You must do this even if you present the data in a new form—for example, you create a graph based on data originally published in a table, add fresh data to a table from another source, or combine data from multiple sources by meta-analysis.

Treat a source line as a footnote to a table (see 26.2.7) or as part of a caption for a figure (see 26.3.2). Introduce the source line with the word *Source(s)* (capitalized, in italics, followed by a colon). If the source line runs onto more than one line, the runovers should be flush left, single-spaced. End a source line with a period.

If you are following bibliography style for your citations, cite the source as in a full note (see chapter 16), including the original table or figure number or the page number from which data were taken. Unless you cite this source elsewhere in your paper, you need not include it in your bibliography.

Source: Data from David Halle, *Inside Culture: Art and Class in the American Home* (Chicago: University of Chicago Press, 1993), table 2.

Sources: Data from Richard H. Adams Jr., "Remittances, Investment, and Rural Asset Accumulation in Pakistan," *Economic Development and Cultural Change* 47, no. 1 (1998): 155–73; David Bevan, Paul Collier, and Jan Gunning, *Peasants and Government: An Economic Analysis* (Oxford: Clarendon Press, 1989), 125–28.

If you are following reference list style for your citations, cite the source as in a parenthetical citation (minus the parentheses) and include full bibliographical information about it in your reference list (see chapter 18).

Source: Data from Halle 1993, table 2.

Sources: Data from Adams 1998, 155–73; Bevan, Collier, and Gunning 1989, 125–28.

If the data is adapted in any way from what is presented in the original source, include the phrase *adapted from* in the source line, as shown in tables 26.1 and 26.3.

For photographs, maps, and other figures that you did not create yourself, include an acknowledgment of the creator in place of a source line.

Map by Gerald F. Pyle.   Photograph by James L. Ballard.

If your dissertation will be submitted to an external dissertation repository, you may also need to obtain formal permission to reproduce tables or figures protected by copyright. See chapter 4 of the *Chicago Manual of Style,* 15th edition (2003). If you need to include credit lines in connection with such permissions, see *CMOS* 12.40–51 (figures) and 13.44 (tables).

26.2 Tables

In many situations, you may choose to present data in a table. Chapter 8 describes criteria for using tables as well as general design principles for them. This section covers most of the issues you are likely to encounter in their preparation. Tables 26.1–26.3 provide examples of the principles discussed here.

Tables vary widely in the complexity of their content and therefore in their structure, but consistency both within and across tables is essential to ensure that readers will understand your data.

Use arabic numerals for all numerical data in tables unless otherwise noted. To save space, you can use abbreviations and symbols more freely than you can in text, but use them sparingly and consistently. If standard abbreviations do not exist, create your own and explain them either in a footnote to the table (see 26.2.7) or, if there are many, in a list of abbreviations in your paper's front matter (see A.2.1).

Table 26.1. Selected churches in Four Corners, Boston

Church	Religious tradition	Attendance	Ethnicity/origin	Class
Church of God	Pentecostal	100	Caribbean, mixed	Middle
Church of the Holy Ghost	Pentecostal	10	Southern Black	Working
Faith Baptist	Baptist	70	Southern Black	Middle
Maison d'Esprit	Pentecostal	50	Haitian	Working
Mt. Nebo Apostolic	Apostolic	30	Southern Black	Working/ middle

Source: Data adapted from Omar M. McRoberts, *Streets of Glory: Church and Community in a Black Urban Neighborhood* (Chicago: University of Chicago Press, 2003), 53.

Table 26.2. Election results in Gotefrith Province, 1950–60

	1950		1956		1960	
Party	% of vote	Seats won	% of vote	Seats won	% of vote	Seats won
			Provincial Assembly			
Conservative	35.5	47	26.0	37	30.9	52
Socialist	12.4	18	27.1	44	24.8	39
Christian Democrat	49.2	85	41.2	68	39.2	59
Other	2.9	0	5.7	1[a]	5.1	0
Total	100.0	150	100.0	150	100.0	150
			National Assembly			
Conservative	32.6	4	23.8	3	28.3	3
Socialist	13.5	1	27.3	3	24.1	2
Christian Democrat	52.1	7	42.8	6	46.4	8
Other	1.8	0	6.1	0	1.2	0
Total	100.0	12	100.0	12	100.0	13[b]

Source: Data from Erehwon 1950, 1956, 1960.

[a]This seat was won by a Radical Socialist, who became a member of the Conservative coalition.

[b]Reapportionment in 1960 gave Gotefrith an additional seat in the National Assembly.

Table 26.3. Unemployment rates for working-age New Yorkers, 2000

	As % of labor force		
Unemployment rate	Female	Male	Both sexes
All workers	6.1	5.4	. . .
By education (ages 25–64)			
Less than high school	11.9	5.8	. . .
High school degree	5.4	5.0	. . .
Some college	4.2	4.5	. . .
BA or more	2.6	2.3	. . .
By age			
16–19	. . .	. . .	19.3
20–34	. . .	. . .	6.5
35–54	. . .	. . .	4.7
55–64	. . .	. . .	2.9

Source: Data adapted from Mark Levitan, "It Did Happen Here: The Rise in Working Poverty in New York City," in *New York and Los Angeles: Politics, Society, and Culture—A Comparative View,* ed. David Halle (Chicago: University of Chicago Press, 2003), table 8.2.

Note: "Working age" is defined as ages 16 to 64. Educational level is not tracked below the age of 25 in census data.

26.2.1 Table Structure

A table has elements analogous to horizontal and vertical axes on a graph. On the horizontal axis are *column heads.* On the vertical axis are headings that constitute what is called the *stub column.*

This grid of columns (vertical) and rows (horizontal) in a table correlates two sets of variables called *independent* and *dependent.* The independent variables are traditionally on the left, in the stub column. The dependent variables are traditionally in the column heads. If you include the same set of variables in two or more tables in your paper, be consistent: put them in the same place in each table, as column heads or in the stub.

The data, which may be words, numbers, or both (see table 26.1), are entered in the cells below the column heads and to the right of the stub column.

26.2.2 Table Numbers and Titles

In general, every table should have a number and a title. Place these items flush left on the line above the table, with the word *Table* (capitalized, in roman type), followed by the table number (in arabic numerals), followed by a period. After a space, give the title without a terminal period. Capitalize the title sentence style (see 22.3.1). If a title runs onto more than one line, the runovers should be flush left, single-spaced.

Table 13. Yen-dollar ratios in Japanese exports, 1995–2005

A simple tabulation that can be introduced clearly in the text, such as a simple two-column list, need not be numbered or titled.

Chicago's population grew exponentially in its first century:

1840	4,470
1870	298,977
1900	1,698,575
1930	3,376,438

TABLE NUMBERS. Number tables separately from figures, in the order in which you mention them in the text. If you have only a few tables, number them consecutively throughout the paper, even across chapters. If you have many tables and many chapters, use double numeration: that is, the chapter number, followed by a period, followed by the table number, as in *Table 12.4.*

When you refer to a table in the text, specify the table number ("in table 3") rather than its location ("below") because you may end up moving the table while editing or formatting the paper. Do not capitalize the word *table* in text references to tables.

·   ·

TABLE TITLES. Keep table titles short but descriptive enough to indicate the specific nature of the data and to differentiate tables from one another. For discussion of good titling practices, see 8.3.1. Table titles may be presented in a smaller typeface than the rest of your text; consult your local guidelines.

26.2.3 Column Rules

Rules separate different types of data and text. Too many rules create a confusing image, so use them sparingly and consistently (see also 8.3.2).

- Insert full-width horizontal rules to separate the title from the column heads (see 26.2.4), the column heads from the body of the table, and the body of the table from footnotes. A rule above a row of totals is traditional but not essential. Two-column tables within the text are best set with no rules, as long as the column heads are set off typographically.
- Use partial-width horizontal rules to indicate which column heads and columns are governed by special types of heads, if you use them (see 26.2.4, table 26.2).
- Leave enough space between columns to avoid using internal vertical or other horizontal rules. Do not use vertical rules to enclose the table in a box. For a long and narrow table positioned in side-by-side format (see 26.1.2), however, use a vertical rule to separate the two halves.
- Avoid using shading in place of rules, except in long or complex tables (see 8.3.2). Also avoid color. Even if you print the paper on a color printer, it may be printed or copied later on a black-and-white machine, and if it is a dissertation, it may be microfilmed. Shading and color do not reproduce well in any of these forms. If you use shading, make sure it does not obscure the text of the table, and do not use multiple shades, which might not reproduce distinctly.

26.2.4 Column Heads

A table must have at least two columns, each with a *head* or *heading* at the top that names the data in the column below.

- Use noun phrases for column heads. Keep them short (or set them to wrap, as in tables 26.1 and 26.2) to avoid an excessively wide table.
- Make column heads singular or plural depending on the data below. Stub heads, if present, are usually singular (see 26.2.5).
- Capitalize column heads sentence style (see 22.3.1).
- Align stub heads flush left; center other column heads over the widest entry in the column below. Align the bottom of all heads horizontally.

If your data are complex, you may need to include special types of heads in addition to the column heads. Such a head may apply to two or more columns of data. Center the head over the relevant columns with a partial-width horizontal rule beneath (and, if necessary, above) it. Table 26.2 shows heads both above ("1950") and below ("Provincial Assembly") the column heads.

Heads may have explanatory tags to clarify or to indicate the unit of measure for data in the column below. Enclose such tags in parentheses. You may use abbreviations and symbols for such tags (mpg, km, lb., %, $M, and so on), but be consistent within and among your tables.

Responses (%)   Pesos (millions)

26.2.5 The Stub

The leftmost column of a table, called the *stub,* lists the categories of data in each row.

- Include a column head for the stub whenever possible, even if it is generic ("Typical Characteristic" or "Variable"). Omit the head only if it would merely repeat the table title or if the categories in the stub are too diverse for a single head.
- Make *stub entries* nouns or noun phrases whenever possible, and keep them consistent in form: "Books, Journal articles, Manuscripts" rather than "Books, Articles published in journals, Manuscripts." Use the same word for the same item in all of your tables (for example, if you use *Former USSR* in one table, do not use *Former Soviet Union* in another).
- Capitalize all stub entries sentence style (see 22.3.1), with no terminal periods.
- Set the stub head and entries flush left, and indent any runovers (as in table 26.1).
- To show the sum of the numbers in a column, include an indented stub entry entitled *Total* (see table 26.2).

If the stub column includes subentries as well as main entries (see table 26.3), distinguish them through indentation, typography (such as italics), or both. Follow the same principles listed above for main entries for capitalization and so forth.

26.2.6 The Body of a Table

The body of a table consists of *cells* containing your data, which may be words, numbers, or both (see table 26.1).

If the data are numerical and all values in a column or in the entire table are in thousands or millions, omit the rightmost zeros and note the unit in an explanatory tag in the relevant column head (see 26.2.4), in the table title (26.2.2), or in a footnote (26.2.7). Indicate an empty cell with three spaced periods (ellipsis dots), centered as in table 26.3.

HORIZONTAL ALIGNMENT. Align the data in each row with the stub entry for that row.

■ If the stub entry runs over onto two or more lines but the related data does not, align the row with the bottom line of the stub entry (see the row beginning "Church of the Holy Ghost" in table 26.1).
■ If both the stub entry and the data run over onto two or more lines, align the row with the top line of the stub entry (see the row beginning "Mt. Nebo Apostolic" in table 26.1).
■ If necessary, insert *leaders* (lines of periods, or dots) to lead the reader's eye from the stub to the data in the first column. (For an example of leaders in a similar context, see fig. A.5.)

VERTICAL ALIGNMENT. Align a column of numbers vertically on their real or implied decimal points by aligning on the rightmost numeral, so that readers can compare the values in the column. If all numerical values in a column have a zero before a decimal point, you may omit the zeros (see figure A.13).

Align dollar signs, percent signs, degrees, and so on. But if they occur in every cell in the column, delete them from the cells and give the unit as a tag in the column head (see 26.2.4, table 26.2, and figure A.13).

If the data consist of words, center each column under the column head. If any items have runovers, align each column flush left (see table 26.1).

26.2.7 Footnotes

If a table has footnotes, position them flush left, single-spaced. Leave a blank line between the bottom rule of the table and the first note, and also between notes. Footnotes may be presented in a smaller typeface than the rest of the text; consult your local guidelines.

Footnotes for tables can be of four kinds: (1) source lines (discussed in 26.1.3), (2) general footnotes that apply to the whole table, (3) footnotes that apply to specific parts of the table, and (4) notes on levels of statistical significance. If you have more than one kind of note, put them in that order.

GENERAL NOTES. General notes apply to the entire table. They define abbreviations, expand on the table title, specify how data were collected or derived, indicate rounding of values, and so on. Gather all such remarks into a single note. Do not put a note number (or other symbol) anywhere in the table or the table title, or with the note itself. Simply begin the note with the word *Note* (capitalized, in italics, followed by a colon). See also table 26.3.

Note: Since not all data were available, there is disparity in the totals.

SPECIFIC NOTES. Notes to explain specific items in a table can be attached to any part of the table except the table number or title. Designate such notes with lowercase, superscript letters rather than numbers, both within the table and in the note itself. Do not begin the note with the word *note* but with the same superscript letter, with no period or colon following.

[a]Total excludes trade and labor employees.

If you include more than one such note in a table (as in table 26.2), use letters in sequential order, beginning at the upper left of the table, running left to right and then downward, row by row. If a note applies to two or more items in a table, use the same letter for each item; if it applies to all items in a column or row, put the letter in the relevant column head or stub entry.

NOTES ON STATISTICAL SIGNIFICANCE. If you include notes on the statistical significance of your data (also called *probability notes*), and if the significance levels are standard, designate notes with asterisks, both within the table and in the note itself. Use a single asterisk for the lowest level of probability, two for the next higher, and three for the next higher. If, however, you are noting significance levels other than standard ones, use superscript letters instead. Because these footnotes are short and they share a single purpose, you may combine them on the same line, spaced, without intervening punctuation. The letter p (for *probability*, no period after it) should be lowercase and italic. Omit zeros before decimal points.

*p<.05　　　　**p <.01　　　　***p<.001

26.3 Figures

The term *figure* refers to a variety of images, including charts, graphs, diagrams, photographs, maps, musical examples, and drawings. Most such materials can now be prepared and inserted into a paper electronically.

The technical details are software-specific and too complex to be covered in this book, but some general guidelines are presented in A.3.1 in the appendix.

This section describes some principles for presenting two types of figures created from data: charts and graphs. It also discusses captions for figures of all kinds. ·

Treat videos, animations, or other multimedia files that cannot be presented in print form as an appendix (see A.2.3).

26.3.1 Charts and Graphs

In many situations, you may choose to present data in a chart or graph. Chapter 8 describes criteria for using these graphic forms as well as general design principles for them. It also provides examples of several different types of graphics. For detailed guidance on constructing charts and graphs, consult a reliable authority.

Each chart and graph in your paper should take the form that best communicates its data and supports its claim, but consistency both within and across these items is essential in ensuring that readers will understand your data. Keep in mind the following principles when presenting charts and graphs of any type:

- Represent elements of the same kind—axes, lines, data points, bars, wedges—in the same way. Use distinct visual effects only to make distinctions, never just for variety.
- Use arabic numerals for all numerical data.
- Label all axes using sentence-style capitalization. Keep the labels short, following practices for good table titles (see 8.3.1). Use the figure caption (see 26.3.2) to explain any aspects of the data that cannot be captured in the labels. To save space, you can use abbreviations and symbols more freely than you can in text, but use them sparingly and consistently. If standard abbreviations do not exist, create your own and explain them either in the caption or, if there are many, in a list of abbreviations in your paper's front matter (see A.2.1).
- Label lines, data points, or other items within the chart or graph that require explanation using either all lowercase letters (for single words) or sentence-style capitalization (for phrases). If phrases and single words both appear, they should all be styled the same (as in fig. 8.3). The other principles described above for axis labels also apply to labels of this type.
- Avoid shading and color. Even if you print the paper on a color printer, it may be printed or copied later on a black-and-white machine, and the shading and color might not reproduce well. If you use shading, make

sure it does not obscure the text of the figure, and do not use multiple shades, which might not reproduce distinctly.

26.3.2 Figure Numbers and Captions

In general, every figure in your paper should have a number and a caption. If you include only a few figures in your paper and do not specifically refer to them in the text, omit the numbers. Figure captions may be presented in a smaller typeface than the rest of your text; consult your local guidelines.

On the line below the figure, write the word *Figure* (flush left, capitalized, in roman type), followed by the figure number (in arabic numerals), followed by a period. After a space, give the caption, usually followed by a terminal period (but see below). If a caption runs onto more than one line, the runovers should be flush left, single-spaced.

Figure 6. The Great Mosque of Cordoba, eighth to tenth century.

In musical examples only, place the figure number and caption above the figure.

FIGURE NUMBERS. Number figures separately from tables, in the order in which you mention them in the text. If you have only a few figures, number them consecutively throughout the paper, even across chapters. If you have many figures and many chapters, use double numeration: that is, the chapter number, followed by a period, followed by the figure number, as in *Figure 12.4.*

When you refer to a figure in the text, specify the figure number ("in figure 3") rather than its location ("below") because you may end up moving the figure while editing or formatting the paper. Do not capitalize the word *figure* in text references to figures, and do not abbreviate it as *fig.* except in parenthetical references—for example, "(see fig. 10)."

FIGURE CAPTIONS. Figure captions are more varied than table titles. In some cases, captions can consist solely of a noun phrase, capitalized sentence style (see 22.3.1), without a terminal period.

Figure 9. Mary McLeod Bethune, leader of the Black Cabinet during this era

More complex captions begin with a noun phrase followed by one or more complete sentences. Such captions are also capitalized sentence style but have terminal periods, even after the initial incomplete sentence. If your captions include a mix of both types, you may include a terminal period after those of the first type for consistency.

Figure 16. Benito Juárez. Mexico's great president, a contemporary and friend of Abraham Lincoln, represents the hard-fought triumph of Mexican liberalism at mid-century. Courtesy of Bancroft Library, University of California at Berkeley.

When a figure has a source line, put it at the end of the caption, following the guidelines in 26.1.3.

Figure 2.7. The Iao Valley, site of the final battle. Photograph by Anastasia Nowag.

Sometimes a caption is attached to a figure consisting of several parts. Identify the parts in the caption with terms such as *top, bottom, above, left to right,* or *clockwise from left* (italicized to distinguish them from the caption itself) or with lowercase italic letters.

Figure 6. *Above left,* William Livingston; *right,* Henry Brockholst Livingston; *below left,* John Jay; *right,* Sarah Livingston Jay.

Figure 15. Four types of Hawaiian fishhooks: *a,* barbed hook of tortoise shell; *b,* trolling hook with pearl shell lure and point of human bone.

If the caption for a figure will not fit on the same page as the figure itself, put it on the nearest preceding text page (see A.3.1), with placement identification in italics before the figure number and caption.

Next page: Figure 19. A couple with a newly purchased 20-inch color TV. The economic reforms of the 1980s encouraged rampant consumerism in China.

Appendix
Paper Format and Submission

When you are writing a thesis, a dissertation, or a class paper, you must observe certain format and style requirements for the paper. For a thesis or dissertation, these requirements are set by your department or your university's office of theses and dissertations; for a class paper, they are set by your instructor. You may also have to follow specific procedures for submitting the paper, whether in hard copy or electronically.

Be particularly aware of these requirements if you are writing a thesis or dissertation. You will be judged on how well you follow the academic conventions of your field. Also, many of the rules for format and submission are intended to make the preserved copy, bound or electronic, as accessible as possible for future readers.

The guidelines presented here are widely accepted for the format and submission of theses and dissertations, but most universities have their own requirements, which are usually available from the office of theses and dissertations. *Review the specific guidelines of your department or university before you submit your thesis or dissertation. They take precedence over the guidelines suggested here.*

In general, the requirements for a class paper are less extensive and strict than those for a thesis or dissertation. Such papers usually have fewer elements, and since they are not likely to be bound or preserved electronically, there are fewer submission requirements. Even so, you should observe the conventions of your field for formatting the paper, because those conventions help your reader quickly identify items such as footnotes and long quotations. If you have questions about the format of your paper, ask your instructor or consult your department.

This appendix assumes that you will prepare your paper on a computer. Although word-processing programs vary, most can automatically set margin size, number pages, and place and number footnotes. If, however, you must follow specific guidelines, particularly regarding margins and other placement issues, check the printout of your paper (preferably with ruler in hand) before submitting it. Software has simplified the task of formatting a paper, but it can never fully replace your own judgment.

A.1 General Format Requirements

This section describes general format issues that apply to your paper as a whole. For discussion of specific elements and their individual format requirements, see A.2. Your instructor, department, or university may have guidelines that differ from the advice offered here. If so, those guidelines take precedence.

A.1.1 Margins

Nearly all papers in the United States are produced on standard pages of 8½ × 11 inches. Leave a margin of at least one inch on all four edges of the page. For a thesis or dissertation intended to be bound, you may need to leave a bigger margin on the left side—usually 1½ inches.

Be sure that any material placed in headers or footers, including page numbers and other identifiers (see A.1.4), falls within the margins specified in your local guidelines.

A.1.2 Typeface

Choose a readable typeface designed for text, such as Times Roman or Palatino, and use it throughout. Avoid ornamental typefaces that distract readers and make your work seem less serious. (For the characteristics of specific typefaces, see Robert Bringhurst, *The Elements of Typographic Style* [Point Roberts, WA: Hartley & Marks, 2004].) For most papers, use at least ten-point and preferably twelve-point type. Some universities require twelve-point type for text and ten-point for footnotes or endnotes, table titles, and figure captions.

A.1.3   Spacing and Indentation

Double-space all text in papers except the following items, which should be single-spaced:

- block quotations (see 25.2.2)
- table titles and figure captions

The following items should be single-spaced internally but with a blank line between items:

- certain elements in the front matter (see A.2.1), including the table of contents and any lists of figures, tables, and abbreviations
- footnotes or endnotes
- bibliographies or reference lists

Instead of requesting double or single spacing, some departments and universities define the amount of vertical space between items in terms of points ("exactly 24 points"), an option given in many word processors.

Put only one space, not two, following the terminal punctuation of a sentence. Use tabs rather than spaces for indentation, columns of text, and other content requiring consistent alignment.

Indent all paragraphs consistently. Block quotations have their own rules for indentation, depending on whether they are prose or poetry (see 25.2.2).

A.1.4   Pagination

NUMBERING. If your only front matter is a title page, do not number that page. Number pages in the body of the paper and the back matter with arabic numerals, starting on the first page of text.

If you are writing a thesis or dissertation, number front matter separately from the rest of the text.

- Front matter includes the title page and various other elements (see A.2.1). Number these pages consecutively with lowercase roman numerals (i, ii, iii, etc.; see table 23.1). Every page of front matter except the submission page is usually counted in numbering, but not all of these pages have numbers displayed on them. Departments and universities often provide specific directions for numbering front matter pages; if they do not, follow the guidelines described in this appendix.
- The rest of the text, including back matter (see A.2.3), is numbered consecutively with arabic numerals.

If your thesis or dissertation is very long, your department or university may bind it in multiple volumes. Your local guidelines should indicate the maximum number of pages per volume as well as any special requirements for numbering a multivolume paper.

PLACEMENT. Page numbers are usually placed in one of three locations: centered in the *footer* (at the bottom of the page), centered in the *header* (at the top of the page), or flush right in the header. For class papers, choose one of these locations and follow it consistently.

Traditionally, page numbers for theses and dissertations have been placed in different locations depending on the part of the paper (as shown in the samples in this appendix).

- *In the footer (centered):* All front matter pages; pages in the text and back matter that bear titles, such as the first page of a chapter or an appendix
- *In the header (consistently either centered or flush right):* All other pages in the text and back matter

Many departments and universities have eliminated these distinctions and now require consistent placement of page numbers throughout a thesis or dissertation. Some specify one of the three locations, while others allow students to choose one. Check your local guidelines.

OTHER IDENTIFIERS. In some settings, you may be allowed or even encouraged to include identifying information besides the page number in the header or footer. For a class paper, your instructor may ask you to include your last name, the date of the paper, or a designation such as "First Draft." For longer papers, chapter or section titles help readers keep track of their location in the text. The requirements for headers and footers in theses and dissertations are still evolving, so consult your local guidelines.

A.1.5 Titles

Depending on its complexity, your paper may consist of many elements, as described in A.2, and most of them should have a title. Use the same typography and format for the titles of all elements, traditionally centered roman type with all capital letters (as shown in the samples in this appendix). Any number designations that precede a title (for example, *Part II: The Early Years*) should match the title in typography and format .

If your paper includes chapters, make the chapter titles and number designations typographically consistent but different from the titles of elements. In most cases, use roman type with headline-style capitalization unless your local guidelines require sentence-style capitalization (see 22.3.1 for the two styles). For subheadings within chapters, see A.2.2.

If your local guidelines are flexible, you may use different typography and format from those described here for various types of titles. All titles of a given type should be consistent, and each type should be different from all others. Titles of larger divisions (parts, chapters) should be more visually prominent than subheadings. In general, titles are more prominent when centered, in boldface or italic type, in all capital letters, or capitalized headline style than when flush left, in regular type, or capitalized sentence style.

The most efficient way to ensure consistency in titles is to define and apply a style for each type of title (including typeface, capitalization, position, and so forth) using a common software function (see A.3.1).

A.2 Format Requirements for Specific Elements

In addition to the general requirements outlined in A.1, specific elements of a paper have specific format requirements. This section describes elements most commonly found in class papers, theses, and dissertations, and it provides samples of many of them. All of the samples except figures A.1 and A.8 are pages drawn from dissertations written at the University of Chicago. As needed, the pages have been edited to match the style and format recommendations in this manual. If your instructor, department, or university has specific guidelines that differ from these samples, they take precedence.

Most long papers and all theses and dissertations have three main divisions: (1) front matter, (2) the text of the paper itself, and (3) back matter. The front and back matter are also divided into elements that vary, depending on your paper.

In a class paper, the front matter will probably be a single title page and the back matter just a bibliography or reference list.

A.2.1 Front Matter

The front matter of your thesis or dissertation may include some or all of the following elements. Departments and universities usually provide specific directions for the order of elements; if they do not, follow the order described here.

SUBMISSION PAGE. Most theses and dissertations include a submission page, usually as the first page of the document. If it appears in this position, it does not bear a page number and is not counted in paginating the front matter.

The submission page states that the paper has been submitted in partial fulfillment of the requirements for an MA or PhD degree (the wording varies), and it includes space for the signatures of the examining commit-

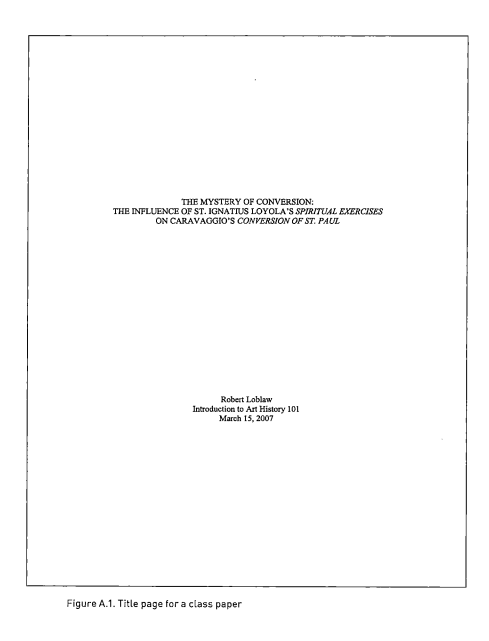

THE MYSTERY OF CONVERSION:
THE INFLUENCE OF ST. IGNATIUS LOYOLA'S *SPIRITUAL EXERCISES*
ON CARAVAGGIO'S *CONVERSION OF ST. PAUL*

Robert Loblaw
Introduction to Art History 101
March 15, 2007

Figure A.1. Title page for a class paper

THE UNIVERSITY OF CHICAGO

ADAM SMITH AND THE CIRCLES OF SYMPATHY

A DISSERTATION SUBMITTED TO

THE FACULTY OF THE DIVISION OF THE SOCIAL SCIENCES

IN CANDIDACY FOR THE DEGREE OF

DOCTOR OF PHILOSOPHY

DEPARTMENT OF POLITICAL SCIENCE

BY

FONNA FORMAN-BARZILAI

CHICAGO, ILLINOIS

DECEMBER 2001

Figure A.2. Title page for a dissertation. Reprinted with permission from Fonna Forman-Barzilai, "Adam Smith and the Circles of Sympathy" (PhD diss., University of Chicago, 2001).

CONTENTS

Figure A.3. Table of contents. Reprinted with permission from Fonna Forman-Barzilai, "Adam Smith and the Circles of Sympathy" (PhD diss., University of Chicago, 2001).

Figure A.4. Second page of a complex table of contents. Reprinted with permission from Dana Jean Simmons, "Minimal Frenchmen: Science and Standards of Living, 1840–1960" (PhD diss., University of Chicago, 2004).

TABLES

Figure A.5. List of tables. Reprinted with permission from Mark R. Wilson, "The Business of Civil War: Military Enterprise, the State, and Political Economy in the United States, 1850–1880" (PhD diss., University of Chicago, 2002).

ILLUSTRATIONS

Figures

Figure A.6. List of illustrations. Reprinted with permission from Dana Jean Simmons, "Minimal Frenchmen: Science and Standards of Living, 1840–1960" (PhD diss., University of Chicago, 2004).

ABBREVIATIONS

AD	*Annales danici*
APL	*Acta processus litium inter regem Danorum et achiepiscopum lundensem*
BD	*Bullarium danicum*
CIC	*Corpus iuris canonici*
DBL	*Dansk biografisk leksikon*
DD	*Diplomatarium danicum*
DGL	*Danmarks gamle Landskabslove*
DMA	*Danmarks middelalderlige Annaler*
GD	Saxo Grammaticus, *Gesta Danorum*
KLNM	*Kulturhistorisk leksikon for nordisk middelalder*
LDL	*Libri memoriales capituli lundensis: Lunde Domkapitels Gavebøger (= Liber daticus lundensis)*
PL	*Patrologia latina*
SD	*Svenskt diplomatarium*
SMHD	*Scriptores minores historiae danicae medii aevi*
SRD	*Scriptores rerum danicarum*
VSD	*Vitae sanctorum Danorum*

Figure A.7. List of abbreviations. (Note that the items in this list are italicized only because they are titles of published works.) Reprinted with permission from Anthony Perron, "Rome and Lund: A Study in the Church History of a Medieval Fringe" (PhD diss., University of Chicago, 2002).

arabic numeral. One of the familiar digits used in arithmetical computation (1, 2, 3, etc.).

block quotation. Quoted material set off typographically from the text by indentation.

boldface type. Type that has a darker and heavier appearance than regular type (**like this**).

italic type. Slanted type suggestive of cursive writing (*like this*), as opposed to roman type.

lowercase letter. An uncapitalized letter of a font (a, b, c, etc.).

roman numeral. A numeral formed from a traditional combination of roman letters, either capitals (I, II, III, etc.) or lowercase (i, ii, iii, etc.).

roman type. The primary type style (like this), as opposed to italic type.

run-in quotation. Quoted material set continuously with text, as opposed to a block quotation.

Figure A.8. Glossary

tee members. Most departments and universities provide model submission pages that should be followed exactly for wording and form.

TITLE PAGE. Class papers should begin with a title page (though some put the title on the first page of the text; consult your instructor). Place the title of the paper a third of the way down the page, usually centered. If the paper has both a main title and a subtitle, put the main title on a single line, followed by a colon, and begin the subtitle on the next line. Several lines below it, place your name along with any information requested by your instructor, such as the course title (including its department and number) and the date. Figure A.1 shows a sample title page for a class paper. For most such papers, this is the only front matter needed.

For a thesis or dissertation, most departments and universities provide model title pages that should be followed exactly for wording and form. Otherwise, use figure A.2 as a model. Count the title page as page i, but do not put that number on it.

If your thesis or dissertation will be bound in more than one volume (see A.1.4), you will probably need to provide separate title pages for each volume. Consult your local guidelines.

COPYRIGHT OR BLANK PAGE. In a thesis or dissertation, insert a copyright page after the title page. Count this page as page ii, but do not put that number on it unless directed by your local guidelines. Include the copyright notice near the bottom of this page, usually flush left, in this form:

Copyright © 20XX by Your Name
All rights reserved

You need not apply for a formal copyright because this notice legally establishes your copyright.

If you do not need to include a copyright notice in your paper, you may insert a blank sheet in its place or omit this element, depending on your local guidelines.

DEDICATION. If your department or university allows dedications, you may include a brief one to acknowledge someone who has been especially important to you. Count the dedication page in paginating the front matter, but do not put a page number on it unless directed by your local guidelines. Place the dedication a third of the way down, usually centered, and set it in roman type with no terminal punctuation. You need not include the words *dedication* or *dedicated;* simply say *to:*

To Anika

You may identify the person to whom you dedicate the work ("To my father, Sebastian Wells") or give other information such as birth and death dates. More extravagant dedications are outdated, and humorous ones rarely stand the test of time.

EPIGRAPH. If your department or university allows epigraphs, you may include a brief one in addition to or instead of a dedication. An epigraph is a quotation that establishes a theme of the paper. It is most appropriate when its words are especially striking and uniquely capture the spirit of your work. Count the epigraph page in paginating the front matter, but do not put a page number on it unless directed by your local guidelines. You need not include the word *epigraph* on the page.

Place the epigraph a third of the way down the page, either centered or treated like a block quotation (see 25.2.2). Do not enclose it in quotation marks. On the line following the epigraph, usually flush right, give its source—the author's name, the title of the work (see 22.3.2), and, if you wish, the date of the quotation, preceded by an em dash (or two hyphens; see 21.7.2):

Thus out of small beginnings greater things have been produced by His hand . . . and, as one small candle may light a thousand, so the light here kindled hath shone unto many, yea in some sort to our whole nation.

—William Bradford

Some people think the women are the cause of modernism, whatever that is.

—*New York Sun*, February 13, 1917

Epigraphs may also appear at the beginning of a chapter or section; see 25.2.2 and figure A.9.

TABLE OF CONTENTS. All papers divided into chapters require a table of contents. Number all pages of this element with roman numerals. Label the first page *Contents* at the top of the page. If the table of contents is more than one page, do not repeat the title. Leave two blank lines between the title and the first item listed. Single-space individual items listed, but leave a blank line between items.

A table of contents does not list pages that precede it (submission page, title page, copyright or blank page, dedication, epigraph) but should begin with the front matter pages that follow it. Following these items, list in order the parts, chapters, or other units of the text, and then the elements of the back matter. If you have subheads in the text (see A.2.2), include only the first and second levels unless further levels are specific enough to give readers an accurate overview of your paper. Be sure that the wording, capitalization, number style (arabic, roman, or spelled out), and typography of all titles and subheads (see A.1.5) match exactly those in the paper.

Give page numbers only for the first page of each element (not the full span of pages), and use lowercase roman or arabic numerals as on the pages themselves. List page numbers flush right and, if you choose, use a line of periods or dots (called *leaders*) to lead a reader's eye from each title to the page number.

Figure A.3 shows a sample table of contents for a paper with a simple structure. Part and chapter titles appear flush left, with page numbers flush right.

For a more complex paper, follow the logic of your paper's organization unless your local guidelines require a specific format. Figure A.4 shows the second page of a long table of contents. Note that you may center part titles or volume numbers (if relevant; see A.1.4) above the relevant chapters and use the word *Chapter* as a heading above the column listing chapter numbers. To distinguish chapter titles and subheadings more clearly, you may indent the subheadings, with each level consistently indented a half inch to the right of the preceding level.

If your thesis or dissertation will be bound in more than one volume, you may need to repeat the table of contents, or at least the relevant listings from it, in each volume after the first. Consult your local guidelines.

LIST OF FIGURES, TABLES, OR ILLUSTRATIONS. If your thesis or dissertation (or, in some cases, your class paper) includes figures, tables, or both, list them in the front matter. Number all pages of such a list with roman numerals. If your paper includes only figures (see chapter 26 for definitions), label the first page *Figures* at the top of the page; if it includes only tables, label it *Tables* instead. If the list is more than one page, do not repeat the title. Leave two blank lines between the title and the first item listed. Single-space individual items listed, but leave a blank line between items. Figure A.5 shows a sample list of tables.

If your paper includes both figures and tables, your local guidelines may allow you to combine them into a single list. Label the list *Illustrations* (following the pattern described above), but divide it into two sections labeled *Figures* and *Tables,* as in figure A.6.

Give each table or figure number in arabic numerals, and vertically align the list on the period following. If you are using double numeration (as in fig. A.5), align the numbers on the decimals instead.

Figure captions and table titles should match the wording and capitalization of those in the paper itself, but if they are very long, shorten them in a logical way in this list. Indent runovers by a half inch. (See 26.2.2 and 26.3.2 for more on table titles and figure captions.) List page numbers flush right and, if you choose, use leaders to connect the captions and titles to page numbers.

PREFACE. In a thesis or dissertation, you may include a preface to explain what motivated your study, the background of the project, the scope of the research, and the purpose of the paper. The preface may also include acknowledgments, unless they are so numerous and detailed that they merit their own section (see below). Number all pages of this element with roman numerals. Label the first page *Preface* at the top of the page. If the preface is more than one page, do not repeat the title. Leave two blank lines between the title and the first line of text. Double-space the text of the preface, and format it to match the main text.

ACKNOWLEDGMENTS. In a thesis or dissertation, you may have a separate section of acknowledgments in which you thank mentors and colleagues or name the individuals or institutions that supported your research or provided special assistance (such as consultation on technical matters or aid in securing special equipment and source materials). If your only acknowledgments are for routine help by an advisor or a committee, include them in the preface (see above) or omit them entirely. Number all pages of the acknowledgments with roman numerals. Label the first page *Acknowledgments* at the top of the page. If the acknowledgments are more than one page, do not repeat the title. Leave two blank lines between the title and the first line of text. Double-space the text of the acknowledgments, and format it to match the main text.

LIST OF ABBREVIATIONS. If your thesis or dissertation (or, in some cases, your class paper) includes an unusual number of abbreviations other than the common types discussed in chapter 24, list them in the front matter. Examples of items to include would be abbreviations for sources cited frequently (see 16.4.3) or for organizations that are not widely known (24.1.2).

Number all pages of such a list with roman numerals. Label the first page *Abbreviations* at the top of the page. If the list is more than one page, do not repeat the title. Leave two blank lines between the title and the first item listed. Single-space individual items listed, but leave a blank line between items. Figure A.7 shows a sample list of abbreviations. (The items in this sample are italic only because they are titles of published works.)

Note that the items are arranged alphabetically by the abbreviation, not by the spelled-out term. The abbreviations themselves are flush left;

spelled-out terms (including runovers) are set on a consistent indent that allows about a half inch of space between the longest abbreviation in the first column and the first word in the second column.

GLOSSARY. You may need a glossary if your thesis or dissertation (or, in some cases, your class paper) includes many foreign words or technical terms and phrases that may be unfamiliar to your readers. Some departments and universities allow or require the glossary to be placed in the back matter, after any appendixes and before the endnotes and bibliography or reference list. If you are free to choose, put it in the front matter if readers must know the definitions before they begin reading. Otherwise, put it in the back matter (see A.2.3).

If it appears in the front matter, number all pages of a glossary with roman numerals. Label the first page *Glossary* at the top of the page. If the glossary is more than one page, do not repeat the title. Leave two blank lines between the title and the first item listed. Single-space individual items listed, but leave a blank line between items. Figure A.8 shows a sample glossary.

Note that the terms are arranged alphabetically, flush left and followed by a period (a colon or dash is sometimes used). You may put the terms in boldface or italics to make them stand out. The translation or definition follows, with its first word capitalized and a terminal period. If, however, the definitions consist of only single words or brief phrases, do not use terminal periods. If a definition is more than one line, indent the runovers by a half inch.

EDITORIAL OR RESEARCH METHOD. If your thesis or dissertation requires an extensive preliminary discussion of your editorial method (such as your choices among variant texts) or research method, include it as a separate element. You can also briefly discuss method in the preface. If you only state that you have modernized capitalization and punctuation in quoted sources, put that in the preface or in a note attached to the first such quotation.

Number all pages of a note on method with roman numerals. Label the first page *Editorial Method* or *Research Method* at the top of the page. If the section is more than one page, do not repeat the title. Leave two blank lines between the title and the first line of text. Double-space the text of this section, and format it to match the main text.

ABSTRACT. Many departments or universities require that a thesis or dissertation include an abstract summarizing its contents. (Sometimes the abstract is submitted as a separate document.) This abstract will likely be submitted to the publication *Dissertation Abstracts International.* Number all pages of this element with roman numerals. Label the first page *Abstract* at the top of the page. If the abstract is more than one page, do not repeat the title. Leave two blank lines between the title and the first line of text. Most departments or universities have specific models for abstracts that you should follow exactly for content, length, format, and placement.

A.2.2 Text

The text of a paper includes everything between the front matter and the back matter. It begins with your introduction and ends with your conclusion, both of which may be as short as a single paragraph or as long as several pages. In a thesis or dissertation, the text is usually separated into chapters and sometimes into parts, sections, and subsections. Many longer class papers are also divided in this way.

Since most of the text consists of paragraphs laying out your findings, there are few format requirements beyond those discussed in A.1. The only additional issues are how to begin divisions of the text, how to format notes or parenthetical citations, and how to position tables and figures within the text.

Begin the arabic numbering of your paper with the first page of the text.

INTRODUCTION. Many theses and dissertations (and, in some cases, class papers) begin with a section that previews the contents and argument of the entire paper and is so distinct that the writer separates it from the rest of the paper. (The background of the project and any issues that informed the research should be covered in the preface; see A.2.1.) If you begin with such an introduction, label the first page *Introduction* at the top of the page. Do not repeat the title on subsequent pages of the introduction. Leave two blank lines between the title and the first line of text. If the substance of your introductory material is not clearly distinct from the following chapters, consider incorporating it into your first chapter.

PARTS. If you divide the text of your thesis or dissertation into two or more parts, each including two or more chapters, begin each part with a part-title page. The first part-title page follows the introduction (even if the introduction is labeled chapter 1). Count a part-title page in paginating, but do not put a page number on it except in the case described below or unless directed by your local guidelines. Label this page *Part* followed by the part number at the top of the page. Depending on your local guidelines, give the part number either in capitalized roman numerals (II) or spelled

Chapter 1

The Conflicted Self

> And what a malignant philosophy must it be that will not allow to humanity and
> friendship the same privileges which are undisputedly granted to the darker
> passions of enmity and resentment. Such a philosophy is more like a satyr than a
> true delineation or description of human nature, and may be a good foundation for
> paradoxical wit and raillery, but is a very bad one for any serious argument.
> —David Hume, *An Enquiry Concerning the Principles of Morals*

Since the closing years of the nineteenth century, scholarship on Adam Smith has

addressed the extent to which his two seminal books can be reconciled. The question,

which has come down to us as the "Adam Smith problem," turns on how we might

reconcile his *Theory of Moral Sentiments* (1759) and its moral philosophical emphasis on

sympathy with *The Wealth of Nations* (1776) and its economic emphasis on self-interest.[1]

Are the books consistent or continuous? And if not, which in Smith's mind was prior?

As I mentioned in the introduction, scholarship on Smith was long the province of

economists and historians of economics, with the consequence that his moral philosophy

was regularly subordinated.[2] Self-interest trumped sympathy, most insisted, giving little

thought to how the two ideas related in Smith's mind. Though their evaluations of the

"Smithian legacy" radically diverged, Chicago-school types like Hayek, Friedman, and

Becker and Marxists like Macpherson and Dumont generally agreed that in *The Wealth of*

Nations Smith had come to embrace an essentially materialist, Hobbesian orientation to

human motivation checked only by an equally celebratory optimism that human

1. For a useful history, see Richard Teichgraeber III, "Rethinking *Das Adam Smith Problem,"*
Journal of British Studies 20, no. 2 (Spring 1981): 106–23.

2. For discussion, see Donald Winch, introduction to *Adam Smith's Politics: An Essay in*
Historiographic Revision (Cambridge: Cambridge University Press, 1978), 1–27; and Winch, "Adam
Smith and the Liberal Tradition," in *Traditions of Liberalism: Essays on John Locke, Adam Smith, and*
John Stuart Mill, ed. Knud Haakonssen (Sydney: Center for Independent Studies, 1988), 82–104.

20

Figure A.9. First page of a chapter. Reprinted with permission from Fonna Forman-Barzilai, "Adam Smith and the Circles of Sympathy" (PhD diss., University of Chicago, 2001).

influence alone. In fact, the Democrats did not win control of the House until 1875, and it

was Republican-controlled Congresses that passed most of the cuts.[66] Support for a small

peacetime military was widespread, on both sides of the aisle in Congress and among the

public at large. A tradition of antimilitary sentiment among Americans, which had been

well established by the antebellum era, survived into the postwar era.[67] In December

1865, soon after President Johnson delivered his address to Congress, the pro-Republican

Cincinnati Daily Commercial newspaper argued,

> It is not in accordance either with our national interest or the principles of our
> Government, to keep up a heavy standing army in time of peace. The enormous
> expense of standing armies is perhaps their least evil. They absorb and withdraw
> from useful occupations a large class of citizens who would otherwise be engaged
> in productive industry. They foster a spirit of restlessness, ambition, and
> discontent. They create and maintain national jealousies and animosities, and
> minister to that spirit of domination and passion for conquest which is fatal to the
> steady growth and permanent prosperity of a people.[68]

On the subjects of the peacetime military establishment and national government

expenditures, many Republicans could find common ground with their Democratic

colleagues. There were many fiscal conservatives in Republican ranks; these included

Elihu Washburne, the former Van Wyck committee member, who in 1870 wrote from

Paris to his brother (another Congressman) in Washington to say that he was dismayed by

the recent Court of Claims awards to war contractors. "I hope your committee,"

continued Washburne, "will put the knife to the throats of every appropriation not

absolutely necessary."[69] Although most Congressmen and their constituents naturally

---

66. Utley, *Frontier Regulars,* 59–68.

67. Marcus Cunliffe, *Soldiers and Civilians: The Martial Spirit in America, 1775–1865* (Boston: Little, Brown & Co., 1968).

68. *Cincinnati Daily Commercial,* December 16, 1865.

69. Elihu Washburne to C. C. Washburn, February 5, 1870, C. C. Washburn Papers, SHSW.

Figure A.10. Page of text with footnotes. Reprinted with permission from Mark R. Wilson, "The Business of Civil War: Military Enterprise, the State, and Political Economy in the United States, 1850–1880" (PhD diss., University of Chicago, 2002).

The conclusions of scholars who argue that the welfare state has "survived" its crisis (Pierson 1994; Piven and Cloward 1988; Schwab 1991; Ruggie 1996) are undeniable if what is being discussed is the first segment of the welfare state, old age pensions: Reagan's positions on cutting Social Security were so unpopular that he quickly drew back from any sustained attempt to reduce it, and Social Security not only maintained its strength, it actually grew in size. As Pierson succinctly explains it,

> Welfare states have created their own constituencies. If citizens dislike paying taxes, they nonetheless remain fiercely attached to public social provision. That social programs provide concentrated and direct benefits while imposing diffuse and often indirect costs is an important source of their continuing political viability. (Pierson 1994, 2)

Of course this is only true for those programs that do concentrate benefits and diffuse costs, like Social Security. The opposite is the case for those programs that benefit a minority by taxing the majority, like means-tested AFDC, for better or worse the symbol of the other part of America's welfare state. The Reagan administration managed a first strike against AFDC in the form of the Omnibus Budget Reconciliation Act of 1981 (OBRA), which tightened program eligibility and put a time limit on the "30 and 1/3 rule." In addition to AFDC, Reagan achieved cuts in the food stamp program, subsidized housing, the school lunch program, child care and housing assistance, public mental health and counseling services, legal aid, and other smaller means-tested programs (Rochefort 1986; Trattner [1974] 1999).

That these cuts were not larger has led most scholars to conclude that the conservative attack was not successful: "These programs remained substantially larger in 1985 than in 1966—the Reagan Revolution was a skirmish when viewed in its historical context" (Gottschalk 1988). This is the conclusion that one would come to after a

Figure A.11. Page of text with parenthetical citations. Reprinted with permission from Monica Prasad, "The Politics of Free Markets: The Rise of Neoliberal Economic Policy in Britain, France, and the United States" (PhD diss., University of Chicago, 2000).

Figure 1. Léonce Reynaud, "Prison Mazas," *Traité d'architecture* (1863), vol. 2, plate 58.

    The Mazas prison, which replaced an aging detention center in Paris's Faubourg Saint Antoine, was one of the first to implement the government's new prescriptions on cellular design (see fig. 1).[35] The Prefect of Paris called upon Dumas, Boussingault, Leblanc, and their colleagues on the commission to set a scientific standard for the prison's air supply. By trial and error, as we have seen, they settled on an hourly figure of ten cubic meters of air per person. This standard was consecrated by the commission and determined the government's choice of building and ventilation plan.

    In May of 1850, the new prison opened its doors. Bentham's Panopticon had

---

35. The Conciergerie contained a few individual holding cells, and the La Roquette prison for youth had experimented with solitary confinement. Mazas, however, was the first large-scale project of its kind in France. Benjamin Appert, *Bagnes, prisons et criminals*, 2nd ed. (Paris: Guilbert, 1836), 1:155.

Figure A.12. Page with text and a figure. Reprinted with permission from Dana Jean Simmons, "Minimal Frenchmen: Science and Standards of Living, 1840–1960" (PhD diss., University of Chicago, 2004).

68

Table 2.2. The largest regions by employment

	Rank	Number of subcenters	Fraction of regional employment in			Mean annual earnings ($)			
			CBD	Center city	Subcenters	CBD	Center city	Subcenters	Region
New York	1	38	.19	.83	.47	47,217	34,781	37,360	33,984
Los Angeles	2	62	.04	.49	.21	38,238	30,228	31,770	29,719
Chicago	3	67	.09	.44	.16	39,968	30,133	28,137	29,355
Washington	4	46	.08	.33	.22	40,156	35,657	32,329	32,556
Dallas	5	72	.06	.40	.34	35,391	29,107	28,959	27,902
Philadelphia	6	58	.10	.55	.34	32,614	28,393	28,805	27,696
Houston	7	47	.06	.77	.19	37,379	27,863	30,784	27,493
Detroit	8	38	.05	.23	.22	32,219	28,606	32,270	29,305
San Francisco	9	35	.12	.40	.35	37,651	33,559	33,256	31,098
Atlanta	10	38	.07	.55	.19	30,548	28,567	29,210	27,800
Minneapolis	11	52	.08	.22	.30	31,671	27,534	27,918	25,962
Boston	12	37	.14	.39	.24	38,285	33,620	27,653	30,684
San Diego	13	26	.05	.58	.19	29,482	26,973	27,113	25,307
Baltimore	14	32	.10	.46	.25	29,926	26,887	27,223	26,191
Saint Louis	15	36	.08	.29	.24	29,923	26,383	28,503	25,147
Phoenix	16	32	.02	.58	.18	29,529	25,147	24,734	24,600
Denver	17	43	.07	.47	.29	32,725	28,072	26,990	26,305
Miami	18	32	.07	.44	.26	28,345	24,539	24,800	24,462
Seattle	19	18	.12	.50	.25	30,177	27,565	29,579	27,574
Cleveland	20	16	.11	.40	.19	32,461	27,972	29,607	26,108
Pittsburgh	21	26	.14	.42	.28	30,801	26,596	26,561	24,968
Tampa	22	36	.05	.36	.29	27,650	23,974	22,825	22,812
Kansas City	23	34	.07	.43	.18	29,578	25,897	24,835	24,925
Milwaukee	24	20	.11	.47	.19	28,434	24,400	26,176	24,086
Portland, OR	25	32	.12	.48	.18	28,319	25,287	23,317	25,458
Sacramento	26	31	.10	.46	.28	29,996	27,995	26,240	27,118
Orlando	27	37	.05	.30	.31	28,089	22,963	22,476	22,629
Indianapolis	28	17	.11	.80	.22	27,004	25,264	26,930	24,693
Columbus	29	30	.13	.74	.30	29,546	25,046	25,294	26,307
Cincinnati	30	21	.14	.54	.13	30,358	27,615	23,093	25,900

Source: Data from U.S. Bureau of the Census 1990.

Note: The portion of CTPP-defined regions that are closest to the CBD of the largest city defines the geography. This definition does not result in exact matches with metropolitan areas in some cases.

Figure A.13. Page with a landscape table. Reprinted with permission from Nathaniel Baum-Snow, "Essays on the Spatial Distribution of Population and Employment" (PhD diss., University of Chicago, 2005).

out (Two); be sure to number the chapters in a different style. If the part has a descriptive title in addition to its number, place this title two lines down, following a blank line.

If you include text introducing the contents of the part on the part-title page, number the page with an arabic numeral. Leave two blank lines between the title and the first line of text. If the text is more than one page long, do not repeat the part number or title.

Follow a consistent format for all of your part-title pages: if one part has a descriptive title in addition to a number, then give all parts descriptive titles; if one part has introductory text, then include introductory text in all parts.

CHAPTERS. Most theses and dissertations, and many long class papers, consist of two or more chapters. Each chapter begins on a new page. Label this page *Chapter* followed by the chapter number at the top of the page. You may give the chapter number either in arabic numerals (4) or spelled out (Four). If your paper has parts, choose a different style of numbering for the chapter numbers (for example, Part II; Chapter Four). If the chapter has a descriptive title in addition to its number, place this title two lines down, following a blank line. Do not repeat the number or the title on subsequent pages of the chapter. Leave two blank lines between the title and the first line of text. Figure A.9 shows a sample first page of a chapter with an epigraph (see 25.2.2).

An alternative format is to omit the word *Chapter* and use only the chapter number and title, which can then appear on the same line, separated by a colon or a tab space. Do not use this format, however, if your paper has parts as well as chapters, if it does not have chapter titles, or if there is any possibility of confusing a new chapter with any other division of the paper.

SECTIONS AND SUBSECTIONS. Long chapters in theses, dissertations, and long class papers may be further divided into sections, which in turn may be divided into subsections, and so on. If your paper, or a chapter within it, has only a few sections, you may signal the division between sections informally by leaving an extra blank line between paragraphs.

If you create formal sections in a paper or in its chapters, you may give each one its own title, also called a *subheading* or *subhead.* You may have multiple levels of subheads, which are designated *first-level, second-level,* and so on. Unless you are writing a very long and complex paper, think carefully before using more than two or three levels of subheads. Rather than being helpful, they can become distracting. You should have at least two subheads at any level; if you do not, your divisions might not be logically structured.

Unless your local guidelines have rules for subheads, you may devise your own typography and format for them. Each level of subhead should be consistent and different from all other levels, and higher-level subheads should be more visually prominent than lower-level ones. In general, subheads are more prominent when centered, in boldface or italic type, or capitalized headline style than when flush left, in regular type, or capitalized sentence style. Put an extra blank line before and after subheads; do not end them with a period.

Here is one plan for five levels of subheads.

- *First level:* centered, boldface or italic type, headline-style capitalization

Contemporary Art

- *Second level:* centered, regular type, headline-style capitalization

What Are the Major Styles?

- *Third level:* flush left, boldface or italic type, headline-style capitalization

Abstract Expressionism

- *Fourth level:* flush left, roman type, sentence-style capitalization

Major painters and practitioners

- *Fifth level:* run in at beginning of paragraph (no blank line after), boldface or italic type, sentence-style capitalization, terminal period

Pollock as the leader. The role of leading Abstract Expressionist painter was filled by Jackson Pollock. . . .

Never end a page with a subhead. Set your word processor to keep all headings attached to the ensuing paragraph, or if necessary, add an extra blank line or two so that the subhead appears at the top of the next page. Add an extra blank line between two subheads of different levels that appear together without intervening text.

NOTES OR PARENTHETICAL CITATIONS. If you are using bibliography-style citations with footnotes, see 16.3 for a discussion of how to format footnotes. Figure A.10 shows a sample page of text with footnotes.

If you are using reference list–style citations, see 18.3 for a discussion of how to format parenthetical citations. Figure A.11 shows a sample page of text with parenthetical citations.

TABLES AND FIGURES. If your paper includes tables or figures, see chapter 26 for a discussion of how to format tables, some types of figures, and figure captions, and A.3.1 for information about inserting these elements into your paper. Figure A.12 shows a sample page of text with a figure positioned on it, and figure A.13 shows a sample of a table in landscape orientation on its own page.

CONCLUSION. In a thesis or dissertation (or, in some cases, a long class paper), you will probably end with a conclusion that is long enough to treat as a separate element. If you include such a conclusion, label the first page *Conclusion* at the top of the page. Do not repeat the title on subsequent pages of the conclusion. Leave two blank lines between the title and the first line of text.

You may also label the conclusion as the last numbered chapter of your paper if you want to emphasize its connection to the rest of your text. If so, treat the word *Conclusion* as a chapter title (see above, p. 397).

A.2.3   Back Matter

The back matter of your paper may consist of all or some or none of the following elements. Departments and universities usually provide specific directions for the order of elements; if they do not, follow the order described here. Number the back matter continuously with the text using arabic numerals.

ILLUSTRATIONS. If your thesis or dissertation (or, in some cases, your class paper) includes photographs, maps, or similar types of figures that are marginally relevant to your topic or too large to put in the text (see 26.1.1), make them the first element in the back matter. Other types of figures, such as charts and graphs, that meet these criteria should be treated as an appendix, as should tables; see below.

Label the first page of the illustrations section *Illustrations* at the top of the page. If this section is more than one page, do not repeat the title. For information about inserting figures into your paper, see A.3.1.

APPENDIXES. If your thesis or dissertation (or, in some cases, your class paper) includes essential supporting material that cannot be easily worked into the body of your paper, put the material in one or more appendixes in the back matter. (Do not put appendixes at the ends of chapters.)

123. The claims of several states are the subject of Kyle Scott Sinisi, "Civil War Claims and American Federalism, 1861–1880" (PhD diss, Kansas State University, 1997). A variety of war claims are discussed in chapter 8.

Chapter 3

1. Meigs to Wilson, February 20, 1864, pp. 516–17, vol. 74-B, roll 45, Letters Sent by the Office of the Quartermaster General, Main Series, National Archives Microfilm Publications M745 (abbreviated hereafter as QMGLS).

2. Ibid.

3. On the history of the Quartermaster's Department, see Russell F. Weigley, *Quartermaster General of the Union Army: A Biography of M. C. Meigs* (New York: Columbia University Press, 1959); Erna Risch, *Quartermaster Support of the Army: A History of the Corps, 1775–1939* (Washington, DC: Quartermaster Historian's Office, 1962); James A. Huston, *The Sinews of War: Army Logistics, 1775–1953* (Washington, DC: Office of the Chief of Military History, 1966). On the number of quartermaster officers during the war, see Meigs to R. J. Atkinson, October 4, 1861, pp. 485–90, vol. 56, roll 36, QMGLS; Meigs circular, May 16, 1862, pp. 49–54, vol. 60, roll 38, QMGLS; Risch, *Quartermaster Support,* 334–35, 382–87, 390–93.

4. After the war, Johnston worked in the insurance business and served from Virginia in the U.S. House. From 1885 to 1891, he was commissioner of railroads under President Cleveland. Patricia L. Faust, ed., *Historical Times Illustrated Encyclopedia of the Civil War* (New York: Harper & Row, 1986), 400–401.

5. Weigley, *Quartermaster General.*

6. Lincoln to Winfield Scott, June 5, 1861, copy in Box 10, David Davis Papers, Chicago Historical Society. George Templeton Strong, a Wall Street lawyer and treasurer of the U.S. Sanitary Commission, would soon describe Meigs as "an exceptional and refreshing specimen of sense and promptitude, unlike most of our high military officials. There's not a fibre of red tape in his constitution." Strong, *The Civil War, 1860–1865,* vol. 3 of *The Diary of George Templeton Strong,* ed. Allan Nevins and Milton Halsey Thomas (New York: Macmillan, 1952), 173. See also Risch, *Quartermaster Support,* 335–36.

7. Weigley, *Quartermaster General*; Allan Nevins, *War Becomes Revolution, 1862–1863,* part 2 of *The War for the Union* (New York: Charles Scribner's Sons, 1960), 471–78. Meigs also appears as a prominent character in Nevins's discussion of how the war promoted organization in American society. See Nevins, "A Major Result of the Civil War," *Civil War History* 5 (1959): 237–50.

Figure A.14. Endnotes. Reprinted with permission from Mark R. Wilson, "The Business of Civil War: Military Enterprise, the State, and Political Economy in the United States, 1850–1880" (PhD diss., University of Chicago, 2002).

Gallman, J. Matthew. "Entrepreneurial Experiences in the Civil War: Evidence from Philadelphia." In *American Development in Historical Perspective*, ed. Thomas Weiss and Donald Schaefer, 205–22. Stanford: Stanford University Press, 1994.

————. *Mastering Wartime: A Social History of Philadelphia during the Civil War.* Cambridge: Cambridge University Press, 1990.

————. *The North Fights the Civil War: The Home Front.* Chicago: Ivan R. Dee, 1994.

Gallman, Robert E. "Commodity Output, 1839–1899." In *Trends in the American Economy in the Nineteenth Century*, edited by the National Bureau of Economic Research, 13–67. Princeton: Princeton University Press, 1960.

Gamboa, Erasmo. "Mexican Mule Packers and Oregon's Second Regiment Mounted Volunteers, 1855–1856." *Oregon Historical Quarterly* 92 (1991): 41–59.

Gansler, Jacques S. *The Defense Industry.* Cambridge, MA: MIT Press, 1986.

Gardner, Mark L. *Wagons for the Santa Fe Trade: Wheeled Vehicles and Their Makers, 1822–1880.* Albuquerque: University of New Mexico Press, 2000.

Gates, Paul W. *Agriculture and the Civil War.* New York: Alfred A. Knopf, 1965.

————. *The Farmer's Age: Agriculture, 1815–1860.* New York: Holt, Rinehart and Winston, 1960.

————. *Fifty Million Acres: Conflicts over Kansas Land Policy, 1854–1890.* Ithaca: Cornell University Press, 1954.

"General Roeliff Brinkerhoff, 1828–1911." *Ohio Archaeological and Historical Publications* 20 (1911): 353–67.

Gerber, David. "Cutting Out Shylock: Elite Anti-Semitism and the Quest for Moral Order in the Mid–Nineteenth Century American Market Place." *Journal of American History* 69 (1982): 615–37.

Gerleman, David James. "Unchronicled Heroes: A Study of Union Cavalry Horses in the Eastern Theater; Care, Treatment, and Use, 1861–1865." PhD diss., Southern Illinois University, 1999.

Geyer, Michael, and Charles Bright. "Global Violence and Nationalizing Wars in Eurasia and America: The Geopolitics of War in the Mid–Nineteenth Century." *Comparative Studies in Society and History* 38 (1996): 619–57.

Gibson, George H. "The Growth of the Woolen Industry in Nineteenth-Century Delaware." *Textile History Review* 5 (1964): 125–57.

Figure A.15. Bibliography. Reprinted with permission from Mark R. Wilson, "The Business of Civil War: Military Enterprise, the State, and Political Economy in the United States, 1850–1880" (PhD diss., University of Chicago, 2002).

Bréchon, Pierre, ed. 1994. *Le discours politique en France*. Paris: La documentation Française.

Brooks, Clem. Forthcoming. Civil rights liberalism and the suppression of a Republican political realignment in the U.S., 1972–1996. *American Sociological Review*.

Brown, Michael K., ed. 1988. *Remaking the welfare state: Retrenchment and social policy in Europe and America*. Philadelphia: Temple University Press.

Brownlee, W. Elliot, ed. 1996a. *Funding the modern American state, 1941–1995: The rise and fall of the era of easy finance*. Cambridge: Cambridge University Press.

————. 1996b. Tax regimes, national crisis, and state-building in America. In *Funding the modern American state, 1941–1995: The rise and fall of the era of easy finance*, ed. W. Elliot Brownlee, 37–106. Cambridge: Cambridge University Press.

Burawoy, Michael. 1979. *Manufacturing consent: Changes in the labor process under monopoly capitalism*. Chicago: University of Chicago Press.

————. 1989. Two methods in search of science: Skocpol versus Trotsky. *Theory and Society* 18, no. 6:759–805.

Burstein, Paul. 1998. Bringing the public back in: Should sociologists consider the impact of public opinion on public policy? *Social Forces* 77:27–62.

Business Week. 2000. Unions campaign to shrink work time. April 24.

Butler, David, and Dennis Kavanagh. 1984. *The British general election of 1983*. London: Macmillan.

————. 1988. *The British general election of 1987*. New York: St. Martin's Press.

Butler, David, and Michael Pinto-Duschinsky. 1971. *The British general election of 1970*. London: Macmillan.

Cameron, David. 1991. Continuity and change in French social policy: The welfare state under Gaullism, liberalism, and socialism. In *The French welfare state: Surviving social and ideological change*, ed. John S. Ambler. New York: New York University Press.

Campbell, John. 1993. *Edward Heath: A biography*. London: Random House.

Campbell, John L., and Michael Patrick Allen. 1994. The political economy of revenue extraction in the modern state: A time series analysis of U.S. income taxes, 1916–1986. *Social Forces* 72, no. 3:643–69.

Figure A.16. Reference list. Reprinted with permission from Monica Prasad, "The Politics of Free Markets: The Rise of Neoliberal Economic Policy in Britain, France, and the United States" (PhD diss., University of Chicago, 2000).

Examples of such material would be tables and some types of figures, such as charts and graphs, that are marginally relevant to your topic or too large to put in the text; schedules and forms used in collecting materials; copies of documents not available to the reader; and case studies too long to put into the text.

Label the first page *Appendix* at the top of the page. If the appendix is more than one page, do not repeat the title. Leave two blank lines between the title and the first line of text or other material.

If the appendix material is of different types—for example, a table and a case study—divide it among more than one appendix. In this case, give each appendix a number or letter and a descriptive title. You may give the numbers in either arabic numerals (1, 2) or spelled out (One, Two), or you may use single letters of the alphabet in sequential order (A, B). Put the number or letter following the word *Appendix,* and place the descriptive title on the next line. (If your paper has only one appendix, you may also give it a descriptive title, but do not give it a number or letter.)

If the appendix consists of your own explanatory text, double-space it and format it to match the main text. If it consists of a primary document or a case study, you may choose to single-space the text, especially if it is long.

Treat supporting material that cannot be presented in print form, such as a large data set or a multimedia file, as an appendix. Include a brief description of the material and its location, including a hyperlink (if relevant). Consult your local guidelines for specific format and presentation requirements; see also A.3.1.

GLOSSARY. If your thesis or dissertation (or, in some cases, your class paper) needs a glossary (see A.2.1), you may include it in either the front or back matter, where it follows any appendixes and precedes endnotes and bibliography or reference list. All of the special format requirements described in A.2.1 apply, except that the back-matter glossary pages should be numbered with arabic instead of roman numerals. Figure A.8 shows a sample glossary (formatted to appear in front matter).

ENDNOTES. If you are using bibliography-style citations, you may include notes in the back matter as endnotes (see 16.3.4 for formatting endnotes). Label the first page of this element *Notes* at the top of the page. Do not repeat the title on subsequent pages of the endnotes section. Leave two blank lines between the title and the first note, and one blank line between notes. Figure A.14 shows a sample page of endnotes for a paper divided into chapters.

If you are using reference list–style citations, you will not have endnotes.

BIBLIOGRAPHY OR REFERENCE LIST. If you are using bibliography-style citations, you will probably include a bibliography in the back matter. Label the first page of this element Bibliography at the top of the page. Do not repeat the title on subsequent pages of the bibliography. Leave two blank lines between the title and the first item listed, and one blank line between items. Figure A.15 shows a sample page of a bibliography.

For some types of bibliographies, you should use a different title, such as *Sources Consulted.* If you do not arrange the bibliography alphabetically by author, include a headnote, subheadings (formatted consistently), or both to explain the arrangement. See 16.2 for these variations.

If you are using reference list–style citations, you must include a reference list in the back matter. Label the first page of the list *References* at the top of the page. Do not repeat the title on subsequent pages of the reference list. Leave two blank lines between the title and the first item listed, and one blank line between items. Figure A.16 shows a sample page of a reference list.

In the rare case that you do not arrange the reference list alphabetically by author (see 18.2.1), include a headnote, subheadings (formatted consistently), or both to explain the arrangement.

A.3 Submission Requirements

A.3.1 Preparing Your Files

Following some basic practices for good electronic file management and preparation will help you avoid problems and produce a legible, properly formatted paper in any situation. These practices are especially important if you need to submit the paper electronically (see A.3.3).

FILE MANAGEMENT. Try to minimize the risk that data in your files will be lost or corrupted at some point.

- Prepare your paper as a single electronic file, regardless of its length. Working with a single file allows you to search and make changes globally, to use your word processor's automated numbering functions accurately (for footnotes and the like), and to define and apply styles consistently (see below). Papers submitted electronically must almost always be in a single file.
- Name the file simply and logically. If you save different versions of the file over time, name them consistently (always ending in the date, for example) to avoid confusion of versions.

- Avoid working on the file in more than one type of software. Conversions always involve some risk of errors and lost data, even when moving between standard word processors.
- Save the file often during each writing session.
- Back up the file in more than one location after each writing session. In addition to your local hard drive, save it to a local network (if available) or a removable storage medium, such as a CD.
- Print out the file before your submission date. Look it over for any software glitches, such as special characters that are not supported by your printer, while there is time to correct them. Label the printout "Draft" and keep it at least until you submit the final version. In an emergency (such as a computer malfunction or a serious illness), you can use it to show that you did indeed produce a draft.

TEXT COMPONENTS. Present all components of your text clearly and consistently.

- Format each text component consistently, including regular text, block quotations, footnotes, and each type of title and subhead. The most efficient way to ensure consistency is to define and apply a style for each component (including typeface, capitalization, position, and so forth) using a common software function.
- Set your word processor to left justify (with a "ragged" right margin), and do not use its automated hyphenation feature (see 20.4.1).
- Create diacritics using key strokes or from the symbol font in your basic font set. Create other special characters (such as Greek letters, mathematical symbols, and paragraph or section marks) from the symbol font.
- Avoid color fonts. Even if you print the paper on a color printer, it may be printed or copied later on a black-and-white machine, and the color might not reproduce well.
- Create equations and formulas with the equation editor in your word processor, if possible. If not, create these items in the relevant program and insert them into your file as images (see below). Leave at least one blank line between an image and the text (if any) both above and below.

TABLES. Use your software to present tables that are clear, focused, and relevant.

- Create tables with the table editor in your word processor, if possible. If not, create them in a spreadsheet program and insert them into your file as unlinked tables. Format them to match the surrounding text. See chapter 26 for discussion of table structure, format, and placement in text.
- Put a table number and title on the line above a table (see 26.2.2). Run

the title the full width of the table, and do not indent any runovers. Table titles may be presented in a smaller typeface than the rest of the text; consult your local guidelines.

- Put table footnotes (if any) under the bottom rule of a table, with a blank line between the rule and the first note, and also between notes. Footnotes may be presented in a smaller typeface than the rest of the text; consult your local guidelines.

- Leave at least one blank line between the table title and any text above it on the page, and also between the bottom rule (or last footnote) and any text below it. If the table appears at the top or bottom of a page, put it flush with the top or bottom margin.

- Avoid shading, except in long or complex tables (see 8.3.2). Also avoid color. Even if you print the paper on a color printer, it may be printed or copied later on a black-and-white machine, and if it is a dissertation, it may be microfilmed. Shading and color do not reproduce well in any of these forms. If you use shading, make sure it does not obscure the text of the table, and do not use multiple shades, which might not reproduce distinctly. Consult your local guidelines for information about resolution and related characteristics.

- Repeat the stub column and all column heads (see 26.2) on every page of a multipage table. Put the table number on a "continued" line at the top left of every page after the first, flush left, in italic letters (*Table 2 continued*). Omit the bottom rule on all pages except the last.

- Maintain your paper's standard margins for a table that takes up an entire page or is in landscape orientation (see 26.1.2). Do not put any regular text on a page containing a landscape table. Set the table title in either landscape or portrait orientation. Number that page as appropriate.

- Keep a table that cannot be presented in print form, such as one containing a large data set, as a separate file, and treat it as an appendix to your paper (see A.2.2).

FIGURES. Take care that your graphics are easy to read, accurate, and to the point.

- Create charts, graphs, and diagrams with your word processor, if possible. If not, create them in the relevant program and insert them into your file as images. Format them to match the surrounding text. See chapter 26 for discussion of figure types, format, and placement in text.

- Insert photographs, maps, and other types of figures into your file as images. If the item is available to you only in hard copy, scan and insert it, if possible. Images affixed to the hard copy of your paper do not reproduce well on photocopies and will be lost from any copies subsequently printed from your file.

- Put a figure number and caption on the line below a figure (see 26.3.2). (For musical examples only, put these items on the line above a figure.) Run the caption the full width of the figure, and do not indent any runovers. If there is not room for both figure and caption within the margins of a page, put the caption at the bottom (or, if necessary, the top) of the nearest preceding text page. Figure captions may be presented in a smaller typeface than the rest of your text; consult your local guidelines.
- Leave at least one blank line between the figure and any text above it on the page, and also between the caption and any text below it. If the figure appears at the top or bottom of a page, put it flush with the top or bottom margin.
- Avoid shading and color. Even if you print the paper on a color printer, it may be printed or copied later on a black-and-white machine, and if it is a dissertation, it may be microfilmed. Shading and color do not reproduce well in any of these forms. If you use shading, make sure it does not obscure the text of the figure, and do not use multiple shades, which might not reproduce distinctly.
- Consult your local guidelines for information about resolution and related characteristics of all figures.
- Maintain your paper's standard margins for a figure that takes up an entire page or is in landscape orientation (see 26.1.2). Do not put any regular text on a page containing a landscape figure. Set the figure caption in either landscape or portrait orientation. Number that page as appropriate.
- Keep a figure that cannot be presented in print form, such as a multimedia file, as a separate file, and treat it as an appendix to your paper (see A.2.3).

A.3.2 Submitting Hard Copy

If you are writing a class paper, submitting it may be as simple as printing out a single hard copy and handing it in to your instructor. You may instead be asked to submit it electronically (see A.3.3), or to submit multiple copies to multiple individuals (your classmates, or other faculty members). Follow instructions exactly, and always keep both a hard copy and the electronic file for your records. All copies should exactly match the original.

Although producing your paper double-sided may save paper and is now technologically simple, most instructors find it easier to read and comment on papers printed on only one side of a page. Unless instructed otherwise, submit your paper single-sided.

The requirements for theses and dissertations are more stringent because such papers will most likely be preserved in bound or electronic form by the university and possibly by an external dissertation repository.

Well in advance of the submission deadline, review the specific guidelines of your department or university regarding such matters as the medium of submission (hard copy, electronic, or both), the number of copies required, and any paperwork or procedures that must be completed before you can submit the paper. If possible, have an official review the paper for proper format before you produce the final copies.

Nearly all departments and universities require you to submit one or more hard copies of your thesis or dissertation on a specific paper stock. Such paper should be 8½ × 11 inches (in American universities) and must be suitable for long-term preservation of the work, which means it should be acid free. If the guidelines do not specify the paper stock, follow the American Library Association's recommendation for twenty-pound weight, neutral-pH paper that is labeled either "buffered" or as having a minimum 2 percent alkaline reserve. Some but not all stock referred to as "dissertation bond" meets these requirements, so be sure to examine the paper specifications before making the copies.

Most universities are served by one or more copy centers, either on or near campus, that are familiar with the requirements for copies of theses and dissertations. Although using their services may be more expensive than producing the copies on your own, it reduces the risk that your paper will be rejected for incorrect paper stock or copy quality problems. Copy center workers generally do not check for errors in format, such as incorrect margins, so be sure your paper reflects all the necessary guidelines before you have it copied. Inspect the copies carefully before you leave the copy center, and notify a worker if you see any problems with them.

A.3.3   Submitting Electronic Files

Many departments and universities now require electronic submission of a thesis or dissertation in addition to or instead of hard copy. Instructors may also request electronic copies of class papers.

Consult your local guidelines for technical specifications, and seek assistance well in advance of the submission deadline if you need it. If required to submit a paper as a PDF file, be sure to embed the fonts to preserve the paper's appearance and format. Test all hyperlinks for accuracy. If the paper contains illustrations, set the resolution and other characteristics of the images depending on how the file will be used (preserved archivally, printed, posted online, and so forth). Check with the office of theses and dissertations or your instructor for handling of material that cannot be put into a single-file format, such as large data sets or multimedia files.

Bibliography

There is a large literature on finding and presenting information, only some of which can be listed here. For a larger and more current selection, consult the Library of Congress catalog and commercial Web sites that provide customer reviews of books. If there is no date listed for an item, the publication appears annually. Sources available online or as a CD-ROM (in addition to or in place of traditional print formats) are so indicated. Online sources for which no URL is given are readily available from multiple online databases. This list is divided as follows:

For most of those areas, six kinds of resources are listed:

1. specialized dictionaries that offer short essays defining concepts in a field
2. general and specialized encyclopedias that offer more extensive overviews of a topic
3. guides to finding resources in different fields and using their methodologies
4. bibliographies, abstracts, and indexes that list past and current publications in different fields
5. writing manuals for different fields
6. style manuals that describe required features of citations in different fields

Internet Databases (Bibliographies and Indexes)

General

ArticleFirst. Dublin, OH: OCLC, 1990–. http://oclc.org/.

The Booklist. Chicago: American Library Association. 1969–. http://www.ala.org/booklist/.

ClasePeriodica. Mexico, D.F.: UNAM, 2003–. http://oclc.org.

Digital Dissertations. Ann Arbor, MI: UMI, [19—]–. http://wwwlib.umi.com/dissertations/.

Electronic Resources Review. Bradford, UK: MCB University Press, 1997–2000. http://www.emeraldinsight.com/1364–5137.htm.

ERIC. Educational Resources Information Center. Ipswich, MA: EBSCO Pub., 1994–; Bethesda, MD: Cambridge Scientific Abstracts, 1998–. http://www.lib.umt.edu/laser/cdalpo.htm.

Essay & General Literature. Bronx, NY: H. W. Wilson Co., 1900–. http://wilson-web2.hwwilson.com.

FirstSearch Dissertations. Ann Arbor, MI: University Microfilms. http://wwwlib.umi.com/dissertations/.

FRANCIS. Institut de l'information scientifique et technique (France); Getty Information Institute; Research Libraries Group. Mountain View, CA: Research Libraries Group, 1984–. http://connectsciences.inist.fr/internes/oldi/baseSearch.php.

General Reference Center Gold. Farmington Hills, MI: The Gale Group, 1999–. http://infotrac.galegroup.com/.

InfoTrac OneFile. Farmington Hills, MI: Gale Group. http://web5.infotrac.galegroup.com/itw/infomark.

ISI Web of Knowledge. Philadelphia: Institute for Scientific Information, 2000–. http://isinet.com/webofknowledge.

LexisNexis Academic Universe. Dayton, OH: LexisNexis. http://web.lexis-nexis .com/universe/.

Library Literature & Information Science Full Text. Bronx, NY: H. W. Wilson Co., 1900–. http://wilsonweb2.hwwilson.com.

Periodicals Index Online. ProQuest Information and Learning Company, 1990–. http://pio.chadwyck.co.uk/home.do.

ProQuest Research Library. Ann Arbor, MI: ProQuest Information and Learning Co., 1998–. http://proquest.umi.com/pqdweb?RQT=306&DBld=4138#sform.

Wilson Omnifile Full Text. Mega edition. Bronx, NY: H. W. Wilson Company, 1990–. http://hwwilsonweb.com.

WorldCat. Dublin, OH: Online Computer Library Center. http://www.oclc.org/ worldcat/.

Humanities

Arts & Humanities Search. Philadelphia, Institute for Scientific Information; Dublin, OH: OCLC, 1990–. http://oclc.org.

Bibliography of the History of Art. Santa Monica, CA: J. Paul Getty Trust; Vandoeu-vre-lès-Nancy, France: Centre national de la recherche scientifique, 1990–. http:// www.eureka.rig.org.

History Resource Center U.S. Farmington Hills, MI: Gale Group, ca. 2000–. http:// www.galenet.com/servlet/HistRC.

Humanities Full Text. Bronx, NY: H. W. Wilson Co., 1990–. http://hwwilsonweb .com/.

Social Sciences

Anthropological Literature. Cambridge, MA: Tozzer Library, Harvard University, 1984–. telnet://cobalt.rig.org.

LawDesk. http://lawlibrary.ucdavis.edu/lawlib/august02/0095.html.

On-Line Index to Indian Social Science Journals and Press Clippings Files. New Delhi: ISID. http://isidev.nic.in/odb.html.

PAIS International. Public Affairs Information Service. Norwood, MA: SilverPlatter International, 1900–. http://www.bowdoin.edu/dept/library/erl/spirs/pais.

PAISArchive. Public Affairs Information Service. Dublin, OH: OCLC, 2004–. http://www.oclc.org.

Political Science Resources on the Web. Ann Arbor, MI: Document Center, University of Michigan, 1996–. http://www.lib.umich.edu/govdocs/polisci.html.

PsycARTICLES. Washington, DC: American Psychological Association, 2001–. http://psycinfo.com/library/fulltext.cfm.

PsycINFO. American Psychological Association. New York, NY: Ovid Technologies, 1900–. http://www.apa.org/psycinfo/.

Social Sciences Abstracts. Bronx, NY: H. W. Wilson Co., 1997–. http://www.oclc .org.

Social Sciences Citation Index with Abstracts. Philadelphia: Institute for Scientific In-formation, ca. 1992–. http://www.isinet.com/products/citation/ssci/.

Sociological Abstracts. Sociological Abstracts, Inc. Dublin, OH: OCLC, 1990–. http://www.oclc.com.

Natural Sciences

AGRICOLA (AGRICultural OnLine Access). Beltsville, MD: The Library, 1970–. http://purl.access.gpo.gov/GPO/LPS1292.

Applied Science and Technology Abstracts. Bronx, NY: H. W. Wilson; Dublin, OH: OCLC, 1983–. http://www.oclc.org.

ISI Web of Science. Philadelphia: Institute for Scientific Information, ca. 1998–. http://isiknowledge.com.

PubSCIENCE United States. Washington, DC: U.S. Dept. of Energy, Office of Scientific and Technical Information, 1999–2002. http://purl.access.gpo.gov/GPO/LP3399.

Science Citation Index. Philadelphia: Institute for Scientific Information, ca. 1988–. http://isi01.isiknowledge.com/portal.cgi/wos.

Web of Science. Philadelphia: Institute for Scientific Information, 1998–. http://isiknowledge.com, http://www.webofscience.com/.

Print and Electronic Resources

General

1. Bowman, John S., ed. *The Cambridge Dictionary of American Biography*. Cambridge: Cambridge University Press, 1995.

1. Garraty, John A., and Mark C. Carnes, eds. *American National Biography*. New York: Oxford University Press, 1999.

1. Matthew, H. C. G., and Brian Howard Harrison, eds. *Oxford Dictionary of National Biography, in Association with the British Academy: From the Earliest Times to the Year 2000*. New York: Oxford University Press, 2004. Also at http://www.oxforddnb.

2. Jackson, Kenneth T., Karen Markoe, and Arnie Markoe, eds. *The Scribner Encyclopedia of American Lives*. 6 vols. covering 1981–2002. New York: Charles Scribner's Sons, 1998–ca. 2004.

2. Lagassé, Paul, ed. *The Columbia Encyclopedia*. 6th ed. New York: Columbia University Press, 2000. Also at http://www.bartleby.com/65/.

2. *New Encyclopaedia Britannica*. 15th ed. 32 vols. Chicago: Encyclopaedia Britannica, 2005. Also at http://www.eb.com.

3. Balay, Robert, ed. *Guide to Reference Books*. 11th ed. Chicago: American Library Association, 1996.

3. Hacker, Diana, and Barbara Fister. *Research and Documentation in the Electronic Age*. 3rd ed. Boston: Bedford/St. Martins, 2002. Also at http://www.dianahacker.com/resdoc/.

3. Kane, Eileen, and Mary O'Reilly-de Brún. *Doing Your Own Research*. New York: Marion Boyars, 2001.

3. Lipson, Charles. *Doing Honest Work in College: How to Prepare Citations, Avoid Plagiarism, and Achieve Real Academic Success*. Chicago: University of Chicago Press, 2004.

3. Mann, Thomas. *Oxford Guide to Library Research*. 3rd ed. New York: Oxford University Press, 2005.

3. Preece, Roy A. *Starting Research: An Introduction to Academic Research and Dissertation Writing*. London: Continuum, 2000.

3. Rowely, Jennifer, and John Farrow. *Organizing Knowledge: An Introduction to Managing Access to Information.* 3rd ed. Aldershot, Hampshire, England: Gower, 2000.

3. Sears, Jean L., and Marilyn K. Moody. *Using Governmental Information Sources: Electronic and Print.* 3rd ed. Phoenix, AZ: Oryx Press, 2001.

3. Whiteley, Sandra, ed. *The American Library Association Guide to Information Access: A Complete Handbook and Directory.* New York: Random House, 1994.

4. *Alternative Press Index.* College Park, MD: Alternative Press Centre, 1969.

4. *Bibliographic Index.* New York: H. W. Wilson. Also at http://hwwilsonweb.com.

4. *Book Review Index.* Detroit: Gale Research Co., 1965–.

4. *Book Review Index: A Master Cumulation.* Detroit: Gale Research Co., 1980–.

4. *Books in Print.* New Providence, NJ: R. R. Bowker. Also at http://www.booksinprint.com/bip.

4. Brigham, Clarence S. *History and Bibliography of American Newspapers, 1690–1820.* 2 vols. Westport, CT: Greenwood Press, 1976.

4. *Conference Papers Index.* Louisville, KY: Data Courier, Inc., 1978–.

4. *Current Book Review Citations* in English. New York: H. W. Wilson Co., 1976–1982.

4. *Current Book Review Citations* in multiple languages. Bronx, NY: H. W. Wilson Co., 1976–1982.

4. Fanning, C. E., Margaret Jackson, Mary Katharine Reely, and Mertice May James. *Book Review Digest. Annual Cumulation.* 1905–. New York: The H. W. Wilson Co.

4. Farber, Evan Ira, and Ruth Matteson Blackmore, eds. *Combined Retrospective Index to Book Reviews in Scholarly Journals, 1886–1974.* Arlington: Carrollton Press, 1979–.

4. Gregory, Winifred, ed. *American Newspapers 1821–1936: A Union List of Files Available in the United States and Canada.* New York: H. W. Wilson, 1937.

4. *Kirkus Reviews.* New York: Kirkus Service, 1991–.

4. *Library of Congress Subject Catalog.* Washington, DC: Library of Congress. Also at http://catalog.loc.gov/.

4. *National Newspaper Index.* Menlo Park, CA: Information Access. Also online from multiple sources.

4. *New York Times Index.* New York: New York Times.

4. *Newspapers in Microform.* Ann Arbor, MI: University Microfilms International.

4. *Periodical Abstracts & General Periodicals. Research II.* University Microfilms International. 1990s–.

4. Poole, William Frederick, and William Isaac Fletcher. *Poole's Index to Periodical Literature.* Rev. ed. Gloucester, MA: Peter Smith, 1970.

4. *Popular Periodical Index.* Camden, NJ: Rutgers University.

4. *ProQuest Digital Dissertations.* Ann Arbor, MI: University Microfilms International. Also at http://wwwlib.umi.com/dissertations/.

4. *Readers' Guide to Periodical Literature.* New York: H. W. Wilson. Also at http://hwwilsonweb.com/.

4. *Reference Books Bulletin.* Chicago: American Library Association, 1984–.

4. *Serials in Microform.* Ann Arbor, MI: University Microfilms International.

4. *Serials Review.* San Diego: Pergamon. Also by subscription through Science Direct. 1975–.

4. *Subject Guide to Books in Print.* New York: R. R. Bowker. Also at http://www
   .booksinprint.com/bip/.
4. *Wall Street Journal Index.* New York: Dow Jones. Also at http://www.il.proquest
   .com/products/pt-product-WSJ.shtml.
5. Bolker, Joan, ed. *Writing Your Dissertation in Fifteen Minutes a Day: A Guide to
   Starting, Revising, and Finishing Your Doctoral Thesis.* New York: H. Holt, 1998.
5. Miller, Jane E. *The Chicago Guide to Writing about Numbers.* Chicago: University
   of Chicago Press, 2004.
5. Sternberg, David Joel. *How to Complete and Survive a Doctoral Dissertation.* New
   York: St. Martin's Griffin, 1981.
5. Strunk, William, and E. B. White. *The Elements of Style.* 4th ed. New York: Longman, 2004.
5. Williams, Joseph M. *Style: Toward Clarity and Grace.* Chicago: University of Chicago Press, 1990.
6. *The Chicago Manual of Style.* 15th ed. Chicago: University of Chicago Press,
   2003.

Visual Representation of Data (Tables, Figures, etc.)

2. Harris, Robert L. *Information Graphics: A Comprehensive Illustrated Reference.*
   New York: Oxford University Press, 2000.
3. Cleveland, William S. *The Elements of Graphing Data.* 2nd ed. Summit, NJ: Ho-
   bart Press, 1994.
3. ————. *Visualizing Data.* Summit, NJ: AT&T. Bell Laboratories, 1993.
3. Monmonier, Mark. *Mapping It Out: Expository Cartography for the Humanities
   and Social Sciences.* Chicago: University of Chicago Press, 1993.
3. Tufte, Edward R. *Envisioning Information.* Cheshire, CT: Graphics Press, 1990.
3. ————. *The Visual Display of Quantitative Information.* Cheshire, CT: Graphics
   Press, 1983.
3. ————. *Visual & Statistical Thinking: Displays of Evidence for Decision Making.*
   Cheshire, CT: Graphics Press, 1997.
3. Wainer, Howard. *Visual Revelations: Graphical Tales of Fate and Deception from
   Napoleon Bonaparte to Ross Perot.* New York: Copernicus, Springer-Verlag,
   1997.
5. Briscoe, Mary Helen. *Preparing Scientific Illustrations: A Guide to Better Posters,
   Presentations, and Publications.* 2nd ed. New York: Springer-Verlag, 1996.
5. Kosslyn, Stephen M. *Elements of Graph Design.* New York: W. H. Freeman,
   1994.
5. National Institutes of Health, Division of Research Services, Medical Arts and
   Photography Branch. *Graphics User Guide.* Bethesda, MD: The Branch, 1986?.
5. Nicol, Adelheid A. M., and Penny M. Pexman. *Presenting Your Findings: A Practical Guide for Creating Tables.* Washington, DC: American Psychological Association, 1999.
5. Robbins, Naomi, B. *Creating More Effective Graphs.* New York: John Wiley &
   Sons, 2004.
5. Ross, Ted. *The Art of Music Engraving and Processing: A Complete Manual, Reference, and Text Book on Preparing Music for Reproduction and Print.* Miami: Han-
   sen Books, 1970.

5. Zweifel, Frances W. *A Handbook of Biological Illustration*. 2nd ed. Chicago: University of Chicago Press, 1988.
6. CBE Scientific Illustration Committee. *Illustrating Science: Standards for Publication*. Bethesda, MD: Council of Biology Editors, 1988.

Posters

Corbin, Nancy C. "The Well-dressed Poster Board." In *A Mission to Communicate: Proceedings, 32nd International Technical Communication Conference, May 19–22, 1985, Houston, Texas*, VC 26–29. Washington, DC: Society for Technical Communication, 1985.

Dubois, Betty Lou. "Poster Sessions at Biomedical Meetings: Design and Presentation." *English for Special Purposes Journal* 4.1 (1985): 37–48.

Esposito, Mona, Kaye Marshall, and Fredericka L. Stoller. "Poster Sessions by Experts." In *New Ways in Content-based Instruction*, edited by Donna M. Brinton and Peter Master, 115–18. Alexandria, VA: Teachers of English to Speakers of Other Languages, 1997.

George Mason University, Department of Biology. "A Guide to Writing in the Biological Sciences: The Poster Session." http://classweb.gmu.edu/biologyresources/writingguide/Poster.htm.

Griffith, George W. "Poster Sessions: One-to-One Technical Communication." In *Proceedings: 28th International Technical Communication Conference, May 20–23, 1981, Pittsburgh, PA*, G26–G27. Pittsburgh: Society for Technical Writing, 1981.

Larkin, Greg. "Storyboarding: A Concrete Way to Generate Effective Visuals." *Journal of Technical Writing and Communication* 26.3 (1996): 273–90.

Rice University, Cain Project in Engineering and Professional Communication. "Designing Scientific and Engineering Posters." http://www.owlnet.rice.edu/~cainproj/ih_posters.html.

Shalom, Celia. "Established and Evolving Spoken Research Process Genres: Plenary Lecture and Poster Session Discussions at Academic Conferences." *English for Specific Purposes Journal* 12.1 (1993): 37–50.

Stanford University, Visual Art Services. "Posters Templates." http://stanford.edu/dept/VAS/posters/poster_temps.html.

University of California, Davis, Nutrition Department. "Poster Printer." http://teaching.ucdavis.edu/poster/template.htm.

White, J. T. "Technical Poster Fabrication." In *Proceedings: 28th International Technical Communication Conference, May 20–23, 1981, Pittsburgh, PA*, G64–G65. Pittsburgh: Society for Technical Writing, 1981.

Humanities

General

1. Murphy, Bruce, ed. *Benet's Reader's Encyclopedia*. 4th ed. New York: HarperCollins, 1996.
3. Kirkham, Sandi. *How to Find Information in the Humanities*. London: Library Association, 1989.
4. *American Humanities Index*. Troy, NY: Whitston Pub. Co.
4. *Arts & Humanities Citation Index*. Philadelphia: Institute for Scientific Information, 1976–.

4. *Arts & Humanities Index.* Philadelphia: Institute for Scientific Information. Also at http://www.isiknowledge.

4. Blazek, Ron, and Elizabeth Smith Aversa. *The Humanities: A Selective Guide to Information Sources.* 5th ed. Englewood, CO: Libraries Unlimited, 2000. Also at http://www.netlibrary.com.

4. *British Humanities Index.* London: Library Association; Bethesda, MD: Cambridge Scientific Abstracts.

4. *Humanities Index.* New York: H. W. Wilson Co., 1974. Also at http://hwwilsonweb.com.

4. *Index to Book Reviews in the Humanities.* Williamston, MI: P. Thomson, 1960–90.

4. *Index to Social Sciences & Humanities Proceedings.* Philadelphia: Institute for Scientific Information, 1979–.

4. Harzfeld, Lois A. *Periodical Indexes in the Social Sciences and Humanities: A Subject Guide.* Microform. Metuchen, NJ: Scarecrow Press, 1978.

4. Walford, Albert J., Anthony Chalcraft, Ray Prytherch, and Stephen Willis, eds. *Walford's Guide to Reference Material. Vol. 3, Generalia, Language and Literature, The Arts.* 7th ed. London: Library Association, 1998.

5. Northey, Margot, and Maurice Legris. *Making Sense in the Humanities: A Student's Guide to Writing and Style.* Toronto: Oxford University Press, 1990.

Art

1. Chilvers, Ian, and Harold Osborne, eds. *The Oxford Dictionary of Art.* 3rd ed. Oxford: Oxford University Press, 2004. Also at http://www.oxfordreference.com.

1. Myers, Bernard L., and Trewin Copplestone, eds. *The Macmillan Encyclopedia of Art.* Rev. ed. London: Macmillan, 1981.

1. Myers, Bernard S., and Shirley D. Myers, eds. *McGraw-Hill Dictionary of Art.* 5 vols. New York: McGraw-Hill, 1969.

2. Myers, Bernard S., ed. *Encyclopedia of World Art.* 17 vols. New York: McGraw-Hill, 1987.

3. Arntzen, Etta, and Robert Rainwater. *Guide to the Literature of Art History.* Chicago: American Library Association, 1980.

3. Jones, Lois Swan. *Art Information and the Internet: How to Find It, How to Use It.* Phoenix, AZ: Oryx Press, 1999.

3. ———. *Art Information: Research Methods and Resources.* 3rd ed. Dubuque, IA: Kendall/Hunt, 1990.

3. Marmor, Max, and Alex Ross. *Guide to the Literature of Art History 2.* Chicago: American Library Association, 2005.

3. Minor, Vernon Hyde. *Art History's History.* 2nd ed. Upper Saddle River, NJ: Prentice Hall, 2001.

4. *Art Abstracts.* Bronx, NY: H. W. Wilson Co., 1984–. Also at http//wilsonweb2.hwwilson.com.

4. *Art Index.* New York: H. W. Wilson. Also at http://hwwilsonweb.

4. *Art Index Retrospective.* Bronx, NY: H. W. Wilson Co., 1997–. Also at http://wilsonweb2.hwwilson.com.

5. Barnet, Sylvan. *A Short Guide to Writing about Art.* 8th ed. New York: Pearson/Longman, 2005.

History

1. Cook, Chris. *A Dictionary of Historical Terms.* 3rd ed. Houndmills, UK: Macmillan, 1998.
1. Ritter, Harry. *Dictionary of Concepts in History.* Westport, CT: Greenwood Press, 1986.
2. Breisach, Ernst. *Historiography: Ancient, Medieval & Modern.* 2nd ed. Chicago: University of Chicago Press, 1994.
3. Benjamin, Jules R. *A Student's Guide to History.* 9th ed. Boston: Bedford/St. Martin's, 2004.
3. Brundage, Anthony. *Going to the Sources: A Guide to Historical Research and Writing.* 3rd ed. Wheeling, IL: Harlan Davidson, 2002.
3. Frick, Elizabeth. *History: Illustrated Search Strategy and Sources.* 2nd ed. Ann Arbor, MI: Pierian Press, 1995.
3. Fritze, Ronald H., Brian E. Coutts, and Louis Andrew Vyhnanek. *Reference Sources in History: An Introductory Guide.* 2nd ed. Santa Barbara, CA: ABC-Clio, 2004.
3. Higginbotham, Evelyn Brooks, Leon F. Litwack, and Darlene Clark Hine. *The Harvard Guide to African-American History.* Cambridge, MA: Harvard University Press, 2001.
3. Kyvig, David E., and Myron A. Marty. *Nearby History: Exploring the Past Around You.* 2nd ed. Walnut Creek, CA: AltaMira Press, 2000.
3. Prucha, Francis Paul. *Handbook for Research in American History: A Guide to Bibliographies and Other Reference Works.* 2nd ed. Lincoln: University of Nebraska Press, 1994.
4. *America: History and Life.* Santa Barbara, CA: ABC-Clio. Also at http://serials.abc-clio.
4. Blazek, Ron, and Anna H. Perrault. *United States History: A Selective Guide to Information Sources.* Englewood, CO: Libraries Unlimited, 1994. Also at http://www.netlibrary.
4. Danky, James Philip, and Maureen E. Hady. *African-American Newspapers and Periodicals: A National Bibliography.* Cambridge, MA: Harvard University Press, 1998.
4. *Historical Abstracts.* Santa Barbara, CA: ABC-Clio. Also at http://serials.abc-clio.
4. Kinnel, Susan K., ed. *Historiography: An Annotated Bibliography of Journal Articles, Books, and Dissertations.* 2 vols. Santa Barbara, CA: ABC-Clio, 1987.
4. Mott, Frank Luther. *A History of American Magazines.* 5 vols. Cambridge, MA: Belknap Press of Harvard University Press, 1930–1968.
5. Barzun, Jacques, and Henry F. Graff. *The Modern Researcher.* 6th ed. Belmont, CA: Thomson/Wadsworth, 2004.
5. Marius, Richard, and Melvin E. Page. *A Short Guide to Writing about History.* 5th ed. New York: Pearson Longman, 2005.

Literary Studies

1. Abrams, M. H. *A Glossary of Literary Terms.* 8th ed. Boston: Thomson/Wadsworth, 2005.
1. Baldick, Chris, ed. *The Concise Oxford Dictionary of Literary Terms.* 2nd ed. Oxford: Oxford University Press, 2001.

1. Brogan, Terry V. F., ed. *The New Princeton Handbook of Poetic Terms*. Princeton: Princeton University Press, 1994.

1. Groden, Michael, Martin Kreiswirth, and Imre Szeman, eds. *The Johns Hopkins Guide to Literary Theory and Criticism*. 2nd ed. Baltimore: Johns Hopkins University Press, 2005.

1. Preminger, Alex, and Terry V. F. Brogan, eds. *The New Princeton Encyclopedia of Poetry and Poetics*. Princeton: Princeton University Press, 1993.

2. Drabble, Margaret, ed. *The Oxford Companion to English Literature*. 6th ed. New York: Oxford University Press, 2000. Also at http://www.oxfordreference.com.

2. Hart, James David, and Phillip W. Leininger, eds. *The Oxford Companion to American Literature*. 6th ed. New York: Oxford University Press, 1995. Also at http://www.oxfordreference.com.

2. Lentricchia, Frank, and Thomas McLaughlin, eds. *Critical Terms for Literary Study*. 2nd ed. Chicago: University of Chicago Press, 1995.

2. Parini, Jay, ed. *The Oxford Encyclopedia of American Literature*. 4 vols. New York: Oxford University Press, 2004.

2. Ward, Sir Adolphus William, A. R. Waller, William Peterfield Trent, John Erskine, Stuart Pratt Sherman, and Carl Van Doren. *The Cambridge History of English and American Literature: An Encyclopedia in Eighteen Volumes*. New York: G. P. Putnam's Sons, 1907–21. Also at http://www.bartleby.com/cambridge/.

3. Altick, Richard Daniel, and John J. Fenstermaker. *The Art of Literary Research*. 4th ed. New York: Norton, 1993.

3. Harner, James L. *Literary Research Guide: An Annotated Listing of Reference Sources in English Literary Studies*. 4th ed. New York: Modern Language Association of America, 2002.

3. Klarer, Mario. *An Introduction to Literary Studies*. 2nd ed. London: Routledge, 2004.

3. Vitale, Philip H. *Basic Tools of Research: An Annotated Guide for Students of English*. 3rd ed., rev. and enl. New York: Barron's Educational Series, 1975.

4. *Abstracts of English Studies*. Boulder, CO: National Council of Teachers of English.

4. Blanck, Jacob, Virginia L. Smyers, and Michael Winship. *Bibliography of American Literature*. 9 vols. New Haven: Yale University Press, 1955–1991. Also at http://lion.chadwyck.co.uk/.

4. *Index of American Periodical Verse*. Metuchen, NJ: Scarecrow Press, 1971–.

4. *MLA International Bibliography of Books and Articles on the Modern Languages and Literature*. New York: Modern Language Association of America. Also online from multiple sources.

5. Barnet, Sylvan, and William E. Cain. *A Short Guide to Writing about Literature*. 10th ed. New York: Longman/Pearson, 2005.

5. Griffith, Kelley. *Writing Essays about Literature: A Guide and Style Sheet*. 7th ed. Boston: Heinle & Heinle, 2005.

6. Gibaldi, Joseph. *MLA Handbook for Writers of Research Papers*. 6th ed. New York: Modern Language Association of America, 2003.

Music

1. Randel, Don Michael, ed. *The Harvard Dictionary of Music*. 4th ed. Cambridge: Belknap Press of Harvard University Press, 2003.

1. Sadie, Stanley, and John Tyrrell, eds. *The New Grove Dictionary of Music and Musicians*. 2nd ed. 29 vols. New York: Grove, 2001. Also at http://www.grovemusic.com.

2. Netti, Bruno, Ruth M. Stone, James Porter, and Timothy Rice, eds. *The Garland Encyclopedia of World Music*. 10 vols. New York: Garland, 2002.

2. Sadie, Stanley, ed. *The Norton/Grove Concise Encyclopedia of Music*. Rev. and enl. ed. New York: W. W. Norton, 1994.

3. Brockman, William S. *Music: A Guide to the Reference Literature*. Littleton, CO: Libraries Unlimited, 1987.

3. Duckles, Vincent H., Ida Reed, and Michael A. Keller, eds. *Music Reference and Research Materials: An Annotated Bibliography*. 5th ed. New York: Schirmer Books, 1997.

4. *The Music Index*. Detroit, MI: Information Service. Also at http://www.hppmusicindex.com.

4. *RILM Abstracts of Music Literature*. New York: RILM. Also online from multiple sources.

5. Druesedow, John E., Jr. *Library Research Guide to Music: Illustrated Search Strategy and Sources*. Ann Arbor, MI: Pierian Press, 1982.

5. Herbert, Trevor. *Music in Words: A Short Guide to Researching and Writing about Music*. London: Associated Board of the Royal Schools of Music, 2001.

5. Wingell, Richard. *Writing about Music: An Introductory Guide*. 3rd ed. Upper Saddle River, NJ: Prentice Hall, 2002.

6. Bellman, Jonathan. *A Short Guide to Writing about Music*. New York: Longman, 2000.

6. Holoman, D. Kern. *Writing about Music: A Style Sheet from the Editors of 19th Century Music*. Berkeley: University of California Press, 1988. Also at http://www.netlibrary.com.

Philosophy

1. Blackburn, Simon. *The Oxford Dictionary of Philosophy*. 2nd ed. Oxford: Oxford University Press, 2005. Also at http://www.oxfordreference.com.

2. Edwards, Paul. *The Encyclopedia of Philosophy*. 8 vols. New York: Simon & Schuster Macmillan, 1996.

2. Parkinson, George H. R. *The Handbook of Western Philosophy*. New York: Macmillan, 1988.

2. Urmson, J. O., and Jonathan Rée, eds. *The Concise Encyclopedia of Western Philosophy and Philosophers*. 3rd ed. London: Routledge, 2005.

3. List, Charles J., and Stephen H. Plum. *Library Research Guide to Philosophy*. Ann Arbor, MI: Pierian Press, 1990.

4. *The Philosopher's Index*. Bowling Green, OH: Philosopher's Information Center. Also at http://www.ovid.com/site/catalog/DataBase/.

5. Martinich, Aloysius. *Philosophical Writing: An Introduction*. 3rd ed. Malden, MA: Blackwell Publishers, 2005.

5. Watson, Richard A. *Writing Philosophy: A Guide to Professional Writing and Publishing*. Carbondale: Southern Illinois University Press, 1992. Also at http://www.netlibrary.com.

Social Sciences

General

1. Calhoun, Craig, ed. *Dictionary of the Social Sciences*. New York: Oxford University Press, 2002. Also at http://www.oxfordreference.com.
1. *Statistical Abstract of the United States*. Washington, DC: U.S. Census Bureau. Also at http://www.census.gov/statab/www/.
2. Sills, David, ed. *International Encyclopedia of the Social Sciences*. 19 vols. New York: Macmillan, 1991.
3. Herron, Nancy L. *The Social Sciences: A Cross-Disciplinary Guide to Selected Sources*. 3rd ed. Englewood, CO: Libraries Unlimited, 2002.
3. Light, Richard J., and David B. Pillemer. *Summing Up: The Science of Reviewing Research*. Cambridge: Harvard University Press, 1984.
3. Øyen, Else, ed. *Comparative Methodology: Theory and Practice in International Social Research*. London: Sage, 1990.
4. *Bibliography of Social Science Research and Writings on American Indians*. Compiled by Russell Thornton and Mary K Grasmick. Minneapolis: Center for Urban and Regional Affairs, University of Minnesota, 1979.
4. *Book Review Index to Social Science Periodicals*. Ann Arbor, MI: Pierian Press, 1964–70.
4. *CommSearch*. Annandale, VA: Speech Communication Association, 1995–.
4. *C.R.I.S.: The Combined Retrospective Index Set to Journals in Sociology, 1895–1974*. Compiled by Annadel N. Wile and Arnold Jaffe. Washington, DC: Carrollton Press, 1978.
4. *Current Contents: Social & Behavioral Sciences*. Philadelphia: Institute for Scientific Information, 1974–.
4. *Document Retrieval Index*. U.S. Dept. of Justice, Law Enforcement Assistance Administration, National Institute of Law Enforcement and Criminal Justice, 1979–. Microfiche.
4. Grossman, Jorge. *Indice general de publicaciones periódicas latinoamericanas: Humanidades y ciencias sociales; Index to Latin American periodicals: Humanities and social sciences*. Metuchen, NJ: Scarecrow Press, 1961–70.
4. Harzfeld, Lois A. *Periodical Indexes in the Social Sciences and Humanities: A Subject Guide*. Metuchen, NJ: Scarecrow Press, 1978.
4. *Index of African Social Science Periodical Articles*. Dakar: Council for the Development of Economic and Social Research in Africa, ca. 1989–.
4. *Index to Social Sciences & Humanities Proceedings*. Philadelphia: Institute for Scientific Information, 1979–.
4. *PAIS International in Print*. New York: OCLC Public Affairs Information Service, 1991–.
4. *PAIS International*. New York: SilverPlatter Information, Inc.; OCLC Public Affairs Information Service, 1900s–.
4. *Social Sciences Citation Index*. Philadelphia: Institute for Scientific Information, 1969–.
4. *Social Sciences Index*. New York: H. W. Wilson. Also at http://hwwilsonweb.com.

4. Walford, A. J., Alan Day, and Michael Walsh, eds. *Walford's Guide to Reference Material.* Vol. 2, *Social and Historical Sciences, Philosophy, and Religion.* 8th ed. London: Library Association, 2000.

5. Becker, Howard S. *Writing for Social Scientists: How to Start and Finish Your Thesis, Book, or Article.* Chicago: University of Chicago Press, 1986.

5. Bell, Judith. *Doing Your Research Project: A Guide for First-time Researchers in Education, Health, and Social Science.* 4th ed. Maidenhead, UK: Open University Press, 2005.

5. Krathwohl, David R. *How to Prepare a Research Proposal: Guidelines for Funding and Dissertations in the Social and Behavioral Sciences.* 3rd ed. Syracuse, NY: Syracuse University Press, 1988.

5. Northey, Margot, Lorne Tepperman, and James Russell. *Making Sense: Social Sciences; A Student's Guide to Research and Writing.* Updated 2nd ed. Ontario: Oxford University Press, 2005.

Anthropology

1. Barfield, Thomas J., ed. *The Dictionary of Anthropology.* Oxford: Blackwell, 2000. Also at http://www.netlibrary.com.

1. Winthrop, Robert H. *Dictionary of Concepts in Cultural Anthropology.* New York: Greenwood Press, 1991.

2. Barnard, Alan, and Jonathan Spencer, eds. *Encyclopedia of Social and Cultural Anthropology.* London: Routledge, 2004.

2. Ember, Melvin, Carol R. Ember, and Ian A. Skoggard, eds. *Encyclopedia of World Cultures: Supplement.* New York: Gale Group/Thomson Learning, 2002.

2. Ingold, Tim, ed. *Companion Encyclopedia of Anthropology: Humanity, Culture, and Social Life.* New ed. London: Routledge, 2002.

2. Levinson, David, ed. *Encyclopedia of World Cultures.* 10 vols. Boston: G. K. Hall, 1996.

2. Levinson, David, and Melvin Ember, eds. *Encyclopedia of Cultural Anthropology.* 4 vols. New York: Henry Holt, 1996.

3. Bernard, H. Russell, ed. *Handbook of Methods in Cultural Anthropology.* Walnut Creek, CA: AltaMira Press, 2000.

3. ————. *Research Methods in Anthropology: Qualitative and Quantitative Approaches.* 4th ed. Lanham, MD: AltaMira Press, 2005.

3. *Current Topics in Anthropology: Theory, Methods, and Content.* 8 vols. Reading, MA: Addison-Wesley, 1971–.

3. Glenn, James R. *Guide to the National Anthropological Archives, Smithsonian Institution.* Rev. and enl. ed. Washington, DC: National Anthropological Archives, 1996.

3. Poggie, John J., Jr., Billie R. DeWalt, and William W. Dressler, eds. *Anthropological Research: Process and Application.* Albany: State University of New York Press, 1992. Also at http://www.netlibrary.com.

4. *Abstracts in Anthropology.* Amityville, NY: Baywood Publishing.

4. *Annual Review of Anthropology.* Palo Alto, CA: Annual Reviews. Also online from multiple sources.

Business

1. Friedman, Jack P. *Dictionary of Business Terms.* 3rd ed. Hauppauge, NY: Barron's Educational Series, 2000. Also at http://www.netlibrary.com.
1. Link, Albert N. *Link's International Dictionary of Business Economics.* Chicago: Probus, 1993.
1. Nisberg, Jay N. *The Random House Dictionary of Business Terms.* New York: Random House, 1992.
1. Wiechmann, Jack G., and Laurence Urdang, eds. *NTC's Dictionary of Advertising.* 2nd ed. Lincolnwood, IL: National Textbook Co., 1993.
2. Folsom, W. Davis, and Rick Boulware. *Encyclopedia of American Business.* New York: Facts on File, 2004.
2. *The Lifestyle Market Analyst: A Reference Guide for Consumer Market Analysis.* Wilmette, IL: Standard Rate & Data Service.
2. McDonough, John, and Karen Egolf, eds. *The Advertising Age Encyclopedia of Advertising.* 3 vols. New York: Fitzroy Dearborn, 2003.
2. Vernon, Mark. *Business: The Key Concepts.* New York: Routledge, 2002. Also at http://www.netlibrary.com.
2. Warner, Malcolm, and John P. Kotter, eds. *International Encyclopedia of Business and Management.* 2nd ed. 8 vols. London: Thomson Learning, 2002.
3. Amor, Louise, ed. *The Online Manual: A Practical Guide to Business Databases.* 6th ed. Oxford: Learned Information, 1997.
3. Daniells, Lorna M. *Business Information Sources.* 3rd ed. Berkeley: University of California Press, 1993.
3. Kervin, John B. *Methods for Business Research.* New York: HarperCollins, 1992.
3. Moss, Rita W., and Diane Wheeler Strauss. *Strauss's Handbook of Business Information: A Guide for Librarians, Students, and Researchers.* 2nd ed. Westport, CT: Libraries Unlimited, 2004.
3. Sekaran, Uma. *Research Methods for Business: A Skill Building Approach.* 4th ed. New York: John Wiley & Sons, 2003.
3. Woy, James B., ed. *Encyclopedia of Business Information Sources.* 19th ed. Farmington Hills, MI: Gale Group, 2004.
4. *Business Periodicals Index.* New York: H. W. Wilson. Also at http://hwwilsonweb.com.
5. Farrell, Thomas J., and Charlotte Donabedian. *Writing the Business Research Paper: A Complete Guide.* Durham, NC: Carolina Academic Press, 1991.
6. Vetter, William. *Business Law, Legal Research, and Writing: Handbook.* Needham Heights, MA: Ginn Press, 1991.

Communication, Journalism, and Media Studies

1. Miller, Toby, ed. *Television: Critical Concepts in Media and Cultural Studies.* London: Routledge, 2003.
1. Newton, Harry. *Newton's Telecom Dictionary: Covering Telecommunications, Networking, Information Technology, the Internet, the Web, Computing, Wireless, and Fiber.* 21st ed. San Francisco, CA: CMP Books, 2005.
1. Watson, James, and Anne Hill. *A Dictionary of Communication and Media Studies.* 4th ed. London: Arnold, 1997.
1. Weik, Martin H. *Communications Standard Dictionary.* 3rd ed. New York: Chapman & Hall, 1996.

1. Weiner, Richard. *Webster's New World Dictionary of Media and Communications.* Rev. and updated ed. New York: Macmillan, 1996.
2. Barnouw, Erik, ed. *International Encyclopedia of Communications.* 4 vols. New York: Oxford University Press, 1989.
2. Johnston, Donald H., ed. *Encyclopedia of International Media and Communications.* 4 vols. San Diego, CA: Academic Press, 2003.
2. Jones, Steve, ed. *Encyclopedia of New Media: An Essential Reference to Communication and Technology.* Thousand Oaks, CA: Sage, 2003.
2. Paneth, Donald. *The Encyclopedia of American Journalism.* New York: Facts on File, 1983.
2. Stern, Jane, and Michael Stern. *Jane and Michael Stern's Encyclopedia of Pop Culture: An A to Z Guide of Who's Who and What's What, from Aerobics and Bubble Gum to Valley of the Dolls and Moon Unit Zappa.* New York: HarperPerennial, 1992.
3. Clark, Vivienne, James Baker, and Eileen Lewis Key. *Concepts and Skills for Media Studies.* London: Hodder & Stoughton, 2003.
3. Stokes, Jane. *How to Do Media and Cultural Studies.* London: Sage, 2003.
3. Storey, John. *Cultural Studies and the Study of Popular Culture: Theories and Methods.* 2nd ed. Athens: University of Georgia Press, 2003.
4. Block, Eleanor S., and James K. Bracken. *Communication and the Mass Media: A Guide to the Reference Literature.* Englewood, CO: Libraries Unlimited, 1991.
4. Blum, Eleanor, and Frances Goins Wilhoit. *Mass Media Bibliography: An Annotated Guide to Books and Journals for Research and Reference.* 3rd ed. Urbana: University of Illinois Press, 1990.
4. Cates, Jo A. *Journalism: A Guide to the Reference Literature.* 3rd ed. Westport, CT: Libraries Unlimited, 2004.
4. *CD Review.* Hancock, NH: WGE Pub., 1989–96.
4. *Communications Abstracts.* Los Angeles: Dept. of Journalism, University of California, Los Angeles.
4. *Film Review Annual.* Englewood, NJ: J. S. Ozer, 1981–.
4. Matlon, Ronald J., and Sylvia P. Ortiz, eds. *Index to Journals in Communication Studies through 1995.* Annadale, VA: National Communication Association, 1997.
4. *Media Review Digest.* Ann Arbor, MI: Pierian Press, 1974–.
4. *New York Theatre Critics' Reviews.* New York: Critics' Theatre Reviews, 1943–1995.
4. *New York Times Directory of the Film.* New York: Arno Press, 1971–.
4. *Records in Review.* Great Barrington, MA: Wyeth Press, 1957–1981.
4. Sterling, Christopher H., James K. Bracken, and Susan M. Hill, eds. *Mass Communications Research Resources: An Annotated Guide.* Mahwah, NJ: Erlbaum, 1998.
6. Goldstein, Norm, ed. *Stylebook and Briefing on Media Law.* 40th ed. New York: Associated Press, 2005.

Economics

1. Pearce, David W., ed. *MIT Dictionary of Modern Economics.* 4th ed. Cambridge, MA: MIT Press, 1992.

2. Eatwell, John, Murray Milgate, Peter K. Newman, and Sir Robert Harry Inglis Palgrave, eds. *The New Palgrave: A Dictionary of Economics.* 4 vols. New York: Palgrave, 2004.

2. Greenwald, Douglas, ed. *The McGraw-Hill Encyclopedia of Economics.* 2nd ed. New York: McGraw-Hill, 1994.

2. Mokyr, Joel, ed. *The Oxford Encyclopedia of Economic History.* 5 vols. Oxford: Oxford University Press, 2003.

3. Fletcher, John, ed. *Information Sources in Economics.* 2nd ed. London: Butterworths, 1984.

3. Johnson, Glenn L. *Research Methodology for Economists: Philosophy and Practice.* New York: Macmillan, 1986.

4. *Journal of Economic Literature.* Nashville, TN: American Economic Association. Also at http://www.jstor.org.

5. McCloskey, Deirdre Donald N. *The Writing of Economics.* New York: Macmillan, 1987.

5. Thomson, William. *A Guide for the Young Economist.* Cambridge, MA: MIT Press, 2001.

Education

1. Barrow, Robin, and Geoffrey Milburn. *A Critical Dictionary of Educational Concepts: An Appraisal of Selected Ideas and Issues in Educational Theory and Practice.* 2nd ed. New York: Teacher's College Press, 1990.

1. Collins, John Williams, and Nancy P. O'Brien, eds. *The Greenwood Dictionary of Education.* Westport, CT: Greenwood, 2003.

1. Gordon, Peter, and Dennis Lawton. *Dictionary of British Education.* 3rd ed. London: Woburn Press, 2003.

2. Alkin, Marvin C., ed. *Encyclopedia of Educational Research.* 6th ed. 4 vols. New York: Macmillan, 1992.

2. Guthrie, James W., ed. *Encyclopedia of Education.* 2nd ed. 8 vols. New York: Macmillan Reference USA, 2003. Also at http://www.netlibrary.com.

2. Husen, Torsten, and T. Neville Postlethwaite, eds. *The International Encyclopedia of Education.* 2nd ed. 12 vols. Oxford: Pergamon, 1994.

2. Levinson, David L., Peter W. Cookson, and Alan R. Sadovnik, eds. *Education and Sociology: An Encyclopedia.* New York: RoutledgeFalmer, 2002.

2. Unger, Harlow G. *Encyclopedia of American Education.* 2nd ed. 3 vols. New York: Facts on File, 2001.

3. Bausell, R. Barker. *Advanced Research Methodology: An Annotated Guide to Sources.* Metuchen, NJ: Scarecrow Press, 1991.

3. Keeves, John P., ed. *Educational Research, Methodology, and Measurement: An International Handbook.* 2nd ed. New York: Pergamon, 1997.

3. Tuckman, Bruce W. *Conducting Educational Research.* 5th ed. Fort Worth, TX: Harcourt Brace, 1999.

4. *Education Index.* New York: H. W. Wilson. Also at http://hwwilsonweb.

4. *The ERIC Database.* Lanham, MD: Educational Resources Information Center. Also at http://www.eric.ed.gov/.

4. O'Brien, Nancy P. *Education: A Guide to Reference and Information Sources.* 2nd ed. Englewood, CO: Libraries Unlimited, 2000. Also at http://www.netlibrary.com.

5. Carver, Ronald P. *Writing a Publishable Research Report: In Education, Psychology, and Related Disciplines.* Springfield, IL: C. C. Thomas, 1984.

Geography

1. Witherick, M. E., Simon Ross, and John Small. *A Modern Dictionary of Geography.* 4th ed. London: Arnold, 2001.
2. Dunbar, Gary S. *Modern Geography: An Encyclopedic Survey.* New York: Garland, 1991.
2. McCoy, John, ed. *Geo-Data: The World Geographic Encyclopedia.* 3rd ed. Detroit, MI: Thomson-Gale, 2003. Also at www.netlibrary.com.
2. Parker, Sybil P., ed. *World Geographical Encyclopedia.* 5 vols. New York: McGraw-Hill, 1995.
3. Walford, Nigel. *Geographical Data Analysis.* New York: John Wiley & Sons, 1995.
4. Conzen, Michael P., Thomas A. Rumney, and Graeme Wynn. *A Scholar's Guide to Geographical Writing on the American and Canadian Past.* Chicago: University of Chicago Press, 1993.
4. *Current Geographical Publications.* New York: American Geographical Society of New York.
4. *Geographical Abstracts.* Norwich, UK: Geo Abstracts.
4. Okuno, Takashi. *A World Bibliography of Geographical Bibliographies.* Japan: Institute of Geoscience, University of Tsukuba, 1992.
5. Durrenberger, Robert W., John K. Wright, and Elizabeth T. Platt. *Geographical Research and Writing.* New York: Crowell, 1985.
5. Northey, Margot, and David B. Knight. *Making Sense: A Student's Guide to Research and Writing: Geography & Environmental Sciences.* 2nd updated ed. Ontario: Oxford University Press, 2005.

Law

1. Curzon, L. B. *Dictionary of Law.* 6th ed. Harlow, UK: Pearson Education Limited, 2002.
1. Garner, Bryan A., and Henry C. Black, eds. *Black's Law Dictionary.* 8th ed. St. Paul, MN: Thomson/West, 2004.
1. Martin, Elizabeth A., ed. *A Dictionary of Law.* 5th ed. Oxford: Oxford University Press, 2003. Also at http://www.oxfordreference.com.
2. Baker, Brian L., and Patrick J. Petit, eds. *Encyclopedia of Legal Information Sources.* 2nd ed. Detroit, MI: Gale Research, 1993.
2. *Corpus Juris Secundum.* St. Paul, MN: West Publishing Company.
2. Hall, Kermit, and David Scott Clark, eds. *The Oxford Companion to American Law.* New York: Oxford University Press, 2002. Also at http://www.oxfordreference.com.
2. Lehman, Jeffrey, and Shirelle Phelps. *West's Encyclopedia of American Law.* 2nd ed. 13 vols. Detroit, MI: Thomson/Gale, 2005. Also online from multiple sources.
3. Campbell, Enid Mona, Lee Poh-York, and Joycey G. Tooher. *Legal Research: Materials and Methods.* 4th ed. North Ryde, Australia: LBC Information Services, 1996.

3. Long, Judy A. *Legal Research Using the Internet*. Albany, NY: West Legal Studies/ Thomson Learning, 2000. Also at http://www.netlibrary.com.

4. *Current Index to Legal Periodicals*. Seattle: M. G. Gallagher Law Library and Washington Law Review. Also at http://lib.law.washington.edu/cilp/cilp.html.

4. *Current Law Index: Multiple Access to Legal Periodicals*. Farmington Hills, MI: Gale Group, 2001.

4. *Index to Legal Periodicals & Books*. New York: H. W. Wilson. Also at http:// hwwilsonweb.

5. Bast, Carol M., and Margie Hawkins. *Foundations of Legal Research and Writing*. 2nd ed. Albany, NY: West/Thomson Learning, 2002.

5. Garner, Bryan A. *The Elements of Legal Style*. 2nd ed. New York: Oxford University Press, 2002.

6. *The Bluebook: A Uniform System of Citation*. 18th ed. Cambridge, MA: Harvard Law Review Association, 2005.

Political Science

1. Robertson, David. *A Dictionary of Modern Politics*. 4th ed. London: Europa, 2005.

2. *The Almanac of American Politics*. Washington, DC: National Journal. Also at http://nationaljournal.com/members/almanac.

2. Hawkesworth, Mary E., and Maurice Kogan, eds. *Encyclopedia of Government and Politics*. 2nd ed. 2 vols. London: Routledge, 2004.

2. Lal, Shiv, ed. *International Encyclopedia of Politics and Laws*. 17 vols. New Delhi: The Election Archives, 1987.

2. Miller, David, ed. *The Blackwell Encyclopaedia of Political Thought*. Oxford: Black-. well, 1998. Also at http://www.netlibrary.com.

3. Green, Stephen W., and Douglas J. Ernest, eds. *Information Sources in Political Science*. 5th ed. Santa Barbara, CA: ABC-Clio, 2005.

3. Johnson, Janet Buttolph, and H. T. Reynolds. *Political Science Research Methods*. 5th ed. Washington, DC: Congressional Quarterly Press, 2005.

4. *ABC PolSci*. Santa Barbara, CA: ABC-Clio.

4. *PAIS International Journals Indexed*. New York: Public Affairs Information Service.

4. *United States Political Science Documents*. Pittsburgh: University of Pittsburgh, University Center for International Studies, 1975–1991.

4. Wynkoop, Sally. *Subject Guide to Government Reference Books*. Littleton, CO: Libraries Unlimited, 1972.

5. Biddle, Arthur W., Kenneth M. Holland, and Toby Fulwiler. *Writer's Guide: Political Science*. Lexington, MA: D. C. Heath, 1987.

5. Lovell, David W., and Rhonda Moore. *Essay Writing and Style Guide for Politics and the Social Sciences*. Sydney: Australasian Political Studies Association, 1992.

5. Schmidt, Diane E. *Writing in Political Science: A Practical Guide*. 3rd ed. New York: Pearson Longman, 2005.

5. Scott, Gregory M., and Stephen M. Garrison. *The Political Science Student Writer's Manual*. 5th ed. Upper Saddle River, NJ: Pearson/Prentice Hall, 2004.

6. American Political Science Association. *Style Manual for Political Science*. Rev. Washington, DC: American Political Science Association, 2001.

Psychology

1. Colman, Andrew M. *Oxford Dictionary of Psychology*. Oxford: Oxford University Press, 2003. Also at http://www.oxfordreference.com.

1. Eysenck, Michael, ed. *The Blackwell Dictionary of Cognitive Psychology*. Oxford: Blackwell, 1997.

1. Hayes, Nicky, and Peter Stratton. *A Student's Dictionary of Psychology*. 4th ed. London: Arnold, 2003.

1. Wolman, Benjamin B., ed. *Dictionary of Behavioral Science*. 2nd ed. San Diego, CA: Academic, 1989.

2. Colman, Andrew M., ed. *Companion Encyclopedia of Psychology*. 2 vols. London: Routledge, 1997.

2. Craighead, W. Edward, Charles B. Nemeroff, and Raymond J. Corsini, eds. *The Corsini Encyclopedia of Psychology and Behavioral Science*. 3rd ed. 4 vols. New York: Wiley, 2002.

2. Kazdin, Alan E., ed. *Encyclopedia of Psychology*. 8 vols. Washington, DC: American Psychological Association; Oxford: Oxford University Press, 2000.

3. Breakwell, Glynis M., Sean Hammond, and Chris Fife-Schaw. *Research Methods in Psychology*. 2nd ed. London: Sage, 2004.

3. Elmes, David G., Barry H. Kantowitz, and Henry L. Roediger III. *Research Methods in Psychology*. 8th ed. Belmont, CA: Wadsworth, 2005.

3. Reed, Jeffrey G., and Pam M. Baxter. *Library Use: A Handbook for Psychology*. 3rd ed. Washington, DC: American Psychological Association, 2003.

3. Shaughnessy, John J., Eugene B. Zechmeister, and Jeanne S. Zechmeister. *Research Methods in Psychology*. 7th ed. Boston: McGraw-Hill, 2005.

3. Wilson, Christopher. *Research Methods in Psychology: An Introductory Laboratory Manual*. Dubuque, IA: Kendall-Hunt, 1990.

4. *Annual Review of Psychology*. Palo Alto, CA: Annual Reviews. Also at http://arjournals.annualreviews.org.

4. *Compact Cambridge MEDLINE*. Bethesda, MD: NLM by Cambridge Scientific Abstracts. Also at http://www.ncbi.nlm.nih.gov/entrez/query.fcgi/.

4. *NASPSPA Abstracts*. Champaign, IL: Human Kinetics Publishers.

4. *PsycINFO*. Washington, DC: American Psychological Association. Also online from multiple sources.

4. *The Web of Science Citation Databases*. Philadelphia: Institute for Scientific Information. Also at http://isiknowledge.com.

5. Solomon, Paul R. *A Student's Guide to Research Report Writing in Psychology*. Glenview, IL: Scott, Foresman, 1985.

5. Sternberg, R. J. *The Psychologist's Companion: A Guide to Scientific Writing for Students and Researchers*. 4th ed. Cambridge: Cambridge University Press, 2003.

6. *Publication Manual of the American Psychological Association*. 5th ed. Washington, DC: American Psychological Association, 2003.

Religion

1. Bowker, John, ed. *The Concise Oxford Dictionary of World Religions*. Oxford: Oxford University Press, 2000. Also at http://www.oxfordreference.com.

1. Pye, Michael, ed. *Continuum Dictionary of Religion*. New York: Continuum, 1994.

2. Jones, Lindsay, ed. *Encyclopedia of Religion*. 15 vols. Detroit, MI: Macmillan Reference USA, 2005.

2. Routledge Encyclopedias of Religion and Society (series). New York: Routledge.

3. Kennedy, J. *Library Research Guide to Religion and Theology: Illustrated Search Strategy and Sources*. 2nd ed., rev. Ann Arbor, MI: Pierian, 1984.

4. Brown, David, and Richard Swinbourne. *A Selective Bibliography of the Philosophy of Religion*. Rev. ed. Oxford: Sub-Faculty of Philosophy, 1995.

4. Chinvamu, Salms. *An Annotated Bibliography on Religion*. Malawi: Malawi Library Association, 1993.

4. *Guide to Social Science and Religion in Periodical Literature*. Flint, MI: National Library of Religious Periodicals, 1970–1988.

4. *Index to Book Reviews in Religion*. Chicago: American Theological Library Association. Also at http://www.ovid.

4. *Islamic Book Review Index*. Berlin: Adiyok, 1982–.

4. O'Brien, Betty A., and Elmer J. O'Brien, eds. *Religion Index Two: Festschriften, 1960–1969*. Chicago: American Theological Library Association, 1980. Also at http://www.ovid.com.

4. *Religion Index One: Periodicals*. Chicago: American Theological Library Association, 1977–.

4. *Religion Index Two: Multi-author Works*. Chicago: American Theological Library Association. Also at http://www.ovid.

Sociology

1. Abercrombie, Nicholas, Stephen Hill, and Bryan S. Turner. *The Penguin Dictionary of Sociology*. 4th ed. London: Penguin, 2000.

1. Johnson, Allan G. *The Blackwell Dictionary of Sociology: A User's Guide to Sociological Language*. 2nd ed. Oxford: Blackwell, 2002.

1. Scott, John, and Marshall Gordon, eds. *A Dictionary of Sociology*. 3rd ed. New York: Oxford University Press, 2005.

2. Beckert, Jens, and Milan Zafirovksi, eds. *Encyclopedia of Economic Sociology*. London: Routledge, 2005.

2. Borgatta, Edgar F., ed. *Encyclopedia of Sociology*. 2nd ed. 5 vols. New York: Macmillan Reference USA, 2000.

2. Levinson, David L., Peter W. Cookson, and Alan R. Sadovnik, eds. *Education and Sociology: An Encyclopedia*. New York: RoutledgeFalmer, 2002.

2. Ritzer, George, ed. *Encyclopedia of Social Theory*. 2 vols. Thousand Oaks, CA: Sage, 2005.

2. Smelser, N., ed. *Handbook of Sociology*. Newbury Park, CA: Sage, 1988.

3. Aby, Stephen H., James Nalen, and Lori Fielding, eds. *Sociology: A Guide to Reference and Information Sources*. 3rd ed. Westport, CT: Libraries Unlimited, 2005.

3. Lieberson, Stanley. *Making It Count: The Improvement of Social Research and Theory*. Berkeley: University of California Press, 1987.

4. *Annual Review of Sociology*. Palo Alto, CA: Annual Reviews. Also at http://www.jstor.org and at http://arjournals.annualreviews.org/loi/soc/.

4. *Applied Social Sciences Index and Abstracts (ASSIA)*. Bethesda, MD: Cambridge Scientific Abstracts. Also at http://www.csa.

4. *Social Science Research*. San Diego, CA: Academic Press. Also at http://www.sciencedirect.com.

4. *Sociological Abstracts.* Bethesda, MD: Sociological Abstracts. Also at http://www
.csa.

5. Sociology Writing Group. *A Guide to Writing Sociology Papers.* 5th ed. New York:
Worth, 2001.

5. Tomovic, Vladislav A., ed. *Definitions in Sociology: Convergence, Conflict, and Alternative Vocabularies: A Manual for Writers of Term Papers, Research Reports, and
Theses.* St. Catharines, ON: Diliton Publications, 1979.

Women's Studies

1. Bataille, Gretchen M., and Laurie Lisa, eds. *Native American Women: A Biographical Dictionary.* 2nd ed. New York: Routledge, 2001.

1. Mills, Jane. *Womanwords: A Dictionary of Words about Women.* New York:
H. Holt, 1993.

1. Salem, Dorothy C., ed. *African American Women: A Biographical Dictionary.* New
York: Garland, 1993.

1. Uglow, Jennifer S., Frances Hinton, and Maggy Hendry, eds. *The Northeastern
Dictionary of Women's Biography.* 3rd ed. Boston: Northeastern University Press,
1999.

2. Hine, Darlene Clark, Elsa Barkley Brown, and Rosalyn Terborg-Penn, eds. *Black
Women in America: An Historical Encyclopedia.* 2 vols. Bloomington: Indiana
University Press, 1994.

2. Kramarae, Cheris, and Dale Spender, eds. *Routledge International Encyclopedia
of Women: Global Women's Issues and Knowledge.* 4 vols. New York: Routledge,
2000.

2. Tierney, Helen, ed. *Women's Studies Encyclopedia.* Rev. and expanded ed. 3 vols.
Westport, CT: Greenwood Press, 1999. Also at http://www.gem.greenwood
.com/.

2. Willard, Frances E., and Mary A. Livermore, eds. *American Women: Fifteen Hundred Biographies with Over 1,400 Portraits.* 2 vols. Rev. ed. Detroit, MI: Gale
Research, 1973.

3. Atkinson, Steven D., and Judith Hudson. *Women Online: Research in Women's
Studies Using Online Databases.* New York: Haworth, 1990.

3. Carter, Sarah, and Maureen Ritchie. *Women's Studies: A Guide to Information
Sources.* London: Mansell, 1990.

3. Searing, Susan E. *Introduction to Library Research in Women's Studies.* Boulder,
CO: Westview Press, 1985.

4. *Studies on Women and Gender Abstracts.* Oxfordshire, UK: Carfax. Also at http://
www.tandf.co.uk/swa/.

4. *Women Studies Abstracts.* Rush, NY: Rush Publishing Company.

4. *Women's Review of Books.* Wellesley, MA: Wellesley College Center for Research
on Women, 1983–2004.

4. *Women's Studies International.* Baltimore, MD: National Information Services
Corp. Also at http://www.nisc.com.

Natural Sciences

General

1. *McGraw-Hill Dictionary of Scientific and Technical Terms.* 6th ed. New York: Mc-Graw-Hill, 2003. Also at http://www.accessscience.com.
1. Morris, Christopher, ed. *Academic Press Dictionary of Science and Technology.* San Diego, CA: Academic, 1992.
1. Porter, Ray, and Marilyn Bailey Ogilvie, eds. *The Biographical Dictionary of Scientists.* 3rd ed. 2 vols. New York: Oxford University Press, 2000.
1. *Science Navigator.* New York: McGraw-Hill, 1998. CD-ROM, version 4.0.
1. Walker, Peter M. B., ed. *Chambers Dictionary of Science and Technology.* London: Chambers, 2000.
2. Heilbron, J. L., ed. *The Oxford Companion to the History of Modern Science.* Oxford: Oxford University Press, 2003. Also at http://www.oxfordreference.com.
2. *McGraw-Hill Encyclopedia of Science and Technology.* 9th ed. New York: McGraw-Hill, 2002. Also at http://www.accessscience.com.
2. *Nature Encyclopedia: An A-Z Guide to Life on Earth.* New York: Oxford University Press, 2001.
2. *Van Nostrand's Scientific Encyclopedia.* 9th ed. New York: Wiley-Interscience, 2002.
3. *Directory of Technical and Scientific Directories: A World Bibliographic Guide to Medical, Agricultural, Industrial, and Natural Science Directories.* 6th ed. Phoenix, AZ: Oryx Press, 1989.
3. Hurt, Charlie Deuel. *Information Sources in Science and Technology.* 3rd ed. Englewood, CO: Libraries Unlimited, 1998. Also at http://www.netlibrary.com.
3. Nielsen, Harry A. *Methods of Natural Science: An Introduction.* Englewood Cliffs, NJ: Prentice-Hall, 1967.
4. *Applied Science & Technology Index.* New York: H. W. Wilson. Also at http://hwwilsonweb.
4. *British Technology Index.* London: Library Association, 1962–1980.
4. *Compumath Citation Index.* Philadelphia: Institute for Scientific Information, 1981–.
4. Fanning, C. E., Margaret Jackdon, Mary Katharine Reely, and Mertice May James. *Book Review Digest: Annual Cumulation.* New York: The H. W. Wilson Co., 1905–.
4. *General Science Index.* New York: H. W. Wilson, 1978–. Also at http://hwwilsonweb.com.
4. *Genetics Citation Index: Experimental Citation Indexes to Genetics with Special Emphasis on Human Genetics.* Comp. Eugene Garfield and Irving H. Sher. Philadelphia: Institute for Scientific Information, 1963.
4. *Index to Scientific Reviews: An International Interdisciplinary Index to the Review Literature of Science, Medicine, Agriculture, Technology, and the Behavioral Sciences.* Philadelphia: Institute for Scientific Information, 1974.
4. *ISI Web of Science: Science Citation Index.* Philadelphia: Institute for Scientific Information. Also at http://www.isiknowledge.
4. *Science and Technology Annual Reference Review.* Phoenix, AZ: Oryx Press, ca. 1989–.
4. *Science Citation Index.* Philadelphia: Institute for Scientific Information, 1961–.

4. *Technical Book Review Index.* New York: Special Libraries Association, 1935–. Available on microfilm and microfiche from University Microfilms.

5. Booth, Vernon. *Communicating in Science: Writing a Scientific Paper and Speaking at Scientific Meetings.* 2nd ed. Cambridge: Cambridge University Press, 1993.

5. Gilpin, Andrea A., and Patricia Patchet-Golubev. *A Guide to Writing in the Sciences.* Toronto: University of Toronto Press, 2000.

5. Valiela, Ivan. *Doing Science: Design, Analysis, and Communication of Scientific Research.* Oxford: Oxford University Press, 2001.

5. Wilson, Anthony, et al. *Handbook of Science Communication.* Bristol: Institute of Physics Pub., 1998. Also at http://www.netlibrary.com.

6. Rubens, Phillip, ed. *Science and Technical Writing: A Manual of Style.* 2nd ed. New York: Routledge, 2001. Also at http://www.netlibrary.com.

Biology

1. *A Dictionary of Biology.* 5th ed. Oxford: Oxford University Press, 2004. Also at http://www.oxfordreference.com.

1. Allaby, Michael, ed. *The Oxford Dictionary of Natural History.* Oxford: Oxford University Press, 1985.

1. Lawrence, Eleanor, ed. *Henderson's Dictionary of Biology.* 13th ed. Harlow, UK: Prentice Hall, 2005.

1. Singleton, Paul, and Diana Sainsbury. *Dictionary of Microbiology and Molecular Biology.* 3rd ed. New York: Wiley, 2001.

1. Smith, Anthony D., ed. *Oxford Dictionary of Biochemistry and Molecular Biology.* Rev. ed. Oxford: Oxford University Press, 2003.

2. *Biology Encyclopedia.* New York: HarperCollins, 1991. Videodisc.

2. Creighton, Thomas E., ed. *Encyclopedia of Molecular Biology.* 4 vols. New York: John Wiley & Sons, 1999.

2. Dulbecco, Renato, ed. *Encyclopedia of Human Biology.* 2nd ed. 9 vols. San Diego, CA: Academic Press, 1997.

2. Eldredge, Niles, ed. *Life on Earth: An Encyclopedia of Biodiversity, Ecology, and Evolution.* 2 vols. Santa Barbara, CA: ABC-Clio, 2002.

2. Hall, Brian Keith, and Wendy M. Olson, eds. *Keywords and Concepts in Evolutionary Developmental Biology.* Cambridge, MA: Harvard University Press, 2003.

2. Pagel, Mark D., ed. *Encyclopedia of Evolution.* 2 vols. Oxford: Oxford University Press, 2002.

3. Boorkman, Jo Anne, Jeffrey T. Huber, and Fred W. Roper. *Introduction to Reference Sources in the Health Sciences.* 4th ed. New York: Neal-Schuman, 2004.

3. Wyatt, H. V., ed. *Information Sources in the Life Sciences.* 4th ed. London: Bowker-Saur, 1997.

4. *Biological Abstracts.* Philadelphia: BioSciences Information Service of Biological Abstracts. Also at http://www.ovid.

4. *Biological and Agricultural Index.* New York: H. W. Wilson. Also at http://hwwilsonweb.com.

4. *Environment Sciences & Pollution Management.* Bethesda, MD: Cambridge Scientific Abstracts. Also at http://www.csa.com.

4. *Genetics Citation Index; Experimental Citation Indexes to Genetics with Special Emphasis on Human Genetics.* Comp. Eugene Garfield and Irving H. Sher. Philadelphia: Institute for Scientific Information, 1963.

5. McMillan, Victoria E. *Writing Papers in the Biological Sciences*. 3rd ed. Boston: Bedford/St. Martin's, 2001.

6. *CBE Style Manual: A Guide for Authors, Editors, and Publishers in the Biological Sciences*. 5th ed. Bethesda: Council of Biology Editors, 1983.

Chemistry

1. Hawley, Gessner Goodrich, and Richard J. Lewis Sr. *Hawley's Condensed Chemical Dictionary*. 14th ed. New York: Wiley, 2002.

2. Kroschwitz, Jacqueline, and Arza Seidel, eds. *Kirk-Othmer Encyclopedia of Chemical Technology*. 5th ed. Hoboken, NJ: Wiley-Interscience, 2004.

2. Lide, David R. *CRC Handbook of Chemistry and Physics*. 86th ed. Boca Raton, FL: CRC Press, 2005.

2. Meyers, Robert A., ed. *Encyclopedia of Physical Science and Technology*. 3rd ed. 18 vols. San Diego, CA: Academic, 2002. Also at http://www.sciencedirect.com.

3. *CRC Handbook of Chemistry and Physics*. Cleveland, OH: CRC.

3. Leslie, Davies. *Efficiency in Research, Development, and Production: The Statistical Design and Analysis of Chemical Experiments*. Cambridge: Royal Society of Chemistry, 1993.

3. Wiggins, Gary. *Chemical Information Sources*. New York: McGraw-Hill, 1991.

4. *ACS Publications*. Columbus, OH: American Chemical Society. Also at http://pubs.acs.org.

4. *Chemical Abstracts*. Columbus, OH: American Chemical Society. Also at http://www.cas.org.

4. *Composite Index for CRC Handbooks*. 3rd ed. 3 vols. Boca Raton, FL: CRC Press, 1991.

4. *CrossFire Beilstein*. San Leandro, CA: MDL Information Systems. Also at http://www.beilstein.com/products/xfire/.

4. *ScienceDirect*. New York: Elsevier Science. Also at http://www.sciencedirect.com/.

5. Beall, Herbert, and John Trimbur. *A Short Guide to Writing about Chemistry*. 2nd ed. New York: Longman, 2001.

5. Ebel, Hans Friedrich, Claus Bliefert, and William E. Russey. *The Art of Scientific Writing: From Student Reports to Professional Publications in Chemistry and Related Fields*. 2nd ed. Weinheim, Germany: Wiley-VCH, 2004.

5. Schoenfeld, Robert. *The Chemist's English, with "Say It in English, Please!"* 3rd rev. ed. New York: Wiley-VCH, 2001.

6. Dodd, Janet S., ed. *The ACS Style Guide: A Manual for Authors and Editors*. 2nd ed. Washington, DC: American Chemical Society, 1997.

Computer Sciences

1. Gattiker, Urs E. *The Information Security Dictionary: Defining the Terms That Define Security for E-Business, Internet, Information, and Wireless Technology*. Boston: Kluwer Academic, 2004.

1. LaPlante, Phillip A. *Dictionary of Computer Science, Engineering, and Technology*. Boca Raton, FL: CRC Press, 2001.

1. Pfaffenberger, Bryan. *Webster's New World Computer Dictionary*. 10th ed. Indianapolis, IN: Wiley, 2003.

1. *Random House Concise Dictionary of Science and Computers.* New York: Random House Reference, 2004.
1. South, David W. *The Computer and Information Science and Technology Abbreviations and Acronyms Dictionary.* Boca Raton, FL: CRC Press, 1994.
2. Henderson, Harry. *Encyclopedia of Computer Science and Technology.* New York: Facts on File, 2003.
2. Marins, Brigham, ed. *World of Computer Science.* 2 vols. Detroit, MI: Gale Group/Thomson Learning, 2002.
2. Reilly, Edwin D., Anthony Ralston, and David Hemmendinger, eds. *Encyclopedia of Computer Science.* 4th ed. Chichester, UK: Wiley, 2003.
3. Ardis, Susan B., and Jean A. Poland. *A Guide to the Literature of Electrical and Electronics Engineering.* Littleton, CO: Libraries Unlimited, 1987.
4. *Directory of Library Automation Software, Systems, and Services.* Medford, NJ: Learned Information.
5. Eckstein, C. J. *Style Manual for Use in Computer-Based Instruction.* Brooks Air Force Base, TX: Air Force Human Resources Laboratory, Air Force Systems Command, 1990.

Geology and Earth Sciences

1. Clark, John O. E., and Stella Stiegeler, eds. *The Facts on File Dictionary of Earth Science.* New York: Facts on File, 2000.
1. Jackson, Julia A., and Robert Latimer Bates, eds. *Glossary of Geology.* 4th ed. Alexandria, VA: American Geological Institute, 1997.
1. *McGraw-Hill Dictionary of Geology and Mineralogy.* 2nd ed. New York: McGraw Hill, 2003.
2. Bishop, Arthur C., Alan R. Woolley, and William R. Hamilton. *Cambridge Guide to Minerals, Rocks, and Fossils.* Rev. ed. Cambridge: Cambridge University Press, 2001.
2. Bowes, Donald R., ed. *The Encyclopedia of Igneous and Metamorphic Petrology.* New York: Van Nostrand Reinhold, 1989.
2. Dasch, E. Julius, ed. *Macmillan Encyclopedia of Earth Sciences.* 2 vols. New York: Macmillan Reference USA, 1996.
2. Good, Gregory A., ed. *Sciences of the Earth: An Encyclopedia of Events, People, and Phenomena.* 2 vols. New York: Garland, 1998.
2. Hancock, Paul L., and Brian J. Skinner, eds. *The Oxford Companion to the Earth.* Oxford: Oxford University Press, 2000. Also at http://www.oxfordreference.com.
2. Nierenberg, William A., ed. *Encyclopedia of Earth System Science.* 4 vols. San Diego, CA: Academic, 1992.
2. Selley, Richard C., L. R. M. Cocks, and I. R. Plimer, eds. *Encyclopedia of Geology.* 5 vols. Amsterdam: Elsevier Academic, 2005.
2. Seyfert, Carl K., ed. *The Encyclopedia of Structural Geology and Plate Tectonics.* New York: Van Nostrand Reinhold, 1987.
2. Singer, Ronald, ed. *Encyclopedia of Paleontology.* 2 vols. Chicago: Fitzroy Dearborn, 1999.

2. Steele, John H., S. A. Thorpe, and Karl K. Turekian, eds. *Encyclopedia of Ocean Sciences.* 6 vols. San Diego, CA: Academic Press, 2001. Also at http://www .sciencedirect.com/science/referenceworks/.

4. *Bibliography and Index of Geology.* Alexandria, VA: American Geological Institute. Also at http://georef.cos.com/.

4. *Geobase.* New York: Elsevier Science. Also online from multiple sources.

4. Wood, David N., Joan E. Hardy, and Anthony P. Harvey. *Information Sources in the Earth Sciences.* 2nd ed. London: Bowker-Saur, 1989.

5. Bates, Robert L., Marla D. Adkins-Heljeson, and Rex C. Buchanan, eds. *Geowriting: A Guide to Writing, Editing, and Printing in Earth Science.* Rev. 5th ed. Alexandria, VA: American Geological Institute, 2004.

5. Dunn, J., et al. *Organization and Content of a Typical Geologic Report.* Rev. ed. Arvada, CO: American Institute of Professional Geologists, 1993.

Mathematics

1. Borowski, E. J., and J. M. Borwein, eds. *Collins Dictionary: Mathematics.* 2nd ed. Glasgow: HarperCollins, 2002.

1. James, Robert Clarke, and Glenn James. *Mathematics Dictionary.* 5th ed. New York: Van Nostrand Reinhold, 1992.

1. Schwartzman, Steven. *The Words of Mathematics: An Etymological Dictionary of Mathematical Terms Used in English.* Washington, DC: Mathematical Association of America, 1994.

2. Darling, David J. *The Universal Book of Mathematics: From Abracadabra to Zeno's Paradoxes.* Hoboken, NJ: Wiley, 2004.

2. Ito, Kiyosi, ed. *Encyclopedic Dictionary of Mathematics.* 2nd ed. 2 vols. Cambridge: MIT Press, 1993.

2. Weisstein, Eric W. *CRC Concise Encyclopedia of Mathematics.* 2nd ed. Boca Raton, FL: Chapman & Hall/CRC, 2003.

3. Pemberton, John E. *How to Find Out in Mathematics: A Guide to Sources of Information.* 2nd rev. ed. Oxford: Pergamon, 1969.

4. *East European Scientific Abstracts.* Arlington, VA: Joint Publications Research Service.

4. *Mathematical Reviews: 50th Anniversary Celebration.* Providence, RI: American Mathematical Society, 1990.

4. *MathSci.* Providence, RI: American Mathematical Society. Also at http://www .ams.org/mathscinet/.

5. *A Manual for Authors of Mathematical Papers.* Rev. ed. Providence, RI: American Mathematical Society, 1990.

5. Miller, Jane E. *The Chicago Guide to Writing about Multivariate Analysis.* Chicago: University of Chicago Press, 2005.

Physics

1. Basu, Dipak, ed. *Dictionary of Pure and Applied Physics.* Boca Raton, FL: CRC Press, 2001.

1. Isaacs, Alan, ed. *A Dictionary of Physics.* 4th ed. Oxford: Oxford University Press, 2000.

1. Sube, Ralf. *Dictionary: Physics Basic Terms; English-German.* Berlin: A. Hatier, 1994.

1. Thewlis, James. *Concise Dictionary of Physics and Related Subjects.* 2nd ed. rev. and enl. Oxford: Pergamon, 1979.
2. Lerner, Rita G., and George L. Trigg, eds. *Encyclopedia of Physics.* 3rd ed. Weinheim, Germany: Wiley-VCH, 2005.
2. *McGraw-Hill Concise Encyclopedia of Physics.* New York: McGraw-Hill, 2005.
2. Meyers, Robert A., ed. *Encyclopedia of Modern Physics.* San Diego, CA: Academic Press, 1990.
2. Trigg, George L., ed. *Encyclopedia of Applied Physics.* Weinheim, Germany: Wiley-VCH, 2004.
2. Woan, Graham. *The Cambridge Handbook of Physics Formulas.* 2003 ed. Cambridge: Cambridge University Press, 2003.
3. Shaw, Dennis F. *Information Sources in Physics.* 3rd ed. London: Bowker-Saur, 1994.
4. *American Institute of Physics Journals.* College Park, MD: AIP. Also at http://www.aip.org/ojs/service.html.
4. *Astronomy and Astrophysics Abstracts.* Berlin: Springer-Verlag.
4. *Current Physics Index.* New York: American Institute of Physics. Also at http://ojps.aip.org/spinweb/.
4. *IEEE Xplore.* New York: Institute of Electrical and Electronics Engineers. Also at http://www.ieee.org/ieeexplore/.
4. *Inspec.* Stevenage, UK: Institution of Electrical Engineers. Also at http://www.iee.org/Publish/INSPEC/.
4. *Institute of Physics Electronic Journals.* London: IOP. Also at http://www.iop.org/EJ/.
4. *Physics Abstracts.* London: Institution of Electrical Engineers.
5. Katz, Michael J. *Elements of the Scientific Paper.* New Haven: Yale University Press, 1985.
6. American Institute of Physics. *AIP Style Manual.* 4th ed. New York: American Institute of Physics, 1990. Also at http://www.aip.org/pubservs/style/4thed/toc.html.

Authors

Wayne C. Booth was the George M. Pullman Distinguished Service Professor Emeritus at the University of Chicago. His many books include *The Rhetoric of Fiction, For the Love of It: Amateuring and Its Rivals,* and *The Essential Wayne Booth,* each published by the University of Chicago Press. Professor Booth died in 2005.

Gregory G. Colomb is professor of English at the University of Virginia. He is the author of *Designs on Truth: The Poetics of the Augustan Mock-Epic.*

Joseph M. Williams is professor emeritus of English and linguistics at the University of Chicago. He is the author of *Style: Lessons in Clarity and Grace,* currently in its ninth edition.

Together Booth, Colomb, and Williams have written *The Craft of Research,* currently in its second edition (University of Chicago Press, 2003). Colomb and Williams have also written *The Craft of Argument,* currently in its third edition.

Index